JAZZ AND THE PHILOSOPHY OF ART

Co-authored by three prominent philosophers of art, *Jazz and the Philosophy of Art* is the first book in English to be exclusively devoted to philosophical issues in jazz. It covers such diverse topics as minstrelsy, bebop, Voodoo, social and tap dancing, parades, phonography, musical forgeries, and jazz singing, as well as Goodman's allographic/autographic distinction, Adorno's critique of popular music, and what improvisation is and is not.

The book is organized into three parts. Drawing on innovative strategies adopted to address challenges that arise for the project of defining art, Part I shows how historical definitions of art provide a blueprint for a historical definition of jazz. Part II extends the book's commitment to social-historical contextualism by exploring distinctive ways that jazz has shaped, and been shaped by, American culture. It uses the lens of jazz vocals to provide perspective on racial issues previously unaddressed in the work. It then examines the broader premise that jazz was a socially progressive force in American popular culture. Part III concentrates on a topic that has entered into the arguments of each of the previous chapters: what is jazz improvisation? It outlines a pluralistic framework in which distinctive performance intentions distinguish distinctive kinds of jazz improvisation.

This book is a comprehensive and valuable resource for any reader interested in the intersections between jazz and philosophy.

Lee B. Brown was Professor of Philosophy at The Ohio State University and a specialist in the history of modern philosophy, general aesthetics, and the philosophy of music. Contemporaneously, he also worked as a professional jazz critic in Columbus, Ohio. His publications span 45 years in major philosophy journals. With David Goldblatt, he was co-editor of the highly successful textbook *Aesthetics: A Reader in Philosophy of the Arts*, now in its 4th edition (Routledge, 2017).

David Goldblatt is Emeritus Professor of Philosophy at Denison University and the author of *Art and Ventriloquism* (2006) in the Routledge series Critical Voices in Art, Theory and Culture. He is co-editor of *Aesthetics: A Reader in Philosophy of the Arts*, with Lee B. Brown and Stephanie Patridge, now in its 4th edition (Routledge, 2017) and is co-editor with Roger Paden of *The Aesthetics of Architecture: Philosophical Investigations into the Art of Building* (2011).

Theodore Gracyk is Professor of Philosophy at Minnesota State University Moorhead and, since 2013, co-editor of the *Journal of Aesthetics and Art Criticism*. His book *I Wanna Be Me: Rock Music and the Politics of Identity* (2001) was selected as co-winner of the 2002 Woody Guthrie Award and he is the author of four other books on the aesthetics of music, as well as co-editor of two books, including *The Routledge Companion to Philosophy and Music* (2011).

JAZZ AND THE PHILOSOPHY OF ART

Lee B. Brown, David Goldblatt and Theodore Gracyk

Routledge
Taylor & Francis Group

NEW YORK AND LONDON

First published 2018
by Routledge
711 Third Avenue, New York, NY 10017

and by Routledge
2 Park Square, Milton Park, Abingdon, Oxon OX14 4RN

Routledge is an imprint of the Taylor & Francis Group, an informa business

© 2018 Taylor & Francis

The right of Lee B. Brown, David Goldblatt, and Theodore Gracyk to be identified as authors of this work has been asserted by them in accordance with sections 77 and 78 of the Copyright, Designs and Patents Act 1988.

Library of Congress Cataloging-in-Publication Data
A catalog record for this book has been requested

ISBN: 978-1-138-24135-0 (hbk)
ISBN: 978-1-138-24136-7 (pbk)
ISBN: 978-1-315-28061-5 (ebk)

Typeset in Bembo
by Taylor & Francis Books

Lee B. Brown (1932–2014)

CONTENTS

FOREWORD

Lee Brown: A Recollection

Like a lot of kids of his generation, my husband Lee Brown grew up with a spinet in the family living room in Salt Lake City. His brother Wilson, with a lot of talent and perfect pitch, took summer jobs playing piano at the El Tovar Hotel at the Grand Canyon; he became a lifelong musician, teacher, and arranger. Lee never got beyond Thompson's Third Grade piano book.

But even without a scintilla of performing talent he had a highly cultivated ear for music. Catholic in taste, he liked everything from Mozart to Wagner to Alban Berg to AC/DC, the Talking Heads, and Ernesto Lecuona. But most of all, jazz.

Listening to Roy Eldridge perform at Jimmy Ryan's in the 1970s, he had to collar Eldridge and remind him of a 1949 performance in Salt Lake City when Lee was fresh out of high school and tasting live jazz for the first time. An idyllic couple of years in San Francisco after he left the Navy in the early 50s introduced him to the Thirsty I and the Brubeck Quartet. In the 90s, Blossom Dearie at Danny's Skylight Room would bring him to tears of joy. We never went to New York City without checking out the scene at Sweet Basil, The Blue Note, Iridium and St. Nick's Pub in Harlem, where we'd share a table with singer Ruth Brisbane and her husband Claude. We never went anywhere that didn't include jazz, from Ronnie Scott's in London to the smoky top floor of El Perron in Cadaques, Spain. No philosophy conventioneers were safe from a night out with Lee at local dives in cities all over the U.S.

As my stepson pointed out at Lee's memorial service in 2014, our basement had (sadly, still has) the entire history of recorded music, from piano rolls, cylinder records and 78s through reel-to-reel tapes, cassettes, vinyl, and CDs. Like a gerbil on an exercise wheel, he raced to keep his collection up to date by transferring from one medium to another and devising one organizing scheme after another.

Lee studied philosophy under Bill Earle and Erich Heller at Northwestern University. Under the influence of his mentors, for many years his philosophical interests ranged from Kant, Hegel, and Nietzsche to the French existentialists and to philosophical questions in the arts and literature. Strangely, he was late coming to a realization that music, and especially jazz, should be the center of his philosophical enterprise, that there were interesting and complex aesthetic issues around the study of jazz music. It was when he started to write a jazz column for a local alternative paper and discovered the rich jazz scene in Columbus, Ohio, that I think he first realized the philosophical potential in this medium. He tapped into a whole lifetime of deep listening that he had never before mined philosophically.

I remember when he became fascinated with defining the essential elements of jazz, including the role of improvisation. He almost drove me mad playing over and over the opening bars of Louis Armstrong's 1928 performance of "West End Blues," where Armstrong rips into his intro too fast to be able to negotiate the 16th notes that lay in wait. Just as Armstrong reaches the expected cascade of notes, he brilliantly substitutes a series of triplets instead. The knife-edge improv is thrilling. Well, for me maybe not so much the thirtieth or fortieth time. For Lee, of course, the repetition raised even more philosophical questions about phonography and jazz.

He is missed. I am delighted that this book can be his life-extender.

Emily Foster

ACKNOWLEDGEMENTS

The authors gratefully acknowledge permission to republish the following material.

A shorter predecessor of Chapter 2 was published by Lee B. Brown as "The Theory of Jazz Music: 'It Don't Mean a Thing…'" *The Journal of Aesthetics and Art Criticism* 49:2 (1991): 115–127. All but two paragraphs of the previously published material have been modified through expansion by Lee B. Brown, David Goldblatt, and Theodore Gracyk. Generally, the modifications involve addition of further examples, updating of examples, expansion of theoretical explanations, and engagements with more recent scholarship. First person singular became plural. Used by permission of the copyright holder: Copyright © 1991 The American Society for Aesthetics (Wiley-Blackwell, Publisher).

A shorter predecessor of Chapter 5 was published by Lee B. Brown as "Can American Popular Vocal Music Escape the Legacy of Blackface Minstrelsy?" *The Journal of Aesthetics and Art Criticism* 71:1 (2013): 91–100. Approximately one of every three paragraphs of the previously published material has been modified through expansion by David Goldblatt and Theodore Gracyk. Generally, the modifications involve addition of further examples, updating of examples, expansion of theoretical explanations, and engagements with more recent scholarship. Goldblatt and Gracyk contributed the opening eight paragraphs and sections 7 and 8. First person singular became plural. Used by permission of the copyright holder: Copyright © 2013 The American Society for Aesthetics (Wiley-Blackwell, Publisher).

A shorter predecessor of Chapter 6 was published by Lee B. Brown as "Adorno's Case against Popular Music," *Aesthetics: A Reader in Philosophy of the Arts*, ed. David Goldblatt, Lee Brown, Stephanie Patridge, 4th edition (Routledge, 2017): 392–397. The material has been modified through expansion by David Goldblatt and Theodore Gracyk, including the incorporation of portions of

Theodore Gracyk, "Adorno," *The Routledge Companion to Aesthetics*, ed. Berys Gaut and Dominic Lopes, 3rd edition (Routledge, 2013): 137–147. Used by permission of the copyright holder: Copyright © 2017 Lee B. Brown (Taylor & Francis, Publisher), and copyright © 2013 Theodore Gracyk (Taylor & Francis, Publisher).

A shorter predecessor of Chapter 7 was published by Lee B. Brown as "Improvisation," *The Routledge Companion to Philosophy and Music*, ed. Theodore Gracyk and Andrew Kania (Routledge, 2011): 59–69. The material has been modified through expansion by David Goldblatt and Theodore Gracyk. Used by permission of the copyright holder: Copyright © 2011 Lee B. Brown (Taylor & Francis, Publisher).

A shorter predecessor of Chapter 8 was published by Lee B. Brown as "Musical Works, Improvisation, and the Principle of Continuity," *The Journal of Aesthetics and Art Criticism* 54:4 (1996): 353–369. The previously published material has been modified. Paragraphs have been re-ordered in sections 3 and 4. Two paragraphs were removed from section 6, one from section 7, and two from section 8. Every remaining paragraph has been modified through expansion by David Goldblatt and Theodore Gracyk. Generally, the modifications involve addition of further examples, updating of examples, expansion of theoretical explanations, and engagements with more recent scholarship. Goldblatt and Gracyk contributed a new opening paragraph to section 8. First person singular became plural. Used by permission of the copyright holder: Copyright © 1996 The American Society for Aesthetics (Wiley-Blackwell, Publisher).

A shorter predecessor of Chapter 9 was published by Lee B. Brown as "Phonography, Repetition and Spontaneity," *Philosophy and Literature* 24:1 (2000): 111–125. © 2000 The Johns Hopkins University Press. Revised by Lee B. Brown, David Goldblatt, and Theodore Gracyk, and reprinted with permission of Johns Hopkins University Press. All material from the last two paragraphs of section 4 to the end is previously unpublished.

A shorter predecessor of Chapter 10 was published by Lee B. Brown as "'Feeling My Way': Jazz Improvisation and Its Vicissitudes – A Plea for Imperfection," *The Journal of Aesthetics and Art Criticism* 58:2 (2000): 113–123. The previously published material has been modified by the addition of section 2, deletion of two paragraphs in section 3, deletion of five paragraphs in section 4, deletion of three paragraphs in section 5, and deletion of one paragraph in section 6, as well as an addition of the opening three paragraphs, the final paragraph of section 5, and last two paragraphs of section 6. Almost all paragraphs have been modified by David Goldblatt and Theodore Gracyk. Generally, the modifications involve addition of further examples, updating of examples, expansion of theoretical explanations, and engagements with more recent scholarship. First person singular became plural. Used by permission of the copyright holder: Copyright © 2000 The American Society for Aesthetics (Wiley-Blackwell, Publisher). Section 2 is a revised version of the concluding section of Lee B. Brown, "Improvisation," *The*

Routledge Companion to Philosophy and Music, ed. Theodore Gracyk and Andrew Kania (Routledge, 2011): 59–69. Used by permission of the copyright holder: Copyright © 2011 Lee B. Brown (Taylor & Francis, Publisher).

Chapters 1, 3, and 4 do not contain previously published material.

When using quotations from any part of *Jazz and the Philosophy of Art*, all three scholars—Lee B. Brown, David Goldblatt, and Theodore Gracyk–should be listed as authors.

Individual Acknowledgements

Collectively, we thank Emily Foster for providing the impetus to pursue publication of this book, and for providing Lee Brown's working notes and draft material for portions of the book that do not derive from previously published work. At Routledge, we thank Andrew Beck for his strong support for the project; we also extend our thanks to his editorial assistant, Vera Lochtefeld. We would like to thank Aili Bresnahan for advice on Chapter 1, and Michael Rings, Margaret Moore, and Thomas Adajian for their comments on the ideas in Chapter 3.

Lee B. Brown thanks Phil Alperson for helpful suggestions with the argument of Chapter 2. For assistance with Chapter 5, he thanks Barry Shank for his responses, in personal correspondence, to queries about his study of Bob Dylan, and Joel Rudinow, who identified valuable sources on the topic, and Terry Waldo, a professional ragtime and jazz composer and musician whose knowledge of minstrel theater proved invaluable. Additionally, he thanks Jeanette Bicknell and John Andrew Fisher for their editorial advice. For discussion of ideas incorporated into Chapter 9, he thanks Stephen Davies, Andrew Kania, and, above all, Diana Raffman.

David Goldblatt thanks Garry Hagberg, Tom Carroll, Rhonda Lubka, Markus Kruse, and Fred Ditirro for general discussions on jazz and specific suggestions on the text. Lee Brown's influence on my interest in jazz, up front and personal as well as theoretical, could not be overestimated.

Theodore Gracyk thanks Lee Brown and Ted Cohen, without whose encouragement he would have stayed far away from the topic of jazz.

INTRODUCTION

> Progress in the philosophy of art in the immediate future is to be made not by theorizing in the grand manner, but by careful and imaginative philosophical scrutiny of the individual arts and their individual problems, seen as somewhat unique, individual problems and not necessarily as instances of common problems of some monolithic thing called "ART."
>
> — *Peter Kivy*

We are now more than a quarter century beyond a Presidential Address at the American Society for Aesthetics at which the late Peter Kivy, one of our most distinguished and insightful philosophers of music, called for a turn away from a unitary philosophy of art in favor of a pluralistic pursuit. Recognizing that art is not a monolith, conceptually or in practice, Kivy proposed that an exploration of differences is more enlightening than a focus on similarities. Unfortunately, not much has changed in the decades since Kivy's proposal. Consulting the indexes of a score of recent books in the philosophy of music, we find no entries – or only incidental ones – for "jazz." For the most part, philosophers continue to theorize about music by talking about Bach and Beethoven and Wagner and, in more adventurous moments, John Cage and perhaps the Beatles. We grant that there are important exceptions, many of which we discuss throughout this book. There are, however, scores of books on jazz by jazz critics, musicians, and historians. And, we acknowledge that this book could not have been written without them. But while there are individual articles appearing in scholarly journals by philosophers, there has not been a full-length book in English devoted to philosophical issues in jazz by philosophers, until now.

What, then, do we believe we have accomplished by bringing philosophical theorizing to bear on jazz? For one thing, we bring together many of the issues on jazz presented in books that have been, for us, excellent sources of historical accounts as well as personal anecdotes from the long history of jazz. Those who have not read much about jazz will appreciate our exploration and synthesis of so much of the literature on jazz and the philosophy of music. For another, we offer our own theories regarding many of the philosophical issues surrounding jazz as it is embedded in the philosophy of music and, more generally, the philosophy of art. Most importantly, we argue that a contextual theory of jazz, which this book offers, has the best chance to clarify, with a certain degree of insight, the muddy waters of many of the issues raised in the broader literature of jazz, that saw jazz as a subject worthy of criticism and analysis. Philosophically, jazz is a dramatically conspicuous example of the poverty of trying to understand any of the arts from a purely synchronic or acontextual point of view.

At the same time, we will, in regard to many of the issues broached in this book, do our best to accept the standard philosophical job-description – that is, to take rough conceptual terrain, map it, and explain where its boundaries, both internal and external, lie. Although philosophical thinking about jazz sometimes mirrors concerns with philosophy of music generally, many aspects of jazz are aesthetically different from the music that has been treated as paradigmatic within philosophy of art. However, the route historically traced by jazz was not fore-ordained or fated. Nor was jazz the product of a teleological, goal-oriented historical process. What we see is that jazz has been beset by a set of cultural constraints about the practice of the music that have actually been inconsistent. Furthermore, the essence of its short life, to put the point paradoxically, has consisted almost from the start in its continual struggle with its own past. Jazz still carries its history on its sleeve, so to say, by comparison with European concert music. The dance forms that served as its source materials have been almost completely lost to the ear, through the combined action of artistic transfiguration and the decay of historical memory. Because jazz is preserved for the most part in recordings rather than scores, nothing is lost to the ear – or so it may seem. Nonetheless, jazz has been with us long enough that changes in the social alignment and uses of jazz have encouraged a decay of relevant memory here, as well.

Every art encapsulates a set of evolved skills, practices, and standards of evaluation. From the viewpoint of a participant inside any one of them, the parameters of its practice are fixed. But, imagine a speeded up film, so to say, of any art, from well before the first signs of its appearance on earth, up through its eventual disappearance. Some pass away with the rise of new technologies, some due to cultural quakes within the sphere of aesthetic values assumed for that art form, some from cultural annihilation, and some from just plain boredom. From this hypothetical point of view, commitment to the longevity of the concepts or principles that govern the production and reception practices of the art form would begin to look foolish. The foregoing also holds, as well, for the overall life of the overarching concept, not of this or that art form, but of *art* in general – a favored if perpetually wearying opening chapter in treatises and textbooks in philosophy of art. However, the general nature of *art* is not one that we intend to spend our time exploring. We take it for granted that jazz is an art form – a complex and important one that has issues that belong to it alone.

Beyond the inherent interest that we jazz lovers may have in these topics, we think that our analysis of them is an important corrective within philosophy of art. Above all, we think that several of these apparent dichotomies are shown to differ as matters of degree, rather than mutually exclusive categories of activity. It is our hope that many of our detailed discussions of jazz-oriented issues will help to reorganize a reader's thinking about this spirited and moody form of music.

Organization of *Jazz and the Philosophy of Art*

What follows is an explanation of how we have grouped our chapters and how they relate to one another.

This book is organized into three parts, which pursue three broad ways that philosophizing about jazz intersects with traditional philosophy of art. Part I explores the issue of whether there is an essence of jazz – some set of necessary and sufficient features that constitute its proper definition. Our conclusion, in Chapter 3, is that such a definition can be given, but *not* by reference to the music's purely musical features.

Chapter 1 makes an inclusive case for understanding dancing to the music of jazz, and the places at or in which the dancing occurred, as essential elements of jazz during one long stretch of its history. Then, sometime around the late 1940s and into the 1950s, there was a reinvention of the social practices surrounding jazz, and these relationships were severed. There is good reason, therefore, to regard subsequent jazz, while still jazz, as a different kind of art. Severing jazz from social dancing and its venues also severed the functional connection between the music and the form of life that shaped it. Its omission would render any explanation of jazz seriously incomplete. We end the chapter with an endorsement of Duke Ellington's claim that jazz fans who never dance to it have a different experience of the music – that the difference for reception theory between bodies in motion and those that are static is a relevant one.

Chapter 2 evaluates the prospects for defining jazz by identifying what is musically distinctive about jazz, apart from the social practices that nurtured it. We make the case that André Hodeir's theory of jazz is unjustly neglected. Rather than improvisation, the centerpiece of the definition is an analysis of the conditions of swing as an underlying pulsation and a rhythmic overlay that pulls against it. Detailing performance goals rooted in rhythm, Hodeir identifies a plausible essentialist account of jazz in its initial five decades. However, the theory does not extend to some jazz beginning around 1960, and we again find a decisive discontinuity that undercuts an essentialist theory of jazz.

Despite widespread skepticism about the prospects for a unified definition of jazz, Chapter 3 argues that recent philosophy of art has developed a suitable definitional strategy. Historical definitions of art provide a blueprint for a historical definition of jazz. Despite notable discontinuities in musical practice, later jazz styles count as jazz by virtue of reflexive practice, either in the intentional preservation of established jazz styles or in innovation grounded in respect for appreciative practices established in earlier jazz. Although we acknowledge that there will be particular music performances with an ambiguous status, the definition sidesteps the pitfalls of traditional essentialist definitions in order to embrace a plurality of styles and performance goals.

Given our argument that a definition of jazz should recognize that the music is embedded in social-historical developments, we must take account of jazz as an intervention in *American* culture. And this, in turn, brings us to topics of race and gender. Part II explores these issues within the context of the diachronic, pluralistic analysis established in Part I. However, instead of advancing a single argument that culminates in the third of three chapters, this set proceeds more dialectically. Chapters 4 and 5 use the lens of jazz vocals to provide perspective on racial issues previously set to one side, after which Chapter 6 examines the broader premise that jazz might be a socially progressive force in American culture in the twentieth century.

Chapter 4 examines and offers support for two claims: jazz stands for, or expresses, a certain species of freedom, and jazz is – in the right circumstances – a Dionysian practice that goes beyond the mimetic art of expressive communication. We propose that these claims are best understood in relation to jazz singing. We argue that Nietzsche's interpretation of the ancient Dionysian festivals has significant parallels in nineteenth-century African-American rituals in and around New Orleans. These parallels continue to resonate in jazz, especially in scat vocal performances by African-American women. In opposition to theories of jazz vocal performance that stress the singer's expressive interpretation of song, we argue that the activity of jazz singing is frequently more significant than that, for it can be a liberating activity made possible by a cultural space provided within the jazz tradition.

Chapter 5 considers the charge that American white popular music is pervasively indebted to minstrel theater in a manner that perpetuates racism. White jazz vocalists such as Bing Crosby and dancers such as Fred Astaire built careers on their appropriation from African-American jazz resources. However, we challenge the hypothesis that these and all similar appropriations are to be understood and evaluated as extensions of blackface minstrelsy, a claim put forward by certain scholars. Just as we think that Dionysian practices inform different jazz practices and eras in varying degrees, the legacy of blackface is genuine yet polymorphous.

White appropriation would not merit extended discussion were it not for the way that these appropriations were successfully packaged and sold as mass entertainment. Chapter 6 examines Theodor Adorno's thirty-year engagement with jazz, which he criticizes as a paradigm of deceptive consumer marketing and as a corrosive tool of social conformity and class exploitation. Adorno casts doubt on the positive achievements that we explored in Chapters 4 and 5 by arguing that the commercialization of jazz robs it of the artistic autonomy that characterizes resistive, "difficult," authentic culture. Jazz is highly standardized music, and it produces predictable, standardized responses. After presenting Adorno's critique, we explore typical responses to it, together with his counter-responses. However, as we did with the minstrel hypothesis in Chapter 5, we resist adoption of an overarching historical narrative that imposes uniform evaluative criteria on all jazz. In particular, jazz should not be evaluated by comparison to the supposed progress of "serious" music. Some of the joyful noise of jazz has a genuine cathartic potential despite its commercialization.

Finally, Part III concentrates on a topic that has entered into the arguments of each of the previous chapters: what is jazz improvisation? Here, the issues are primarily ontological and evaluative. The arc of the argument across the four chapters begins with an exploration of the nature of improvisational music performance, and what this entails for jazz in particular. This position leads us to reject typical assumptions about art and about the nature of musical performance. Next, we pursue further complications that arise from the cultural, historical, and aesthetic importance of *recorded* jazz – a state of affairs in which the opportunity to hear improvisations from the past is undermined by the repeatability of the very technological process that lets us hear it. Finally, we confront the question of how the ubiquitous musical imperfections and errors in jazz improvisations are to be factored into the evaluation of a jazz performance.

More specifically, Chapter 7 grapples with the issue that a principled analysis of the concept of improvisation has been elusive. Although we explained in Part I why improvisation cannot be regarded as essential to a jazz performance, we also acknowledged that improvisation became increasingly important in jazz performance. We examine and discard some of the most common platitudes about improvisation, especially the idea that it is a mode of musical composition. Specifically, we reject the thesis that a jazz improvisation is necessarily a performance or an instantiation of a musical work. Instead, we recommend a pluralistic framework in which jazz performances range from expressive embellishment during the performance of a musical work to spontaneous performance that is not the performance of any work. Distinctive performance intentions distinguish distinctive kinds of jazz improvisation.

Chapter 8 engages directly with recent theories of artwork identity in order to show that they do not describe what takes place in some jazz improvisations. Specifically, a model that bifurcates art works into two basic kinds – enduring objects and structural types – mispresents some jazz performances by asserting that an improvisation is, in principle, an instantiation of a musical work that can be performed again by other musicians. Nelson Goodman's distinction between autographic art and allographic art serves as an example of the position we reject. Against this model, we defend the intuition that jazz improvisations do not generate works that can be performed again. Otherwise, we would have to regard the appreciative stance that jazz fans adopt toward improvisation as a misguided, if not irrational, stance.

Since 1917, recording has been an indispensable tool of jazz's dissemination and reception. Chapter 9 addresses the problem that recorded jazz encourages listening practices that are antithetical to the appreciation of improvisation. The ability to listen repeatedly to the same, recorded improvisation encourages hearing an improvisation as a repeatable, composed structure, reintroducing the model of musical works that we resisted in Chapter 8. We begin by addressing the complaint that repeated playback of recorded music is generally antithetical to music appreciation; we argue that this complaint has limited plausibility. However, we find that the problem is more serious in the case of improvised music, and therefore it is a genuine issue for jazz.

The salient features of jazz are resultants of the intersection of distinct practices and intentions, which become transfigured in the music by their interaction. Given the caveat that not every jazz performance is improvised to the same degree or within the same intentional framework, Chapter 10 examines the idea that jazz improvisations are typically flawed in multiple ways. We separate the unhelpful claim that they are flawed from a Eurocentric standard of good music from the claim that they are typically flawed when evaluated by appropriate standards (e.g., including standards typically applied by jazz musicians). Given the degree of risk taking and forced choices that occur in good improvisation, we recognize that jazz improvisation typically reflects a hierarchy of regulative ideals. Consequently, both the musicians and the audience must accept a significant amount of musical imperfection for the sake of other aesthetic rewards.

Finally, we acknowledge that there are many important issues and perspectives that we do not have room to address. That much is inevitable, as the history of jazz infiltrates history generally. However, we have provided a framework that should make it clear that we are attracted to jazz, in part, because it provides evidence that it is best to reject essentialisms of every kind in the cultural arena of the arts. Jazz does not sound, essentially, one way. Jazz is not, functionally, all of one piece. Jazz is not performed with any one meaning, goal, or regulative ideal. Perhaps that is the deeper meaning of the many clichés that link jazz and the free spirit of its musicians and audiences.

PART I

How is Jazz Distinctive?
Essence and Definition

1

DANCING, DWELLING, AND RHYTHMIC SWING

How music works, or doesn't work, is determined not just by what it is in isolation (if such a condition can ever exist) but in large part by what surrounds it, where you hear it and when you hear it.

— *David Byrne*, How Music Works

Who the hell wants to dance in Carnegie Hall?

— *Leonard Feather*

Philosophers tend to analyze music as a set of sounds, or an abstract recipe for directing those sounds, or the performance of those sounds, or recorded instances of performances. However, we want to say that, for all the philosophical value of each of those contributing theories, what is often missing is part of a culture in which those sounds are created and manifested. An aspect of culture may adhere so closely to the music itself that it is definitional — it so intimately identifies with the music that it would be a conceptual error to omit it from an account of its nature.[1]

For jazz, one such socio-historical factor is dancing. Another is the physical locations, the buildings and other forums, the architecture of jazz — the *where* of the music. What we argue in this chapter, in the context of jazz, can be set against a purely sonic conception of music such as one taken by Roger Scruton, one of the more prominent contemporary aestheticians. Scruton says, "Music relies neither on linguistic order nor on physical context, but on organization that can be perceived in sound itself, without reference to physical context or to semantic conventions."[2] In contrast, this chapter makes an inclusive case for understanding dancing to the music of jazz, and the places at or in which the dancing occurred, as an essential element of jazz during one long stretch of its history. Then there was a reinvention of the social practices surrounding jazz, and these relationships were severed. There is reason, therefore, to ask whether subsequent jazz is really a different art, with different aims, and so whether there is any definition or characterization of jazz that unites its different eras.[3] In this opening chapter we review some pertinent facts from jazz history. Debates about the nature and value of jazz arise, in part, from factual disputes. Consequently, we are engaged in a descriptive project as well as a conceptual one.[4] In this chapter and the next two, we examine the prospects for a definition that makes sense of the common assumption that jazz is still with us.

1. Dancing and the Essence of Jazz

The first reference to "jazz" in print describes it as dance music. According to Alyn Shipton, the San Francisco *Bulletin* in March 1913 called jazz "dance music full of vigor and 'pep.'"[5] We know usage can change quickly and, says Shipton, while ragtime and blues did not, jazz came to have scatological connotations and stayed disreputable as the music entered the twenties and the Jazz Age. In the middle years of the century, philosopher William Fontaine seems to have been the only African-American professor at an Ivy League college. Recalling his teen years in the 1920s in Chester, Pennsylvania, he says:

> The word 'jazz' sounded everywhere. Shoeshine boys would greet a prospect with, 'Hey! Git a jazz shine!' Bosomy, young brown girls, in two's and three's, strolled the streets at sundown singing, 'Um a jazz baby!' Silk-shirted pimps and loafers lolling on the corners carnivorously eying the budding brown beauties answering, 'Hi, sugar. Would you like to be my jazz baby?'[6]

Above all, jazz was associated with the decadence that went along with prohibition and speakeasies.[7] As one early article asked, "Does Jazz Put the Sin in Syncopation?" Evidently, it did, largely by setting the tone for "barbaric" and "immoral" dancing.[8] As it spread through popular culture, the music came to mean different things to black and white America. But from its beginnings and through its raunchiest periods, jazz was linked to dance. Jazz respectability was, in part, a matter of severing this connection.

For a long stretch of its history, the popularity of jazz was intimately connected with social dancing for which much of the music was created, and with the places in which dancing happened. Although types of dances and kinds of places changed over time, ballrooms were paradigms of places to dance – public places like Roseland or the Savoy Ballroom, that were large enough to house hundreds of in-off-the-street patrons, who would dance to the music of big bands and jazz orchestras and with them scores of jazz vocalists. As a popular art, jazz provided "accessibility with minimum effort, virtually on first contact."[9] As it happens with many art histories, bifurcations within a single art form occur – sharp turns in the evolution of art. At some point jazz changed – its primary point of accessibility disappeared when the music became non-danceable for its audience and its venues became smaller clubs almost exclusively.[10] Its audiences now came to listen to a music that had become increasingly self-conscious. Overall, the change – from large to small places, and from moving bodies to static ones – could be characterized as a shift in kind and in degree. As we explain over the course of this chapter, the shift in kind is from popular art to high art in the music of jazz. The shift in degree is from a high degree of bodily or somatic engagement to a relatively low somatic engagement, approximating the kind of sitting-stillness of a classical concert. Borrowing the words of Richard Shusterman, "an African [-derived] aesthetic of vigorously active and communally impassioned engagement" gradually gave way to a European-style "dispassionate judgmental remoteness."[11] We mark this change as the emergence of bebop in the 1940s. We see it as the most significant historic and aesthetic revolution in jazz history. It arose from socio-cultural forces, but it was also driven by longstanding theoretical assumptions about the arts and the place of jazz within the arts. And it may well be, as several historians propose, that the end of jazz as danceable music, coming at a time when sales of recorded music exploded, opened the doors for rock and roll to fill the void for dancing in a young America.[12]

One way of dividing the diverse periods of the history of jazz is to use criteria that lie outside the music itself and yet are important, as we will argue, for understanding jazz and its stages of development.[13] Jazz as music to dance to characterizes a good deal of jazz up until the 1940s and 1950s when the venues of jazz, its architecture, began to shift as well – not suddenly or everywhere at once – so that, eventually, jazz became a music, live and recorded, to *listen to*. Its central role as paralleling and guiding bodily movement was largely forgotten by its audience. There are two other important ways dancing and jazz are part of a single entity: in addition to dancers out for the evening, professionals were hired to dance as part of the entertainment for those set in place to watch them and then, in a more subtle sense, there is the dancing of the jazz musicians themselves as they play their music, their dancing, for some, literal. In this chapter, then, we widen the perspective in which jazz is understood in order to see it as a cultural phenomenon, part of a form of life that involved professionals and non-professionals alike. Any account of jazz that isolates sounds from bodies is seriously incomplete.

2. Dance Venues

Beginning with the 1920s there were a plethora of jazz clubs, cabarets and ball-rooms, small and large, in which dancing took place. However, any telling of dancing to jazz would do well to focus on the Savoy Ballroom – the Harlem dance emporium that featured some of the best jazz bands in the country. Opening in March of 1926, the huge Savoy turned away 2000 potential customers on its first night, with Fletcher Henderson's orchestra, his band once called

"The Henderson Dance Orchestra," making a guest appearance. Downtown, Roseland was whites-only, but the uptown Savoy was an integrated dance hall, initially the only one in New York City. The Savoy remained the place to be for jazz and dancing almost until it was closed in December 1958. The plaque where it stood begins: "Here stood the Savoy Ballroom, a hothouse for the development of jazz in the Swing Era." But in its heyday it was called "The Home for Happy Feet," placing the emphasis on *dancing* to the music. It was also the pre-eminent social hub in New York City for African-Americans for a night out, and these two phenomena are closely related. The Savoy's reputation as the best place for music was overwhelmed by it being the best place for dancing, with the quality of the dancers themselves a large part of the draw. The Savoy was known for its amazing set of in-off-the-street dancers (amateurs, if you will) who created dances like the Lindy Hop (the steps named after Charles Lindbergh, who had just made the first solo airplane "hop" across the Atlantic in 1927). A partner dance, the Lindy spread all over America and endured for decades. A successor to the Charleston, the Lindy Hop – described by one chronicler as "a symmetrical frenzy" – is still regarded as an essential pattern for jazz social dancing.[14] However, there were many other dances, such as the Shuffle Off to Buffalo. When she was fourteen and fifteen, Ella Fitzgerald was regularly taking the subway ten miles to visit the Savoy to learn the latest new dance steps. Back home in Yonkers, she earned money recreating those dances on street corners and in local clubs.[15] Her rhythmic acuity as one of jazz's greatest vocalists was unquestionably shaped by the dance culture of the Savoy.

The Savoy was remarkable for many reasons. It featured virtually every star of jazz in America, black and white, at one point or another. Even if its occupancy was largely African-American, it was a racially integrated forum during a time of segregated social life in the United States. It was managed by a black man, Charles Buchanan, but was owned by two white men, Moe Gale and Jay Faggen, the latter also the owner of the downtown Roseland, the other great ballroom for dancing to jazz in New York City. Unlike many smaller Harlem dance clubs, the Savoy was a "class" place – an enormous emporium with two bandstands and pink and mirrored walls, which boasted special nights for contests and prizes, including battles of the bands.

Albert Murray's *Stomping the Blues* contains several pages of black and white photographs from Harlem dance halls, one of which shows the street side, the outside of the Savoy Ballroom. The marquee advertises: "BREAKFAST DANCE XMAS EVE SUNDAY DEC 24 HAWKINS MACHITO & JIMMY RUSHING ORCHS." The caption reads "A world-renowned stomping place on Lenox Avenue at 140th Street, from 1926–59, where the music of the great dance orchestras was always at its best. ... The ballroom floor was a block long with a double bandstand to accommodate the two orchestras that usually played alternating sets."[16] Other photos in Murray's book offer a telling glimpse of what went on inside the Savoy. One shows a packed dance floor – entirely African-American – and what looks like slow dancing. Men and women are dressed to the nines and we see a uniformed orchestra on a slightly raised bandstand. The photos are stills, of course, but some suggest the swirling, swift movement of the dancers, their faces exhibiting the thrill of the ride. In the living presence of jazz orchestras, the best means of beating whatever may be downcast for any individual was by stomping the blues at the Savoy on a Saturday night.[17]

Soon after the Savoy opened in 1926, another Harlem jazz venue opened its doors. As social history, the contrast could not have been greater. Located at Lenox Avenue and 125th Street, for years the upscale Cotton Club featured virtually every star of the new "jazz" era. From 1927 to 1931, Duke Ellington's eleven-piece orchestra was on stage, and radio broadcasts from the club gave Ellington a national audience. However, the club was a whites-only forum, with black musicians supporting carefully selected groups of young "Nubian" or "sepia" (African-American) showgirls dancing in a kind of "jungle" act for the white patrons. The set design and choreography was, not surprisingly, by whites.[18] The club was run by gangsters and openly served alcohol during prohibition. The police were happy to cooperate by looking the other way. It was, for New York celebs, a social magnet.

Of course, there were other kinds of clubs, and other kinds of jazz venues. The common story that jazz arose in brothels is now discredited.[19] But Harlem apartments were the site of house parties, where social dancing played an important role in the development of jazz piano. A more notorious setting was the taxi dance hall, perhaps the predecessor of lap dancing. The Rodgers and Hart song "Ten Cents a Dance" (1930) characterizes the sad plight of the female taxi-dancers, who were paid commissions on the basis of their number of dances. The taxi dance halls were popular in urban areas in the 1920s and 1930s: there were over one-hundred in New York at one time. "Ten Cents a Dance" also gave its name to a movie starring Barbara Stanwyck (1931), who began her real life career as a dancer.

However, we have emphasized two different jazz forums featuring dancing as exemplars of their kinds – the first, the Savoy, being an example of a space dedicated to non-professional, non-entertainers who came for social dancing and a good time. Some dancers were better than others, and the best came to be watched and admired as if they provided the entertainment for a song or two. Granted, some jazz fans went to the Savoy and other dance halls strictly for the music, but if they took up space near the bands, bouncers dispersed them to make more room for the dancers.[20] The second, the Cotton Club, is an example of a venue where hired dancers were part of an exotic show and were there to be watched by white audiences. While the ballrooms hardly provided for those sitting one out, nightclubs combined dance floors with food and drink and waiter service: the floor show was a bigger draw than the dance floor. Both kinds of dancing – social and professional – are essential to jazz history. But because it was primarily a space for social dancing, we take the Savoy to be the more typical venue for thinking about the social uses of, and thus central meanings of, jazz.

This emphasis is in line with Murray's account, where there is no hard distinction between jazz and the blues. Having "the blues" is taken to be a serious condition of a depressed spirit, an infectious down in the human condition.[21] It can be of virtually any duration and it is not a condition to be taken lightly. The "blues," the word, is not a term to be used casually. In relation to this condition, stomping means dancing, but it means something like dancing *upon* – stamping out. With an eye on African-American culture, Murray emphasizes that dancing to the music of jazz arose as a powerful antidote to the blues, for as long as its ecstatic, Dionysian energy, its spiritual catharsis embodies the dancers who are, at the same time, hearers of if not listeners to, the music.[22]

However, while there are important sonic and historical relationships between the music of the blues and jazz, the motion of its reception is one way of clarifying the distinct nature of each. Jazz, in the eras we are discussing generated bodies in motion primarily through dance, while the blues was a friend of gravity – its music sinking its listeners into an empathetic stasis.

Murray's interest is on African-American forms of life over the span of several decades. The way he sees it, there is a fundamental conflict between religion, performed at African-American Sunday morning services, and the dancing to the music the night before, the Saturday night dance hall temptations that would be admonished the very next morning. It is a division and contest between a philosophy of life and an aesthetic, with the aesthetic never losing; sermons were ignored come another weekend. Taking this background seriously, the spread of jazz into mainstream "white" culture – fully in place with the Swing Era of the 1930s – severed the functional connection between the music and the form of life that shaped it. As philosopher Paul Taylor observes, African-American entertainment and music of the 1920s and 1930s addressed needs and values "drawn from poor and working-class [African-American] communities," rather than aspirational, bourgeoisie values.[23] To the extent that the early decades of blues and jazz were informed by such values, the mainstreaming of jazz brought it to an audience that appreciated the music, but never again in quite the same way. (We expand on our reasoning in support of this position in section 8 of this chapter.)

We must also take notice of a very different jazz forum of the 1920s and 1930s: the movie theater and its representations of jazz and jazz dance.[24] For example, Murray's idea about music stomping the blues did not go unnoticed by Stanley Cavell, who lauds as poetry the lyrics to the Irving Berlin tune, "Cheek to Cheek": "And the cares that hung around me through the week/Seem to vanish like a gambler's lucky streak/When we're out together dancing cheek to cheek."[25] Although both sales of recorded jazz and movie attendance plummeted during the Great Depression, popular entertainment offered endless representations of escape from the pervasive economic blues. The song "Cheek to Cheek" is from the 1935 movie *Top Hat*, the title alone offering the suggestion of apparel as an emblem of social class. While they are dancing, Fred Astaire sings this song to Ginger Rogers. The depicted dance floor looks very unlike the scene at the

Savoy. Yet the fairy-tale world of *Top Hat* offers an uptown parallel to stomping the blues, symbolically addressing real-world problems in song and dance.[26] (Yet, we again acknowledge that, given the pervasive discrimination and oppression that has characterized American race relations, the blues of the dominant culture was not identical with the blues of poor and working-class black communities.) Astaire and Rogers dance among other couples on the floor of the nightclub until everyone else seems to vanish like a gambler's lucky streak. Although the dancing is strictly choreographed, in the fiction the two represent dancers who happen to be out on the dance floor. However, as we still acknowledge, the two dance like no one else when it comes to grace with deceptive ease. Astaire and Rogers are not depicted as entertainers, just part of an audience that got up to dance. However, at times the dancers become transformed into performers as other, less skilled dancers, the extras, break around them, giving them adequate room to perform for their admirers, fictional nightclubbers and real moviegoers watching with smiles. "Cheek to Cheek" was written specifically for Astaire and the film, and his commercial recording of the song stayed at number one on the charts for five weeks. Despite its length and unusually complex structure, it became a standard for jazz singers, including notable recordings by Billie Holiday, Sarah Vaughan, and Louis Armstrong with Ella Fitzgerald. As it often does, jazz comes full circle: black performers reclaim mainstream appropriations of African-American cultural resources.

White nightclubs are frequently depicted in old black and white musicals like *Top Hat*. Movies like *Shall We Dance* (1937) and *Swing Time* (1936), also with Astaire/Rogers, record some of the best dance routines ever. And, they often take place in clubs where the floors shine as brightly as the diamonds adorning the women at the well-lit tables that seat the audience. The impression is clear – these are folks who spend their nights at such clubs. Formal attire is required, natural evening wear for regular patrons, with the nightclub most times an important part of the narrative. There is, then, an obvious gap between the moviegoers' evenings and the depicted clubbers and so any generalizing about the state of American late nights, say as seen in China and other global markets for American entertainment, should be taken with a grain of salt. This was not your grandpa's late night. That being said, we should add that there have been and still are nightclubs that approximate the class acts of the movies. The Savoy, not a nightclub at all, was of an entirely different ilk. The Savoy provided a participatory solution to the blue moods. In contrast, as seen in the movies, nightclubs screened a fantasy America during dark times, depicting a complex escape, an unreachable way of life, for its viewers.

In an important sense, the idealized film depiction represented a mainstream endorsement of the world of jazz and dancing. Todd Decker reminds us that ten of the Astaire films in which he sings and dances are situated in nightclubs and in seven of those he performs in nightclubs only. But he also notes that before Astaire, in George Raft movies for example, the nightclub was a seedy, dark realm, full of danger. Raft's *Dancing in the Dark* (1932) or his *Stolen Harmony* (1935) are examples of these "desperate worlds" where "jazz carried the mark of menace or sexual laxity."[27] But in Astaire's cleaned-up films all that changed and the nightclub became this bright and wholesome place for café society. We read this transformation not simply as Hollywood escapism, but also as a symbolic appropriation of the jazz world for a larger (white) American audience. Astaire's commitment to jazz is sometimes explicit: in the lyrics of "The Ritz Roll and Rock," his closing song and tap performance in *Silk Stockings* (1957), he sings that rock'n'roll is "square" and "dead" in comparison with jazz.

At the same time that the Astaire/Rogers dance movies filled cinemas, America made movies with all black casts and several featured nightclubs as the architecture for jazz. In *The Duke is Tops* (1938), for example, Lena Horne was a club singer before she made it to Broadway. *Paradise in Harlem* (1938) prominently represents both professional and social dancing in Harlem, in both elegant clubs and downscale honky-tonks. Cab Calloway was a band leader in *Murder with Music* (1941) and *Hi De Ho* (1947) where jazz was integrated and expected in the plots. A few mixed-race nightclubs existed in New York, most notably Connie's Inn and the Paradise. One of the most famous lent its name to a film: the "orchestras" of Count Basie and Benny Goodman both appear in *Stage Door Canteen* (1943), which sets a fictional romance in a stage-set recreation of the famous New York nightclub reserved for enlisted servicemen during World War II. The Canteen provided food and an opportunity to dance with young "hostesses," and racial segregation was prohibited.

Although no one knew it at the time, *Stage Door Canteen* depicts a social practice that was approaching its final days. Eventually, when jazz moved almost exclusively to small clubs in the 1940s and 1950s, the audiences, the patrons, came closer to being listeners only, rather than hearers who focused on dancing. Once that happened, dancing and jazz came together far less often. Increasingly, jazz was present only in the bodily movements of the musicians themselves. We get to this third mode of dancing in section 7.

3. Tapping Into Jazz

Jazz was dance music with a beat. Although we will not dwell on it, we should take note of an important development of jazz dance that was popular in both participatory and professional forms: tap. There is a large variety of dances and dancers that are part of the world of jazz music, but tap has a special place and it helps to understand why one might say that jazz is a dance. What makes the jazz from the 1920s to the 1940s so ripe for tap dancing is percussion. The sounds of dancing with metal taps on shoes was tantamount to playing an instrument with one's feet. In a 1973 obituary for the great tap dancer, Baby Laurence, Whitney Balliett wrote, "A great drummer tap dances sitting down. A great tap-dancer drums standing up."[28] When the music was on, this form of dancing was like another instrument and so, with tap dancing, we have the *sound* of dancing. Tap dancing intervals sometimes replaced the drums and were often solos with metal taps clicking on to hard, polished floors.

Introduced to white America in 1921 in the all-black Broadway hit *Shuffle Along*, tap dancing quickly became a staple of theater entertainment. With the advent of "talkies" in 1927, tap was frequently showcased in Hollywood films and became the rage among non-professionals, as well. Hollywood screened tap dancers such as Bill "Bojangles" Robinson, the Nicholas Brothers, John W. Bubbles, Ralph Brown, and, later, Gregory Hines and Savion Glover. But here, again, we have a dimension of the art that did not remain exclusively African-American. Among the greats were Fred Astaire and Eleanor Powell. Astaire's dancing perfection, as we saw above, went well beyond tap. Yet Astaire's first appearance in film, in the movie *Flying Down to Rio* (1933), was "a genuine jazz encounter" – it was not a dance with Ginger Rogers, but a solo tap dance to the song, "Music Makes Me."[29] In his essay, "Astaire Asserts the Right to Praise," Stanley Cavell reproduces seventeen frames from the film *The Band Wagon* (1953) as the basis of a detailed analysis of a tap dance routine between a somewhat older Astaire and an African-American shoeshine man (Leroy Daniels) in an arcade. Cavell reads this encounter as a "dance of praise" in which Astaire pays homage to African-American dance, specifically tap dance. The dance is a wordless acknowledgement of the roots of something in which Astaire excels. But the essay is really a defensive against the charge that the routine is really a gesture of domination of the white culture over the black – a claim made by Michael Rogin in his book *Blackface, White Noise*. While granting some ambiguity in the sequence, Cavell understands it as "dance of identity" in which "Astaire provides himself with an occasion for acknowledging his indebtedness for his existence as a dancer – his deepest identity – to the genius of black dancing."[30]

If film brought tap to the larger American culture, no such mediation was necessary in the world of black entertainment. At the Apollo Theater in New York's Harlem, tap dancing was on the stage and infectious throughout the audience. Sandman Sims recalls that, "Up in the balcony, dancers, and the first six rows, you saw nothing but tap dancers, wanna-be tap dancers, gonna-be tap dancers, tried-to-be tap dancers. That's the reason a guy would want to dance at the Apollo."[31] In the face of such intense scrutiny, it is no wonder that an aspiring dancer – Ella Fitzgerald, still a teenager – canceled her dancing debut at the Apollo just before her scheduled performance and sang, instead.[32]

Looking back at this era, Francis Ford Coppola's movie *The Cotton Club* (1984) depicts many of the aspects of the Harlem emporium – racial divisions, gangsters, dancing "jungle" routines, and jazz. But whatever one thinks of the movie, its tap dancing was a key feature and, with Gregory Hines in a substantial role in the film and lots of screen time dancing, it was first class in that respect. The movie depicts tap dancing, at the fabled Hoofer's Club (with blacks-only membership, in a small back room of a comedy and gambling club) and elsewhere, as a major aspect of African-American culture of the Jazz Age and to that end it does it well.

4. Initial Reflections on Definitions

Dancing may not be definitional of jazz in the strict sense of being one element in a list of necessary and sufficient conditions. However, dancing to jazz in many of its various incarnations is as important to capture the spirit of the music as any trait one might find inside a purported essence that probes the music alone. If you were telling the proverbial martian about jazz, trying to explain what jazz is, your explanation would be frustrated if you left out the part about dancing to the music. Dancing has accompanied the proto-music of jazz since its beginning and through its most important phases, at least until about 1960.[33] And, if we assume that dancing without music makes no sense except in an avant-garde tradition of modern dance, then music is a necessary condition for dancing. But if for commercial purposes, jazz orchestras worked only if dancers made it to their bandstands, then for the big bands, dancing was a necessary condition for their existence as well. Even so, it would be a mistake to think that the relationship was simply commercial. It would be another mistake to think that the dancers simply took their cues from the rhythms provided by the musicians.[34] In fact, jazz musicians frequently took their cues from the dancers. To return to the example of the Savoy Ballroom, bands rehearsed in the afternoon, sharing their space with non-professional dancers who practiced their steps for the coming evening. The musicians were aware of the dancers, and if they saw the dancers quit "and walk off," recalls trombonist Dicky Wells, "the rhythm's wrong. But when you get that beat he's right in there saying, 'Play that again!'"[35] So a symbiotic relationship between jazz and dancing existed during the heyday of jazz popularity, before the small clubs became the scene for jazz.

There is a suggestion, in Ludwig Wittgenstein's *Philosophical Investigations*, that for many cases, meaning can be found by looking for use. Use, in turn, can sometimes be explained by locating a word or phrase in the language game in which it has a home. And, in this extended sense, to learn a language is to learn a form of life and only in its use does a sign take on meaning. Wittgenstein put it this way: "Every sign *by itself* seems dead. *What* gives it life? In its use it is *alive*. Is life breathed into it there? Or is the *use* its life?"[36] Put another way, Wittgenstein is emphasizing that meaning is more than just syntax and semantics. There are also always pragmatic elements – the things we are trying to *do* by using a particular word or phrase in a particular context, over and above describing the world. Differences in pragmatic force are easily obscured when a word has distinct multiple uses. The criteria for sameness change in different situations, and so the meaning, or use, of "same" varies with the context of use.

However, it is not just language that has meaning in relation to an associated form of life. Art forms do, too. Applying the Wittgensteinian approach to the concept of jazz, what it means – saying what it is – we must look for the form of life in which "jazz" has its role. An explanation of what jazz is must therefore include an account of jazz in its life situations. That life, we note, is contingent, not necessary, and like biological life may change or come to an end. That is one reason art history is important in understanding the lives of artworks – some styles and genres come to their end while others live on. What we are saying about jazz, then, is that from its inception it was a music intending to move bodies, created for and with the consequence of dancing to it, and by that we mean popular social dancing, dancing that came as natural to many as running or talking. Dancing was part of our form of life when jazz was in the air, backgrounding and coloring our immediate world. Perhaps the best way to say this, is to say that with jazz, it took an effort *not* to dance. But as the music became associated with other forms of life, dance rhythms became less central, and new forms of life have come to dominate the jazz world. Change was fed by numerous economic and social factors, and while we will mention some, we will make no effort to survey all of them. The important point is that, serving new functions, new sounds emerged; as these became the established sound of jazz, older forms of life were no longer supported.

5. Dancing in the Streets

Jazz, as a novel kind of twentieth-century dance music, had an efficacious past. Yet, the earliest jazz remains shrouded in mystery. In the absence of contemporary accounts and detailed original sources, most of what we know about it was assembled long after the fact by fans, critics, and (more recently) music historians. Much of what we know is found in interviews conducted with first-generation jazz musicians. However, their stories include many questionable claims and occasional outlandish fabrications, ranging from conflicting stories by various musicians about where and how the term "jazz" became the name for a new kind of music,[37] to Jelly Roll Morton's hyperbolic boasts that he invented both ragtime and jazz.[38] If a great deal about early jazz is uncertain, disputed, and subject to historical reappraisal, at least one thing appears beyond dispute: its origins link it inexorably to bodily motion. If we go back to the earliest aspects of jazz in America, what is not yet jazz, but what is considered proto-jazz by many, say back to the nineteenth century, jazz and dancing were linked even then.

As we suggest throughout this chapter, place is important for what happens.[39] To know when jazz appeared, we must know where: "What jazz was – for friend and foe alike – [included] where it was performed."[40] If we ask *where* did jazz begin, the answer may well be, in the streets. Or at least in the out of doors, sometimes in designed or designated areas, sometimes just negative spaces, and sometimes, as in farms and fields, just there for other reasons or no reason at all.

By most accounts dancing in the street, in New Orleans, at least since the beginning of the nineteenth century, is part of the answer. There, at *Place Congo*, what is pretty much today's Louis Armstrong Park, African slaves moving to rhythmic drums, handclapping, and to strange string instruments (something like a calabash), took part by the hundreds in Ring Dances, on Sunday, their day off.

It was one piece of a strong cultural tradition, an outgrowth of religious custom that survived as spirit in their Afro/Caribbean transport. So, it was not an event incubated from an overall worldview – was not art set separately from life. And the participatory aspect of this rhythmic music should be emphasized along with the availability of dancing out of doors.

In 1817, New Orleans, in an amazing gesture, officially designated the area, Congo Square, for slaves to do their singing and dancing on Sundays – legitimizing a place for their traditional music but prohibiting it anywhere else. Still a far cry from any music of the twentieth century, jazz historians attribute these weekly New Orleans slave rituals as an important component of the social and artistic mixture that eventually became jazz. Slave dancing in Congo Square would regularly include hundreds, sometimes thousands of dancers dancing the Bamboula or Calinda, "in their gay, picturesque finery."[41] These dances were often connected with Voodoo, which means ecstatic bodily movements, with contortions and trances, whirling, delirium, and trembling. Shipton notes that, "The ecstatic element of the slave and Voodoo dances described by 19th century historians was carried forward into the atmosphere of early jazz dances in New Orleans and Chicago."[42] As is typical, African-American culture became white entertainment. Grace King, whose history of New Orleans Shipton relied upon, "describes the street entertainment and food stalls set up round and about for white onlookers."[43] One can only wonder what went through the minds of the participants and, more so, what a white observer might have been thinking watching slaves dancing in public to a music as different radically from its current status as we today might imagine.

By definition, marches and funerals are also out-of-doors events. These two also came together in New Orleans. Originating as a white phenomenon before being taken up by African-Americans, funeral marches or jazz funerals – mournful one way while upbeat on the return from the graveyard – may have been the first instance of brass instruments being inserted into the fledgling history of jazz. Portability determines the kinds of instruments used and the instruments in turn determine the limits of the music. Whether with respect to dancing or marching, the proto-jazz form of New Orleans funeral music was intimately connected with motion. Marches were linear in motion with the participants tied to musical instruments, while audiences, if we can call them that, were whoever might happen to be street side. Bands became so prevalent and marches of all sorts such frequent outdoor phenomena it was like boom boxes being carried across neighborhoods in more recent times. It is important to emphasize that the march steps strongly resembled dancing, as if moving forward by dancing in one direction.

According to Arthur Singleton, black youth gained an identity by belonging to a band and so to a larger community association. Children were trained to play musical instruments so that they could function in many of the social activities of the black communities, and family bands became an institution and hung on until well after slavery became tenant farming. Black associations sponsored funeral marches so that, "When the member died, he had to have a band. He was nothing if he didn't have a band."[44] Associations such as "the Masons, Odd Fellows, Druids, Eagles, Moose, Knights of St. Pythias, and trade unions" sponsored black groups that played funerals but also dance halls and outdoor events such as picnics and baseball games. The funeral tradition continues today and is one of the icons of New Orleans, continually cementing the relationship between that city and music.[45]

Jazz also became the music of New Orleans parades. The difference between marches and parades is simply one of context. It is analytic of a parade that it is ceremonial, that there is an occasion prompting its forward motion. Marches can happen anytime and in New Orleans they seemed to happen with music almost daily. Needless to say, Mardi Gras, through hundreds of years of New Orleans life, remains the most celebrated, imitated, and Dionysian of American parades. In any case, it was marches, generally, that played a most dynamic and prevalent part of the history of the Crescent City, immersing it in a type of music that was largely an outdoor phenomenon. Bands and marching became synonymous and young blacks joined bands, which later became part of the social aspects of New Orleans, clubs and organizations being represented by their own bands.

Following in the footsteps of marching musicians was what came to be called "the second line." Murray describes this practice, which is an important supplement to parades and marches:

> In the context of the history of jazz music in the United States, the second line refers to that element of the traditional New Orleans street parade which consists of groups of admirers and protégés who march and prance and dance along the curb and sidewalk beside their favorite bands, sometimes for the length of the street in their neighborhoods and sometimes as far as escorting traffic policemen permit, with other enthusiasts joining in all along the route of the procession to the ceremonial destination.[46]

Keeping in mind the largely unavailable prospects of indoor space for music and the extremely poor unemployment circumstances of musicians, marching in the streets took on a daily musical presence and a competitive status. Bands would march and, as street accidents happen, would intersect at cross streets, sometimes resulting in violent meetings. One has to think here of con-temporary turf wars in African-American neighborhoods as a matter of who owned the streets.

Brass bands played at every imaginable event and venue in New Orleans, in large tents at parks and plazas. Steamboats regularly floated dancing up and down the Mississippi. To get an idea of the ubiquitous use of musical instruments in New Orleans consider this particular visit, noted by Ken Burns and Geoffrey C. Ward: "When Patrick Sarsfield Gilmore, the master cornetist and bandleader, who was as celebrated as John Philip Sousa in his day, presented a Grand National Concert at Lafayette Square, five hundred New Orleans brass players turned out to play with him."[47]

We will discuss the centrality of race to jazz in an analysis later in this book. In a racially segregated nation, it is no surprise to find that forums for performing jazz and dancing to its music also had their own institutionalized mechanisms for keeping the races separated. Segregation did not, however, prevent whites from taking on aspects of black music that they could imitate, perhaps in a spirit of envy. Here, in the out of doors, it is *dancing* that we find being copied in this description by Murray:

> [B]ack during the years when black dance and stage show bands became nationally famous because of their recordings and radio broadcasts, when their schedules took them into the then widely and strictly segregated South, there was in effect a practice that amounted to a fourth line: a small number of white musicians and fans would arrange with the local legal authorities to have the venue owners and operators provide a special roped-off area from which there was a good view of the bandstand and within which they could dance with dates which some of them sometimes brought along, especially if they wanted to try out some of the new movements that the regular clientele were playing around with at the time.[48]

6. Moving Indoors

Almost from the beginning, jazz was as much indoors music as out. Although against the rules, slaves danced regularly in taverns (and with proper passes could attend the opera, having their own special section). By 1841 there were over eighty ballrooms in New Orleans that housed dancers entertained by musician marchers who now doubled as indoor entertainers. Before the Civil War, some of these ballrooms held the markets for sales of slaves.

The biggest difference between music indoors and out of doors was the contained sound. The intimacy, the closeness of an indoor night in New Orleans before and after the Civil War, made the music personal. Stages were built for acoustical purposes and to oversee the mobile audience. Burton Peretti makes note of this transition from outside to inside:

> [A]s bands shifted more rapidly indoors, acoustical standards were developed and articulated. The drummer Warren "Baby" Dodds indicated that early bands cared deeply about how their music sounded amid noise, noting that they preferred to play on platforms about four feet high. "Music is more even when it comes down on people's heads, because it hits the ceiling and comes down on them," and "a band will sound better if the best place in the room is picked out to set up the band."[49]

Of course, much later, in the twentieth century, intimacy was upended by the vast festival concerts and overhead projections, common in rock arenas, but also true of many gatherings for jazz.

After 1915, about the same time as the word "jazz" began to be used widely to refer to the music, increasing numbers of African-Americans migrated from South to North. Many musicians settled in Chicago's South Side and in the Midway section just outside downtown and played in numerous clubs and enormous dance halls, but also in vaudeville and movie theaters, where audiences watched, made noise, but didn't dance, like the standard audiences at solemn classical concerts. One can imagine, however, that even with jazz groups playing theaters, dancing in the aisles was not unknown. In the Swing Era, it may even have been commonplace. In 1937, teenagers flocked to New York's Paramount Theater when Benny Goodman appeared, purchased tickets for seats, and then many, lifted by the music, abandoned their seats to jitterbug in the aisles.[50] At this point, the music was making its way out of the dance halls into other venues. But the dance hall was still present in its rhythms.

7. The Turn

As we have argued thus far, in its infancy and then in the period during which jazz developed a distinctive identity, jazz was dance music, and the dancing varied according to the places in which it was embedded. That is, until the 1950s, when social dancing to jazz slowed to a standstill.

There are several accounts as to what happened to jazz at about this point. They vary according to the weight they assign to artistic, economic, social, and demographic developments. In any case, jazz underwent a revolution of sorts: changing music, changing locations, and there was also a change in what happened to the body when jazz was in the air.

Here are two contrasting stories about that revolution. The first account might be described as the standard account.

With the entry of the United States into World War II, many swing musicians were drafted into the armed forces. The war years were hard on jazz. With rationing, it was difficult for jazz groups to stage multi-city tours. At the same time, the American Federation of Musicians organized its member musicians and launched a ban on newly recorded music. The ban was an attempt to provide more paid work for musicians by limiting the use of recorded music by radio networks. Put simply, the result was that no new jazz was recorded for release to the general public from August 1, 1942 until February 16, 1944, when Coleman Hawkins and his orchestra recorded several sides, with Dizzy Gillespie as arranger.[51] A year later, Gillespie had a contract to record small combo bebop under his own name. Charlie Parker was a member of Gillespie's septet. A flurry of bop recordings followed, often for new independent labels, and America finally got to hear the music that had arisen in New York City jam sessions while the war limited touring and kept the boppers-to-be place-bound and in continuous contact. Their new style of jazz was the antithesis of swing. Bop's fans embraced it, in part, as a symbol of progress within jazz. However, it was not just *musical* progress: "the bebop revolution in the mid-1940s" constitutes "[t]he historical transformation of jazz from entertainment music to an art music."[52] In other words, bop is a renunciation of mainstream commercial entertainment, and of the "whitening" of jazz in the Swing Era.[53] According to a recent college-level textbook, bebop is "complex, dense, and difficult to grasp," and its emergence marks the point at which jazz becomes "self-conscious art music."[54] An anthology on jazz dance agrees that bop "propel[s] ... jazz music into the status of an art form."[55] Until then, jazz had been overwhelmingly created as dance music. In contrast, bop was decidedly non-danceable (although some people will dance to their busy signal). In David Ake's apt description, it is "precarious" for social dancing.[56] Relocated from dance halls to small nightclubs and the concert stage, jazz turned its back on "popular music."[57] Aspiring to transform modern jazz into "art-music," the boppers and their successors produced "a recital music" – "not ... played for dancing, but for listening."[58] In short, jazz developed "art" credentials by reducing accessibility and by transforming its primary function into providing the aesthetic rewards of attentive listening.

Here is the second account. It emphasizes that jazz has almost always been produced as an element of a commercial enterprise, subject to market forces, and that bop is no exception.

Six weeks after the American Federation of Musicians settled with most record companies and lifted the recording ban, the federal government raised the long-standing "cabaret tax" to 30%. The change imposed a new 25% surcharge on all receipts in establishments where food was served and where there was either dancing or staged entertainment. The tax applied to any "public place" offering both "refreshments" and "dancing privileges or any other entertainment, except instrumental or mechanical music alone."[59] Throughout the country, the tax undercut profits at clubs with small dance floors. Most clubs and dance halls closed. To remain in business, most of those staying open did so by banning the activities that were subject to the tax: they filled their dance floors with tables and eliminated all taxable "entertainment."[60] Since "mechanical" music included all recorded music, jukeboxes could play vocal music. And patrons could dance to a jukebox without creating a tax liability for the owners. Jukeboxes became ubiquitous. But in many establishments that continued to feature live music, vocalists were banned. Aside from jukebox operators and the record companies that stocked them, the surprising "winners" were the small instrumental combos.[61] It was an advantage if the music was *not* danceable. Bebop was suddenly high profile in New York City nightclubs. "You couldn't have a big band," explained drummer Max Roach, "because the big band played for dancing." Instrumental prowess became central, "because people came to hear music."[62] On 52nd Street, signs that proclaimed "No Tax" were soon understood to mean that the club featured only small combo, instrumental jazz.[63] Solo pianists also gained. Although it is seldom mentioned, another obvious consequence of the elevated tax (which persisted at a 20% levy through the 1950s) was that it limited work for jazz vocalists, who either had to appear in concert settings or appeal to the taste of the clientele of expensive hotels and nightclubs.

The standard account tells us that jazz was elevated to an art form, which made it less suitable for dancing, and so it was no longer presented in dance halls and clubs that catered to dancing. The complexity of the new music drove away the dancers. The second account tells us that club owners had economic incentives to ban dancing, which meant abandoning swing rhythm, and this gave them an incentive to hire and promote bebop. The loss of dancing – both social dance and staged entertainment – was a victim of circumstances on either account. What remained, for some jazz musicians, was doing a kind of dance while playing their music.

The two narratives, we propose, are contrasting but not mutually exclusive. All modern artworlds include an economic web. In painting, for example, galleries and auction houses, dollar amounts on paintings, patrons as well as artists exist parallel to each other in artworld wheeling and dealing. In jazz, the narrative of the connection between sound and body is grounded in situations of taxes and fees, of politicos and real estate, all happening simultaneously in our everyday lives. We can isolate them for purposes of "analysis," but in a "real world" the two accounts we have suggested are mixed as one.

The dual accounts we have presented are partial descriptions of our form of life at a particular turning point in jazz history. Jazz, we have said, is not merely an art of sound. Different styles of music and different rhythms imply different embodiments and physical responses, and these in turn are structured, in part, by the places and social practices in which the music develops and is presented. Taken together, the art contributes to and is an element of a particular form of life. Although we by no means want to imply a dichotomy of body and mind, social practices are also influenced by ideas and ideals, including ideas about the proper role of art in our lives. Artworks, in particular, as Arthur Danto has argued, are embodied meanings.[64] In Danto's view, it is one of the characteristics that differentiate "mere real things" from artworks, the latter of which require some degree of interpretation. Jazz, we have argued, was initially and for many years an art that invited active, *participatory* interpretation, primarily in the form of social dancing. High art, in contrast, is designed to facilitate a different kind of encounter – the adoption of an attitude of aesthetic disinterest, a mode of thinking about what performances are about – that no one characterizes as directly participatory. The standard account of the bebop revolution draws on longstanding ideas about art's incompatibility with entertainment and popular art, which in turn aligns with assumptions about the divide between aesthetic disinterest, interpretation, and bodily engagement – between, say, listening to music and dancing to it. Even if the standard account is corrected by the second account, so that economic factors bear more of the burden in the explanation of bebop's rise, we still have to account for the widespread view that it constitutes the point at which jazz becomes self-conscious art music. Eurocentric, modernist assumptions about the non-participatory nature of art and art music were already in place, and they encourage the judgment that jazz "becomes" art once the masses no longer dance to it. And when the artists were no longer responsible for providing rhythms for dancing, jazz could develop in many directions stylistically.

However, it is fairly easy to refute the idea that bop was simply music for listening and not music for dancing. It had merely ceased to be music for social dancing; with the rise of bop, "Latin" rhythms became increasingly common for social dancing at the Savoy.[65] Although there were fewer venues for them, professional dancers developed new steps and routines to accompany bop groups in theatrical variety shows. Dancing to jazz, we might say, became professionalized. Intended for African-American cinemas, the film *Jivin' in Be-bop* (1947) features Dizzy Gillespie's orchestra – indeed, his name is almost as prominent as the film title on surviving posters. Today, jazz fans may be surprised to find bop standards, such as "Salt Peanuts," "A Night in Tunisia," and "Ornithology," being used as the support for entertaining dance routines. Ralph Brown, who paid his dues at the Cotton Club in the 1930s, tap dances to "Ornithology" by syncopating rapid eighth notes against the basic meter. The duo Johnny and Henny combine tap, shuffle, splits, and backflips. Two couples adjust the Lindy Hop to bop (to a tune that appears to be called "Shoot Me a Little Dynamite Eight"). Ray Sneed, who receives third billing, improvises to Milt Jackson's vibraphone.[66] Gillespie himself can be seen swaying and gyrating to the music at a few points in the film.

Gillespie was certainly not the only bop star to move with the music. When working with Thelonious Monk, another of the style's founders, other musicians knew that they were meeting his high expectations because he left the piano and danced around the stage. Drummer Ben Riley recalls that Monk's dancing was sometimes a sign of praise, and at other times a method of directing the group: "when his music was happening, then he'd get up and do his little dance. ... he knew you knew where you were and the music was swinging, and that's what he wanted. So [by dancing] he said, 'Well, I don't have to play now. You're making it happen.'" At the same time, it could indicate that Monk wanted the rhythm section to swing harder, pushing him: "when he got up and danced ... we need to just give it some more energy."[67] Monk's dance is on full display in the opening minutes of *Straight, No Chaser*, the 1988 documentary film about Monk and his music. The film footage opens mid-tune, with Charlie Rouse's tenor saxophone solo in the middle of Monk's composition "Evidence." Dressed to the nines, Monk is away from his piano, spinning – almost marching – in place, swinging his arms to the beat. Suddenly, he leaves the stage. His band shows no concern and keeps swinging. Monk sprints back in view and hits the keys before he's even seated at his piano. The amazing thing is that he resumes dancing. Anchored by his left heel against the bottom of his piano bench, his entire right leg bounces to the music while his right foot taps a more complex syncopated rhythm, heel to toe. Ellington, also, in his sixties danced in front of his band.

Unlike, say, Louis Armstrong, there is no evidence that Monk ever danced to entertain the audience. Working at Chicago's Sunset Cafe in 1926, Armstrong routinely closed the show in "the wee hours of the morning" by moving to the dance floor with several other musicians. They fanned out and, to the delight of the audience, became the floor show by doing the Charleston.[68] If we now find it hard to imagine a time when jazz musicians danced for the customers, it is *not* because the music became genuinely undanceable. As demonstrated by the 1947 clip of Ralph Brown tap dancing to Gillespie's "Ornithology," any music with a predictable, accented pulse is danceable. But where there is no groove, however incidental it may be to the non–musician, jazz performers cannot create the rhythmic play that is characteristic of jazz. (We discuss this at length in Chapter 2.) Kenny Clarke moved timekeeping from the bass drum to the ride cymbal – "a tectonic shift"[69] – and the crucial cues for social dancing were no longer prominent in the sound. Yet they were still there for the musicians. Once a performing group locks together around a basic pulse, it no longer has to be explicit. Granted, it becomes easier for an individual to lose the pulse once it becomes downplayed or merely implicit. Miles Davis valued the restrained playing of pianist Bill Evans, but Evans provided limited rhythmic support to soloists, sometimes dropping out altogether. Evans' restraint was especially problematic for saxophonist Cannonball Adderley, who counted on a solid rhythm section in which the pianist worked with the drummer to provide "direction" without "lead[ing]" him during his soloing.[70] Adderley, it seems, was not ready to follow Davis and Evans into a more "subdued" form of jazz; he still wanted to swing, and he was happy when Evans departed and Wynton Kelly joined, because Kelly was strong with "both the subdued things and the swingers."

Despite the challenges of playing to a pulse that is sometimes only implicit, post-bop jazz is no less dependent on rhythmic interplay than earlier jazz. It is more dependent, therefore, on less overt clues, and it relies more heavily on entrainment among the players in the absence of their participatory entrainment with an audience or with trained dancers. (In conspicuous cases, entrainment is physical synchronization to a rhythm in one's environment, but there can also be genuine synchronization without physical display of it.) If a seated audience still has the freedom to entrain with jazz musicians through foot tapping and head nodding, the musicians themselves are often dancing silently, entraining in the virtual dance floor of their imaginations. But these responses can seem like mere vestigial structures of getting up and dancing and an audience that does not dance, for whatever reason, may be missing out on, holding back from, what was once a socially sanctioned form of letting oneself go: stomping the blues.

8. Concluding Reflections on a Form of Life

In *The Book of Jazz*, written in the 1950s, Leonard Feather is questioning trumpeter Don Ellis. Summing up their conversation, Ellis tells Feather:

> Many people have not yet figured out exactly what music is. They don't realize that it is closely related to dancing – either popular or classical dancing; there is a relationship between the bodily movements and the essence of a lot of music. Along with an expansion of the rhythmic facets of jazz, there should be a great broadening of the concepts of dancing in coordination with it.[71]

Unfortunately, dancing and jazz continued to drift farther apart. For complex reasons, the bebop revolution relocated jazz from large to small places, and participatory social dancing gave way to seated spectators. When jazz was presented in larger venues, it was no longer the ballroom but Carnegie Hall or Lincoln Center.[72] The management no longer hung signs that said "No Dancing Allowed," as they did when the cabaret tax jumped in 1944. The idea that jazz is now art music has the same effect. In large part, Duke Ellington's performance at the 1956 Newport Jazz Festival became noteworthy and revitalized interest in his music because a single individual, a trained dancer named Elaine Anderson, got up to dance during "Diminuendo and Crescendo in Blue," inspiring both soloist Paul Gonsalves and other dancers.[73] At a 1950s jazz concert, musical interaction with dancers was remarkable, not the norm. Sure enough, we see that the liner notes to *Ellington at Newport* (1956) take pains to reassure jazz fans that Anderson and the crowd "were listening," and not engaged in a "rock'n'roll reaction."[74] This shift is less significant for conferring cultural respectability on jazz than for the attendant loss of a shared form of life: we deny that this shift represents progress.

The diminishing of the role of dancing to the music of jazz, even at its transformation into a "higher" form of art, cannot be a good thing. Among many other things, dancing for fun and participatory social dancing to jazz – dancing in-off-the streets as we have put it earlier – has always been at the heart of the vernacular side of the art. Sadly, that side of the art/entertainment divide is all but unknown in the *lived experiences* of most jazz fans that came of age after 1950. There are attendant changes in the communities in which jazz arose and initially developed, some of which Albert Murray has outlined. There is another, more subtle change, and it lies within the brains, and thus the receptive processes and assessments, of the audience. As Duke Ellington observes, "people who don't dance, or who never did dance, don't really understand the beat."[75] Although the neuroscience of music listening is still in its infancy, we have increasing evidence that Ellington is right: people who've never danced to a particular rhythm will have a limited, more "mechanical" response to it. In a very real sense, they will not fully understand it.

The significance of this claim is hard to overstate. Musicological and critical discussions of the bebop revolution emphasize that it represents progress because it introduced harmonic complexity into jazz.[76] However, harmonic variance and complexity is only meaningful to listeners who are anticipating (albeit unconsciously) specific harmonic events. Stylistically attuned listeners generally expect specific note sequences in melodies and specific chord changes at specific points in the music's development, such as on the first beat of a particular measure. Music's emotional effect is largely a product of how it is designed to both fulfill and violate these expectations.[77] Notice, however, that these expectations depend on a listener's understanding of, and expectations about, meter and rhythm: "deciphering the metrical structure of a piece is a critically important aspect of understanding" any given piece of music.[78] That is because mental processing of melody and harmony is separate from rhythm processing.[79] In jazz, as in metrical music more generally, a listener's competence in rhythmic anticipation creates the basic musical "space" or metrical grouping that underlies melodic and harmonic affect. Listeners with a limited sense of rhythmic anticipation cannot be surprised by Herbie Hancock's thematic prolongation in "Watermelon Man" (1962) (making it a 16-bar blues) if they have no prior experience with 12-bar blues, and cannot be impressed that Dizzy Gillespie provides eight chords where there should be only four in two bars of "I Can't Get Started" in 1945.

So what has all this to do with dancing? Psychologically, we process rhythms by *anticipating* stress and grouping; when our psychological expectations align with what we hear, we achieve entrainment – we "lock" into music's metrical and rhythmic organization. What we can now say with confidence (but many long suspected) is that listeners who do not entrain with metrically structured music do not know how to locate its rhythms. We "hear" metrical regularity only by entraining with it. (Gregorian chant is probably the most familiar case of Western nonmetrical music.) Entraining does not mean that someone passively "follows" metrical groupings. That gets it the wrong way around. To borrow from musicologist Justin London, "Musical meter is the *anticipatory* schema that is the result of our inherent abilities to entrain to periodic stimuli in our environment."[80] The important point is *how* we unconsciously anticipate metrical stress: the anticipatory schema is a mental representation of sensory-guided action involving the listener's own musculoskeletal system. To summarize: to grasp the metrical and thus rhythmic organization of music, one must entrain to it. To entrain to it, one must imagine moving to it, by thinking about how we would move our own bodies to that music. We do not locate the beat unless we have a clear sense of how we ourselves would move – and at what speed – in synchronizing our movements to its reoccurring accents.[81] Even if the audience is sitting still, not moving a muscle, their perception of rhythm (and therefore harmonic placement) is grounded in their kinesthetic response.

To vindicate Ellington's claim that people who never dance don't grasp the beat of his music, we need only bring these points together with another recent finding of neuroscience. The physical act of moving in certain ways enriches the ability to move *imaginatively* in those ways. Writing about appreciation of dance performances, Renee Conroy states our point quite forcefully:

> in virtue of the way they are crafted, [kinesthetic artworks] demand of viewers that they attend to their bodily responses. With respect to these works, failure to become corporeally engaged and to reflect on the nature of that engagement is tantamount to failure to grasp some artistic properties of the work and to appreciate it in light of its maker's intentions.[82]

The evidence? Even when they are not allowed to move to music, the kinesthetic response of professional dancers is more complex than that of "amateur" dancers, whose response, in turn, is more complex than that of non-dancers.[83] In other words, people who dance regularly have a richer engagement with the music even when merely listening – in one very important dimension, at any rate – than listeners who never or seldom engage in social dancing. Granted, the key research about training and appreciation involves people who watch video of dancers moving to music, but it is almost certainly true that, given the basics of entrainment outlined above, the same results hold when dancers and non-dancers listen to a familiar style of music.

Although Wittgenstein argues that psychological research is irrelevant to the philosophy of art,[84] we will end by noticing a place where Wittgenstein's reflections on music and its appreciation dovetails with the relevant recent science. Generalizing from his own experience with music, Wittgenstein proposes that some aspects of music do not have to be appreciated conceptually: "with some people, me especially, the expression of an emotion in music, say, is a certain gesture."[85] The gesture is indescribable. It is rooted in, if not identical to, a kinesthetic experience. As we have just seen, Wittgenstein's experience was not really a special case. But it explains an important phenomenon. Discuss music with the average music lover and you quickly discover that most people are unable to describe what moves or excites them about a particular piece of music. Wittgenstein proposes that this is not a deficit or a sign of lack of understanding: there is no reason to think the gesture in a particular bar of music can be described. On the contrary, attempts to describe what is most valuable about the experience may be futile, and those who insist on them as a sign of understanding or musical competence are the ones who have it wrong. To understand music, what matters is one's understanding of the way it moves and the gestures it makes – the gestures the musicians are making by means of the music – and this depends on one's ability to imagine how one should move to that music. As with most things, practice makes a difference.

We are not claiming that dancing is the whole story behind jazz and how it arose, how it was transformed, and how it came to be viewed as "legitimate" art. We have, instead, argued that participatory dancing is an important but neglected aspect of what jazz was and is. Jazz was originally dance music, but this fell by the wayside, and therefore recent audiences, who have seldom or never danced to jazz, have a reduced kinesthetic understanding of jazz rhythms than did earlier generations. Consequently, jazz is frequently performed for an audience with a limited capacity to hear and appreciate those rhythms, and therefore everything else that is musically erected upon a distinctive jazz approach to the hierarchy of meter and rhythm. (One might argue that knowing how to dance to other popular music, such as rock'n'roll, is all that one needs. However, this reply fails if jazz rhythms are distinctive, a topic we explore in Chapter 2.) We are not restricting our thesis to jazz styles that arose before the bebop revolution. Furthermore, we recognize there is still a great deal of jazz with an explicit dance beat. Most obviously, New Orleans jazz is still performed in the French Quarter, and one can still book the Duke Ellington Orchestra for a performance, decades after Ellington's death. And, as we noted, there's a danceable groove to Monk's compositions, if you let yourself feel it, and those compositions continue to be among the most performed works in the jazz repertoire. Finally, some new post-bop jazz styles continued to be informed by dance rhythms, including the hard bop that was the staple of the Blue Note label. So the dance tradition remains central to jazz even if performing for social dancing is now a relative rarity, and therefore our speculative thesis applies to much, but not all, contemporary jazz.

Notes

1   In recent philosophy of music, formalist opposition to our thesis can be found in Nick Zangwill, "In Defence of Moderate Aesthetic Formalism," *Philosophical Quarterly* 50:201 (2000): 476–493, and Julian Dodd, *Works of Music: An Essay in Ontology* (Oxford: Oxford University Press, 2007), e.g., at 268–269.
2   Roger Scruton, *Understanding Music: Philosophy and Interpretation* (London: Continuum, 2009), 5.
3   Catharine Abell argues that art genres are best understood "as categories distinguished by certain of the purposes that the works belonging to them are intended to serve" ("II – Genre, Interpretation and Evaluation," *Proceedings of the Aristotelian Society* 115 (1:1) (2015): 25–40). To the extent that we endorse this idea, our reasons are distinct, since Abell does not draw on Wittgenstein's philosophy.
4   Our use of these terms follows a distinction advanced by Sally Haslanger, "Gender and Race: (What) Are They? (What) Do We Want Them to Be?" in *Feminist Theory: A Philosophical Anthology*, ed. Ann E. Cudd and Robin O. Andreasen (Malden: Blackwell, 2005), 154–170. Methodologically, we are aligned with David Davies' pragmatic constraint, which holds that theorizing about art should be constrained by artistic practice (*Art as Performance* (Oxford: Blackwell, 2004), 16–20).
5   Alyn Shipton, *A New History of Jazz*, rev. and updated ed. (London: Bloomsbury, 2007), 1.
6   Quoted in Bruce Kuklick, *Black Philosopher, White Academy: The Career of William Fontaine* (Philadelphia: University of Pennsylvania Press, 2008), 11.
7   A detailed account of negative attitudes toward jazz is Neil Leonard, *Jazz and the White Americans: The Acceptance of a New Art Form* (Chicago: University of Chicago Press, 1962). See also Kathy. J. Ogren, *The Jazz Revolution: Twenties America and the Meaning of Jazz* (New York: Oxford University Press, 1989), chap. 5.

8 Anne Shaw Faulkner, "Does Jazz Put the Sin in Syncopation?" *Ladies Home Journal* 38:8 (August 1921): 16, 34.

9 Noël Carroll, *A Philosophy of Mass Art* (Oxford: Clarendon Press, 1998), 196.

10 See Vincent Pelote, "Jazz Clubs," in *The Oxford Companion to Jazz*, ed. Bill Kirchner (Oxford: Oxford University Press, 2000), 722–733.

11 Richard Shusterman, *Pragmatist Aesthetics: Living Beauty, Rethinking Art*, 2nd ed. (Lanham: Rowman & Littlefield, 2000), 184.

12 Elijah Wald, *How the Beatles Destroyed Rock and Roll: An Alternative History of American Popular Music* (Oxford: Oxford University Press, 2009), 169; Robert P. Crease, "Jazz and Dance," in *The Oxford Companion to Jazz*, ed. Bill Kirchner (Oxford: Oxford University Press, 2000), 696–705, at 704; Paul Chevigny, *Gigs: Jazz and the Cabaret Laws in New York City*, 2nd ed. (New York: Routledge, 2005), 48.

13 In this respect, we partially endorse Krin Gabbard's view that the sites of jazz performance should be included in its definition, as well as his observation that a definition should be based on socio-cultural analysis ("Introduction: The Jazz Canon and Its Consequences," in Gabbard, ed., *Jazz Among the Discourses* (Durham: Duke University Press, 1995), 1–28, at 22n1). However, as we argue in Chapters 2 and 3, it is a mistake to reject "internal aesthetics" (*ibid.*).

14 Black Hawk Hancock, *American Allegory: Lindy Hop and the Racial Imagination* (Chicago: University of Chicago Press, 2013), 4. Hancock is responding to Ralph Ellison's more negative characterization.

15 Stuart Nicholson, *Ella Fitzgerald: A Biography of the First Lady of Jazz* (New York: Scribner's, 1994), 13–14.

16 Albert Murray, *Stomping the Blues*, 2nd ed. (New York: Da Capo, 2000), 11. In its literal meaning, stomping is foot-stomping.

17 Examples of specific cities and clubs can be generalized to some extent. For a discussion of blues, jazz, and dance clubs in Atlanta in this period, see Tera W. Hunter, "'Sexual Pantomimes,' the Blues Aesthetic, and Black Women in the New South," in *Music and the Racial Imagination*, ed. Ronald Radano and Philip V. Bohlman (Chicago: University of Chicago Press, 2000), 145–164.

18 Although he struggled against the racial restrictions of his time, Ellington's years at the Cotton Club were "influenced very much by remnants of the minstrel tradition" (Olly W. Wilson and Trevor Weston, "Edward Kennedy Ellington as a Cultural Icon," in *The Cambridge Companion to Duke Ellington*, ed. Edward Green (Cambridge: Cambridge University Press, 2014), 67–84, at 72). We discuss this tradition in detail in Chapter 5.

19 Ted Gioia, *The History of Jazz*, 2nd ed. (Oxford: Oxford University Press, 2011), 29.

20 Crease, "Jazz and Dance," 702.

21 Murray, *Stomping the Blues*, 64–70.

22 Murray, *Stomping the Blues*, 17.

23 Paul C. Taylor, *Black is Beautiful: A Philosophy of Black Aesthetics* (Malden, MA: Wiley-Blackwell, 2016), 16. See also Paul C. Taylor, "… So Black and Blue: Response to Rudinow," *Journal of Aesthetics and Art Criticism* 53:3 (1995): 313–316.

24 For a comprehensive study of jazz in film, see Krin Gabbard, *Jammin' at the Margins: Jazz and the American Cinema* (Chicago: University of Chicago Press, 1996).

25 Stanley Cavell, *Disowning Knowledge: In Seven Plays of Shakespeare*, updated ed. (Cambridge: Cambridge University Press, 2003), 32.

26 See Margaret T. McFadden, "Shall We Dance?: Gender and Class Conflict in Astaire-Rogers Dance Musicals," *Women's Studies* 37:6 (2008): 678–706.

27 Todd Decker, *Music Makes Me: Fred Astaire and Jazz* (Berkeley: University of California Press, 2011), 105.

28 Whitney Balliett, quoted in Jacqui Malone, "Jazz Music in Motion: Dancers and Big Bands," in *The Jazz Cadence of American Culture*, ed. Robert G. O'Meally (New York: Columbia University Press, 1998), 278–297, at 281. Ellington "would introduce his

drummers saying they would be dancing for the audience" (Louis Bellson, quoted in Malone, 280). Malone provides a list of jazz drummers who were also tap dancers (281).

29 Todd Decker, *Music Makes Me: Fred Astaire and Jazz* (Berkeley: University of California Press, 2011), 1.
30 Stanley Cavell, *Philosophy the Day after Tomorrow* (Cambridge, MA: Harvard University Press, 2005), 76.
31 Quoted in Malone, "Jazz Music in Motion," 285.
32 For details, see Nicholson, *Ella Fitzgerald*, 17–20.
33 See Danielle Robinson, *Modern Moves: Dancing Race During the Ragtime and Jazz Eras* (Oxford: Oxford University Press, 2015).
34 Surprisingly, Benny Goodman seems to have thought so. See Wald, *How the Beatles Destroyed Rock and Roll*, 120.
35 Quoted in Gary Giddins and Scott DeVeaux, *Jazz* (New York: W. W. Norton, 2009), 176–177.
36 Ludwig Wittgenstein, *Philosophical Investigations*, trans. G. E. M. Anscombe (New York: Macmillan, 1953), 128e.
37 Alan P. Merriam and Fradley H. Garner, "Jazz – The Word," in O'Meally, ed., *The Jazz Cadence of American Culture*, 7–31.
38 Joachim E. Berendt with Günther Huesmann, *The Jazz Book: From Ragtime to the 21st Century*, 7th ed. (Chicago: Lawrence Hill Books, 2009), 6.
39 Ogren, *Jazz Revolution*, 55. Ogren develops this insight at length in Chapter 2 of the book. Another interesting exploration of the same point is Patrick Burke, *Come in and Hear the Truth: Jazz and Race on 52nd Street* (Chicago: University of Chicago Press, 2008).
40 Daniel Hardie, *Jazz Historiography: The Story of Jazz History Writing* (Bloomington: iUniverse LLC, 2013), 252.
41 Grace Elizabeth King, *New Orleans: The Place and the People* (New York and London: Macmillan, 1896), 340.
42 Shipton, *New History of Jazz*, 21.
43 Shipton, *New History of Jazz*, 19.
44 A recollection of drummer Arthur "Zutty" Singleton in the Columbia University Jazz Oral History Collection, quoted in Burton W. Peretti, *The Creation of Jazz: Music, Race, and Culture in Urban America* (Chicago: University of Illinois Press, 1994), 34.
45 Peretti, *Creation of Jazz*, 34.
46 Albert Murray, *Murray Talks Music: Albert Murray on Jazz and Blues* (Minneapolis: University of Minnesota Press, 2016), 120.
47 Geoffrey C. Ward and Ken Burns, *Jazz: A History of America's Music* (New York: Knopf, 2000), 10
48 Murray, *Murray Talks Music*, 121.
49 Peretti, *Creation of Jazz*, 37.
50 Shipton, *New History of Jazz*, 240. Other examples, dating as late as 1944, are noted in Lewis A. Erenberg, *Swingin' the Dream: Big Band Jazz and the Rebirth of American Culture* (Chicago: University of Chicago Press, 1999), 47.
51 Marc Myers, *Why Jazz Happened* (Berkeley: University of California Press, 2012): 23–28.
52 Bernard Gendron, "'Moldy Figs' and Modernists: Jazz at War (1942–1946)," in *Jazz Among the Discourses*, ed. Gabbard, 31–56, at 31.
53 Steven B. Elworth, "Jazz in Crisis, 1948–1958: Ideology and Representation," *Jazz Among the Discourses*, ed. Gabbard, 57–75, at 61.
54 Giddins and DeVeaux, *Jazz*, 296. A more nuanced analysis is Scott DeVeaux, *The Birth of Bebop: A Social and Musical History* (Berkeley: University of California Press, 1997).
55 Jill Flanders Crosby and Michèle Moss, "Jazz Dance from Emancipation to 1970," in *Jazz Dance: A History of the Roots and Branches*, ed. Lindsay Guarino and Wendy Oliver (Gainesville: University Press of Florida, 2015), 35–58, at 52.

56 David Ake, *Jazz Cultures* (Berkeley: University of California Press, 2002), 53. A similar sentiment is expressed in Chevigny, *Gigs*, 48.

57 Giddins and Deveaux, *Jazz*, 296. See also Scott DeVeaux, "North American Jazz," in *The Other Classical Musics: Fifteen Great Traditions*, ed. Michael Church (Woodbridge: Boydell Press, 2015), 198–215.

58 Eric Hobsbawm, *The Jazz Scene* (New York: Pantheon, 1993), 97–98.

59 "Jukes Escape Cabaret Taxes," *Billboard* (March 11, 1944), 61, 65.

60 Paul Tanner, David W. Megill, and Maurice Gerow, *Jazz*, 10th ed. (New York: McGraw-Hill, 2005), 145; Constance Valis Hill, *Tap Dancing America: A Cultural History* (Oxford: Oxford University Press, 2010), 158–159; Malone, "Jazz Music in Motion," 293.

61 Chuck Haddix, *Bird: The Life and Music of Charlie Parker* (Chicago: University of Illinois Press, 2013), 67; Charles A. Sengstock, *That Toddlin' Town: Chicago's White Dance Bands and Orchestras, 1900–1950* (Chicago: University of Illinois Press, 2004), 172.

62 Quoted in Dizzy Gillespie with Al Fraser, *To Be, Or Not … to Bop: Memoirs* (Minneapolis: University of Minnesota Press, 2009), 232.

63 DeVeaux, *Birth of Bebop*, 285.

64 Arthur C. Danto, *The Transfiguration of the Commonplace: A Philosophy of Art* (Cambridge, MA: Harvard University Press, 1981). See also R. A. Sharpe, *Philosophy of Music: An Introduction* (Montreal: McGill-Queen's University Press, 2004), 53.

65 Hill, *Tap Dancing America*, 159. It is worth noting that in a Langston Hughes short story written in 1961, a Dizzy Gillespie record is put on the phonograph so that couples can dance to it in a Harlem apartment ("Seven People Dancing," *The New Yorker* (June 6 and 13, 2016), 60–61).

66 Alan Gevinson, ed., *AFI: American Film Institute Catalog: Within Our Gates: Ethnicity in American Films, 1911–1960* (Berkeley: University of California Press, 1997), 527.

67 Quoted in Quincy Troupe and Ben Riley, "Remembering Thelonious Monk: When the Music was Happening Then He'd Get Up and Do His Little Dance," in O'Meally, *Jazz Cadence of American Culture*, 102–110, at 106. Riley also says that playing for Monk was like playing with a tap dancer (ibid).

68 Armstrong interviewed in Nat Shapiro and Nat Hentoff, *Hear Me Talkin' to Ya* (New York: Dover, 1966), 111.

69 Ralph Peterson, quoted in Michael J. West, "The Drummer Who Invented Jazz's Basic Beat," *A Blog Supreme, NPR* (January 9, 2014), http://www.npr.org/sections/a blogsupreme/.

70 Julian "Cannonball" Adderley, "Paying Dues: The Education of a Combo Leader," *The Jazz Review* (1960): 12–15, at 15.

71 Leonard Feather, *The Book of Jazz* (New York: Horizon, 1957), 262.

72 As with vaudeville generally, the parallel institution of black vaudeville had declined in the 1930s. The major booking agency for black musicians and dancers, the Theater Owners Booking Association, folded in 1930. See Marshall Stearns and Jean Stearns, *Jazz Dance: The Story of American Vernacular Dance*, 2nd ed. (New York: Da Capo, 1994), 254–256.

73 David Schiff, *The Ellington Century* (Berkeley: University of California Press), 170. The moment is so iconic that a photo of Anderson dancing was placed on the back cover of the concert recording, *Ellington at Newport* (1956).

74 Liner notes by George Avakian, *Ellington at Newport*, Columbia Records CL 934, 1956. Ironically, Gonsalves' famous saxophone solo is basically rock'n'roll.

75 Quoted in Stanley Dance, *The World of Duke Ellington* (New York: Scribner's, 1970), 13. Along these lines, see Vijay Iyer, "Embodied Mind, Situated Cognition, and Expressive Microtiming in African-American Music," *Music Perception* 19:3 (2002): 387–414.

76 E.g., DeVeaux, *Birth of Bebop*, 171.

77 The classic text on this topic is Leonard B. Meyer, *Emotion and Meaning in Music* (Chicago: University of Chicago Press, 1956). Meyer is hardly the final word on the matter, and rival versions of this general approach can be found in Eugene Narmour, *The Analysis and Cognition of Basic Melodic Structures: The Implication-Realization Model* (Chicago: University of Chicago Press, 1990), and David Huron, *Sweet Anticipation: Music and the Psychology of Expectation* (Cambridge, MA: MIT Press, 2006).
78 Joel Lester, *The Rhythms of Tonal Music* (Carbondale: University of Southern Illinois Press, 1986), 52.
79 Narmour, *Analysis and Cognition*, 60.
80 Justin London, *Hearing in Time: Psychological Aspects of Musical Meter* (Oxford: Oxford University Press, 2004), 12, emphasis added.
81 See N. P. M. Todd, D. J. O'Boyle, and C. S. Lee, "A Sensory-Motor Theory of Rhythm, Time Perception, and Beat Induction," *Journal of New Music Research* 28:1 (1999): 5–28, especially 26; and Justin London, "Musical Rhythm: Motion, Pace and Gesture," in *Music and Gesture: New Perspectives on Theory and Contemporary Practice*, ed. Anthony Gritten and Elaine King (Aldershot: Ashgate, 2006), 126–141.
82 Renee M. Conroy, "Responding Bodily," *Journal of Aesthetics and Art Criticism* 71:2 (2013): 203–210, at 208.
83 Beatriz Calvo Merino, et al., "Action Observation and Acquired Motor Skills: An fMRI Study with Expert Dancers," *Cerebral Cortex* 15:8 (2005): 1243–1249. For a defense of the philosophical relevance of such experiments, see Noël Carroll and William P. Seeley, "Kinesthetic Understanding and Appreciation in Dance," *Journal of Aesthetics and Art Criticism* 71:2 (2013): 177–186.
84 Ludwig Wittgenstein, *Lectures and Conversations on Aesthetics, Psychology, and Religious Belief*, ed. Cyril Barrett (Oxford: Basil Blackwell, 1966), 11, 38.
85 Wittgenstein, *Lectures and Conversations*, 37.

References

Abell, Catharine. "II – Genre, Interpretation and Evaluation." *Proceedings of the Aristotelian Society* 115(1:1) (2015): 25–40.
Adderley, Julian "Cannonball." "Paying Dues: The Education of a Combo Leader." *The Jazz Review* (1960): 12–15.
Ake, David. *Jazz Cultures*. Berkeley: University of California Press, 2002.
Avakian, George. Liner notes, Ellington at Newport. Columbia Records CL 934, 1956.
Berendt, Joachim E., with Günther Huesmann. *The Jazz Book: From Ragtime to the 21st Century*, 7th edition. Chicago: Lawrence Hill Books, 2009.
Burke, Patrick. *Come in and Hear the Truth: Jazz and Race on 52nd Street*. Chicago: University of Chicago Press, 2008.
Byrne, David. *How Music Works*. San Francisco: McSweeney's, 2012.
Carroll, Noël. *A Philosophy of Mass Art*. Oxford: Clarendon Press, 1998.
Carroll, Noël, and William P. Seeley. "Kinesthetic Understanding and Appreciation in Dance." *Journal of Aesthetics and Art Criticism* 71:2 (2013): 177–186.
Cavell, Stanley. *Disowning Knowledge: In Seven Plays of Shakespeare*, updated ed. Cambridge: Cambridge University Press, 2003.
Cavell, Stanley. *Philosophy the Day after Tomorrow*. Cambridge, MA: Harvard University Press, 2005.
Chevigny, Paul. *Gigs: Jazz and the Cabaret Laws in New York City*, 2nd ed. New York: Routledge, 2005.
Conroy, Renee M. "Responding Bodily." *Journal of Aesthetics and Art Criticism* 71:3 (2013): 203–210.

Crease, Robert P. "Jazz and Dance." In *The Oxford Companion to Jazz*, ed. Bill Kirchner. 696–705. Oxford: Oxford University Press, 2000.

Crosby, Jill Flanders and Michèle Moss. "Jazz Dance from Emancipation to 1970." In *Jazz Dance: A History of the Roots and Branches*, ed. Lindsay Guarino and Wendy Oliver, 35–58. Gainesville: University Press of Florida, 2015.

Dance, Stanley. *The World of Duke Ellington.* New York: Scribner's, 1970.

Danto, Arthur C. *The Transfiguration of the Commonplace: A Philosophy of Art.* Cambridge, MA: Harvard University Press, 1981.

Davies, David. *Art as Performance.* Oxford: Blackwell, 2004.

Decker, Todd. *Music Makes Me: Fred Astaire and Jazz.* Berkeley: University of California Press, 2011.

DeVeaux, Scott. *The Birth of Bebop: A Social and Musical History.* Berkeley: University of California Press, 1997.

DeVeaux, Scott. "North American Jazz." In *The Other Classical Musics: Fifteen Great Traditions*, ed. Michael Church, 198–215. Woodbridge: Boydell Press, 2015.

Elworth, Steven B. "Jazz in Crisis, 1948–1958: Ideology and Representation." In *Jazz Among the Discourses*, ed. Krin Gabbard, 57–75. Durham: Duke University Press, 1995.

Erenberg, Lewis A. *Swingin' the Dream: Big Band Jazz and the Rebirth of American Culture.* Chicago: University of Chicago Press, 1999.

Faulkner, Anne Shaw. "Does Jazz Put the Sin in Syncopation?" *Ladies Home Journal* 38 (August 1921): 16, 34.

Feather, Leonard. *The Book of Jazz.* New York: Horizon, 1957.

Gabbard, Krin, ed. *Jammin' at the Margins: Jazz and the American Cinema.* Chicago: University of Chicago Press, 1996.

Gabbard, Krin. *Jazz Among the Discourses.* Durham: Duke University Press, 1995.

Gendron, Bernard. "'Moldy Figs' and Modernists: Jazz at War (1942–1946)." In *Jazz Among the Discourses*, ed. Krin Gabbard, 31–56. Durham: Duke University Press, 1995.

Gevinson, Alan, ed. *AFI: American Film Institute Catalog: Within Our Gates: Ethnicity in American Films, 1911–1960.* Berkeley: University of California Press, 1997.

Giddins, Gary, and Scott DeVeaux. *Jazz.* New York: W. W. Norton, 2009.

Gillespie, Dizzy, with Al Fraser. *To Be, or Not … to Bop: Memoirs.* Minneapolis: University of Minnesota Press, 2009.

Gioia, Ted. *The History of Jazz*, 2nd ed. Oxford: Oxford University Press, 2011.

Haddix, Chuck. *Bird: The Life and Music of Charlie Parker.* Chicago: University of Illinois Press, 2013.

Hancock, Black Hawk. *American Allegory: Lindy Hop and the Racial Imagination.* Chicago: University of Chicago Press, 2013.

Hardie, Daniel. *Jazz Historiography: The Story of Jazz History Writing.* Bloomington: iUniverse LLC, 2013.

Haslanger, Sally. "Gender and Race: (What) Are They? (What) Do We Want Them to Be?" In *Feminist Theory: A Philosophical Anthology*, ed. Ann E. Cudd and Robin O. Andreasen, 154–170. Malden: Blackwell, 2005.

Hill, Constance Valis. *Tap Dancing America: A Cultural History.* Oxford: Oxford University Press, 2010.

Hobsbawm, Eric. *The Jazz Scene.* New York: Pantheon, 1993.

Hughes, Langston. "Seven People Dancing." *The New Yorker* (June 6 and 13, 2016), 60–61.

Hunter, Tera W. "'Sexual Pantomimes,' the Blues Aesthetic, and Black Women in the New South." In *Music and the Racial Imagination*, ed. Ronald Radano and Philip V. Bohlman, 145–164. Chicago: University of Chicago Press, 2000.

Huron, David. *Sweet Anticipation: Music and the Psychology of Expectation.* Cambridge, MA: MIT Press, 2006.

Iyer, Vijay. "Embodied Mind, Situated Cognition, and Expressive Microtiming in African-American Music." *Music Perception* 19:3 (2002): 387–414.

"Jukes Escape Cabaret Taxes." *Billboard* (March 11, 1944), 61, 65.

King, Grace Elizabeth. *New Orleans: The Place and the People.* New York and London: Macmillan, 1896.

Kuklick, Bruce. *Black Philosopher, White Academy: The Career of William Fontaine.* Philadelphia: University of Pennsylvania Press, 2008.

Leonard, Neil. *Jazz and the White Americans: The Acceptance of a New Art Form.* Chicago: University of Chicago Press, 1962.

Lester, Joel. *The Rhythms of Tonal Music.* Carbondale: University of Southern Illinois Press, 1986.

London, Justin. *Hearing in Time: Psychological Aspects of Musical Meter.* Oxford: Oxford University Press, 2004.

London, Justin. "Musical Rhythm: Motion, Pace and Gesture." In *Music and Gesture: New Perspectives on Theory and Contemporary Practice*, ed. Anthony Gritten and Elaine King, 126–141. Aldershot: Ashgate, 2006.

McFadden, Margaret T. "Shall We Dance?: Gender and Class Conflict in Astaire-Rogers Dance Musicals." *Women's Studies* 37 (2008): 678–706.

Malone, Jacqui. "Jazz Music in Motion: Dancers and Big Bands." In *The Jazz Cadence of American Culture*, ed. Robert G. O'Meally, 278–297. New York: Columbia University Press, 1998.

Merino, Beatriz Calvo, et al. "Action Observation and Acquired Motor Skills: An fMRI Study with Expert Dancers." *Cerebral Cortex* 15:8 (2005): 1243–1249.

Merriam, Alan P., and Fradley H. Garner. "Jazz – The Word." In *The Jazz Cadence of American Culture*, ed. Robert G. O'Meally, 7–31. New York: Columbia University Press, 1998.

Meyer, Leonard B. *Emotion and Meaning in Music.* Chicago: University of Chicago Press, 1956.

Murray, Albert. *Murray Talks Music: Albert Murray on Jazz and Blues.* Minneapolis: University of Minnesota Press, 2016.

Murray, Albert. *Stomping the Blues*, 2nd ed. New York: Da Capo, 2000.

Myers, Marc. *Why Jazz Happened.* Berkeley: University of California Press, 2012.

Narmour, Eugene. *The Analysis and Cognition of Basic Melodic Structures: The Implication-Realization Model.* Chicago: University of Chicago Press, 1990.

Nicholson, Stuart. *Ella Fitzgerald: A Biography of the First Lady of Jazz.* New York: Scribner's, 1994.

Ogren, Kathy J. *The Jazz Revolution: Twenties America and the Meaning of Jazz.* New York: Oxford University Press, 1989.

Pelote, Vincent. "Jazz Clubs." In *The Oxford Companion to Jazz*, ed. Bill Kirchner, 722–733. Oxford: Oxford University Press, 2000.

Peretti, Burton W. *The Creation of Jazz: Music, Race, and Culture in Urban America.* Chicago: University of Illinois Press, 1994.

Robinson, Danielle. *Modern Moves: Dancing Race during the Ragtime and Jazz Eras.* Oxford: Oxford University Press, 2015.

Rogin, Michael. *Blackface, White Noise: Jewish American Immigrants in the Hollywood Melting Pot.* Berkeley: University of California Press, 1996.

Schiff, David. *The Ellington Century.* Berkeley: University of California Press.

Scruton, Roger. *Understanding Music: Philosophy and Interpretation.* London: Continuum, 2009.

Sengstock, Charles A. *That Toddlin' Town: Chicago's White Dance Bands and Orchestras, 1900–1950.* Chicago: University of Illinois Press, 2004.

Shapiro, Nat, and Nat Hentoff. *Hear Me Talkin' to Ya.* New York: Dover 1966.

Sharpe, R. A. *Philosophy of Music: An Introduction.* Montreal: McGill-Queen's University Press, 2004.

Shipton, Alyn. *A New History of Jazz*, rev. and updated ed. London: Bloomsbury, 2007.

Shusterman, Richard. *Pragmatist Aesthetics: Living Beauty, Rethinking Art*, 2nd ed. Lanham: Rowman & Littlefield, 2000.

Stearns, Marshall, and Jean Stearns. *Jazz Dance: The Story of American Vernacular Dance*, 2nd ed. New York: Da Capo, 1994.

Tanner, Paul, David W. Megill, and Maurice Gerow, *Jazz*, 10th ed. New York: McGraw-Hill, 2005.

Taylor, Paul C. *Black is Beautiful: A Philosophy of Black Aesthetics.* Malden, MA: Wiley-Blackwell, 2016.

Taylor, Paul C. "… So Black and Blue: Response to Rudinow." *Journal of Aesthetics and Art Criticism* 53:3 (1995): 313–316.

Todd, N. P. M., D. J. O'Boyle, and C. S. Lee. "A Sensory-Motor Theory of Rhythm, Time Perception, and Beat Induction." *Journal of New Music Research* 28:1 (1999): 5–28.

Troupe, Quincy, and Ben Riley. "Remembering Thelonious Monk: When the Music was Happening Then He'd Get Up and Do His Little Dance." In *The Jazz Cadence of American Culture*, ed. Robert G. O'Meally, 102–110. New York: Columbia University Press, 1998.

Wald, Elijah. *How the Beatles Destroyed Rock and Roll: An Alternative History of American Popular Music.* Oxford: Oxford University Press, 2009.

Ward, Geoffrey C., and Ken Burns. *Jazz: A History of America's Music.* New York: Knopf, 2000.

West, Michael J. "The Drummer Who Invented Jazz's Basic Beat." *A Blog Supreme, NPR* (January 9, 2014): http://www.npr.org/sections/ablogsupreme/.

Wilson, Olly W., and Trevor Weston. "Edward Kennedy Ellington as a Cultural Icon." In *The Cambridge Companion to Duke Ellington*, ed. Edward Green, 67–84. Cambridge: Cambridge University Press, 2014.

Wittgenstein, Ludwig. *Lectures and Conversations on Aesthetics, Psychology, and Religious Belief*, ed. Cyril Barrett. Oxford: Basil Blackwell, 1966.

Wittgenstein, Ludwig. *Philosophical Investigations*, trans. G. E. M. Anscombe. New York: Macmillan, 1953.

2

A THEORY OF JAZZ MUSIC: "IT DON'T MEAN A THING ..."

And just as there is no wet without water, there is no jazz without its swing.
— *Billy Taylor*

By our definition, jazz consists essentially of *an inseparable but extremely variable mixture of relaxation and tension* (that is, of swing and the hot manner of playing).
— *André Hodeir*

André Hodeir's 1956 book, *Jazz: Its Evolution and Essence*, became a staple in jazz literature for many years, raising detailed issues that remain pertinent today even if Hodeir's book has lost some of its presence in jazz circles. In this chapter we make the case that Hodeir's theory of jazz is now unjustly neglected. A critic as well as jazz composer, Hodeir discusses the usual musical and cultural features. He opens his major study of jazz with the point that jazz is a global phenomenon;[1] but nonetheless, "jazz is the Negro's art."[2] And, of course, it is highly improvisational. Yet any such list of contributory features, however accurate, leaves us with a nagging question: What is it about the interaction of these several factors that transforms them into jazz? The ideal definition, in short, ought to be able to explain the distinctive unified effect created by the various elements that contribute to the making of jazz. It might be less important to know which individual features are either necessary or typical than to recognize that something noteworthy emerges from their interaction and synthesis.[3]

This insight underlies Hodeir's bold essentialism. His boldness is matched only by his almost perverse willingness to bruise commonplace ideas about jazz, particularly our sense that jazz has some vital connection with both improvisation and blues tonality. Although a good deal of jazz history has gone by since the classically trained Hodeir published *Jazz: Its Evolution and Essence*, his overarching analysis of the history, culture, and spirit of the music of jazz remains as insightful and provocative today as when it appeared in 1954. In particular, Hodeir's analysis resonates with our own exploration, in Chapter 1, of the appearance and cultural prominence of jazz within a particular social-historical context. However, even if that were not the case, his discussion of what is musically distinctive about jazz deserves the philosophical attention we provide in this chapter. Hodeir, as we shall see, invites us to consider such jazz binaries as, "hot playing" and swing, sound and rhythm, and tension and relaxation – all providing insights into some of jazz's fundamental concepts and the relationships between them.

Despite its virtues, Hodeir's exposition is complicated and sometimes confused. He does not always cling to his own best insights. Further, his theory is indecisive on one rather fundamental point. For these reasons, we will not defend Hodeir outright, but will cherry-pick his better insights in order to reconstruct the most defensible version of his argument. Following this approach, Hodeir makes an interesting case for the thesis that jazz is an essentially rhythmic matter. To a great extent, the argument proceeds by elimination, by arguing that most of what is standard for a jazz performance is dispensable, because it is either not special to jazz or it is simply not necessary. We do not propose that the argument is beyond criticism, but even in its shortcomings it provide insights.

Shockingly, Hodeir defends the following negative propositions:[4] jazz music is not defined (1) by any special relationship to tonality, (2) by its use of special metrical devices, (3) by a connection with its "architecture" (meaning, roughly, "form," e.g., theme-and-variations, sonata-allegro, etc.), (4) by any fundamental connection with "sound" (matière sonore),[5] or (5) by its use of improvisation. Hodeir's defense of these negative claims may seem obscure because he's guided by a curious ground-rule regarding necessary and sufficient conditions: If any musical element discoverable in jazz can also be found elsewhere, then it cannot be part of a definition of jazz.[6] Odd as this rule seems, an important insight underlies it. A definition of jazz should be a unitary one, it should identify something unique to jazz, it should involve something perceivable, and it should be related to our primary criteria for evaluating jazz performances.[7] For example, improvisation is important to jazz, but it does not enter the definition itself. Improvisation is also important in other traditions, from the raga tradition of Indian classical music to the "jam band" tradition founded by the Grateful Dead, but it serves a different function in those traditions. Its role in jazz becomes clear only if we can see how it is a means to an end that is central to jazz.[8] The definition centers on the nature of that end, or its telos. At least since Aristotle, the idea of telos is a powerful one. Under certain conditions, Aristotle's acorn will develop into an oak tree and it implies a kind of inevitable and obvious success, given the proper conditions. With respect to artifactual events, like jazz performances, we imagine, with Hodeir, a description of conditions under which a musical performance would be successful as jazz. We shall examine this web of ideas by first considering Hodeir's negative claims.

1. Purism

At first it isn't clear what's at stake when Hodeir denies that (1) tonal considerations are essential to our understanding of jazz. Nor is it clear why he thinks it's important that (2) jazz is not meter "specific," or why (3) an understanding of musical form is of no use in getting at its nature.

Interpreted narrowly, the issue about tonality is an issue about the blues, a type of music that has fed so thoroughly into jazz music that jazz seems unthinkable without its relationship to blue notes. In part, it was Hodeir's shocking denial of this connection that prompted some members of a jazz symposium – which included Whitney Balliett, Billy Taylor, and Leonard Feather – to teach Hodeir the errors of his ways.[9] In reply, Hodeir scolded his critics for employing a superficial idea of essence, and neatly countered the main argument his critics advanced against him.[10] Taylor had maintained that since "society" or hotel band saxophone playing is on the whole devoid of blues effects, and since the playing of a genuine jazz musician such as Coleman Hawkins is very different from such society band playing, then the blues must inform Hawkins' sound and be definitive of jazz music. This, Hodeir smartly replies, is like trying to prove that the Chinese language is essentially German because it has nothing in common with Russian.

Hodeir's defense of his assertion is simple: there are decisive counterexamples to the supposed dependence of jazz on the blues, most notably Hawkins' classic Victor recording of "Body and Soul" (1939) and Stan Getz's treatment of "These Foolish Things" (1952).[11] It must be understood that Hodeir is not denying the tonal and expressive value of the blues. He is simply saying that a jazz performance can lack blues tonality and still be jazz.[12] However, as neat as the argument is, it may not have put the issue to rest. Given that Hodeir's definitional strategy is not the standard philosophical quest for necessary and sufficient conditions, a pair of examples cannot deliver a knock-out blow. After all, he doesn't exclude swing from his analysis despite its absence from most jazz during its "primitive" early stage. Instead, Hodeir's well-chosen examples invite us to think of other examples of jazz without blues tonality – both actual and imaginary.

Two very different examples are saxophonist Joe Maneri's "Balance + Pulse" (2004) and the Thelonious Monk standard "Misterioso" (1958). In the latter case, Monk teases us by composing a 12-bar "blues" that has no blue notes. We can also think about the general careers of particular performers. Günter Christmann's free jazz sextet frequently eschews every trace of the blues, as evidenced by the live set documented on the *Vario 34–2* album (2003). However, we don't have to wait for free jazz. Dizzy Gillespie observes that "the real blues" require a tonality that he could never achieve, and that was absent from the voices of Ella Fitzgerald and Sarah Vaughan and, more generally, from his own "strain" of "modern," Latin-influenced jazz.[13] Ella Fitzgerald is certainly an interesting case. Pieces like "The E and D Blues" and "C Jam Blues" show that she could improvise over blues changes, but more frequently her jazz prowess rests on her ability to take a standard pop tune and swing it through melodic embellishment and "intricate off-beat attacks."[14] Finally, we can take one of the most famous performances in jazz history, Keith Jarrett's 1975 Köln concert, which involved nearly an hour of extemporaneous, continuous solo piano. Yet the performance features very little in the way of blues tonality or technique, and we can imagine an equally compelling performance despite their total absence. It would be no less jazz had Jarrett consistently avoided its occasional blues elements.[15]

With Hodeir, the issue about the blues is part of a deeper issue regarding a kind of purism that is obsessed with jazz origins. An over-simplified explanation of the phenomenon of blue notes is that when early African-Americans were first taught songs in Western scales, they experienced a cognitive dissonance resulting from the imprint of a European, tempered scale upon a tonality that emphasizes pentatonism. The result is a tendency to flatten notes at the third, the seventh, and possibly the fifth intervals. These notes in the cracks between the piano keys are the blue notes.[16] Hodeir knows this, but he believes it gives too much comfort to an obnoxious purism that tries to reduce the essentials of jazz to its earliest forms. On the purist's view, jazz styles that arose after the 1920s are an adulteration of the real thing.[17] For Hodeir, as for many of us, jazz came of age between 1935 and 1955, and he sees the jazz historian's task as one of identifying continuities despite change, rather than searching for pure forms that remain faithful to jazz's (disputed) origins.[18] On this much we agree.

However, Hodeir's strategy against this purism is to push it to absurdity. In the interest of consistency, purism ought to countenance only the original, non-European musical materials from which "impure" jazz originated. It should tolerate only such uses of melodic and harmonic materials as are completely disconnected from the entire logic of European tonality and chord progressions. For instance, the blues effects that are achieved on a tempered instrument such as the piano are distortions of the notes that would be played without the overprinting of European tonality. Although Hodeir doesn't say so, it is clear that the argument against Afropurism can be adapted to refute Europurism as well. (It would undermine the old-fashioned idea, for instance, that jazz is just a vulgarization of music that is European in essence.) In general, it doesn't follow from the fact that jazz has inherited either European or non-European elements, that it is either European or non-European in its essence.

This enables us to understand and appreciate Hodeir's ground rule about necessary and sufficient conditions. He is tacitly appealing to the fact that there are two different ways in which qualities are essential. In one sense, to say that the familiar notes of the tempered scale are a necessary condition of jazz music is just to say that the music systematically uses that idiom. For Hodeir, this is not a very interesting sense in which a characteristic is essential. It's a little like saying that bats and balls are the essence of – that is, necessary for – baseball. True, but so obvious as to be uninformative. We have not yet articulated success conditions. We get at the more interesting sense if we ask what the telos of the music is.

"Telos" is Aristotle's term, we'll recall, for one's purpose or end in pursuing a particular course of action. More importantly, it constitutes the defining essence of that action *by making sense of it*, and it does so even if the purpose is not achieved. Hodeir grants that a jazz concert that contains neither improvisation nor blues tonality "is not desirable," but it could still be jazz.[19] The purist fails to see that the citation of musical materials, European or African, does not tell us what the jazz musician *does* with those materials. If jazz shares neither African nor European tonal goals, then what are its tonal goals? The tempting answer is that it uses these resources in order to create blues effects. Since Hodeir thinks there are counterexamples to this generalization, he concludes that the telos of jazz music is not a tonal one at all. Jazz performances should not be evaluated by reference to the presence or absence of "blues." Nothing would be gained or lost if we conceded that Ella Fitzgerald "cannot sing the blues" and only "decorates them" in performances like "The E and D Blues" and "C Jam Blues."[20]

Hodeir applies the same thinking to purist views about rhythm. Much of the scholarship suggests that European music has simply not explored some of the complex rhythmic matters that preoccupy African musicians.[21] Hodeir accepts this truism, but wants to prevent the purist from taking any comfort from it. He argues that a consistent Afropurism should legislate against the input of *every* unAfrican rhythmic element, including the constant *variation* encouraged in jazz drumming.[22] Nor do African musicians "imprison their figurations in the framework of the four-bar unit of construction and the four beat measure."[23] In the course of using the rhythmic materials it receives whatever the source, jazz music, *qua* jazz, transmogrifies them into something else.

At first, Hodeir's discussion of jazz architecture seems almost contradictory. On the one hand, he tells us that the dominant form in jazz is the variation form; jazz typically involves improvised solos based on the chords of a tune.[24] On the other hand, Hodeir draws attention to performances that don't use this form. He notes that Duke Ellington's famous "concerto" for trumpet player Cootie Williams is not a set of variations on a single theme at all.[25] Even when he turns to works that might be regarded as using the variation form, Hodeir balks. In some cases, the initial statement is already a variation on a theme. In "Body and Soul" for instance, Hawkins begins, not with the tune as written by Johnny Green, but with a spontaneous paraphrase of it.[26] Further, there are many blues performances simply called, for example, "Blues in B" that aren't prefaced by any statement of theme at all. Consider Charlie Christian's "Blues in B" (1941). Waiting for Benny Goodman to arrive for a studio session, someone calls out, "Charlie, Charlie, let's play the blues in B." And they do, sequentially improvising without a preset theme. Hodeir might have added that in jazz, there is often no thematic continuity between the initial statement and the improvised choruses. Because of this, such "variations" do not generate markedly distinct variants on a theme.[27]

Unfortunately, Hodeir conflates several different points. Six, in fact, of which only one is really fundamental. The other five are either (relatively) uninteresting or questionable. He holds that (1) the so-called variation form in jazz music is really quite different from the European form that goes by the same name. He also maintains that (2) we can't define jazz music in terms of its use of any single musical form. From this rather innocuous point, he passes to the conclusion that (3) form in general is not a necessary condition of jazz. Not only does the third claim not follow from the second; it isn't true. Jazz performances do exhibit musical forms. Witness the many refinements of the AABBACCDD ragtime pattern (or some variant thereof) used by jazz composers from Jelly Roll Morton to Duke Ellington. Furthermore, jazz has persistently and consciously tested the limits of previously accepted formal conventions of the music. Hodeir did not really have to ignore plain facts in order to stick to his central idea, which is simply that experimentation in form is not definitive of jazz. The reason he does ignore them is that he blurs the factual claims with an evaluative one: (4) the exploitation of musical forms has not, in jazz, been carried to the great heights that it has in European music. (In this spirit, Hodeir would probably argue that the open-ended nature of jazz "variations" deprives the music of any capacity for organizational drama and climax.) Hodeir finally blurs this normative matter with a different point: (5) jazz's use of the "variation" form is routine, that is, common. None of these points, however, has much to do with Hodeir's basic insight that (6) whatever the sources of jazz music are, jazz bends those sources to its own tasks.

We can see how Hodeir lets the evaluative concern about musical form (4) skew his whole discussion. He acerbically notes that a Strauss waltz probably has more architectural interest than any jazz piece.[28] (He does admit, however, that the compositions by Duke Ellington and Thelonious Monk are important exceptions to this rule.[29]) Since the fate of form and tonality are, in European music, closely bound together, it is natural that Hodeir would make similarly disparaging remarks about the poverty of jazz tonality. He says that jazz pieces are harmonically static, lacking even as much interest as results, say, from the brightening modulations in a piece by Vivaldi.[30] Furthermore, whereas European music has persistently probed the possibilities of tonality inherent in the tempered scale, jazz has remained harmonically boxed in from a developmental point of view. Hodeir might have added that jazz music does not possess any of the orchestral richness that in European music is as much a function of music's harmonic sophistication as of its resources in instrumental timbre.

Hodeir also misrepresents his position to justify another invidious normative distinction. He marginalizes non-European sources of jazz music in comparison with jazz proper. African conceptions of rhythm are, Hodeir says, incantatory and developmentally "static."[31] He notes that a typical African harmonic idiom is one in which the same harmonic intervals are repeated over and over again "untiringly."[32] In such remarks, Hodeir not only verges on inaccuracy,[33] but is also putting a normative spin on his thesis which is both objectionable and irrelevant to his basic insight: jazz should not be judged in terms of its sources, but only in terms of how it transforms those sources to its own ends. This does not mean, however, that when jazz abandons its distinct concerns for the sake of creating second-rate impressionism or atonalism, we cannot say so.

As we shall see, Hodeir places rhythm at the center of his positive theory. This is not inconsistent with his objections to purism, however, for his view is that in jazz rhythmic sources are in the service of distinctive rhythmic goals of jazz. This leaves us with a question to which we return in section 5. What are those goals, and what do tonality and form have to do with these goals?

2. Sound

Roland Barthes was fascinated by the elements of music that have escaped institutionalization.[34] In no sphere of jazz have such elements found a happier home than in the realm of sound. In a broad sense, everything in music is a function of sound. It's the chiaroscuro of light and dark that gives pieces like King Oliver's "Chimes Blues" (1923) its special beauty. Hodeir uses the term "sound" to refer to the many kinds of inflections that jazz players use, e.g., slides, growls, "wa-wa" effects, half-valve trumpet effects, and so on. Even within the sphere of vibrato effects of brass instruments, we can see how many different paths have been taken. Louis Armstrong made an elaborate, exciting terminal vibrato one of his trademarks. Using the same strategy with great subtlety, Dickie Wells gets an effect that is almost the opposite of Armstrong's. Instead of moving from calm to excitement, Wells's trombone vibrato brings the listener from excitement to a period of relative calm.[35] Quite different again is the abrupt ripped release with which Bill Harris would finish off a trombone shake.

Different effects can be achieved with the saxophone depending on whether the vibrato rises from the diaphragm or from the throat. Materials too, such as Ornette Coleman's plastic saxophone, make a difference. Modernists like Eric Dolphy, Ornette Coleman, and Roland Kirk sometimes create an effect by almost vocalizing or "speaking" onomatopoeically, as they blow through their instruments. Archie Shepp and Pharoah Sanders have pushed the distortions to which their instruments can be subjected even further, so that the instrument's sound rises almost to a scream. The voice itself, of course, has been directed toward countless specific effects, often in imitation of favored instruments, as illustrated by the vastly influential singing of Armstrong. Baby Cox, whose voice was used advantageously by Duke Ellington, made a specialty of falsetto effects, as does Joe Williams.

A clear understanding of what these effects have in common, on Hodeir's view of the matter, cannot be obtained by fixating on the sounds per se. Sound can only be understood in terms of a stance that jazz players take toward the acoustic material with which they deal. They regard it as raw stuff to be shaped and modified at will.[36] We will return to this point in section 5.

Now we might expect Hodeir to argue that individualized uses of sound are not really unique to jazz. They can be found in all sorts of folk and popular music that isn't jazz, and if we think about it, they exist in "serious" music as well. However, Hodeir surprises us by simply stating that sound is part of the essence of jazz.[37] If we look closely, though, we see that this admission is highly qualified. Throughout his study, Hodeir admits that his idea of sound plays many valuable roles in jazz, by its contribution to expressiveness and individuality of style. Consider the way Bessie Smith's subtle off-pitch shadings are connected with blues tonality. However, on his view, sound contributes to the essence of jazz only in terms of the contribution it makes to hot playing.[38] Although it plays a central role in his explanation of the essence of jazz, Hodeir never defines "getting hot." However, he suggests that it is a function of such factors as distorted sonority and volume.[39] So, sound is part of the essence of jazz only to the extent that it is in some way extreme. Furthermore, even in this role, sound is not necessary for jazz, since other factors, such as drive, can make for hot playing.[40] To this cluster of ideas, we shall return shortly.

3. Improvisation

Hodeir's strategy for asserting his vexing claim that jazz does not require improvisation is simple: He merely cites a case in which improvisation plays virtually no role, namely the Ellington trumpet "concerto" mentioned earlier.[41] The soloist's job in this piece is not to produce melodic variations, but to display, in miniature, a repertoire of inflections ranging from muted growl, plunger-muted "wa-wa" and closed mute, to open horn. Hodeir terms the piece a "bouquet" of sonorities.[42] Hodeir could have improved his case by citing other examples from Ellington alone, e.g., his "Black, Brown, and Beige." If he had considered an earlier period, he might have noted that alternative recording "takes" of performances by Bessie Smith show that, as improvised as her phrasing sounds, it was probably often worked out in advance. Or he could have pointed to examples of vocalese, the jazz vocal form in which lyrics are composed to fit famous jazz solos, which are then sung as fixed melodies. One of the first big hits in the emerging subgenre was "Twisted" (1952), created when Annie Ross set lyrics to saxophonist Wardell Gray's 1949 performance of the same name. More than twenty years later, it served as Joni Mitchell's first recorded foray into jazz, introducing vocalese to millions of pop fans who bought Court and Spark (1974). If we are tempted to say that Mitchell's "cover" isn't jazz, the absence of improvisation cannot be the reason: it has neither more nor less of it than Ross's recording for Prestige Records. From a later vantage point, Hodeir could have cited Charlie Mingus's "Half-Mast Inhibition" (1960), which lacks a single measure of melodic improvisation. Today, we can cite the phenomenon of transcriptions of jazz improvisations that generate note-for-note recreations of jazz albums, treating improvised music as a fixed composition. Two prominent examples are captured on the albums Blue (2014), a sonic recreation of Miles Davis's Kind of Blue, and Tomasz Trzcinski's recreation of Jarrett's Köln concert Blue Mountains (2006).[43]

There are other dimensions of the issue that Hodeir might have considered as well. The Original Dixieland Jazz Band (ODJB), a group not really representative of the music we know today as Dixieland Jazz, played in the teens, and struck gold when they made the first "jass" recording. This band capitalized upon an absurd but fashionable myth that jazz music was utterly primitive, free, and untutored.[44] In fact, except for the work of their drummer, the ODJB's work was highly predictable. Even when we turn to the much more representative New Orleans jazz of King Oliver's Creole Jazz Band, "free" is hardly the word we should use to describe the control exhibited by this band's playing. Although Oliver and his protégé, Louis Armstrong, do play brief hot breaks, improvisation on the chords was not part of the agenda at all, except in the form of rhythmic paraphrases. If one is used to the sort of long-winded solo performances (often called "blowing sessions") that were encouraged in the modern era by the development of the long playing record, one will be surprised by this music. It is not the wild ensemble improvisation it is often said to be. The myth is also challenged by the work of Jelly Roll Morton, in whose music spontaneity was always a very limited part of an overall conception. Indeed, some of his instrumentalists' solos were undoubtedly worked out in advance.[45]

However, the idea that jazz is a sheer welling up of untutored inspiration will not die. It was given a new lease on life, at the other end of the historical spectrum, by the playing of Eric Dolphy, Ornette Coleman, and others. Even in these cases, though, the extreme spontaneity of which such music seems capable must be seen in the correct light. First, it is not as unlimited as it seems. It might seem that Cecil Taylor played with as much freedom as could be imagined in almost any music. Among his innovations, he was notorious for having eradicated any sense of swing from his piano improvisations. Yet however much his music shocked established jazz musicians, jazz scholars have identified his debts to earlier pianists (most notably Lennie Tristano), and how his improvisation "had a clear structural foundation."[46] Second, even where ideals of "free jazz" came close to being realized, we still have to put this fact in its historical context.[47] By the fifties and sixties, jazz had become burdened with many of the obsessions that the term "modernism" implies, of which freedom was paramount. However, this fact cannot be used to show that jazz simply is an improvisatory art form. That would be like citing similar preoccupations in abstract expressionist painting to show that painting is an essentially improvisatory art form.

Part of what we often assume when we conceive jazz to be essentially improvisational is that jazz is essentially melodic. Is this really so? It is an interesting thought experiment to try to listen to jazz solo choruses as melodies. Jazz vocalese certainly encourages us in this direction. Melody, in a familiar European sense, has an inherently cantabile character. (We can imagine any European tune that isn't cantabile being nudged in that direction.) To the extent that jazz solos retain their jazz quality, the same cannot be said of them. If we try to hear jazz solos as melodies in the European sense, they will seem overly punctuated. The reason for this is the tendency in jazz to bring weak beats up to the level of strong ones. Further, solos will often sound as if they are continually starting, stopping, and starting again. What Miles Davis plays, in uptempo pieces, is many note bursts, each one made up of many little notes and separated from other bursts by a rest. Heard as European melody, such phrases sound choppy. Until one reckons with the fact that jazz players are on constant look-out for rhythmic opportunities, one will not understand such "melodies." Some twenty measures of the solo Louis Armstrong plays on the Hot Five recording of "Muggles" either orbit around (or play nothing but) the tone C. If one listens to it as a tune, one won't get the point of the effort. Armstrong could generate interest by the simple device of ping-ponging a note back and forth within a single harmonic interval for several measures. Count Basie too made extreme melodic asceticism a trademark of his piano playing. These players are not inventing tunes.

If we think about such examples, we will begin to understand why Dizzy Gillespie said that in thinking about what to play, he first gets hold of a rhythmic figure, and then picks out the notes.[48] This will become our theme in the following section.

4. Tension and Relaxation

The centerpiece of Hodeir's definition of jazz is his attempt to isolate the conditions of swing. The first of these conditions has to do with something he calls infrastructure. By some means or other, whether through the efforts of the rhythm section, the pianist's left hand, or some other device, jazz music provides an underlying pulsation. This pulsation has certain rough boundary conditions. It is standardly accentuated by strong and weak beats in 2/4 or 4/4 time. (3/4 and 5/4 also work.) It should be regular and felicitous in tempo. Above certain speeds, performers will find it difficult to maintain a simultaneous grip on accuracy and flexibility. Below certain speeds, the tempo loses its centrifugal force and acts like a "dying roulette ball."[49] Instead of a full-fledged jazz piece, we will then get a ballad performance, as we find on Don Byas's 1952 recording of "Laura." Jazz, we might say, is fully realized somewhere in the middle, between two tempo extremes.

A second musical stratum necessary for the production of jazz music, *the superstructure*, as Hodeir terms it, involves the rhythmic articulation of the line(s) superimposed over the *infrastructure*. However, these two principles really need to be united in a single one, for it is as a result of the internal relation between these two rhythmic levels that the music acquires, in a slightly technical use of the term, swing. "Swing," here, is not the genre of dance-band music of the thirties and forties, but a phenomenological feature of a broader sphere of jazz music that both pre-dated and post-dated the so-called swing era.[50] Thus, musicologists explain how Charlie Parker maintained swing in bebop improvisations, the antithesis of the music of the swing era.[51] Stravinsky was drawing attention to the swing phenomenon when he spoke of the "giddy sensation" we register when jazz music or dancing "persists in marking irregular accentuations but does not succeed in diverting the ear from the metrical pulsation" beaten out by the percussion.[52] Even greater interest can sometimes be aroused if the pulsation is not always beaten out explicitly. One thinks of "stop-time" breaks, used by many players from Armstrong to Charlie Parker, which are suspended over a beat that remains implicit rather than sounded. Hodeir points to an extreme and more extended example: Monk's composition "I Should Care" "disregard[s] the bar line completely, pulverize[s] the musical tissue and yet preserve[s] that 'jazz feeling.'" To accomplish this, the piece draws on "a second, underlying tempo, imperceptible to us but which Monk *hears* in all the complexity of its relationship with the figures he is playing."[53] Finally, there are jazz players who specialize in obscuring the infrastructure/superstructure distinction. In the early 1970s work of Weather Report, it is no longer easy to distinguish them as individual players surface briefly, only to return to the blended textures of the whole, to which every instrument is busy making its contribution.

The general insight is that swing emerges when the two strata catalyze each other, producing the paradoxical impression both of dependence and independence.[54] A good player will achieve this effect by leaving some notes of the superstructure in a strict relationship with the underlying pulsation while displacing some notes away from it.[55] For example, an effective phrase in the superstructure will usually have at least a few syncopated notes alternating with notes played on the beat.[56] In Charlie Parker's playing, swing emerges from "strong forward motion ... created by the uneven temporal progressions of the parts, and by Parker's unexpected accents ... and subtle playing behind the beat."[57] In 1956, Ella Fitzgerald swings the pop standard "Where or When" by initially staying with the beat, gradually introducing delayed entrances and then "syncopated rhythms across the bar line," culminating in "intricate off-beat attacks," all the while "paying proper respect to the tune."[58] A weaker player will treat the pulsation of the infrastructure as a series of slots that dictate an isomorphic placement of notes in the superstructure. Such a soloist may be tempted to use syncopations monotonously, thereby producing a "corny," polka-like beat that undermines the effective interaction between the two levels.

Treating this single integrated idea as if it were two distinct principles, Hodeir adds a third factor, *la mise en place de valeurs*: the player must "get the notes in the right place."[59] Now this seems to say, simply, that players must keep time.[60] Since it seems inappropriate for Hodeir to remind us of so basic a requirement at this stage in the analysis, he is more likely speaking of the placement of notes over the infrastructure in such a way as to generate and maintain swing. In that case, the third principle comes out sounding rather platitudinous: "place the notes in the superstructure in such a way as to produce swing." In explanation of how this is done, Hodeir can only give rules-of-thumb. Still, a consideration of such rules, as well as their limitations, helps us gain insight into his central idea.

For instance, a strict rule about alternating syncopations and notes played on the beat would not account for the playing of Erroll Garner, whose melodic line falls dangerously out of synchrony with the main pulsation for long stretches to the advantage, rather than the disadvantage, of swing. Sometimes, in slower tempos, as in Hawkins' "Body and Soul," the solo phrases can be structured in terms of two beats for every one the rhythm section actually plays.[61] But it would be foolish to insist upon this invariably. Even Hodeir's rule about avoiding too many short or too many very long notes has exceptions. A burst of short notes in a stop-time chorus, for instance, will dramatically profile the pulsation to which the music eventually returns. Furthermore, there are differences in approach between modern and classic jazz. In the latter, phrases will often begin with an emphasis of strong beats and conclude with rhythmically disorienting placements. Modern jazz often reverses the procedure by using a series of displaced accents to draw our interest toward a subsequent strong beat.

Clearly, it's impossible to calculate the daunting number of possible places, and combinations of places, notes might be swingingly placed in reference to a given infrastructure. What we can say is just that jazz playing interweaves metrically "correct" placements of notes with displacements of other notes.[62] The result is that the musical phrases are felt, by turns, as moving independently of the underlying pulse and then as being recaptured by it.

The history of the music is, in large part, a history of individualized experiments in "getting the notes in the right place." Taking their departure from its familiar cross-beat rhythmic organization, ragtime players gradually ironed out the heavy 2/4 beat of the left hand, while rhythmically augmenting the right hand with ever subtler accents. If Morton's way of playing Scott Joplin's "Maple Leaf Rag," on a famous 1938 recording preserved by the Library of Congress, did not prove that he invented jazz, as he liked to claim, it does show how he made a quantum leap beyond ragtime.[63] While Morton's right hand made pointed use of between-the-beat accents, breaks, and abrupt suspensions, his left hand was modified into a walking, melodically figured line that could interact interestingly with the right. The effect was that, while a piece might actually be played more slowly, it could generate great swing. Hodeir proposes that almost all of the devices exploited by Louis Armstrong in his Hot Five recordings, including vibrato and extensions of notes beyond their expected values, can be understood in terms of the generation of swing. Armstrong was thus ahead of his peers in his perception of single beats as decomposable into many sub-divisions.[64] Marshall Stearns says that Pine Top Smith created his "easy, flowing style," not by means of regularity, but by "complicating the rhythm,"[65] that is, by using accents that carry over, around, and about the infrastructure. Modern jazz, which has simply carried this idea further, searches for more daring ways to challenge our expectations without losing touch with the rhythmic continuity that gives these efforts sense. But here, we run into possible obstacles. Bop's use of pure showers of notes, for instance, challenged the ear in new ways to recognize the tempo that remains underneath. With "mad audacity," as Hodeir calls it, Charlie Parker distributed accents now on the beat, now on the off-beat, now just before the beat, while still maintaining contact with indispensable points of rhythmic support.[66] The same can be said of Thelonious Monk.[67] While threatening to pulverize the musical material entirely, he is in constant contact with the underlying pulse.

Hodeir adds two further conditions: relaxation (*décontraction* but frequently *détente*) and drive (*pulsion vitale*). However, they do little work in explaining the phenomenon of swing, given the rather anemic descriptions he gives them. (They have to do with the unmechanical and effortless character of good swing.) These come off sounding more like rather intangible and adventitious values that some jazz has, rather than defining conditions.[68]

Now Hodeir realizes that he needs more fully developed concepts answering to these two terms if he is to complete his theory. Without recognizing that it doesn't jibe with the use of the terminology just cited, he goes on to use one of the same terms, relaxation, to name an element in an overarching duality which, when applied to the concept of swing, is intended to produce, finally, the definition of jazz. The essence of jazz is, in his pithy formulation, the generation and handling of "tension-relaxation duality."[69] (Where Chapter XII of *Jazz* identifies relaxation as a contributing factor in swing, his subsequent identification of the essence of jazz refers to a relaxation phenomenon that characterizes the music more holistically.) While this duality doesn't quite do the work Hodeir wants it to do, his observation on it is trenchant. We can use it to push the theory in a rewarding direction.

European music, he suggests, capitalizes upon meaningful alternations between tension and relaxation. For example, it oscillates between movement and repose, between dissonance and consonance. In jazz, however, tension and relaxation are perpetually bound together within a single structure, and they can co-exist "at the same moment."[70] What are the sources of the tension and relaxation in jazz? Surprisingly, tension is linked to *hot playing*, which is treated as primarily a matter of *sound*. As is often the case, Hodeir conveys his thought not by defining the concept of hot playing, but by giving examples, from which we are presumably invited to generalize: examples include exceptional or continually rising volume, slides or *portamenti*, overblown notes. Amateurs can play hot: "distorted sonorities played *fortissimo* are generally sufficient." He also cites vital drive.[71] Relaxation is associated with swing. Here, Hodeir takes the wrong path. For there are two alternatives.

Alternative I: His official position is to define jazz in terms of a relationship between swing and hot playing, where swing is cast as the source of relaxation, and hot playing the source of tension.[72] The challenge is to keep track of two kinds of relaxation: one is an ingredient of swing (we might call it rhythmic relaxation), and one is the general effect that swing has on the whole performance (which we might call holistic relaxation). For example, "screaming tenor saxophonists like Illinois Jacquet ... re-emphasized the elements of tension, but without sacrificing the quality of swing that the preceding generation had acquired."[73] Yet the overall quality of the solos lacks the quality of relaxation that Hodeir admires in the playing of Lester Young. Once we note it, we can keep track of Hodeir's two levels of relaxation. However, the contrast between the playing of Jacquet and Lester Young leaves Hodeir with a disjunctive definition of jazz. Jazz is either swing or hot playing or, in the best jazz, both. However, there is no direct connection between jazz rhythm and important features of jazz "heat" that are not obviously rhythmic in character – drive and sound, for instance. The obvious disadvantage is that we are left without any central conceptual connection between the two disjuncts. If so, his thesis has lost touch with his central idea that a genuine theory of jazz should give us an account of the central aim or telos of the musical performance. Instead of a unified theory, Hodeir has only isolated two kinds of jazz, or perhaps only two kinds of value in jazz. Indeed, there are likely trade-offs between these characteristics. Music that is too relaxed may lack drive, while music that is too hot – too driving, for instance – may be less swinging, because it leaves less room for the flexible placement of notes in the superstructure.[74] In this spirit, Hodeir suggests that fifties' "cool" bop may be regarded as too relaxed.[75] This very example shows, though, that it is simplistic to correlate relaxation with swing. Who would say that cool jazz was too swinging?

One suspects that Hodeir does not notice the equivocation between two senses of "relaxation," partly on the basis of his highly positive opinion of the laid-back playing of Lester Young. While seeming irrational, Young's rhythmic suspensions and delays are precisely what make him a more thrillingly relaxed producer of rhythmic swing than more "rational" players – Benny Carter, say – whose accents may be almost too even.[76] One might put it this way: Young can maintain less forward drive than other players without losing swing because of the constant rhythmic variation in his playing. With his eye on Young, Hodeir might have come to identify swing as such with a relaxed way of swinging.

Alternative II: Suppose, though, that we treat the theory of swing as telling the whole story about the essence of jazz: we simply define the essence of jazz in terms of its distinctive manner of handling rhythm.[77] Now this radical version of the theory would stand some chance of regaining the unity lost on the more straightforward interpretation of Hodeir's text. The theory of swing, recall, involves an internal relationship between an underlying pulsation and a rhythmic overlay that pulls against it (if only to periodically reconfirm it). On this interpretation, the duality that defines swing is itself the basis for the tension–relaxation duality that Hodeir sees as peculiar to jazz. We can find at least one place in the text where Hodeir invites us to interpret him in just this way. In a footnote, he cites a suggestion made by Lucien Malson in an article in *Les Temps Modernes*. There, Malson suggests that in swing we have, "one of the Freudian paradoxes: an unpleasant tension which is associated with pleasure – that is, with a partial relaxation." Hodeir calls the thesis a "tempting one."[78] Nevertheless, in the main body of the text, he persists in rejecting this view in favor of the official one. Perhaps he should have followed the path suggested by Malson.

Even if we take that route, though, our work is not quite finished. We need to find a place in the theory for *drive*, not as Hodeir anemically described it in the section of his book written under that heading, but in the sense of the forward push or momentum of jazz music. In virtue of such factors as metric regularity and tempo, jazz shares momentum with all music, of course. However, jazz exhibits a peculiar sort of momentum. Regularity and tempo are only partial conditions of it. Hodeir comes closest to describing jazz momentum (without using the term) in his description of a felicitous infrastructure as giving "the impression of moving inexorably ahead (like a train that keeps moving at the same speed but is still being *drawn ahead* by its locomotive)."[79]

Perhaps the solution is that jazz momentum is also a function of the very polyrhythmic interaction between infra- and superstructure that Hodeir uses to define swing. This makes sense, since swing is felt almost as a kind of need to reconcile partly synchronous, partly unsynchronous rhythmic lines. In jazz, the goal of this need is, so to say, promised, realized, and undone at each instant. So, it appears that we can make room in Hodeir's theory for Malson's thesis that swing embraces tension and release in a single structure. Tension and relaxation co-exist. The continuum of disequilibrium in such music is what fires the swing "engine" and moves it forward. We encounter a different approach to "metrical conflict" in the rhythms of the second Miles Davis quintet (1965–1968), producing a jazz feel even when the music does not really swing.[80]

Contrary to Hodeir, there is no danger in embracing a genetic explanation of how this came to be. African musicians in America learned how to correlate the points of emphasis that exist in their native music with European downbeats. Meanwhile, they satisfied their polyrhythmic impulses by means of accents made against the beat.[81] For fully realized examples of the phenomenon, one need only turn to any number of Hot Five's performances, such as the "West End Blues" (1928), in which Armstrong's ecstatic notes seem literally straining to burst the confines of their rhythmic placement. Hodeir is right though that such results cannot be reduced to the factors that combined to generate them.

5. Evaluation

What are the prospects for such a theory? One problem concerns the possibility of counter-examples. A second concerns the conceptual connection between jazz rhythm and the other important dimensions of jazz that have no obvious conceptual connection with it. Of these dimensions, spontaneity is of special importance.

(1) An account that locates an essence in a telos, a performing goal, is not subject to counter-examples in the usual way. It allows for imperfectly realized examples. Having rejected purism and fixed rhythmic and tonal materials, Hodeir's account could be taken to embrace any musical performance that aims

at the proper telos and sound profile. Unlike most essentialist definitions, this is not an ahistorical approach. Adjusted to recognize that later musicians inherit the jazz telos from their predecessors, the theory makes room for incorporation of non-purist developments; an idea we pursue in the following chapter.

Adjusted in this way, are there clear instances of jazz music that violate the account? In particular, have recent developments in jazz simply carried it outside the bounds of any theory that might have been adequate for mainstream jazz? Ornette Coleman, for instance, wanted to work with a very loose sort of "spread" rhythm that would be liberated from any overall metric consistency.[82] Perhaps such music does not swing, at least in the sense we have discussed here. In 1964, Albert Ayler's *Spiritual Unity* abandoned conventional timekeeping. However, it is certainly jazz. On the other hand, the account has explanatory value. It predicts, for example, the resistance of mainstream jazz fans to the rock-slanted rhythms of jazz-fusion. As Mark Gridley puts it, fusion likes to "sit on each beat instead of pulling it along or leading it, as [traditional] jazz does."[83] In minimizing swing, it is jazz for the rock era, rhythmically not so far removed from the Original Dixieland Jazz Band.

(2) What, if anything, is the connection between jazz rhythm and the other important qualities of jazz? While Hodeir doesn't claim that an invariable connection between sound and rhythm can be provided *a priori*, he is ingenious in profiling connections between the two in individual cases. For instance, the way effective jazz manipulates note-placements for the sake of swing constitutes the centerpiece of Hodeir's chapter on Armstrong. Elsewhere, he points out how, in the concerto Ellington wrote for him, Cootie Williams's sonorities have the important effect of deflecting the rhythmic values of the themes that make up the piece.[84] He nicely explains how Miles Davis's refined terminal vibrato has the effect of making the rhythm "rebound."[85] In the same vein, Hodeir points out that the effect of Dickie Wells's trombone vibrato is a rhythmic uncertainty created by the dislocation of syncopated notes.[86] We might feel, though, that not everything about sound can be framed in this light. Consider the expressive function of blues inflections, for instance.

In section 1, we didn't really own up to the questions that need answering about the jazz function of form and tonality. There, we simply asserted, on Hodeir's behalf, that the formal and tonal ingredients in jazz have to be understood, somehow, as serving jazz functions. We know that the history of jazz documents a harmonic and formal evolution. We know, for instance, how the early concentration on melodies strongly governed by tonic and dominant chords was gradually expanded to include the use of wider intervals and more and more complex chords. Was this a contingent fact about jazz or was it somehow connected with developments in the way jazz pursued its rhythmic goals? Similar questions can be raised about the evolution of jazz forms. Should we expect that formal and harmonic decisions will always be made in the service of rhythmic ones? This seems unwarranted.[87]

Perhaps the formal and tonal dimensions of jazz are simply molds into which jazz rhythm is poured. However, this rather dismissive description tempts us to put jazz into conceptually incoherent comparison-classes, to its inevitable disadvantage. As noted earlier, it makes no more sense to evaluate jazz arrangements as European compositions than it would to downgrade European forms because they do not generate swing. Nor does it make sense to compare a jazz arrangement with the whole thing of which it is an arrangement, any more than it would make sense to put the form of a Viennese symphony into competition with the symphony itself. In short, jazz arrangements should only be compared with other jazz arrangements and evaluated on their potentiality to tie diverse solo and ensemble material together in the production of jazz rhythm. If this seems like a small thing, consider the many gems that Jelly Roll Morton alone gave us. In them, he sought to provide the greatest possible variety through the use of multipart forms, modulations, interludes, and countermelodies in the production of swing. But if we think of Morton, we must think too of Don Redmond, Eddie Sauter, and Billy Strayhorn. Is this, then, such a small thing?

It is worth noting, finally, that Hodeir's position about the primacy of rhythm in jazz can be framed in terms of a spectrum of possibilities rather than in terms of a strident bifurcation: to the degree to which a musician's decisions are dictated by considerations other than rhythmic then to that same degree, the player's music will drift away from jazz. However, a special problem remains in regard to one factor, namely flexibility, or more accurately, spontaneity. Indeed, it is a dilemma.

(3) Even if we were to give up the dogma that jazz is essentially improvisatory in a strictly melodic sense, as suggested in section 3, we want to emphasize that it is central to the jazz tradition that players are evaluated for their ability to produce strings of uncomposed tones. Even where jazz lacks invention in this sense, freedom and individuality are essential in a jazz performer's accent and inflection. Hodeir himself draws attention to the importance in jazz of this kind of non-compositional flexibility.[88] However, flexibility is not the same thing as spontaneity. When he tells us that jazz tempos must allow for flexibility, Hodeir means that the tempo must leave room for the soloist to play around, so to speak, in the space between infra- and superstructure. To return to an earlier example, both Annie Ross and Joni Mitchell replicate Wardell Gray's melodic design when they sing "Twisted," but the three performers introduce distinctive accents – not surprisingly, Ross's vocal swings with more confidence than Mitchell's. However, we have also noted examples to which we are supposed to listen knowing full well that every inflection in it is written out.[89] Further, we can imagine such "jazz" as allowing the play-room necessary for swing. Such music would only contain surprises for someone who didn't know the score or who hadn't heard the music. This suggests that the question we should now be asking concerns spontaneity, for that's what this music lacks.

Our intuitions tell us that spontaneity has a jazz function. Can we plausibly save Hodeir by saying that the whole function of spontaneity is a swing function?

But even Hodeir does not think that is the case, for it often functions instead to interject personalized expression.[90] Spontaneity and personalization are, at least to some extent, autonomous characteristics distinct from swing. But now we are either driven back to an unsatisfying pluralistic definition of jazz; or we would have to regard spontaneity as a value that some jazz music happens to share with some folk and popular music. On Hodeir's general approach, neither is a happy result.

However, a qualification may bring us close to a unified theory again, as well as provide some insight into the concept of spontaneity. It may be possible to save Hodeir's theory while bringing it into line with our intuitions. Imagine a jazz-machine with built-in randomizing capabilities. Such a hypothetical case brings out the fact that the spontaneity we prize in jazz is not mere randomness. Jazz spontaneity actually has two aspects. On the one hand, it is an on-the-spot response to problems generated by the interaction between specific musical events and a player's sense of the rhythmic and harmonic possibilities in the music and of his or her own capacities. For example, a soloist may need to reshape a line metrically because its pace would otherwise outrun his or her technical abilities. This is obviously what Armstrong does in his famous introduction to "West End Blues." The unique qualities of Jarrett's Köln concert have been attributed to the fact that he discovered, too late to find a replacement, that he would be giving a solo performance on a piano with a defective pedal and some sticky keys.[91] In this form, spontaneity includes responses to the unanticipated, random, or perverse actions of any player including those of the player in question. The second aspect of jazz spontaneity is correlative to the first aspect. It is a willingness to make precisely the kinds of dangerous moves to which the player must then spontaneously respond in the way first described. Even in this second form, though, spontaneity is not simply randomness. Wynton Marsalis praises this element in the playing of Sonny Rollins, explicitly connecting it to rhythmic invention: "he scrapes the beat, pushes it, leans on it, makes taffy out of it. He takes chances like a great juggler, ... an acrobat ... He plays super-syncopation – the *unexpected* unexpected rhythm."[92]

Now if we wonder why jazz rhythm should stand in such a special relationship with spontaneity, the answer is that jazz musicians are preoccupied with rhythm in a game of tension and release, as Hodeir reminds us. We might then simply observe that spontaneity, as just described, seems perfectly suited to this fact. And there is at least some anecdotal evidence that important jazz figures thought about jazz as, essentially, a music of rhythmic improvisation. Jazz pianist Andrew Hill says he heard from Charlie Parker: "I look at melody as rhythm." Hill's understanding of music was turned upside down; based on a traditional, "Eurocentric" music education, he had regarded rhythm as the least important element of music. "It opened my mind up to many possibilities," Hill said. "If everything is rhythm, then you just have these rhythms on top of each other. But they're not polyrhythms or pyramids of rhythm: they're crossing rhythms."[93] Reflecting on jazz history and innovation, Wynton Marsalis concurs: Parker and bebop represent a rhythmic revolution rather than a harmonic one.[94]

Would it be so wrong to say that a theory of swing is all we need for a theory of what is distinctive in jazz? Would it have the result of placing excessive stress on rhythm – that is, on a distinctively jazz way of handling rhythm? Hill's epiphany is a variation of Hodeir's central insight. It is often assumed that European ideas of harmony and melody are fundamental in jazz, "whereas the truth may be that in jazz, rhythm is fundamental."[95] For all its apparent idiosyncrasies, Hodeir's theory as here formulated finds support in key statements of some leading jazz authorities. We find Martin Williams saying that if attempts to impose innovations in harmony are "not intrinsically bound to innovations in rhythm, they risk distorting some secret but innate balance in the nature of jazz."[96] Most pointed of all is the main thesis of Jan Slawe's *Einführung in die Jazzmusik*, that central to jazz is the conflict between simultaneously executed but distinct segments of musically filled time.[97] Taken as a distinctive telos, rather than a necessary condition, a theory of jazz rhythm has much to recommend it.

In the end, we owe Hodeir plenty. We praise him for taking an evolutionary approach to an essence for jazz – like boarding a moving train. In recognizing the complexity and diversity of the story of jazz up until the 1950s, Hodeir highlights the difficulties in finding a single, simple, underlying element that can ground all of jazz. He recognizes that the invariable mixtures of tension and relaxation or swing and hot are matters of degree and as such can change to the point where one can dominate as the other weakens, fades, and disappears. In a section headed, "Toward a Change of Essence?," Hodeir says, "There is reason ... to consider the possibility that one of the two poles between which the electricity of jazz is concentrated may disappear."[98] That, he says, might bring about the "total effacement" of jazz itself.[99] He balances this observation with the sobering fact that every other musical tradition is temporary, and more or less "just a lucky accident" that eventually gives way to successor art forms. However, we cannot evaluate the vitality of jazz if we cannot demarcate the art form, and therefore an investigation of its essence remains relevant, however unjustly neglected.

In the next chapter we take up this issue of definition with a different approach, one we are calling a historical definition of jazz.

Notes

1 Ted Gioia says that globalization is the "main story, the overwhelming trend" of contemporary jazz (Will Friedwald, Ted Gioia, et al., *The Future of Jazz*, ed. Yuval Taylor (Chicago: Chicago Review Press, 2002), 155). See also Stuart Nicholson, *Is Jazz Dead? (Or Has It Moved to a New Address?)* (New York: Routledge, 2005), chaps. 7 and 8.

2 André Hodeir, *Jazz: Its Evolution and Essence*, trans. David Noakes (New York: Grove Press, 1956), 7; originally *Hommes et problèmes du Jazz: suivi de la Religion du Jazz* (Paris: Parentheses, 1954), later reissued in French in 1981 by Parentheses with a new

avant-propos by Christian Tarting. Amplification of Hodeir's position appears in his
Toward Jazz, trans. Noel Burch (New York: Grove Press, 1962), which consists of
translations of essays that appeared in such periodicals as *Arts*, *DownBeat*, and *Jazz-Hot*
(of which Hodeir was for some time editor).

3   The point that the "essential elements" predate jazz was made in 1938 by Winthrop
Sargeant; see his *Jazz: Hot and Hybrid*, 3rd ed. (New York: Da Capo, 1975), 20. One
author who appreciates Hodeir's approach is Joachim E. Berendt (with Günther
Huesmann), *The Jazz Book: From Ragtime to the 21st Century*, 7th ed. (Chicago: Lawrence
Hill Books, 2009). Berendt defines jazz in terms of three elements (all of which will
figure in this chapter): a relationship to time, namely, "swing," a spontaneity of
musical production, and sonorities. These elements interact to produce a rise and fall
of musical tension (661).

4   Hodeir, *Jazz*, 10, 139–144, 160, 234–235.

5   This is qualified in section 3.

6   Hodeir, *Jazz*, 234–235.

7   The need to locate something distinctive is also emphasized by Peter J. Martin,
"Spontaneity and Organisation," in *The Cambridge Companion to Jazz*, ed. Mervyn
Cooke and David Horn (Cambridge: Cambridge University Press, 2002), 133–152.

8   Jazz improvisation, Hodeir opines, is "simply a *means of expression*," which does not
distinguish jazz from other kinds of music (*Toward Jazz*, 60). But orchestration and
arranging are no less legitimate as musical means (ibid., 59).

9   "A Jazz Seminar: Are Blues Essential to Jazz?" *DownBeat* (June 27, 1957), 15–16.

10   Hodeir, *Toward Jazz*, 60. Hodeir believes his essentialism to be Husserlian in character.

11   Hodeir, *Jazz*, 145, 235, and *Toward Jazz*, 62, respectively.

12   Hodeir does not seem to be aware of Sargeant's analysis of fourteen recorded jazz
works, not all of which are blues in any straightforward sense. By dissecting their
tonalities, Sargeant shows how references to a blues scale appear in the performer's
solos and embellishments (*Jazz*, 168). The weakness in Sargeant's analysis is that he
preselected examples with the right "harmonic circumstances" to "permit the appearance"
of the blues scale.

13   Dizzy Gillespie (with Al Fraser), *To Be, Or Not … to Bop* (Minneapolis: University of
Minnesota Press, 2009 [1979]), 310–311.

14   Norman David, *The Ella Fitzgerald Companion* (Westport, CT: Praeger, 2004), 49;
David offers this characterization while detailing her handling of the Rodgers and Hart
standard "Where or When."

15   As explained by Peter Elsdon, blues inflections appear only sparingly in Jarrett's
improvisation – first in one rhythmic "vamp" and then in a variation on "a purely
diatonic harmony" that adds a bluesy passing note (*Keith Jarrett's* The Köln Concert
(Oxford: Oxford University Press, 2013), 70, 110).

16   The theory of blues tonality involves (1) the theory of the blues scale and (2) the
theory of its typical 12-bar blues format and chord changes. Blues songs also have a
poetics. The iambic pentameter of "I will not be afraid of death or bane/till Birnam
forest come to Dunsinane" will work nicely for a blues verse, if one sings the first line
twice, and the second line once, making space for the customary pauses required in
blues songs.

17   Although there are few such critics any longer, an example of the kind of purist
Hodeir has in mind is the French critic, Hugues Panassié, *The Real Jazz*, trans. Anne
Sorelle Williams (New York: Smith and Durrell, 1942). Amiri Imamu Baraka and
Wynton Marsalis represent another form of origin-based essentialism; see Lee B.
Brown, "Marsalis and Baraka: An Essay in Comparative Cultural Discourse," *Popular
Music* 23:3 (2004): 241–255.

18   Concerning the question of whether the musical origins of jazz are more fundamentally
African or European with African-American innovations, see William H. Youngren,

"European Roots of Jazz," in *The Oxford Companion to Jazz*, ed. Bill Kirchner (Oxford: Oxford University Press, 2000), 17–28.

19 Hodeir: "let us not confuse … the outward form of the thing with its essence" (*Toward Jazz*, 60). The search for an essential end or telos that unifies a set of artistic choices under a common essence should not be confused with a second idea, prominent in Hegel's aesthetic, that different art epochs develop in order to arrive at some end that is inherent in that art; in recent aesthetic theory, Arthur Danto famously argues that the "end" of all art was achieved in the 1960s, when Warhol's work turned art into a philosophical scrutiny of the nature of art (*After the End of Art: Contemporary Art and the Pale of History* (Princeton: Princeton University Press, 1997)).

20 Whitney Balliett, "The First Lady of Song," *New Yorker* (April 26, 1993), 105–106, at 106.

21 In African drumming, rhythmic patterns are typically superimposed over one another, thereby giving rise to hierarchies of lines of such complex interaction that a time lapse between a beat in one line may regularly occur as little as a twelfth of a second after the occurrence of a beat in a parallel line without the former becoming absorbed into the orbit of the second. For a summary of recent scholarship, see Gunther Schuller's masterful *Early Jazz: Its Roots and Musical Development* (Oxford: Oxford University Press, 1968), 6–26.

22 Hodeir, *Jazz*, 42.

23 Hodeir, *Jazz*, 43. Hodeir is not quite right about this matter. See below, note 33.

24 Hodeir, *Jazz*, 139–140.

25 Hodeir, *Jazz*, Chapter VI and 235–236. The piece displays a refined ragtime pattern with an introduction, three themes and their variants, a coda, one key change, and some interesting departures from standard bar-length conventions.

26 Hodeir, *Jazz*, 144.

27 Hodeir may assume that the overall metric consistency of jazz makes this difficult. He would probably also dispute Sargeant's analogy between jazz variations and the chaconne or the passacaglia as being any more useful (Sargeant, *Jazz*, 249). Jazz has neither formal congruence nor any likely historical connection with these forms.

28 Hodeir, *Jazz*, 140.

29 Hodeir, *Toward Jazz*, 164

30 Hodeir, *Jazz*, 146–147.

31 Hodeir, *Jazz*, 43.

32 Hodeir, *Jazz*, 42.

33 Hodeir is both right and wrong that African drumming is static. The master drummer has his drummers repeat something over and over until he signals a change. Ironically for Hodeir, some of jazz's repetitive characteristics, e.g., the "riff," may actually be adapted from African music. (See Schuller, *Early Jazz*, 48.) If Hodeir is simply saying that jazz makes room for more individualism, he is right, but this fact may in the end work against him.

34 His example was probably the grain of the voice of lieder singer, Charles Panzéra.

35 Hodeir, *Jazz*, 72.

36 Hodeir, *Jazz*, 224. This description has implications to be considered in section 5 of this chapter.

37 Hodeir, *Jazz*, 235.

38 Hodeir, *Jazz*, 237–240.

39 Hodeir, *Jazz*, 229–232. Hodeir seems to see this in terms of the raw, expressionistic, almost physical, dimensions of the music.

40 Hodeir, *Jazz*, 231, 238.

41 Hodeir, *Jazz*, 231, 238.

42 Hodeir, *Jazz*, 93.

43 Which raises the obvious question: Why bother? For one answer, see P. D. Magnus, "Kind of Borrowed, Kind of Blue," *Journal of Aesthetics and Art Criticism* 74:2 (2016): 179–185.

44 See Schuller, *Early Jazz*, 180, where he reports some of the provocative claims with which the leaders of the ODJB liked to tease the public, e.g., "I don't know how many pianists we tried before we found one who couldn't read music."

45 Martin Williams agrees. See his *The Jazz Tradition* (Oxford: Oxford University Press, 1971), 37.

46 Jeff Pressing, "Free Jazz and the Avant-garde," in *The Cambridge Companion to Jazz*, ed. Mervyn Cooke and David Horn (Cambridge: Cambridge University Press, 2002), 202–216, at 208.

47 Although normally associated with Ornette Coleman, the first free jazz was actually tried out by Lennie Tristano and his group in the late 1940s. Hodeir appears to have been unaware of this music.

48 Quoted in Hal Galper, "Practice and Performance Goals," *Jazz Education Journal* 35:5 (2003): 60–71, at 69.

49 Hodeir, *Jazz*, 197–199. Hodeir speculates that some of these conditions might not be absolutely necessary for swing. For instance, jazz performances do have a tendency to speed up slightly as they proceed. Furthermore, there is evidence that music can swing in meters other than 2/4 and 4/4. Hodeir also recognizes that even in traditional jazz music, there are at least four basic ways in which strong and weak beats may be variously emphasized.

50 However, Hodeir hypothesizes that the two uses are historically related (*Jazz*, 217).

51 For example, Henry Martin, *Charlie Parker and Thematic Improvisation* (Lanham, MD: Scarecrow Press, 2001), 19–20.

52 Igor Stravinsky, *Poetics of Music in the Form of Six Lessons*, trans. Arthur Knodel and Ingolf Dahl (Cambridge, MA: Harvard University Press, 1942), 45.

53 Hodeir, *Toward Jazz*, 166.

54 Hodeir would probably grant that the relationship between super- and infrastructure is more cybernetic than the description suggests. Rhythm sections and soloists are generally highly reactive to what the other is doing.

55 Hodeir could hardly agree, then, with the judgment of Frederick Kaufman and John P. Guckin (*The African Roots of Jazz* (Sherman Oaks, CA: Alfred Publishing, 1979), 81), where it is claimed that Milhaud's *La Creation du Monde* is a "fully developed classical jazz composition." In fact, the rhythm of this piece is so polyrhythmic in character that the underlying stability required for swing is obliterated. Nor do its blue notes make it jazz, for reasons previously explained.

56 Hodeir, *Jazz*, 200–201. Hodeir takes pains to explain that syncopations in jazz are not quite like the familiar ones we know in European music. In classic jazz, they are typically played a third of a beat ahead of time and last through two thirds of the next beat.

57 Martin, *Charlie Parker*, 20. Hodeir offers similar analyses of swing in the playing of Louis Armstrong and Johnny Hodges (*Jazz*, 201).

58 David, *Ella Fitzgerald Companion*, 49.

59 Hodeir, *Jazz*, 200–201.

60 Hodeir, *Jazz*, 52–53, 205, 212. Hodeir sometimes appears to be faulting some players for sheer time-keeping problems (e.g., 232–233). Still, this can't be the main issue.

61 Hodeir, *Jazz*, 203.

62 Gunther Schuller's contribution to the discussion of swing in *Early Jazz* (6–10, 144) and *The Swing Era: The Development of Jazz, 1930–1945* (Oxford: Oxford University Press, 1989), 222–225, makes points of contact with the treatment discussed here.

63 Alas, Hodeir completely undervalues the work of Morton, and so fails to cite it as part of his evidence.

64 Hodeir, *Jazz*, 161–163.

65 Marshall Stearns, *The Story of Jazz* (Oxford: Oxford University Press, 1956), 273.

66 Hodeir, *Jazz*, 16. Miles Davis described his early frustration trying to understand Parker's practice of what was called "turning the rhythm around." In his solo playing, Parker

would sometimes seem to be emphasizing the wrong beat, as if he had come in too early or too late. Max Roach, who understood, would have to shout at the piano player not to fall into line with Parker, since Parker would eventually reverse himself and fall back into line with the rhythm section. See Miles Davis (with Quincy Troupe), *Miles: The Autobiography* (New York: Simon and Schuster, 1989), 101.

67 Initially, Hodeir misses the boat on Monk, whom he classifies as just another member of the "modern" school. See *Jazz*, 271. In Chapter XVI of *Toward Jazz*, however, he elaborately recants this opinion.

68 He sees these intangibles as reflections of "character" and even of race (e.g., *Jazz*, 207).

69 Hodeir, *Jazz*, 237.

70 Hodeir, *Jazz*, 195–196.

71 Hodeir, *Jazz*, 224–233, quotation at 232.

72 Hodeir, *Jazz*, 240.

73 Hodeir, *Jazz*, 238.

74 Hodeir, *Jazz*, 238.

75 Hodeir, *Jazz*, 238.

76 Hodeir, *Jazz*, 31, 118, 125.

77 Although they do not speak of a jazz "essence," a version of this view is endorsed by Eric Hobsbawm, *The Jazz Scene* (New York: Pantheon, 1993), 87–88, and Gary Giddins and Scott DeVeaux, *Jazz* (New York: W.W. Norton, 2009), 172.

78 Hodeir, *Jazz*, 196.

79 Hodeir, *Jazz*, 196.

80 See Keith Waters, *The Studio Recordings of the Miles Davis Quintet, 1965–68* (Oxford: Oxford University Press, 2011), 67–69.

81 For an utterly simple example, imagine listening to someone play "When the Saints Come Marching In," accenting the first and third beats, while you clap on the second and fourth.

82 Read his own words in Joe Goldberg, *Jazz Masters of the Fifties* (New York: Macmillan, 1965), 239.

83 Mark C. Gridley, "Clarifying Labels: Jazz, Rock, Funk and Jazz-Rock," *Popular Music and Society* 9:2 (1983): 27–34, at 29.

84 Hodeir, *Jazz*, 94.

85 Hodeir, *Jazz*, 124–125. Whereas Miles Davis' playing is often thought of as devoid of vibrato entirely, Hodeir astutely observes that he often uses a rather precise terminal vibrato of four oscillations per beat.

86 Hodeir, *Jazz*, 74.

87 See Schuller, *Early Jazz*, 117, for a good example of the opposite case.

88 E.g., Hodeir, *Jazz*, 205.

89 We pass over well-documented problems about the capacity of notational systems to represent swinging rhythms.

90 Hodeir, *Toward Jazz*, 60.

91 Elsdon, *Jarrett's* The Köln Concert, 6. For an extended discussion of improvisation that copes with such obstacles, see Lydia Goehr, "Improvising Impromptu, Or, What to Do with a Broken String," in *The Oxford Handbook of Critical Improvisation Studies, Volume 1*, ed. George E. Lewis and Benjamin Piekut (Oxford: Oxford University Press, 2014).

92 Wynton Marsalis with Geoffrey Ward, *Moving to Higher Ground: How Jazz Can Change Your Life* (New York: Random House, 2008), 18.

93 Quoted in Ben Ratliff, *The Jazz Ear: Conversations over Music* (New York: Times Books, 2008), 49–50.

94 Wynton Marsalis, "What is Jazz?" *American Heritage Magazine*, October 1995 (46:6), http://www.americanheritage.com/content/what-jazz.

95 Williams, *Jazz Tradition*, 11. See also Francis Newton, *The Jazz Scene* (New York: Monthly Review Press, 1960), 26–27; Newton read and was influenced by Hodeir.

96 Williams, *Jazz Tradition*, 123. Williams is making a point against the harmonically interesting but rhythmically unadventurous work of Lennie Tristano.
97 See part three of Jan Slawe, *Einführung in die Jazzmusik* (Berne: Verlag National-Zeitung, 1948).
98 Hodeir, *Jazz*, 239.
99 Hodeir, *Jazz*, 240; he remarks that others thought jazz was dying, but he saw too much "vitality" in young players to agree. The year was 1954.

References

"A Jazz Seminar: Are Blues Essential to Jazz?" *DownBeat* (June 27, 1957): 15–16.

Balliett, Whitney. "The First Lady of Song." *New Yorker* (April 26, 1993): 105–106.

Berendt, Joachim E., with Günther Huesmann. *The Jazz Book: From Ragtime to the 21st Century*, 7th ed. Chicago: Lawrence Hill Books, 2009.

Brown, Lee B. "Marsalis and Baraka: An Essay in Comparative Cultural Discourse." *Popular Music* 23:3 (2004): 241–255.

Danto, Arthur C. *After the End of Art: Contemporary Art and the Pale of History*. Princeton: Princeton University Press, 1997.

David, Norman. *The Ella Fitzgerald Companion*. Westport, CT: Praeger, 2004.

Davis, Miles, with Quincy Troupe. *Miles: The Autobiography*. New York: Simon and Schuster, 1989.

Elsdon, Peter. *Keith Jarrett's* The Köln Concert. Oxford: Oxford University Press, 2013.

Friedwald, Will, et al., *The Future of Jazz*, ed. Yuval Taylor. Chicago: Chicago Review Press, 2002.

Galper, Hal. "Practice and Performance Goals." *Jazz Education Journal* 35:5 (2003): 60–71.

Giddins, Gary, and Scott DeVeaux. *Jazz*. New York: W.W. Norton, 2009.

Gillespie, Dizzy, with Al Fraser. *To Be, Or Not … to Bop*. Minneapolis: University of Minnesota Press, 2009 [1979].

Goehr, Lydia. "Improvising Impromptu, Or, What to Do with a Broken String." In *The Oxford Handbook of Critical Improvisation Studies*, vol. 1, ed. George E. Lewis and Benjamin Piekut, 458–480. Oxford: Oxford University Press, 2014.

Goldberg, Joe. *Jazz Masters of the Fifties*. New York: Macmillan, 1965.

Gridley, Mark C. "Clarifying Labels: Jazz, Rock, Funk and Jazz-Rock." *Popular Music and Society* 9:2 (1983): 27–34.

Hobsbawm, Eric. *The Jazz Scene*. New York: Pantheon, 1993.

Hodeir, André. *Jazz: Its Evolution and Essence*, trans. David Noakes. New York: Grove Press, 1956.

Hodeir, André. *Toward Jazz*, trans. Noel Burch. New York: Grove Press, 1962.

Kaufman, Frederick, and John P. Guckin. *The African Roots of Jazz*. Sherman Oaks, CA: Alfred Publishing, 1979.

Magnus, P. D. "Kind of Borrowed, Kind of Blue." *Journal of Aesthetics and Art Criticism* 74:2 (2016): 179–185.

Marsalis, Wynton. "What is Jazz?" *American Heritage Magazine* 46:6 (October 1995): http://www.americanheritage.com/content/what-jazz.

Marsalis, Wynton, with Geoffrey Ward. *Moving to Higher Ground: How Jazz Can Change Your Life*. New York: Random House, 2008.

Martin, Henry. *Charlie Parker and Thematic Improvisation*. Lanham, MD: Scarecrow Press, 2001.

Martin, Peter J. "Spontaneity and Organisation." In *The Cambridge Companion to Jazz*, ed. Mervyn Cooke and David Horn, 133–152. Cambridge: Cambridge University Press, 2002.

Newton, Francis. *The Jazz Scene*. New York: Monthly Review Press, 1960.

Nicholson, Stuart. *Is Jazz Dead? (Or Has It Moved to a New Address?)*. New York: Routledge, 2005.

Panassié, Hugues. *The Real Jazz*, trans. Anne Sorelle Williams. New York: Smith and Durrell, 1942.

Pressing, Jeff. "Free Jazz and the Avant-garde." In *The Cambridge Companion to Jazz*, ed. Mervyn Cooke and David Horn, 202–216. Cambridge: Cambridge University Press, 2002.

Ratliff, Ben. *The Jazz Ear: Conversations over Music*. New York: Times Books, 2008.

Sargeant, Winthrop. *Jazz: Hot and Hybrid*, 3rd ed. New York: Da Capo, 1975.

Schuller, Gunther. *Early Jazz: Its Roots and Musical Development*. Oxford: Oxford University Press, 1968.

Schuller, Gunther. *The Swing Era: The Development of Jazz, 1930–1945*. Oxford: Oxford University Press, 1989.

Slawe, Jan. *Einführung in die Jazzmusik*. Berne: Verlag National–Zeitung, 1948.

Stearns, Marshall. *The Story of Jazz*. Oxford: Oxford University Press, 1956.

Stravinsky, Igor. *Poetics of Music in the Form of Six Lessons*, trans. Arthur Knodel and Ingolf Dahl. Cambridge, MA: Harvard University Press, 1942.

Taylor, Billy with Teresa L. Reed. *The Jazz Life of Dr. Billy Taylor*. Bloomington: Indiana University Press, 2013.

Waters, Keith. *The Studio Recordings of the Miles Davis Quintet, 1965–68*. Oxford: Oxford University Press, 2011.

Williams, Martin. *The Jazz Tradition*. Oxford: Oxford University Press, 1971.

Youngren, William H. "European Roots of Jazz." In *The Oxford Companion to Jazz*, ed. Bill Kirchner, 17–28. Oxford: Oxford University Press, 2000.

3

DEFINING JAZZ HISTORICALLY

Hearing that G. E. Moore's younger son, Timothy, had organized a successful jazz "combo," Wittgenstein persuaded him to sit at the piano and explain at great length the structure and development – what Schönberg would have called the "logic" – of jazz.

– *Allan Janik and Stephen Toulmin,* Wittgenstein's Vienna

It is literally true to say that a jazz lover who heard Bix's 'Singing the Blues', then went into a monastery, stayed there till the death of Roosevelt, and then came out to hear Charlie Parker's 'Anthropology' would have real difficulty recognizing any relationship between the two recordings.

– *Benny Green,* The Reluctant Art

In Chapter 1, we highlighted a change in musical style and attendant reception practices that arose with the bop revolution – a change so pronounced that many fans and some critics thought that bop/post-bop "is a form of music distinct from jazz."[1] In Chapter 2, we noted that André Hodeir's theory that jazz requires polyrhythmic interaction runs afoul of some free jazz, yet we do not want to deny that it is jazz. Consequently, we did not reach closure on the topic of the essence of jazz. In this chapter, we turn directly to the general issue of the prospects for securing a general definition of jazz. That search faces three distinct challenges: (1) The stylistic diversity of jazz undercuts reference to essential musical elements. (2) As explained in Chapter 1, different social practices and venues align with different styles of jazz. (3) In addition to those two complications, there are "hard cases" that might be counted as jazz, or might not: jazz-rock fusion as a whole, but also some specific pieces of music, such as Miles Davis's unjazzy ambient tribute to Duke Ellington, "He Loved Him Madly" (1974).[2]

1. Elements and Essences

We live in an age that is deeply suspicious of essences and definitions, and jazz historians and theorists no longer want to face the question, "What is jazz?" For example, jazz historian Scott DeVeaux observes that it is no longer "an article of faith that some central essence named *jazz* remains constant" or unifies its history.[3] Daniel Hardie remarks that the topic of definition has become a "black hole" in jazz criticism and histories.[4] *The Oxford Companion to Jazz* thinks that three sentences are enough to raise and then dismiss the topic.[5] Elsewhere, one discerns contempt for the very idea that a hunk of cultural territory should have a character that is definitive.[6] In much of this anti-essentialist literature, those who seek definitions are treated like fascist border guards busy keeping the right people in and the wrong people out. But where do we find this horde of essentialists busy drawing boundaries around jazz?

In practice, most jazz critics and historians appear to be satisfied if they can identify a few basic characteristics of jazz, no combination of which amounts to an "essence."[7] The typical candidates are some relationship to the blues, the centrality of improvisation, and an essential relationship to notable features of African-American experience. It is also common to find these three features linked together as the proposal that jazz embraces blues and improvisation because it is, at base, African-American music. The following statements, some of them quoted frequently, are typical examples:

- "There would be no jazz without the blues, and if one dismissed them and their effect … jazz would become a sterile and meaningless music."[8]
- "Without blues, as interior animator, jazz has no history, no memory."[9]
- "The moment when the blues ceases to be part of jazz is the moment when jazz, as we know it, ceases to exist."[10]
- "No blues, no jazz, it's that simple."[11]
- "The essence of jazz [is] improvisation."[12]
- "Improvisation is the heart and soul of jazz."[13]
- "Jazz music *is* black history."[14]
- "It's the American Negro's tradition, it's his music. White people don't have a right to play it."[15]

However, these and similar reference to jazz's musical resources and cultural sources do not constitute a definition. Construed as definitions, they disenfranchise a great deal of recent jazz.[16] And, interesting as it may be to trace competing etymologies of "jazz," conclusive evidence that it derives from, say, the slang term "Jezebel" would not show that contemporary jazz supports either idolatry or prostitution.[17] Shifting connotations can be informative, but our focus is the question of whether the music commonly referred to as "jazz" has any shared nature. As G. E. Moore rightly cautions, "No argument from the origin of a thing can be a safe guide as to exactly what the nature of the thing is now."[18] For example, the fact that there would be no United States without the revolution of 1775–1783 does not demonstrate that the United States remains a revolutionary society. Similarly, jazz arose as African-American music and was, for a very long time, dance music, but it does not follow that these attributes remain central in today's global jazz scene. Although we will offer our own account of how historical consciousness is important to jazz, there is a serious error in supposing that historical *origins* constitute a *definition*. We elaborate on this point at length in this chapter, where we face the problem of *how* various originating characteristics retain some relevance as part of jazz's essential nature.

Another questionable approach tells us that we must settle for a plurality of "views," none of which have priority over others.[19] While pluralism has the merit of correcting an overly tidy "evolutionary" model of jazz development, it often swings to the other extreme, describing a flux of "motion, kinesis, agitation," and of "loss, dispossession, opposition, and contradiction."[20]

This reluctance to prioritize is odd. It runs away from the intuition that by the end of the second decade of the twentieth century, a new musical phenomenon with definite features had come into being. This intuition is supported by empirical studies of music reception. In an academic equivalent of the "blindfold test," researchers played samples of jazz, Western classical music, and Chinese classical music for primary school through university-level students in the United States, Hong Kong, and China.[21] They provided no information about the music. Their only goal was to measure and compare patterns of preference for different samples of music displaying distinctive, broad musical characteristics. The jazz samples included Oscar Peterson, Dave Brubeck, and Johnny Hodges. The Western classical music included Satie and Mozart. One of their most unequivocal findings was that the three groups of listeners heard distinct musical characteristics in the samples and these characteristics aligned with the criteria used by the researchers in selecting them. The listeners aligned their preferences accordingly – each group preferred the samples that illustrated a particular style. For example, Americans consistently preferred the three jazz selections over the Western classical, which they preferred over the Chinese classical. Students from mainland China had precisely the opposite response, while those in Hong Kong had the strongest preference for Western classical together with a strikingly low endorsement of Peterson, Brubeck, and Hodges. Independent of any organized exposure to jazz, groups with distinct cultural backgrounds grouped the three jazz recordings together and either preferred or disliked them as a group.[22]

We are not downplaying the difficulty of defining jazz. However, those who are skeptics about the possibility of arriving at a definition – or even of landing in the neighborhood of a definition – generally adopt a simplistic and outmoded framework for any such project.[23] Then, when the simple approach fails, the attempt ends. As philosophers, what we bring to the table are lessons learned from the enormous effort that has been made to solve a parallel problem over the course of the last six decades: the problem of defining art. If it's difficult to fit Cecil Taylor, Peggy Lee, Charlie Christian, and Jelly Roll Morton into one category, it's a cakewalk compared to the task of finding a definition of art that includes the prehistoric cave painters of Altamira and the work of Marcel Duchamp, Katsushika Hokusai, Jack Kerouac, Cindy Sherman, Mozart, George Eliot, John Cage, and Dale Chihuly. And, since jazz is an art, our definition of art must also include pretty much every recording played in *DownBeat*'s Blindfold Tests.

The question, then, is can we pick out something distinctive and uniform about jazz that runs through its history? This could be some manifest property (that is, something listeners directly observe in every instance of the music itself, once they know how to listen for it). We made such an attempt in Chapter 2, but ran into trouble after the 1950s. The important lesson from philosophy of art, however, is that manifest properties are probably not the place to look, and even if some candidates can be located, they will be insufficient to bring closure on the question of what falls within the scope of jazz.[24]

2. Theoretical Interlude

It is worth pausing to think about this problem of definition from a meta-theoretic point of view. Twentieth-century philosophers often write as if a single counter-example can be devastating.[25] In philosophy of art, a single work by Marcel Duchamp is often taken to refute definitions of art that include an aesthetic dimension – *Fountain*, a commercial urinal displayed as sculpture. Duchamp's *Fountain* became of greater significance after Arthur Danto argued that a single gallery exhibition by Andy Warhol in 1964 was sufficient to prove that no reference to observable properties can be required in the definition of art.[26] However, the strategy of argument by hypothesis and counterexample might be completely wrong-headed when it comes to defining cultural achievements.

Consider, by way of example, the proposal that flatness is an essential feature of the art form of painting. Clearly, we can find numerous examples of works by painters in which a physical relief element is saliently exploited – for instance, the "wrecktangle" works of James Terrell, which he also terms "works in 2 1/2 dimensions." Now is it really correct that such a counterexample proves that painting is not basically a two dimensional art form? In fact, we do make room for divergent cases when we speak of an exception that "proves" a rule. One traditional way of understanding this apparently oxymoronic saying is that an exception tests a rule – puts the rule to the test, in other words. The actual Medieval Latin principle, said to derive from Cicero, is the principle *exceptio probat regulam in casibus non exceptis*. It means that the very fact that an exception is allowed serves to confirm that there is a rule. Since cultural rules may have exceptions, they simply are not the kind of things that are marked off by unchanging essences.[27] Now, think about the standard idea that improvisation is essential to jazz, and then consider the existence of non-improvisatory performances of jazz works, played by musicians whose work is securely anchored in the tradition, as Duke Ellington's certainly was. Although Ellington's "Concerto for Cootie" (1940) prominently features the trumpet of Cootie Williams, Ellington leaves no space for Williams to improvise. Still, the most appropriate kind of appreciation of this music would surely situate it within that tradition. Williams was an improvising musician, as were most members of Ellington's band, a fact that informed listeners will know.[28] Interestingly, George Russell – one of the great innovators in jazz arrangement and composition – said that even a jazz composition should have the "intuitive" sound of uncomposed jazz.[29] In other words, it should offer the sound of music "being improvised," that is, of being searched out as it is being played. The question, then, is whether an essentialist's penchant for strictness is simply misplaced, and whether the key ingredients of jazz – improvisation, metrical conflict, the blues, connection to the African-American community – are something other than elements of a definition. There is an important role for the ubiquity of these features, but not the role that is normally discussed, nor sufficiently appreciated. Again, with Moore, there is no reason to suppose that the later music "must resemble the germ out of which it was developed."[30] Jazz is just such a tradition: A lot of jazz does not possess any of the features that characterize earlier jazz. Nonetheless, blues tonality and the other standard features provide a *historical foundation* for later jazz – both stylistically, and as a set of social practices. Yet none of them individually or together need to be present in recent developments. Rather, what matters is how later jazz displays the right causal-historical connections to earlier stages of jazz. To paraphrase Danto, it might be the case that anything musical can be incorporated into jazz, but it is not the case that everything will be: Some later developments could not have been jazz at an earlier stage.[31] Appropriate historical developments have to pave the way to jazz status.

Finally, we recognize that definitions of cultural phenomena will leave us with any number of unresolvable hard cases: Music whose status is controversial based on prevailing ideas about jazz, and for which it may be impossible to distinguish between an artist who pushes boundaries and one who simply abandons them.[32] In this regard, we have already mentioned Miles Davis's "He Loved Him Madly." Others have singled out his posthumous hip-hop album, *Do-Bop* (1992), but we see the problem arising with any number of jazz-pop hybrids, such as Gil Scott-Heron's *Winter in America* (1974). Hard cases do *not* include the parochial challenges that break out among reactionaries and progressives, such as the debate about swing in the 1930s or the 1943 disagreement between John Hammond and Leonard Feather about Duke Ellington's *Black, Brown, and Beige*.[33] Hard cases are usually at the cutting-edge of an art form. They arise when artists consciously challenge basic assumptions. They differ from short-lived disputes about hybrids by continuing to resist classification into any existing category. Another good example is *Book of Angels Vol. 20* (2013), guitarist Pat Metheny's performances of music by saxophonist/composer John Zorn. Arguably, some of it is free jazz.

Arguably, none of it is jazz at all. The mere presence of Metheny does not settle it – witness his contribution to David Bowie's "This Is Not America" (1985).[34] Music isn't jazz simply because a "jazz musician" plays it.

3. A New Definition of Jazz

We will now offer our definition, which is modeled on a three-part definition of art provided by Stephen Davies.[35] His definition arises from the challenge of linking recent avant-garde art to art's Paleolithic origins: How do we define a particular sphere of cultural production where later instances "transcend its origins step by step until it no longer emulates its foundational works?"[36] We face the same problem. It is quite a stretch to suppose that the standard features of jazz that we noted early in this chapter – relationship to the blues, the centrality of improvisation, and an essential relationship to notable features of African-American experience – are equally present in Ella Fitzgerald's version of "Ding-Dong! The Witch Is Dead" (1961) and the Original Dixieland Jazz Band's "Livery Stable Blues" (1917). On our approach, the standard features are not essential in the sense of being features that must be present in every instance. Instead, they are essential to our understanding of the history of jazz, such that music that lacks all of them can be an instance of jazz provided it has an appropriate causal-historical relation to earlier music that has them. This relation does not require them to be temporally juxtaposed.[37]

Here is our definition:

A piece of music is jazz if and only if (1) it was produced before 1920 and falls within the style parameters of early jazz, or (2) it non-accidentally exemplifies a style publicly recognized as jazz within the subsequent jazz tradition (e.g., Dixieland, classic female blues, stride piano, Kansas City swing, cool, hard bop), or (3) it employs or modifies some stylistic traits of earlier jazz and successfully reflects an intention to satisfy appreciative practices governing some period in the jazz tradition.[38]

This definition demands a bit of explanation. Following that, we offer our defense of it. From this point forward, we'll refer to the three conditions as (1) the *proto-jazz condition*, (2) the *style condition*, and (3) the *appreciative-practice condition*.

One of the noticeable features of this kind of historical definition is that "jazz" is mentioned in both the *definiens* and the *definiendum*. That is, it seems we are trying to define jazz by using the word to define it and so it would seem that the definition, at least in part, is circular. This potential objection is answered by Davies: "Historical definitions can be reflexive, taking a recursive form: something is [an instance of a cultural kind] only if it stands in the appropriate relationship to its artistic forebears."[39] However, reflexivity generates its own problem, which is how chronologically "first" members of the category merit that status. We have avoided this problem by dividing our definition into three conditions, where the first condition faces this problem but the other two do not. But then it is not really a problem, since we do not have to explain why Paleolithic origins of art and music come to have the status of art. We do not have a problem of the non-reflexive status of first instances of jazz: We only need to locate its stylistic branching within an existing art, namely, American popular music. We summarize additional merits of this approach at the end of this chapter, but for now, with the above superficial objections removed, we will get on with our explanation.

It is best to begin with the reflexivity conditions, (2) and (3), and the differences between them. The most important difference is that the style condition refers us to performances that reflect established styles, while the appreciative-practice condition covers cases of stylistic innovation by recognizing that jazz is regulated by a series of changing social practices. Therefore the appreciative-practice condition (but not the style condition) will cover transitional and idiosyncratic instances.

4. The Style Condition

We can be brief about the style condition. Performances in this category generate no controversy. They are readily classifiable as jazz.

Jazz styles are arranging and performing styles. However, there is no generic "jazz" quality that they all possess. (We pursued that possibility in Chapter 2, and failed.) Instead, a performance is jazz when it non-accidentally displays high levels of standard properties of one or more of the many different jazz styles. (We say more about the notion of a standard property in section 9 of this chapter.) By "non-accidental" we mean that the performance sounds as it does because it is influenced by other jazz performances. In practice, "non-accidental" is often synonymous with "intentionally."

As we noted at the start of this chapter, many jazz critics and historians emphasize the central importance of blues to jazz. Yet there are many blues styles, only some of which are jazz styles. So however standard they may be, blue notes and a standard 12-bar construction do not constitute a musical *style* called "the blues." In the wake of the blues craze of the early 1920s, blues singers have been routinely divided between jazz singers, most notably Bessie Smith, "Empress of the Blues," and blues singers who do not belong in jazz, such as Son House, Skip James, and Howlin' Wolf. The blues may be one of jazz's central resources, but whatever we select as the *sources* of jazz, jazz musicians stylistically rework those sources.

To approach this idea from another direction: In the vast majority of cases, a musical performance is jazz because there is a genuine causal-historical connection between the music and a publicly recognized style. It is frequently remarked that there are jazz-like passages in the second movement of Beethoven's piano sonata in C minor (Op. 111). This is very different from saying that Beethoven's piano music can be played as jazz, as demonstrated by Dorothy Donegan's "Donegan's Blues" (1961). But when it is claimed that Beethoven "invents jazz" in Op. 111, independent of African-American influence and decades before there is genuine jazz, the claim is either hyperbole or a category mistake.[40] There are no jazz styles *in abstracta*, that is, there are no stylistic rules existing in a Platonic heaven. There was no boogie-woogie or jazz in 1822, and there could not be. Whatever the explanation for the jazzy passages in Op. 111, it will not involve the causal history that informs proto-jazz. Beethoven was not instantiating a jazz style.

Silly as it is, the Beethoven example also calls attention to the fact that jazz styles are *performance* styles. Music's status as jazz cannot be determined by reference to the musical logic of the bare composition.[41] Stylistically, a composition may be a standard blues, yet one performance will be jazz and another will be rock. Listen to the difference between Mose Allison performing his "Young Man Blues," and the hard rock version of The Who. Many Tin Pan Alley standards lend themselves to jazz performance, but they can be done in a non-jazz manner, too: witness David Byrne's "Don't Fence Me In" (1990). A Duke Ellington composition can be given a non-jazz performance: witness The Rumour's "Do Nothing Till You Hear from Me" (1977) and Richard Thompson's "Rockin' in Rhythm" (1981). If Steely Dan's 1974 version of "East St. Louis Toodle-Oo" is jazz, it is jazz thanks to Donald Fagen's credible stride piano and not because it's an Ellington standard.

If jazz is music of freedom and constant innovation, why are there jazz styles? Jazz musicians are (now more than ever) expected to individualize their performance style, and not merely copy others. However, innovations are imitated, and we can hear these influences. It is not mere happenstance that musicians of a particular generation will have a recognizably similar sound: It is a byproduct of the typical process of becoming a jazz musician – listening to others, copying them, and thereby acquiring *shared* strategies for handling rhythm, harmony, timbre, and melody. When Charlie Parker died, in 1955, Lennie Tristano famously quipped that "if Charlie Parker wanted to invoke plagiarism laws he could sue almost everybody who's made a record in the last 10 years."[42] Then it mushroomed: Art Pepper looked back at the late 1950s and complained, "They'd copy these things off the records and practice by the hour Bird's solos and his licks. Everybody sounded like him with the same ugly sound."[43]

More importantly, however, innovations in any art take place within a tradition, and that tradition establishes parameters limiting those innovations. Innovation, in other words, is always innovating relative to a particular context, without which the idea of innovation would lose its sense.

5. The Appreciative-Practice Condition

The appreciative-practice condition keeps the future of jazz open to new musical developments. It does so by addressing cases of innovative music that do not fit within a publicly recognized jazz style, and which many fans cannot appreciate – either initially, or later – as jazz. We must explain how this music establishes an appropriate causal-historical relation to earlier jazz, without falling into the error of thinking that all music that is stylistically derived from jazz is jazz. Consider the case of Duane Allman's and Dickey Betts' guitar solos for "In Memory of Elizabeth Reed," which Allman said were directly influenced by listening to Davis and Coltrane on *Kind of Blue*.[44] The Allman Brothers Band was working in a rock context, however, so their performances of "In Memory of Elizabeth Reed" are not sanctioned as jazz under any of our definition's three conditions. Importing the technique of modal soloing into blues-rock is not enough to transform southern rock into jazz. Mere stylistic influence is only sufficient in the proto-jazz phase.

To reflect on this chapter's epigraph, Wittgenstein's demand for an explanation of the "logic" of jazz is partly justified, yet also too narrow. Musical form is only *part* of the story: there are also extra-musical goals that the musicians accomplish by performing. These goals and values are part of established jazz practice, enhancing and guiding appreciation of the music. Different styles of music generally deploy a distinctive set of musical features in order to reflect particular social practices and communal values – at the outset, anyway. As a style develops through time, some of its stylistic features and associated values might come to be seen as dated and so lose their prominence, and the style is retired from main-stream practice. (Granted, older jazz styles can co-exist alongside newer ones.) At that point, musical innovations can either uphold or challenge established values and goals. Sometimes, they do both. In Chapter 2, we argued in favor of a certain way of handling rhythm as one of the longest-running stabilizing musical features. As we argued in Chapter 1, jazz being music for dancing was initially related to that feature, but it was gradually superseded by new approaches to rhythm, which in turn facilitated a realignment of jazz with standards of artistic modernism and alternative social practices. Another major realignment occurred at the end of the 1960s, with Miles Davis's *Bitches Brew* (1970). Its enormous first-year sales were largely to fans of rock music, and Davis was also taking his new amplified band to rock venues and rock festivals. Knowing that he was sending mixed signals about his intentions, Davis clarified the music's provenance in *DownBeat*, "We're not a rock band."[45] He wanted to be clear that his new music did not align him with the dominant white popular culture.

We are not simply making the point that jazz is embedded in social practice and the music responds to and reflects a web of cultural happenstance, contested practices, and competing values. We are making a point about *defining* jazz. There are crucial junctures and liminal periods when musicians jettison some of their established musical practices and style features. In doing so, they may either challenge or reaffirm higher-order values associated with the older styles. They may do both at the same time. But when innovative music is subsequently understood – often by younger jazz fans and players – as extending the tradition, and imitators arise, a new jazz style appears. After that, new instances are sanctioned by the style condition; as a result, new higher-order values may be sanctioned to guide subsequent innovations.

Of course, innovative music that does not initially appear to be jazz may be recognized at a later time. What was initially thought to be too radically off tradition may come to seem standard and conservative from a retrospective point of view or to a future generation of jazz lovers.

Our proposal is that when musical performance reflects a jazz influence but is not in a style publicly recognized as jazz, jazz status is maintained if the new music can be appreciated as an intentional extension of the jazz tradition, including adherence to some of its extra-musical, appreciation-guiding values. Intention alone is not enough. We are offering a success condition: knowledgeable listeners must be able to appreciate the audible features of the music as reflecting the performers' tradition-appropriate intentions. If the musical innovations subsequently coalesce into a style, the style condition takes over from there. The primary function of the appreciative-practice condition is to confer jazz status in the interim, before the parameters of the new style are clear. It also covers innovations that are dead ends or one-off experiments, remaining stylistically indeterminate and so never securing jazz status under the style condition. However, if the performers are drawing on jazz practices in order to non-trivially pursue established extra-musical goals and values of the jazz tradition, the musicians are performing jazz. Often, the key value is freedom, as expressed in a famous line from Ellington: "Jazz is freedom. Jazz is the freedom to play anything, whether it has been done before or not."[46] Although Ellington does not explicitly say so, the higher-order value of freedom is generally linked directly to the practice of improvisation.[47]

As evidence of the appreciation-guiding role of higher-order values, consider two early validations of free jazz. Mingus denigrated the performing skills of Ornette Coleman ("I doubt he can even play a C scale in whole notes"). In the same breath, Mingus applauds Coleman for his individualism as one of the few post-bop musicians to escape the example of Charlie Parker, and then for locating and exploring jazz antecedents that everyone else ignored ("He's brought a thing in – it's not new. I won't say who started it, but … people overlooked it").[48] Saxophonist Paul Desmond's 1960 defense of Coleman is very similar. He criticizes the jazz scene for too much conformity. Personal expression is an important jazz value – Desmond summarizes his jazz ideal with one word: "Diversityville." On this basis, he praises Coleman's sonic departures as both valuable and intentional: "one thing I like about Ornette. He's such an individualist. I like the firmness of thought and purpose that goes into what he's doing, even though I don't always like to listen it."[49] Both Mingus and Desmond praise Coleman by distinguishing between higher-order values and the means used to advance them.

In proposing that style violations must be appreciable as explorations of extra-musical values that inform jazz appreciation, we are not excluding the introduction of new values. There is no fixed set of performance goals or higher-order values for jazz. Therefore we reject Barry Ulanov's thesis that there are three crucial general values for evaluating jazz: "freshness, profundity, and skill … joined together [with] a tight reciprocal relationship among them."[50] Jazz musicians sometimes jettison one of these in order to achieve broader goals. For example, a number of early critics dismissed the "soul jazz" wing of hard bop as musically regressive in its pursuit of a simpler technique and a "dirtier" horn sound – even Horace Silver worried that it was becoming too "commercialized" and "bastardized" to count as jazz.[51] His worry reflects *one* set of governing values about jazz practice. But others recognized that this musical "regression" was a means to a further, progressive end: a reassertion of African-American community by black musicians.[52] *Bitches Brew* and Davis's subsequent music were likewise dismissed as an attempt to cash in by reaching the pop audience.[53] But, even if true, Davis was reasserting the legitimacy of pre-bop norms. King Oliver's residency at the Dreamland and Ellington's at the Cotton Club are merely two examples of the long tradition of jazz as an explicitly commercial, "entertainment-based musical culture."[54] The huge audience for amplified jazz in the 1970s shows that there was an audience for jazz that was only too happy to make peace with these values.

It appears, therefore, that (1) there is no fixed set of appreciation-guiding values for jazz and (2) some of the established values are in conflict, so that it is difficult or impossible to embrace all of them simultaneously. Thus, throughout jazz's history we find different jazz musicians pursuing conflicting values. As Ted Gioia explains, this is precisely what happened at the dawn of the 1970s, when the newly emerging fusion music "was virtually [the] mirror image" of free jazz: fusion was commercial and "pragmatic," while free jazz "represented economic isolation" and "progressivism."[55] Different musicians and fans align themselves with different values.

Recognition of these points allows us to understand, without condescension, why many jazz fans condemn stylistic innovation. For example, a 1961 article in *DownBeat* attacks a performance by Coltrane and Erik Dolphy as "anti-jazz."[56] This idea, if not the phrase, appears whenever innovations radically violate expectations of listening. One of the most thoughtful first-person accounts of this appreciative resistance is Philip Larkin's explanation of why he was never able to appreciate bebop and post-bop jazz.

> It wasn't like listening to a kind of jazz I didn't care for. ... It wasn't like listening to jazz at all. Nearly every characteristic of the music had been neatly inverted: for instance, the jazz tone, distinguished from 'straight' practice by an almost-human vibrato, had entirely disappeared ... Had the most original feature of jazz been its use of collective improvisation? Banish it ... Had jazz been essentially a popular art, full of tunes you could whistle? Something fundamentally awful had taken place to ensure that there should be no more tunes.[57]

Notice Larkin's emphasis on technique and other manifest properties. He doesn't want music that *sounds* the way jazz had come to sound. However, there is more to the story. Larkin goes on to discuss higher-order values: bop and post-bop reflect the values of artistic modernism. But earlier jazz – the non-commercial stuff, anyway – was regarded as a kind of folk tradition and so incompatible with modernism. From this perspective, bebop was a change in style *and* a realignment of cultural values.[58] From our perspective, there are is no fixed set of higher-order values, so there is no principled objection to bebop if it spiced the gumbo in a new way. Even so, bop's affirmation of modernism wasn't entirely new. It was merely more obvious. Ellington's more complex arrangements already reflected modernist trends, so modernist values entered jazz early in the Jazz Age.[59] Bop was a new practice for highlighting and endorsing these values.

To summarize the role of the appreciative-practice condition: its function is to recognize music that extends the jazz tradition without offering instances of an established jazz style. It covers one-off experiments and dead ends. But it there-fore also covers the initial steps in the emergence of a new style during a liminal period – music that would count as hard cases had the style remained in an embryonic stage through lack of imitation. Music that seems to resist classification will sometimes turn out to be the prototype of a new style, and this music will *initially* fall under the appreciative-practice condition, but will subsequently fall under the style condition.

6. The Proto-Jazz Condition

The remaining point of interpretation is the proto-jazz condition. By "proto-jazz," we mean the prototypes of the music that became popular and spread during the Jazz Age, which is normally dated as beginning 1919 or 1920.

This condition recognizes that the first jazz was not always distinctive in ways that characterize subsequent jazz. Various cases will be included for a mixture of different reasons. Only some of this music was initially marketed as "jazz." Yet we do not want to restrict early jazz to music that fits neatly into the paradigm of early New Orleans jazz. As it made its way out of New Orleans, spreading through the United States and then into Europe, the term "jazz" indicated a new approach to dance music: "a kind of borderline music that was on the verge of becoming jazz."[60] Musicians and listeners recognized that something new was taking place in popular music, but there was still considerable uncertainty about what it was. As musicians popularized the new approach, much of it was only minimally indebted to the New Orleans paradigm.[61] Consequently, a historical definition requires a proto-jazz clause that covers this early period of musical practice, covering everything outside of the original New Orleans style – most notably blues prior to the "blues craze," and the derivatively "jazzy" music that served as the antecedents of the rich musical tradition that blossomed during the Jazz Age.

The obvious question about the proto-jazz condition is the choice of 1920 as a pivotal year. We grant that it is somewhat arbitrary. So why not push back to 1917, with the recording and release of the crucial first "jazz" record, by the Original Dixieland Jazz Band? First, because their music is rather loosely connected to the other jazz of its time: it remains an amalgamation, with strong "echoes of marching bands, ragtime, and pre-jazz dance tunes."[62] Their music is no more jazz-inflected than the very different music of James Reese Europe and other important musicians in this liminal period: not so much jazz as the incorporation of some jazz elements. Although New Orleans jazz is the one coherent jazz style within this proto-jazz era, we do not have other coherent styles that compete with it. Lacking that diversity, the style condition does not baptize any music from this time other than music in the New Orleans style. Hence, the proto-jazz condition is necessary to recognize any other music as jazz in 1917 and just after.

Ultimately, 1920 is the pivotal year because it is the year of Mamie Smith's "Crazy Blues," as well as the year that Joseph "King" Oliver took charge of the Creole Jazz Band and took up residency at Chicago's Dreamland Cafe. On the one hand, Smith's record launched the so-called "blues craze" of the early Jazz Age, setting the template for blues as a musical constant of 1920s jazz. More significantly, it was the record that established that the blues and jazz were African-American music.[63] And, as a recording, it was a milestone in shifting the music industry from selling sheet music to selling records.[64] If "Crazy Blues" had been a minor hit for Smith but a million-selling record by a white imitator, jazz might have turned out very differently. Jazz might have become a composed music (like ragtime), with only superficial connections to the blues. It might have been like rock'n'roll after Elvis Presley became its "King": the African-American originators are sidelined, both in the marketplace and in the historical record, and a different, "whiter" music dominates popular culture. That historical detour was avoided because Smith's "Crazy Blues" launched the record industry's investment in "race records." Consequently, the music of the Jazz Age was firmly and irrevocably rooted in, and then repeatedly shaped by, African-American musical developments.

King Oliver's residency at the Dreamland was not as immediately significant as "Crazy Blues." It is nonetheless an important milestone, because it is the birth of a Chicago style that branches off from the established New Orleans style. Within the course of a few months in 1920, jazz moved from one style (with imitators) to three streams that would unfold into distinct jazz styles. (Add stride piano, unrecorded but emerging in New York at about this time, and we have four streams.) Consequently, 1920 set the stage for the musical proliferation that permits us to invoke the style condition. Finally, we should note that these musical developments fall just after two historical events that influenced the Jazz Age in innumerable ways: the end of the war, and the start of prohibition. Ending proto-jazz with the arrival of the first "jazz" recordings puts us on the wrong side of these major historical markers.

7. Additional Clarifications of the Definition

The remaining issue is *how* music identified by the other two conditions relates to the proto-jazz condition. Among the earliest 1920s styles, the connection is relatively direct: early jazz styles coalesced from proto-material, especially (but not limited to) early blues and the New Orleans style. By the late 1920s, the connection back to proto-jazz becomes indirect due to variation and augmentation of inter-mediate styles. However, the whole point of the three-part definition is that the style condition and the appreciative-practice condition are independent of the proto-jazz condition. This is not to say that the period dating back to the late nineteenth century did not foreground musical elements that would later come to characterize jazz. The function of the proto-jazz condition is to get jazz started, by recognizing that it did not arise *ex nihilo* from Jelly Roll Morton or from Buddy Bolden's cornet. Several jazz styles emerged from proto-jazz at approximately the same time, after which no jazz has had to have a direct tie back to proto-jazz. Even the "moldy figs" of the 1930s were not really defending New Orleans jazz of the proto-jazz period so much as they were championing the classic style of the 1920s.[65]

We end our explanation of the definition with a word of warning. Although our definition is recognizably a historical definition, we endorse neither an evo-lutionary nor a teleological account. The notion that jazz "evolved" is every-where in the jazz literature, but this adoption of a biological metaphor guts the idea of its biological implications. If it means no more than that jazz kept chan-ging in a context of competing alternatives, it adds nothing to the point that new styles of jazz developed out of earlier ones. It does not, however, elucidate why the later styles are still jazz. After all, to the extent that some rhythm and blues music and early rock'n'roll derives directly from jazz (e.g., the jump style of Louis Jordan, the R&B hit "The Hucklebuck"), talk of "evolution" only muddies the water, obscuring the important point that some derived styles belong to different broader categories or genres.[66]

Nor do we find it plausible to suppose, with Hodeir, that the essence of an art form is something toward which history moves: that early jazz had not fully realized the ideal balance of tension and relaxation toward which the music progressed.[67] The Hegelian logic of this view implies that an art form "ends" when it realizes its goal and, thus, artistic closure. Hodeir writes that "a musical form is just like a human being in that it develops, grows larger and more complex, reaches maturity, then declines and dies."[68] But we see no compelling argument that leads us to think that jazz is dead, or that performances in today's jazz clubs are post-jazz music.[69] Therefore we defend the centrality of historical criteria without building in any notions of evolution or teleological completion.

8. Merits of the Definition

Our definition of jazz has the obvious advantage of stressing that jazz is a historical phenomenon. Its three conditions preserve, as relevant but not definitive, all the features that are normally referenced in characterizations of jazz.

At the same time, the definition successfully avoids the major objections that bedevil historical definitions of art. Specifically, the claim that later art must have the right social historical connections back to earlier art conflicts with the idea that art is a universal human phenomenon. The universality of art requires the historical approach to unify a wide range of practices and traditions together into a single grand history of art, identifying one time and place for the emergence of the first art. This complication generates two criticisms of historical definitions of art. First, if the first art, which is presumably Paleolithic art, does not have that status by virtue of the proper connections back to earlier art, then we seem to need an independent reason why it is art.[70] However, if we can offer an independent reason why some Paleolithic artifacts or activities count as art, then that reason should equally apply to some artifacts and activities today, without any need for the required link back into art history.[71] Therefore the historical explanation only applies to some recent art, and so it postulates a requirement for art that is not universal. At best, the theory emphasizes something about what takes place with a lot of recent Western art. The theory is therefore "too parochial."[72] A second problem is that this parochialism is best addressed by conceding that, as Davies puts it, "there is more than one artworld, more than one tradition of making artworks."[73] In line with the evidence that agriculture was initiated and developed independently in several places at approximately the same time, we must allow that distinct artistic traditions may have arisen independently of one another. Just as we then have no reason to suppose that each of these artworlds will have the same structures of relations in place to link later art to earlier art, so we have no reason to think that we have *artworld* histories in place, distinct from other kinds of social relations. Together, these two objections demonstrate that a purely historical definition of art will not succeed.

A historical definition of *jazz*, however, does not face these two objections. Beethoven's Op. 111 aside, no one is claiming that jazz arose independently in different musical cultures. There was music and art in the seventeenth-century courts of the Mughal empire (in present-day India), but no one supposes that they had jazz because they had a tradition of polyrhythmic, improvised music.[74] There is a tradition of improvised songs of mourning among the Kaluli people of Papua New Guinea.[75] However much their musical practice resembles the blues, it makes no sense to claim that there is Kaluli jazz. With jazz, we *do* want to say there is a single tradition, and all subsequent jazz must trace back into that tradition by the right kinds of social historical connections. If there are Kaluli jazz singers today, it is because they became aware of, and imitated, the jazz tradition that arose in the United States around the start of the twentieth century. Miles Davis and Carla Bley have both performed jazz with Indian instruments and influence, so it is likely that their music sounds *something* like the court music of the Mughal "golden age." However, there was no jazz anywhere in the world in the seventeenth century, so it does not matter *how much* similarity or difference there is. There was no Mughal jazz.

Nonetheless, we don't face the problem of "first jazz" in the way that there is a "first art" problem for historical definitions of art. Jazz arose in the United States during a particular period of time. A historical definition of jazz requires no more than its differentiation from other music of that place and time. Jazz histories only have to explain how and when it was differentiated (in the proto-jazz stage), not how it emerged *ex nihilo* among our prehistoric ancestors.

We can also deal with the worry that a historical definition casts too wide a net: we might be accused of certifying too much non-jazz as jazz, simply because it is historically related to, and is influenced by, bona fide jazz. This is certainly a problem for most historical definitions of *art*, especially Jerrold Levinson's. Once a cultural kind is established, the category snowballs. If *mere historical influence* determines classification, then there is no principled way to say that any offshoot or hybrid is excluded under the definition. There is nothing especially jazzy about the music of Brian Eno, but *Bitches Brew* was a major influence on Eno's work as a record producer and Davis's "He Loved Him Madly" influenced Eno's development of ambient music.[76] However, Eno-produced U2 albums are not jazz, nor is ambient music a kind of jazz, something we avoid only by placing the proper constraints on historical continuity. We provide these constraints in intentional style instantiation and intentional preservation of higher-order values.

Rather than snowballing and expanding, the meaning of the term "jazz" narrowed when its popularity waned.[77] Our definition is consistent with this phenomenon; appeal to mere influence is not. Although a chain of musical influence is relevant to continuation and development of the category "jazz," it is never sufficient to confer jazz status. However, this result should not surprise anyone who thinks about the history of jazz. The same holds for jazz offshoots. Transitions to new styles are constrained by the appreciative-practice condition. The fact that a new style of music emerges from jazz is not sufficient to make it jazz. Western swing would not exist without jazz, yet several major histories of jazz do not contain a single reference to Bob Wills, its greatest star.[78] The musical genre of free improvisation grew out of and might be said to overlap with free jazz, but most contemporary free improvisation is not jazz.[79] Closer to the present day, notes Ted Gioia, "It is only a slight exaggeration to claim that the burgeoning market for New Age music grew out of ... the first twenty minutes" of Keith Jarrett's *The Köln Concert* (1975).[80] Yet almost none of that derived music is regarded as jazz. Even George Winston, the paradigm of New Age piano, says, "I am not a jazz player."[81] We are not merely saying that a history of jazz is more than a narrative about an early twentieth-century popular music and its subsequent development. We are also saying that we cannot make sense of the idea of *jazz history* unless we supplement our story of musical continuity and development by reference to social practices that determine when "branches" in that history constitute the emergence of an altogether different musical category, such as New Age music.

9. Why Style Categorization Matters

Our emphasis on style reflects a central insight of contemporary philosophy of art, Kendall Walton's thesis that art reception and evaluation are category-relative.[82]

Accurate aesthetic evaluation requires correct identification of the stylistic category that informs each instance of art-making, including music performance and dancing. The relevant categories are distinct horizons of recognizably shared style, organizing "features that can be perceived in a work when it is experienced in the normal manner."[83] As a product of human agency, a series of performed notes has no fixed aesthetic value: a passage of solo trumpet that is ragged and disorganized in a cadenza for the Joseph Haydn Trumpet Concerto can be adventuresome and witty in a jazz context. The blues may be central to jazz, but it is never enough to hear, for example, that a musician is playing the blues. The blues is not a style in the Waltonian sense. Without any familiarity with bebop, a jazz fan nurtured on the music of the 1920s is likely to recognize that Thelonious Monk's "Ba-lue Bolivar Ba-lues-Are" (1956) is a 12-bar blues – and will hear errors, sour chords, and choppy playing in Monk's piano part. Post-bop audiences will hear it against a different frame of musical reference and will dig his explorations of temporal and harmonic space. The style condition tells us that this latter response is the justified one.

Just as the accuracy of an evaluation is relative to the music's style, the stylistic categories are fixed by past practice. Styles are historically contingent categories. However, perceivable features are not always sufficient to guide us to the correct category, and when they are not, we must consult non-perceptual factors (including musician's intentions, the makeup of the audience, and the venue for reception) to decide which category is the correct one.[84] This insight plays an important role in understanding the difference between the style condition and the appreciative-practice condition. Because Walton's insight applies to all jazz, transitional and radical cases require a level of insight that is not required when hearing music that fits squarely into an established and familiar style.

Against this approach, a jazz essentialist will insist that some standard features of the music are not style-relative. Improvisation is a standard property of jazz, just as two-dimensionality is a standard property of paintings. As we suggested earlier, the essentialist must then deal with cases of composed jazz by allowing for exceptions that – to repeat – "prove," or rather, draw attention to the rule. At that point, there is no comprehensive definition. Our approach is simpler and does not require saying that essences have exceptions. Adopting Walton's terminology, we simply recognize that each style involves a cluster of typical or standard features. Improvisation is a standard feature of jazz styles after about 1925 and Louis Armstrong's Hot Five recordings. That improvisation is a standard feature of jazz is a good example of the merits of our historical model, since there is no claim here that improvisation is related internally to the music, but rather only that it is something that entered jazz practice and endured. After that, fully composed jazz – like a painting in three dimensions – is a *contra-standard property*, that is, one that would tend to place an item outside that category but which does not invariably do so. Under the style category, a performance cannot incorporate a degree of contra-standard properties that would make it unrecognizable as belonging to that style. Under the appreciative-practice condition, a jazz performance can have any number of features that are contra-standard for a style and still be jazz. Otherwise, as we saw in Chapter 1, new styles would not be certifiable as jazz and new higher-order values could not enter jazz.

Here is a rather different example of the importance of style classification. In modern Western art, originality is a virtue, but being boring is (generally) not. In light of this, consider Ted Gioia's point that it is a standard feature of most improvised jazz that parts of it will be boring.[85] Walton's thesis warns us, however, that there is no general standard for being a boring piece of music. Boring-for-jazz will be different than boring-for-opera; original-for-jazz has a different standard than original-for-The Second Viennese School. This insight carries down to the level of style: the criteria for boring improvisations in free jazz and hard bop are very different, and someone who listens to the former with the category expectations of the latter will not hear it properly. As we will see in Chapter 6, this thesis undercuts Theodor Adorno's critique of jazz. And there will be implications for Chapters 7 and 8, which discuss improvisation and the ontology of jazz.

Walton's thesis confirms the importance of understanding the limits of our art categories. If we cannot define jazz or provide criteria for deciding what counts as jazz and what does not, then (1) we cannot determine the aesthetic value of particular examples, and (2) we should refrain from making evaluative comparisons of examples from distinct musical categories, for there will be no generic *jazz* standards to guide those comparisons. In short, if we cannot define jazz in a way that distinguishes it from similar and related kinds of music, our aesthetic judgments are rendered meaningless. And we assume that, if it is anything, jazz is an opportunity for aesthetic engagement.

Notes

1 Hugues Panassié and Madeleine Gautier, *Guide to Jazz*, trans. Desmond Flower (Boston: Houghton Mifflin, 1956), 41. An excellent summary of this perspective is Philip Larkin, *All What Jazz: A Record Diary 1961–1971* (London: Faber and Faber, 1985), 19–28.

2 On the general problem of "hard cases" and options for handling them, see Dominic McIver Lopes, *Beyond Art* (Oxford: Oxford University Press, 2014), chap. 10. For the argument that jazz-rock fusion is not jazz, see Kevin Fellezs, *Birds of Fire: Jazz, Rock, Funk, and the Creation of Fusion* (Durham: Duke University Press, 2011).

3 Scott DeVeaux, "Constructing the Jazz Tradition: Jazz Historiography," *Black American Literature Forum* 25:3 (1991): 525–560, at 528. Similarly, philosopher Jerrold Levinson says that "the prospects of identifying the *essence* of jazz ... are not bright." He offers a very different response than the one we pursue. Jerrold Levinson, *Musical Concerns: Essays in Philosophy of Music* (Oxford: Oxford University Press, 2015), 133.

4 Daniel Hardie, *Jazz Historiography: The Story of Jazz History Writing* (Bloomington: iUniverse LLC, 2013), 4.

5 Bill Kirchner, "Introduction," *The Oxford Companion to Jazz*, ed. Bill Kirchner (Oxford: Oxford University Press, 2000), 3–6, at 5.

6 A number of these writers, mainly academics, are anthologized in Krin Gabbard, ed., *Jazz Among the Discourses* (Durham: Duke University Press, 1995): see especially

William Howland Kenny, "Historical Context and the Definition of Jazz: Putting More of the History in 'Jazz History,'" 100–116.

7   "Introduction," in *Jazz/Not Jazz: The Music and its Boundaries*, ed. David Ake, Charles Hiroshi Garrett, and Daniel Goldmark (Berkeley: University of California Press, 2012), 1–10, at 5. This approach is adopted by Joachim Berendt, *The Jazz Book: From New Orleans to Rock and Free Jazz*, trans. Dan Morgenstern, Helmut Bredigkeit, and Barbara Bredigkeit (New York: Lawrence Hill, 1975), 174, and by Gary Giddins and Scott DeVeaux, for whom the "basic elements" ultimately boil down to three: "polyrhythm, blues phrasing, timbre variation" (*Jazz* (New York: W.W. Norton, 2009), 172). Relative to contemporary philosophy of art, these approaches are similar to the "cluster" strategy of Berys Gaut, "'Art' as a Cluster Concept," in *Theories of Art Today*, ed. Noël Carroll (Madison: University of Wisconsin Press, 2000), 25–44.

8   Martin Williams, "Jelly Roll Morton," in *Jazz: New Perspectives on the History of Jazz by Twelve of the World's Foremost Jazz Critics And Scholars*, ed. Nat Hentoff and Albert J. McCarthy (New York: Da Capo, 1975 [1959]), 59–81, at 66.

9   Amiri Baraka with Amina Baraka, *The Music: Reflections on Jazz and Blues* (New York: Morrow, 1987), 264.

10 Eric Hobsbawm, *The Jazz Scene* (New York: Pantheon, 1993), 61–62.

11 David Wondrich, *Stomp and Swerve: American Music Gets Hot 1843–1924* (Chicago: A Capella Books, 2003), 120.

12 Henry Martin and Keith Waters, *Essential Jazz: The First Hundred Years*, 3rd ed. (New York: Schirmer, 2014), 8.

13 Gunther Schuller, *Early Jazz: Its Roots and Musical Development* (Oxford: Oxford University Press, 1968), 58.

14 Jed Rasula, "The Media of Memory: The Seductive Menace of Recordings in Jazz History," in *Jazz Among the Discourses*, ed. Gabbard, 134–162, at 156.

15 Charles Mingus, *Beneath the Underdog: His World as Composed by Mingus*, ed. Nel King (New York: Vintage, 1991), 351.

16 We have considerably more to say about this issue in Chapter 5.

17 And, if not from "Jezebel," it has been claimed that it derives "from jasmine, a perfume supposedly favored by Jezebels" (Hugh Rawson, "Jazz Is a Four-Letter Word," *Cambridge Dictionary*, June 27, 2011, https://dictionaryblog.cambridge.org/2011/06/27/jazz-is-a-four-letter-word/). For a brief overview, see Krin Gabbard, "'Jazz': Etymology," in *New Grove Dictionary of Jazz*, ed. Barry Kernfeld, 2nd ed., 3 vols. (London: Macmillan, 2002), 2:389. A lengthier treatment is Allan P. Merriam and Fradley H. Garner, "Jazz – The Word," in *The Jazz Cadence of American Culture*, ed. Robert G. O'Meally (New York: Columbia University Press, 1998), 7–31.

18 G. E. Moore, *Ethics* (Oxford: Oxford University Press, 1912), 118.

19 See any edition of Mark C. Gridley, "What is Jazz," in *Jazz Styles: History and Analysis* (Englewood Cliffs, NJ: Prentice Hall, 1978). See also the editors' introduction in *Jazz/Not Jazz*, ed. Ake, Garrett, and Goldmark, 5–6. Whatever one's judgment of an anti-essentialist pluralism, one of its merits is a heightened discussion of the role of women in jazz; fans and histories have too often treated them dismissively. See Monique Guillory, "Black Bodies Swingin': Race, Gender, and Jazz," in *Soul: Black Power, Politics, and Pleasure*, eds. Monique Guillory and Richard C. Green, 191–215 (New York: New York University Press, 1998). The jazz world remains, alas, strongly sexist. Useful correctives are Linda Dahl, *Stormy Weather: The Music and Lives of a Century of Jazzwomen* (New York: Limelight Editions, 1989), and Sherrie Tucker, *Swing Shift: "All-Girl" Bands of the 1940s* (Durham: Duke University Press, 2000).

20 Rasula, "The Media of Memory," 151–152.

21 Steven J. Morrison and Cheung Shing Yeh, "Preference Responses and Use of Written Descriptors among Music and Nonmusic Majors in the United States, Hong Kong, and the People's Republic of China," *Journal of Research in Music Education* 47:1 (1999): 5–17.

22 In a much-cited study of listener-based music *classification*, a wide range of participants categorized jazz, rock, country, and other music samples into one of ten categories in an astonishingly brief amount of time. However, the researchers rejected the premise that listener's classifications could be in error, and so the study only demonstrates the unhesitating rapidity with which American college students will decide (generally, in under one second) whether a recorded sample is jazz, rock, or some other genre. See R. O. Gjerdingen and D. Perrott, "Scanning the Dial: The Rapid Recognition of Music Genres," *Journal of New Music Research* 37:2 (2008): 93–100.

23 For example, consider Mark Gridley, Robert Maxham, and Robert Hoff, "Three Approaches to Defining Jazz," *The Musical Quarterly* 73:4 (1989): 513–531. The article opens with a sampling of twelve earlier definitions of jazz. It identifies three strategies for definition. Of these, the presentation of Wittgensteinian family resemblance misconstrues the core idea of family resemblance. Nonetheless, the discussion is frequently insightful and highlights the many obstacles to producing an adequate definition.

24 A good introductory summary is Stephen Davies, *Definitions of Art* (Ithaca: Cornell University Press, 1991), 67–69. Drawing upon philosophy of art in this manner does *not* mean that we endorse a bifurcation of culture into high and low that locates jazz in the higher, "art" sector.

25 The history of analytic theory of knowledge after 1963 is almost entirely a reaction to the appearance in that year of two famous counterexamples by Edmund Gettier against the classic analysis of knowledge in terms of justified true belief (Edmund Gettier, "Is Justified True Belief Knowledge?" *Analysis* 23:6 (1963): 121–123).

26 Arthur C. Danto, "The Artworld," *Journal of Philosophy* 61:19 (1964): 571–584.

27 Increasingly, the notion of essences is reserved for natural kind terms, such as "water" and "gold," or "giraffe" or "oak," where it is possible to identify an unchanging, underlying structure that accounts for the empirical appearances of instances of the kind. Ordinarily, language speakers succeed in using natural kind terms even if they do not yet understand the "hidden" essence to which they refer. For the implications of these points, and a defense of the view that "it makes no sense to try to begin by understanding what [cultural objects] are independent of our practices," see David Davies, "Descriptivism and its Discontents," *Journal of Aesthetics and Art Criticism* 75:2 (2017): 117–129.

28 Another example is Gil Evans' arrangement of "Moon Dreams" (1950) for the Miles Davis Nonet – one of the "birth of the cool" arrangements. For analysis, see Giddins and DeVeaux, *Jazz*, 344–345.

29 George Russell, "Where Do We Go from Here?" in *The Jazz Word*, ed. Dom Cerulli, Burt Korall, and Mort Nasatir (New York: Ballantine Books, 1960), 238–239.

30 Moore, *Ethics*, 118.

31 Arthur C. Danto, *The Transfiguration of the Commonplace: A Philosophy of Art* (Cambridge, MA: Harvard University Press, 1981), 65.

32 This characterization is adapted from Lopes, *Beyond Art*, 6. The most interesting cases are "free agents," which are cases that seem to belong to more than one category or genre; these will generally arise as liminal cases that will be resolved as early examples of a new kind of art (Lopes, chap. 10).

33 Their exchange is reproduced in Mark Tucker, ed., *The Duke Ellington Reader* (Oxford: Oxford University Press, 1993), 171–175. The ongoing debate about whether swing was a continuation of jazz is explained by Bernard Gendron, *Between Montmartre and the Mudd Club: Popular Music and the Avant Garde* (Chicago: University of Chicago Press, 2002), chap. 6. Views about Ellington that are more like those of Hammond than Feathers are defended by LeRoi Jones [Amiri Baraka], *Blues People: Negro Music in White America* (New York: William Morrow, 1963), 158, 183–184.

34 Subsequent performances of the song by the Pat Metheny Group and Carla Bley's Liberation Music Orchestra are jazz.

35 Stephen Davies, "Defining Art and Artworlds," *Journal of Aesthetics and Art Criticism* 73:4 (2015): 375–384.

36 Davies "Defining Art and Artworlds," 380.

37 To make a technical point: this language mirrors recent theories of reference by emphasizing the need to employ rules about non-manifest properties in order to achieve successful reference to instances of a historically contingent category of music. It does not treat "jazz" as a *description* of the music.

38 The *definiendum* refers to "a piece of music" because we are pluralists about what kinds of things might fall under the definition. Specifically, we allow both live and recorded music. In Part III, it will be clear that we do not think that musical *works* play a decisive role here. We do not regard ragtime as part of what is included in the first disjunct. Finally, our third disjunct is modified to reflect Lopes, *Beyond Art*, chap. 8.

39 Stephen Davies, "Definitions of Art," in *The Routledge Companion to Aesthetics*, 3rd ed., ed. Berys Gaut and Dominic McIver Lopes (London: Routledge, 2013), 213–223, at 216.

40 Seán Street, *Jazz Time* (Belfast: Lapwing, 2014), 15. Our point is supported by Jerrold Levinson, "Artworks and the Future," in *Music, Art, and Metaphysics: Essays in Philosophical Aesthetics* (Oxford: Oxford University Press, 2011), 179–214, at 188.

41 This point is anticipated by Theodor W. Adorno, *Current of Music*, ed. Robert Hullot-Kentor (Cambridge: Polity Press, 2008), 181, 411. We explore its significance in Chapter 4.

42 Eunmi Shim, *Lennie Tristano: His Life in Music* (Ann Arbor: University of Michigan Press, 2007), 75. Copyright does not actually protect artists in this way.

43 Art Pepper and Laurie Pepper, *Straight Life: The Story of Art Pepper* (New York: Schirmer, 1979), 374.

44 Bill Cole, *Miles Davis: The Complete Guide* (New York: Morrow, 1974), 43.

45 Dan Morgenstern, "Miles in Motion," *DownBeat* (September 3, 1970), 16–17, at 17.

46 Anonymous, "Why Duke Ellington Avoided Music Schools," *PM* (December 9, 1945). Reprinted in *The Duke Ellington Reader*, ed. Mark Tucker (Oxford: Oxford University Press, 1993), 252–255, at 253.

47 E.g., explicitly by Paul Rinzler, *The Contradictions of Jazz* (Lanham: Scarecrow Press, 2008), 59.

48 Charles Mingus, "Another View of Coleman," in *DownBeat: the Great Jazz Interviews: A 75th Anniversary Anthology*, ed. Frank Alkyer et al. (New York: Hal Leonard Books, 2009), 77–78, at 78.

49 Quoted in Marion McPartland, "Perils of Paul: A Portrait of Desperate Desmond," in *DownBeat: the Great Jazz Interviews*, ed. Alkyer et al., 78–82, at 82.

50 Barry Ulanov, *A History of Jazz in America* (New York: Viking, 1952), 348.

51 See Jones [Baraka], *Blues People*, 217–218, and Leonard Feather, "Horace Silver Talks to Leonard Feather about Funk Fever," *Melody Maker* (January 28, 1961), 5.

52 E.g., soul jazz is defended by Martin Williams, "The Funky-Hard Bop Regression," in *The Art of Jazz: Essays on the Nature and Development of Jazz*, ed. Martin Williams (New York: Oxford University Press, 1959), 233–236.

53 E.g., Stanley Crouch, "On the Corner: The Sellout of Miles Davis," in *Considering Genius: Writings on Jazz* (New York: Basic Civitas Books, 2006), 240–256.

54 The phrase comes from John Howland, "Ellingtonian Extended Composition and the Symphonic Jazz Model," *Annual Review of Jazz Studies* 14 (2009): 1–64, at 4.

55 Ted Gioia, *The History of Jazz*, 2nd ed. (Oxford: Oxford University Press, 2011), 306.

56 John Tynan, "Take Five," *DownBeat* (November 23, 1961), 40. He also called it "horrifying" and "musical nonsense."

57 Larkin, *All What Jazz*, 19.

58 See our discussion of this topic in Chapter 1.

59 See Jeffrey Magee, "Ellington's Afro-Modernist Vision in the 1920s," in *The Cambridge Companion to Duke Ellington*, ed. Edward Green (Cambridge: Cambridge University Press, 2014), 85–105.

60 Schuller, *Early Jazz*, 71.
61 Good introductions to this liminal stage are Elijah Wald, *How the Beatles Destroyed Rock and Roll: An Alternative History of American Popular Music* (Oxford: Oxford University Press, 2009), chap. 4, and Alyn Shipton, *A New History of Jazz*, rev. ed. (London: Bloomsbury, 2007), chap. 2.
62 Max Harrison, Charles Fox, and Eric Thacker, *Essential Jazz Records: Volume 1: Ragtime to Swing* (London: Mansell, 1984), 22; this is also the source of our term "proto-jazz." See also Schuller, *Early Jazz*, chap. 2.
63 See, for example, Scott Yanow, *Jazz: A Regional Exploration* (Westport: Greenwood Press, 2005), 31. Prior to this point, much if not most "jazz" seems to have been ragtime rather than blues-based; see Lawrence Gushee, "The Nineteenth-Century Origins of Jazz," *Black Music Research Journal* 14:1 (1994): 1–24. Granted, "Crazy Blues" is not a blues of the classic form, but that form had not yet been regularized.
64 Bob Porter, "The Blues in Jazz," in Kirchner, ed., *Oxford Companion to Jazz*, 64–77, at 69.
65 See Shipton, *New History*, chap. 11.
66 An interesting illustration of this problem is Ornette Coleman's initial confusion about the distinction between bebop and rhythm and blues, based on his recognition that "The Hucklebuck" (1949) is a pop version of Charlie Parker's "Now's the Time" (1945). See A. B. Spellman, *Four Lives in the Bebop Business* (New York: Limelight, 1966), 91.
67 André Hodeir, *Jazz: Its Evolution and Essence*, trans. David Noakes (New York: Grove Press, 1956), 35, 231–237.
68 André Hodeir, *Toward Jazz*, trans. Noel Burch (New York: Grove Press, 1962), 39.
69 *Jazz, A Film by Ken Burns* (2001) is especially susceptible to the criticism that it renders all jazz after 1968 as post-jazz. The argument of the documentary also appears in Geoffrey C. Ward and Ken Burns, *Jazz: A History of America's Music* (New York: Alfred A. Knopf, 2000). See Theodore Gracyk, "Jazz After Jazz: Ken Burns and the Construction of Jazz History," *Philosophy and Literature* 26:1 (2002): 173–187.
70 We find it implausible to suppose, as is sometimes claimed, that "first art" has art status retrospectively or retroactively. (E.g., Jerrold Levinson, "Defining Art Historically," *British Journal of Aesthetics* 19:3 (1979): 21–33.) We do not attempt, for example, to claim that there is a cultural kind, jazz, that predates identification of that kind and yet which is jazz retroactively; consequently, we regard it as a mistake to suppose that antecedents of jazz in African music are to be counted as jazz.
71 This objection leads Robert Stecker to propose a hybrid or mixed definition of art (*Artworks: Definition, Meaning, Value* (University Park, PA: Pennsylvania State University Press, 1997), 50–65). However, we do not need to add a non-historical alternative to the definition. We simply deny that it would be jazz if, say, Franz Schubert and his friend, violinist Georg Hellmesberger, had improvised something in 1820 that sounded like Carla Bley improvising with Stéphane Grappelli. If the right history is absent, it simply isn't jazz.
72 Davies, "Definitions of Art," 271.
73 Davies, "Definitions of Art," 271.
74 See Katherine Butler Schofield, "Reviving the Golden Age Again: 'Classicization,' Hindustani Music, and the Mughals," *Ethnomusicology* 54:3 (2010): 484–517.
75 Steven Feld, *Sound and Sentiment: Birds, Weeping, Poetics, and Song in Kaluli Expression*, 2nd ed. (Philadelphia: University of Pennsylvania Press, 1990), 93–99.
76 See George Grella, *Bitches Brew* (New York: Bloomsbury, 2015), 60–62, and Paul Tingen, *Miles Beyond: Electric Explorations of Miles Davis, 1967–1991* (New York: Billboard Books, 2001), 54, respectively.
77 See Hardie, *Jazz Historiography*, 406.
78 E.g., there are no references in Shipton, *New History*. Gioia sees this music as a "distinctive" offshoot of jazz, rather than as jazz (*History of Jazz*, 149), and another major

text mentions it only as a possible influence on Ornette Coleman (Lawrence Kart, "The Avant-Garde, 1949–1967," in *Oxford Companion to Jazz*, ed. Kirchner, 446–458, at 452).

79 John Corbett, *A Listener's Guide to Free Improvisation* (Chicago: University of Chicago Press, 2016), xvi, 17–18.

80 Gioia, *History of Jazz*, 340. For an analysis of the musical connections, see Peter Elsdon, *Keith Jarrett's* The Köln Concert (Oxford: Oxford University Press, 2013), 135–136.

81 Bret Saunders, "George Winston at Home with Folk, Stride, R&B," *Denver Post* (July 12, 2007), http://www.denverpost.com/2007/07/12/george-winston-at-home-with-folk-stride-rb/.

82 Kendall L. Walton, "Categories of Art," *Philosophical Review* 79:3 (1970): 334–367. See also Lopes, *Beyond Art*, 83.

83 Walton, "Categories of Art," 339.

84 Walton, "Categories of Art," 355–359.

85 Ted Gioia, *The Imperfect Art: Reflections on Jazz and Modern Culture* (Oxford: Oxford University Press, 1988), chap. 6.

References

Adorno, Theodor W. *Current of Music*, ed. Robert Hullot-Kentor. Cambridge: Polity Press, 2008.

Ake, David, Charles Hiroshi Garrett, and Daniel Goldmark. "Introduction." In *Jazz/Not Jazz: The Music and its Boundaries*, ed. David Ake, Charles Hiroshi Garrett, and Daniel Goldmark, 1–10. Berkeley: University of California Press, 2012.

Anonymous, "Why Duke Ellington Avoided Music Schools." *PM*, (December 9, 1945). Reprinted in *The Duke Ellington Reader*, ed. Mark Tucker. Oxford: Oxford University Press, 1993.

Baraka, Amiri, with Amina Baraka. *The Music: Reflections on Jazz and Blues*. New York: Morrow, 1987.

Berendt, Joachim. *The Jazz Book: From New Orleans to Rock and Free Jazz*, trans. Dan Morgenstern, Helmut Bredigkeit, and Barbara Bredigkeit. New York: Lawrence Hill, 1975.

Cole, Bill. *Miles Davis: The Complete Guide*. New York: Morrow, 1974.

Corbett, John. *A Listener's Guide to Free Improvisation*. Chicago: University of Chicago Press, 2016.

Crouch, Stanley. "On the Corner: The Sellout of Miles Davis." In *Considering Genius: Writings on Jazz*, 240–256. New York: Basic Civitas Books, 2006.

Dahl, Linda. *Stormy Weather: The Music and Lives of a Century of Jazzwomen*. New York: Limelight Editions, 1989.

Danto, Arthur C. "The Artworld." *Journal of Philosophy* 61:19 (1964): 571–584.

Danto, Arthur C. *The Transfiguration of the Commonplace: A Philosophy of Art*. Cambridge, MA: Harvard University Press, 1981.

Davies, David. "Descriptivism and its Discontents." *Journal of Aesthetics and Art Criticism* 75:2 (2017): 117–129.

Davies, Stephen. "Defining Art and Artworlds." *Journal of Aesthetics and Art Criticism* 73:4 (2015): 375–384.

Davies, Stephen. *Definitions of Art*. Ithaca: Cornell University Press, 1991.

Davies, Stephen. "Definitions of Art." In *The Routledge Companion to Aesthetics*, 3rd ed., ed. Berys Gaut and Dominic McIver Lopes, 213–223. London: Routledge, 2013.

DeVeaux, Scott. "Constructing the Jazz Tradition: Jazz Historiography." *Black American Literature Forum* 25:3 (1991): 525–560.

Elsdon, Peter. *Keith Jarrett's* The Köln Concert. Oxford: Oxford University Press, 2013.

Feather, Leonard. "Horace Silver Talks to Leonard Feather about Funk Fever." *Melody Maker* (January 28, 1961), 5.

Feld, Steven. *Sound and Sentiment: Birds, Weeping, Poetics, and Song in Kaluli Expression*, 2nd ed. Philadelphia: University of Pennsylvania Press, 1990.

Fellezs, Kevin. *Birds of Fire: Jazz, Rock, Funk, and the Creation of Fusion*. Durham: Duke University Press, 2011.

Gabbard, Krin. "'Jazz': Etymology." In *New Grove Dictionary of Jazz*, ed. Barry Kernfeld, 2nd ed., 3 vols., 2:389. London: Macmillan, 2002.

Gaut, Berys. "'Art' as a Cluster Concept." In *Theories of Art Today*, ed. Noël Carroll, 25–44. Madison: University of Wisconsin Press, 2000.

Gendron, Bernard. *Between Montmartre and the Mudd Club: Popular Music and the Avant Garde*. Chicago: University of Chicago Press, 2002.

Gettier, Edmund. "Is Justified True Belief Knowledge?" *Analysis* 23:6 (1963): 121–123.

Giddins, Gary, and Scott DeVeaux. *Jazz*. New York: W.W. Norton, 2009.

Gioia, Ted. *The History of Jazz*, 2nd ed. Oxford: Oxford University Press, 2011.

Gioia, Ted. *The Imperfect Art: Reflections on Jazz and Modern Culture*. Oxford: Oxford University Press, 1988.

Gjerdingen, Robert O. and David Perrott. "Scanning the Dial: The Rapid Recognition of Music Genres." *Journal of New Music Research* 37:2 (2008): 93–100.

Gracyk, Theodore. "Jazz After Jazz: Ken Burns and the Construction of Jazz History." *Philosophy and Literature* 26:1 (2002): 173–187.

Green, Benny. *The Reluctant Art: The Growth of Jazz*. London: MacGibbon and Kee, 1962.

Grella, George. *Bitches Brew*. New York: Bloomsbury, 2015.

Gridley, Mark C. *Jazz Styles: History and Analysis*. Englewood Cliffs, NJ: Prentice Hall, 1978.

Gridley, Mark, Robert Maxham, and Robert Hoff. "Three Approaches to Defining Jazz." *Musical Quarterly* 73:4 (1989): 513–531.

Guillory, Monique. "Black Bodies Swingin': Race, Gender, and Jazz." In *Soul: Black Power, Politics, and Pleasure*, ed. Monique Guillory and Richard C. Green, 191–215. New York: New York University Press, 1998.

Gushee, Lawrence. "The Nineteenth-Century Origins of Jazz." *Black Music Research Journal* 14:1 (1994): 1–24.

Hardie, Daniel. *Jazz Historiography: The Story of Jazz History Writing*. Bloomington: iUniverse LLC, 2013.

Harrison, Max, Charles Fox, and Eric Thacker. *Essential Jazz Records: Volume 1: Ragtime to Swing*. London: Mansell, 1984.

Hobsbawm, Eric. *The Jazz Scene*. New York: Pantheon, 1993.

Hodeir, André. *Jazz: Its Evolution and Essence*, trans. David Noakes. New York: Grove Press, 1956.

Hodeir, André. *Toward Jazz*, trans. Noel Burch. New York: Grove Press, 1962.

Howland, John. "Ellingtonian Extended Composition and the Symphonic Jazz Model." *Annual Review of Jazz Studies* 14 (2009): 1–64.

Janik, Allan, and Stephen Toulmin. *Wittgenstein's Vienna*, rev. ed. Chicago: Ivan R. Dee, 1996.

Jones, LeRoi [Amiri Baraka]. *Blues People: Negro Music in White America*. New York: William Morrow, 1963.

Kart, Lawrence. "The Avant-Garde, 1949–1967." In *The Oxford Companion to Jazz*, ed. Bill Kirchner, 446–458. Oxford: Oxford University Press, 2000.

Kenny, William Howland "Historical Context and the Definition of Jazz: Putting More of the History in 'Jazz History.'" In *Jazz among the Discourses*, ed. Krin Gabbard, 100–116. Durham: Duke University Press, 1995.

Kirchner, Bill. "Introduction." In *The Oxford Companion to Jazz*, ed. Bill Kirchner, 3–6. Oxford: Oxford University Press, 2000.

Larkin, Philip. *All What Jazz: A Record Diary 1961–1971*. London: Faber and Faber, 1985.

Levinson, Jerrold. "Artworks and the Future." In *Music, Art, and Metaphysics: Essays in Philosophical Aesthetics*, 179–214. Oxford: Oxford University Press, 2011.

Levinson, Jerrold. "Defining Art Historically." *British Journal of Aesthetics* 19:3 (1979): 21–33.

Levinson, Jerrold. *Musical Concerns: Essays in Philosophy of Music*. Oxford: Oxford University Press, 2015.

Lopes, Dominic McIver. *Beyond Art*. Oxford: Oxford University Press, 2014.

McPartland, Marion. "Perils of Paul: A Portrait of Desperate Desmond." In *DownBeat: The Great Jazz Interviews: A 75th Anniversary Anthology*, ed. Frank Alkyer et al., 78–82. New York: Hal Leonard Books, 2009.

Magee, Jeffrey. "Ellington's Afro-Modernist Vision in the 1920s." In *The Cambridge Companion to Duke Ellington*, ed. Edward Green, 85–105. Cambridge: Cambridge University Press, 2014.

Martin, Henry, and Keith Waters. *Essential Jazz: The First Hundred Years*, 3rd ed. New York: Schirmer, 2014.

Merriam, Allan P., and Fradley H. Garner. "Jazz – The Word." In *The Jazz Cadence of American Culture*, ed. Robert G. O'Meally, 7–31. New York: Columbia University Press, 1998.

Mingus, Charles. "Another View of Coleman." In *DownBeat: The Great Jazz Interviews: A 75th Anniversary Anthology*, ed. Frank Alkyer et al., 77–78. New York: Hal Leonard Books, 2009.

Mingus, Charles. *Beneath the Underdog: His World as Composed by Mingus*, ed. Nel King. New York: Vintage, 1991.

Moore, G. E. *Ethics*. Oxford: Oxford University Press, 1912.

Morgenstern, Dan. "Miles in Motion." *DownBeat* (September 3, 1970), 16–17.

Morrison, Steven J., and Cheung Shing Yeh. "Preference Responses and Use of Written Descriptors among Music and Nonmusic Majors in the United States, Hong Kong, and the People's Republic of China." *Journal of Research in Music Education* 47:1 (1999): 5–17.

Panassié, Hugues, and Madeleine Gautier. *Guide to Jazz*, trans. Desmond Flower. Boston: Houghton Mifflin, 1956.

Pepper, Art, and Laurie Pepper. *Straight Life: The Story of Art Pepper*. New York: Schirmer, 1979.

Porter, Bob. "The Blues in Jazz." In *The Oxford Companion to Jazz*, ed. Bill Kirchner, 64–77. Oxford: Oxford University Press, 2000.

Rasula, Jed. "The Media of Memory: The Seductive Menace of Recordings in Jazz History." In *Jazz Among the Discourses*, ed. Krin Gabbard, 134–162. Durham: Duke University Press, 1995.

Rawson, Hugh. "Jazz Is a Four-Letter Word." *Cambridge Dictionary* (June 27, 2011): https://dictionaryblog.cambridge.org/2011/06/27/jazz-is-a-four-letter-word/.

Rinzler, Paul. *The Contradictions of Jazz*. Lanham: Scarecrow Press, 2008.

Russell, George. "Where Do We Go from Here?" In *The Jazz Word*, ed. Dom Cerulli, Burt Korall, and Mort Nasatir, 238–239. New York: Ballantine Books, 1960.

Saunders, Bret. "George Winston at Home with Folk, Stride, R&B." *Denver Post* (July 12, 2007): http://www.denverpost.com/2007/07/12/george-winston-at-home-with-folk-stride-rb/.

Schofield, Katherine Butler. "Reviving the Golden Age Again: 'Classicization,' Hindustani Music, and the Mughals." *Ethnomusicology* 54:3 (2010): 484–517.

Schuller, Gunther. *Early Jazz: Its Roots and Musical Development.* Oxford: Oxford University Press, 1968.

Shim, Eunmi. *Lennie Tristano: His Life in Music.* Ann Arbor: University of Michigan Press, 2007.

Shipton, Alyn. *A New History of Jazz*, rev. ed. London: Bloomsbury, 2007.

Spellman, A. B. *Four Lives in the Bebop Business.* New York: Limelight, 1966.

Stecker, Robert. *Artworks: Definition, Meaning, Value.* University Park, PA: Pennsylvania State University Press, 1997.

Street, Seán. *Jazz Time.* Belfast: Lapwing, 2014.

Tingen, Paul. *Miles Beyond: Electric Explorations of Miles Davis, 1967–1991.* New York: Billboard Books, 2001.

Tucker, Mark, ed. *The Duke Ellington Reader.* Oxford: Oxford University Press, 1993.

Tucker, Sherrie. *Swing Shift: "All-Girl" Bands of the 1940s.* Durham: Duke University Press, 2000.

Tynan, John. "Take Five." *DownBeat* (November 23, 1961), 40.

Ulanov, Barry. *A History of Jazz in America.* New York: Viking, 1952.

Wald, Elijah. *How the Beatles Destroyed Rock and Roll: An Alternative History of American Popular Music.* Oxford: Oxford University Press, 2009.

Walton, Kendall L. "Categories of Art." *Philosophical Review* 79:3 (1970): 334–367.

Ward, Geoffrey C., and Ken Burns. *Jazz: A History of America's Music.* New York: Alfred A. Knopf, 2000.

Williams, Martin. "The Funky-Hard Bop Regression." In *The Art of Jazz: Essays on the Nature and Development of Jazz*, ed. Martin Williams, 233–236. New York: Oxford University Press, 1959.

Williams, Martin. "Jelly Roll Morton." In *Jazz: New Perspectives on the History of Jazz by Twelve of the World's Foremost Jazz Critics and Scholars*, ed. Nat Hentoff and Albert J. McCarthy, 59–81. New York: Da Capo, 1975 [1959].

Wondrich, David. *Stomp and Swerve: American Music Gets Hot 1843–1924.* Chicago: A Capella Books, 2003.

Yanow, Scott. *Jazz: A Regional Exploration.* Westport: Greenwood Press, 2005.

PART II
Jazz and American Culture

4

JAZZ SINGING AND TAKING WING

No longer the *artist*, he has himself become *a work of art*; the productive power of the whole universe is now manifest.
— *Friedrich Nietzsche*, The Birth of Tragedy

It is hard to escape the suspicion that no one knows what jazz singing is.
— *Bruce Crowther, Mike Pinfold*

1. The Gramophone Plays and a Woman Sings

In this chapter and the pair that follow, we explore a paradoxical dichotomy. On the one hand, there is the widespread view that jazz plays a special role in relation to American culture. As we saw in our exploration of definitions of jazz in Part I, the connection is frequently articulated in terms of the troubled story of race relations in American history and so in its music. On the other hand, there was a period in the development and popularization of jazz when it became so ubiquitous that it lent its name to an entire decade of American history: the Jazz Age. As a result, there was a period when jazz was more or less synonymous with American popular music. This tension is present in Jean-Paul Sartre's choice of popular music as a plot element in his 1938 novel *Nausea*. In a provincial French city café, Sartre's protagonist, Roquentin, requests the waitress, Madeleine, to play a song he likes and she starts an American jazz recording on the phonograph. On paper, its English lyrics stand out in Sartre's French prose, confirming that the song is "Some of These Days." Sophie Tucker recorded "Some of These Days" in 1911 and Roquentin remembers hearing soldiers whistling it in 1917. Aware of the earlier version, he recognizes this recording as a more recent version: a "jazz" interpretation of a ragtime song. Roquentin assumes he is listening to an

African-American singing a Tin Pan Alley song written by a Jewish composer – but neither of those projected identities fit the facts.[1] Sartre cannot escape our paradox: in a novel that aims to illustrate that experiences are always too rich to conform to our conceptual expectations, Sartre cannot avoid the pull of social categorization. Roquentin's reception of the song is informed by a dream world that allows him to escape from the anxiety, the nausea, of the human condition. The song is simultaneously a social product and an act of free expression.[2] Roquentin finds a momentary glimmer of meaning and value in an otherwise meaningless world. The nausea experienced by Roquentin is nothing less than a particular way of apprehending the contingency of his visceral existence, thus emphasizing the role of music in the relief of that situation. "I seemed to be dancing," he says. The music stops and Roquentin exits the café and enters into the night. The unreality of the song has ended and the reality characterized by the nausea has returned.

In later writings on art and music, Sartre emphasizes that the power of music and art are independent of their mimetic function:

> Aesthetic contemplation is an induced dream and the passing into the real is an actual waking up. ... This discomfort is simply that of the dreamer on awakening; an entranced consciousness, engulfed in the imaginary, is suddenly freed by the sudden ending of the play, of the symphony, and comes suddenly into contact with existence. Nothing more is needed to arouse the nauseating disgust that characterizes the consciousness of reality.[3]

We will see that a similar confrontation with the lived reality of everyday existence shapes Friedrich Nietzsche's provocative account of Dionysian practices and music, which can be fruitfully applied to jazz.

Roquentin's encounter with "Some of These Days" highlights the major themes that we will explore in this central section of the book. We begin with the nature of jazz singing and the context in which it is embedded. Is the singing an *act* of expression or is it the song that expresses through lyrics and music? Does Roquentin's fantasy about the sources of the music prevent him from understanding what is revealed by the performance? Is there a racial aspect ignored by Roquentin in his encounter with this song? Would it matter if he knew that Tucker's pre-jazz song was written by a Canadian, Shelton Brooks, who was, in fact, a black man? That Brooks also composed "Darktown Strutters' Ball?" That Sophie Tucker's background was in blackface minstrel performance? That jazz songs are so standardized that Sartre conflates "Some of These Days" with a Gershwin standard when he describes it?[4] We have emphasized, from the start, that music is a social activity aligned with multiple social practices. We now take up the challenge of exploring some of the consequences for jazz and its reception. We find it helpful to begin with what some writers say about origins.

Part of the paradox of jazz singing is that something as familiar as a blues or Tin Pan Alley song can be, nonetheless, emblematic of freedom in modern, commercial life.[5] One challenge is to determine the extent to which the activity of jazz singing is a free or liberating action, and the degree to which its sense of freedom is an aesthetic artifice, an illusion generated by the expressive surface of the performance. We grant that jazz singing at its best is instrumentality by other means, with lyrics adding a layer of meaning transported to the personal lives, real or imaginary, of its audience. In relation to that phenomenon, a secondary aim of the present chapter is to correct the error, common in jazz writing, of equating the Dionysian with "direct expression of ... emotion."[6] In contrast, we explore the possibility that jazz is – in the right circumstances – a Dionysian practice that goes beyond the mere art of expressive communication.

2. The Dionysian Moment

We begin with a proposal by another existentialist, André Gide:

> The Greeks, who, not only in the multitude of their statues but also in themselves, left us such a beautiful image of humanity, recognized as many gods as there are instincts, and the problem was to keep the inner Olympus in equilibrium, not just to subjugate and subdue any of the gods.[7]

With profound insight, Gide sees that the complex relationships among the gods of antiquity paralleled the inner, sometimes conflicting relations of the instincts of mere mortals. The issue of Olympian equilibrium had entered modern discourse about the arts by way of Nietzsche's attention to the dual aspects of Apollo and Dionysus, with their physical correlates of dreams and intoxication. While Nietzsche was clear about the need for Olympian equilibrium between the two, he was concerned that undue emphasis on tragedy was ignoring the Dionysian ecstatic aspects of its mythical history, especially its musical origins, in accounts of ancient Greece.

Would it be plausible to compare Nietzsche's ideas on the *origins* of tragedy in his *The Birth of Tragedy: Out of the Spirit of Music*, with the *origins* of jazz?[8] Was there some cultural need in nineteenth- and twentieth-century America, as there was for ancient Athens, to engage in collective ecstatic behavior dislocated from business-as-usual morality? There are a number of striking parallels in the two traditions. We've already mentioned how the Jazz Age was understood as a disreputable, uncivilized, even barbaric period of illegal speakeasies (intoxication and gangsters), brothels (Jelly Roll Morton played piano in one in Chicago), and, for that era, unrestricted social dancing, all the while grounded by the music and sassy singing of jazz. The association of jazz with the New Orleans district of Storyville – however embellished and mythologized – embeds the music in a de facto outlaw community primarily centered on sex. Nietzsche's view of the Dionysian festivals to the god of wine was of an amoral ritual, where pre-cultural nature took on an extreme form of behavior. Nietzsche imagines the celebration as follows:

> The central concern of such celebrations was, almost universally, a complete sexual promiscuity overriding every form of established tribal law; all the savage urges of mind were unleashed on those occasions until they reached that paroxysm of lust and cruelty, which has always struck me as the 'witches' cauldron' *par excellence.*[9]

While we caution that we do not regard jazz as "savage," there are similarities having to do with song, which reach deeper into the birth of jazz and the origins of tragedy.[10] It is especially instructive to contrast the Dionysian spirit of the Jazz Age with what we know of the actual rituals that preserved African celebration in nineteenth-century New Orleans. However, to be clear about the connection we are pursuing, they are not Dionysian in quite the same sense, for less ritualistic jazz practices preserved only *some* of the elements of Dionysian ritual.[11]

In Chapter 1 we mentioned the Sunday Afro-Caribbean rhythms, Creole music, of the *Place Congo* in New Orleans, where dancers could abandon, for the time being, their lives as slaves. Nietzsche says something about the Dionysian ritual that sounds very much like the freedom afforded to slaves in their use of *Place Congo*: "Now the slave emerges as a free man; all the rigid, hostile walls which either necessity or despotism has erected between men are shattered. ... Man now expresses himself through song and dance as the member of a higher community."[12] Dionysus is the god who, for a short time, enables you to stop being your daily self, embedded in the music of the dithyramb, a choral song.[13] The uniform group singing and dancing that took place in both Dionysian ritual and at *Place Congo* promoted the dropping of individual wills, that is, the participants losing the interests, goals, and obligations of quotidian existence by virtue of song and rhythmic entrainment. In the Greek practice, the vocality of ordinary speech was replaced by the dithyramb, a wild, ecstatic song that was connected with the appearance of the god Dionysus – a causal relationship, supposedly.[14] The dithyramb was a central concept in Nietzsche's attempt to view Greek life as a whole and to his reevaluation of any interpretation of an aesthetic that places beauty as its core value. Nietzsche scholars M. S. Silk and J. P. Stern summarize the historical roots of classical Greek poetry and tragedy in the dithyramb: "lyric poetry ... in Greece was originally and characteristically sung poetry and which included the dithyramb, that special kind of sung poetry originally employed in the orgiastic worship of the fertility god, Dionysus, and conventionally regarded as ancestral to Greek tragedy."[15] In a parallel manner, jazz arose from – but transformed and constrained – the Sunday music-making of *Place Congo*.

In a nineteenth-century account that has proven invaluable to jazz scholars, Grace King summarizes the *Place Congo* activities as a thoroughly participatory activity:

[T]hey would gather in their gay, picturesque finery, by hundreds, even thousands, under the shades of sycamores, to dance the Bamboula or the Calinda; the music of their Creole songs tuned by the beating of the tam-tam. ... "Badoum! Badoum!" the children, dancing too on the outskirts, adding their screams and romping to the chorus and movement. ... White people would promenade by to look at the scene. ... At nightfall the frolic ceased.[16]

Henry Kmen, in a 1972 study of *Place Congo*, finds it doubtful that song and dance took place there after about 1835. He concludes that we cannot establish any direct connection between the activities there and the formation of jazz.[17] All the same, he documents the origins of the mixing of African and American musics that became jazz:

[A]t first the dancing on the Square was restricted (by custom) to the French-speaking (or Creole) slaves. "To these festivities nègres 'Méricains were not invited." If true, that restriction did not last long. As the American slaves swarmed in [after the Louisiana Purchase], they naturally imposed many of their own customs, and before long among the new songs heard in the Square were "Hey Jim Along," "Get Along Home You Yallow Gals," and "Old Virginia Never Tire." Similarly, among the instruments played were fifes and fiddles, banjos, triangles, jews harps, and tambourines. Thus the original Afro-West-Indian music and dancing were being diluted by the strong surrounding musical culture. Sometime shortly after 1835 the Congo Square dances ceased.[18]

Where King calls the dancing a frolic, earlier descriptions recognized it as worship.[19] In both ancient Greece and in the Ring Dance of New Orleans, the songs were sung while dancing in a circular movement. As in Nietzsche's account of the origins of tragedy in the dithyramb, both ceremonies involve group or choral singing *while* dancing, where audiences and performers were conflated. (Notably, only whites took the stance of audience in King's description.)

We emphasize that much is uncertain about what went on at *Place Congo*, not least of which was when its music died, when it stopped, and if it started up again in the years subsequent to 1847:

What then can we say about Congo Square and the birth of jazz? First, that in the early nineteenth century there most certainly was African-West-Indian music and dancing in the Square. It reached a peak around 1819 when [Benjamin Henry] Latrobe saw it and left us his description and sketches.[20]

Such accounts tell us that there were hundreds, if not thousands of participants dancing and singing on Sundays – this much does not seem to be in doubt. Nor is the contrast between the tolerated and legal goings-on at *Place Congo* and the secretive outlaw rituals of Voodoo.

Another parallel with Dionysian worship arises in King's emphasis on the music-based rituals that were kept hidden from white eyes, the wild singing and stomping and clapping of the Voodoo rituals that were common in Louisiana, and which informed the broader African-American folkways tradition, before and after slavery. Introduced into New Orleans by West Indian slaves and immigrants, "Voudou" meetings took place secretly at night, both in New Orleans and in the surrounding area.[21]

Compared to Sunday worship, Voodoo was a more extreme activity of consciousness changing as a result of dance and song: "the contortions of the body, frenzy, ecstasies ... the low humming sound rising louder and louder, the dancers whirling around, faster and faster, screaming, ... falling down delirious, exhausted."[22] One eyewitness account of a ritual that took place around 1825 describes a strongly Dionysian scene:

> Up sprang a magnificent specimen of human flesh — Ajona, a lithe, tall black woman, with a body waving and undulating like Zozo's snake — a perfect Semiramis from the jungles of Africa. Confining herself to a spot not more than two feet in space, she began to sway on one and the other side. Gradually the undulating motion was imparted to her body from ankles to hips. Then she tore the white handkerchief from her forehead. This was a signal, for the whole assembly sprang forward and entered the dance ... Under the passion of the hour, the women tore off their garments, and entirely nude, went on dancing, but wriggling like snakes.[23]

If the song and dance at *Place Congo* was proto-jazz in a controlled and pleasurable pastime, Voodoo came closer to the ecstasis characterized by Nietzsche. For here we have the rapturous behavior that he attributes to Dionysian rituals. Regarding those ceremonies, Nietzsche imagines the Dionysian reveler, the "primary man," in asking the following: "did those days of superb somatic and psychological health give rise, perhaps, to endemic trances, collective visions, and hallucinations?"[24] Again, we defer to Silk and Stern: "In the dithyramb, but only in the dithyramb, the chorus are oblivious to everyday existence: in their ecstatic state they identify entirely with their proto-dramatic part."[25]

We can only speculate as to what need was filled by the singing and dancing at Voodoo rituals. But it seems clear to us that it was one way of preserving ancient identities in a new world in which cultural identity was threatened by law and assimilation. If this is correct, it would again be a way song interfaces with issues of identity while offering a respite from a harsh reality.

Keep in mind, however, that Nietzsche is tracing the *origins* of Greek tragedy, and jazz relates to origins at *Place Congo* and in Voodoo much as Sophocles's *Oedipus Trilogy* stands to the dithyramb. So we should not take it literally when

Shipton claims, "The ecstatic element of the slave and Voodoo dances described by nineteenth-century historians was carried forward into the atmosphere of early jazz dances in New Orleans and Chicago."[26] The same caution applies to Ted Gioia's characterization of the blues as the Dionysian side of African-American music.[27] A performance of *Oedipus the King* is not an act of worship. In presentation, the roles of performer and audience are sharply differentiated. In the golden age of Greek tragedy, the Dionysian impulse is *represented* but no longer fully present. Today we can see performances in the Theater of Dionysus, the ancient performance space at the foot of the Acropolis in Athens. To put it another way, the Dionysian mode is expressed in the performance for the sake of audience catharsis. The audience is not participating in the manner required for an ecstatic state that will obliterate everyday existence. In the history of jazz, the transformations from nineteenth-century ritual to full-blown jazz bring us back to Sartre, sitting in a café in Le Havre (fictionalized as Roquentin in Bouville), listening to Sophie Tucker or a "Negress" on a phonograph record and finding meaning in her expression of sorrow. His encounter with the music is at the farthest remove from collective ecstatic behavior. He is the audience for a performer giving a performance. In contrast, the dancers of both the chorus at the origins of tragedy and the Ring Dance of *Place Congo* were at once performer, audience, and actor – subject and object – "nothing but chorus," the artist becoming work of art, as Nietzsche says.[28] This chorus, arising out of the spirit of religion, was a matter of the dropping of the will, in Schopenhauer's sense, which meant the dropping of greed, all political concerns, and in fact all quotidian interests and individual identities. It is a case of *abandonment* both in the sense of leaving behind what one was – a personal history – and in the sense of having few restraints.

However, there is another link between Sartre and Nietzsche in this respect, and it concerns the Dionysian echo that is present in some music. Fifteen years after writing *The Birth of Tragedy: Out of the Spirit of Music*, Nietzsche wrote his "A Critical Glance Backwards" as a preface and reevaluation of his analysis of the life and death of Greek tragedy. In that addendum he says he should have *sung* that book rather than written it. In taking the point of view that the author of his book might be a maenadic soul, referring to himself he says, "And, indeed, this 'new soul' should have *sung*, not spoken. What a pity that I could not tell as a poet what demanded to be told!"[29] Here, Nietzsche is at once divorcing himself from the style of current scholarship and aligning his unorthodox book with the lyric poets of whom he writes in *The Birth of Tragedy*, where the chorus sang in unison the poems that he thought held a place at the very beginnings of tragedy – an obvious contrast with the Socratic style that was to come later. By *singing his book*, we think Nietzsche means to express the idea that the book flows, smoothly and without hesitation, unscholarly, a spiritual somewhat improvisational writing, rather than resorting to second guessing, using as a guideline: don't look back. Ideally, then, the writing flows like a good jazz improvisation: "the improviser, if he sincerely attempts to be creative, will push himself into areas of expression which his technique may be unable to handle."[30] And here, as well, we notice the power that Sartre attributes to "Some of These Days." The central issue of the Dionysian mode is the manner in which it allows us to address our pain. Its power is the power to comfort through a gesture of affirmation.[31] A truly Dionysian affirmation is directed at the world despite all its imperfection, rather than at an idealized world (past or present) or an imaginary better future.[32]

Turning his back on the failed promise of Richard Wagner's romantic fantasies, Nietzsche locates the remaining traces of the Dionysian impulse in a woman's song in popular culture: the opera *Carmen*.[33] This impulse is one of abandon or dispossession and intensification. Singing is a dislocation from the rest of one's life, which for Nietzsche is expression – a giving up of the principle of individuation. The body is infused with song. Even so, in *Nausea*, Roquentin is affected as listener, not as singer, and yet we have imagined the greater power of song as embodying the singer. When Nietzsche offers an account of the concept of *resentiment*, he imagines it as a poisoning of the soul, just as we imagine, at least some of jazz, as antidotal to a troubled soul. In the sections that follow, we make a case that this impulse is frequently present in jazz, especially jazz singing, but not as normally construed.

3. Singing and Song Interpretation: Two Models

John Carvalho makes a persuasive case that the improvisational mastery of Miles Davis fits Nietzsche's description of Dionysian affirmation, especially Davis's rhythmic improvisation.[34] Unfortunately, this narrow emphasis on modern instrumental jazz leaves us wondering about earlier jazz, and about jazz singing in particular. Did a phonograph record allow Sartre to hear a Dionysian affirmation in pre-war Le Havre? Do we find this affirmation in the tradition of jazz singing, in the vocal performances of Louis Armstrong, Billie Holiday, and in the other jazz vocal greats, both pre-war and after? Over the course of this chapter, we make the case that this affirmation is most clearly present in the jazz tradition of *scat singing*.

In order to say that jazz singing retained the Dionysian element of African-American ritual in early twentieth-century New Orleans, we must challenge an influential idea about jazz singing, which is that it is primarily an art of expressive singing. We need to disentangle three things here. First, a song may be written in a way that is expressive of a particular emotion, as when the combination of words and melody makes "Mean to Me" a sad song. Second, the performer's performance choices can express a stance *toward the song*. This expressive stance is emphasized in Jerrold Levinson's claim that jazz singing is valuable because "in singing a song a particular way ... a singer conveys her feeling about the song, how she *feels* about a song, expresses her *attitude* toward the song, or presents the song in a certain *light*."[35] So, while Billie Holiday's handling of "Them There Eyes" in 1939 may convey an ironic stance toward the lyrics, Ella Fitzgerald's more ornate decoration of the melody comes across as playful, but never ironic.[36] Third, a singer's performance may reflect his or her own life in some important way. Singing is then self-expression.

Let's take a cynical position here to make a point. The singers that enter our own personal histories are professionals who get paid for what they do and some may well do it for that reason alone, acting as if they have a feeling or attitude toward a song – fakin' it, Ted Gracyk has said[37] – rather than genuinely feeling a mood that they may successfully pass on to their listeners. As John Szwed observes in his autobiography of Holiday:

> The singers we see in performance are not the real persons. Like actors, singers create their identities as artists through words and music. Singers act as singers when they perform, but behave differently in daily life. … We should not be shocked, then, to learn that, whereas onstage Billie Holiday projected a ladylike distance and grace, offstage her manner was sometimes rough, profane, caustic, and vengeful.[38]

We grant Levinson's point that singers may well interpret songs as they relate to their personal lives and to some of the lives of their audience. Staying with Holiday for the moment, Szwed says this: "Holiday developed an acting style, not merely by deciding who she should be in various songs, but by a kind of American Method acting – finding motivation for a song, asking why the song says what it does, drawing on her experiences and memories of emotions."[39] But, even when there is some connection to the singer's own experiences, the professional jazz singer constructs a persona, a performing personality.[40] The construct goes beyond sound, especially in live performance, where gestures of face and body are often part of the act.[41] However, the idea of singers qua actors is not confined to Holiday or even to jazz singing. Jeanette Bicknell located insight in some words by the political economist Adam Smith, who knew nothing of jazz. She says:

> The singer's acting enhances the performance and is indeed necessary for a good performance. As Smith writes, 'there is no comparison between the effect of what is sung coldly from a music-book at the end of a harpsichord, and of what is not only sung but acted with proper freedom, animation, and boldness.'[42]

Given the difference between acting and self-expression, one of the most misleading and distorting assumptions of jazz reception has been the expression theory of art, the Romantic and late-Romantic position that genuine art is always a sincere, cathartic release of felt emotion. Jazz musicians frequently espouse a strong self-expression version of expression theory, most notably in Charlie Parker's much-quoted observation, "If you don't live it, it won't come out of your horn."[43] There is no fakin' it, and so no persona. But surely strongly felt emotion interferes with, rather than facilitates, musical performance, and connecting them is just bad psychology.[44] Bicknell offers the example of three jazz standards with distinct expressive profiles and then notes, "a performer who sang these three songs in succession simply could not go through such a sequence of emotional ups and downs and still complete the songs."[45] But one song is enough to make the point. One ethnomusicologist witnessed a Ukrainian funeral service where two sisters were expected to sing a lamentation for their father, but one was too grief-stricken to perform; afterwards the villagers praised the behavior of the sister who sang, not the one who was too "distraught" to sing.[46] When sung grief is called for, real grief is a liability.

Although singing normally has something to do with emotion and expression, we have argued that the expression of emotion is logically and psychologically independent of what performers go around feeling in everyday life, outside of their singing. Therefore, self-expression is independent of the other two kinds of expression. To have an emotionally powerful and successful performance, it is sufficient if, while singing, performers offer a convincing display of the emotion they see fit in interpreting the song.

An alternative account of musical expression is considered and rejected in Plato's *Republic*, and it informs the earliest modern definition of art. It tells us that art is fundamentally mimetic, that is, an imitation or representation of existing things, selected and "perfected" to give us pleasure.[47] Art is the product of imitative genius.[48] (If we want to praise the "genius" of Parker and Holiday, this approach is certainly more appealing than the Romantic expression theory.) Instrumental music fits into this scheme by imitating select elements of human expressive behavior, representing a human persona and thereby succeeding as an art that is primarily concerned with the representation of human emotion.[49] The pinnacle of musical performance, on this model, is a selective representation that is so perfect that the performance *seems* to be a sincere expression of real emotion.[50] And, this, we note, is precisely the "genius" that many critics and jazz historians attribute to Billie Holiday:

> Holiday's great performances are the fruit of her experience of her own life. ... She just happened to have the natural musician's ear for harmonic movement combined with the actor's aptitude for word combinations. ... [H]er singing possessed an extraordinary validity intensified by the fact that throughout a tempestuous life she experienced on a personal level all the situations used as themes in the lyrics of the songs she sang.[51]

That is, her innate musicality allowed her to draw on her own experiences as the model for her expressive interpretation of song; there is a virtual collapse of person and persona. Benny Green, whose praise we just quoted, goes on to argue that Holiday is consequently a better jazz singer than Ella Fitzgerald and Sarah

Vaughan. Holiday concentrates on maximizing the *expressive* possibilities of the songs she sings (generally improving them in the process). In contrast, Fitzgerald and Vaughan are so concerned with display of vocal prowess that they disregard the meaning of the song; they frequently generate "gibberish whose emotive content is roughly nil ... amusing and skillful though they may be, [they] have nothing to do with the art of remoulding a melody without at the same time strangling its lyric."[52] Writing about opera rather than jazz, Peter Kivy names this model of songs and singing a theory of expressive eloquence.[53]

A good deal has been written about music and language, and jazz and language in particular. As we would expect when the eloquence model is applied to song performance, writers about this subject tend to articulate those aspects of music that are akin to spoken or written language. The obvious subclass of music, where language can be understood both literally and metaphorically, is song. Language can be used to obfuscate what is being said, say in the lyrics of Bob Dylan's "Sad Eyed Lady of the Lowlands" or his "Visions of Johanna," but in most cases the words sung offer us a good indication of what the song expresses and the relationship between the music and the lyrics has the potential to reinforce one another. Benny Green's discussion of Holiday is especially insightful on the challenge that song lyrics pose for jazz singers.[54]

However, no matter how successful it may be, the eloquent persona is not Dionysian, an insight that informs Nietzsche's reversal of his early estimation of Wagner's operas. The Dionysian impulse fuels a creative act in which the artist "has forgotten how to walk, *how to speak*, and is on the brink of taking wing as he dances. ... No longer the artist, he has himself become a work of art; the productive power of the whole universe is now manifest."[55] Pacified as art, rather than Dionysian bacchanal, the result is "the abrogation of the *principium individuationis* [as] an esthetic event" in which the artist "is incited to strain his symbolic faculties to the utmost," expressing the "oneness of nature," rather than an articulation of human nature and clearly the opposite of expressing himself.[56] Dionysian song performance is the antithesis of the eloquence model of persona construction, which focuses on the construction and presentation of a clearly articulated personal identity.

In keeping with the model of jazz pluralism that we advanced in Chapter 3, we are decidedly *not* saying that Dionysian performance is essential in jazz, or that it is superior to the eloquence of Holiday's best performances or, certainly, that it exists in jazz alone. We are saying, instead, that it is an error to suppose that the values that describe Holiday's performances are *the* model for evaluating jazz singing. Jazz has Dionysian roots, and models of jazz performance that do not make room for the incoherence of a Dionysian aesthetic event are selling jazz short. The next stage of the argument is to examine the eloquence model in greater detail, and to explain why it is not appropriate to the full range of jazz singing. We then offer the jazz scatting tradition as a core example of the Dionysian tradition in jazz.

4. Levinson and the Eloquence Model

As we have seen, the Dionysian jazz singer will use the creative act of performance as an act of affirmation. One might find this, to some degree, when jazz vocalists improvise on standards, breaking free from what the song seems to dictate. A suggestion of this sort is present in the account of jazz singing offered by Jerrold Levinson, who describes a change of identity that could take place while singing – the temporary spiritual embodiment, much like laughter, that happens to a singer in the act of singing, lyrics and music efficacious in the process. Levinson's general model, however, is the eloquence model: the jazz singer imparts an expressive character to the song and thus reveals something about the song. On some occasions, the singer may even engage in sincere personal expression, singing sadly because she is sad or sad because she is singing a sad song.[57] In all these cases, the performative act aims at communicating emotion and personality to an audience. By showing that this model is not adequate as a general theory of jazz singing, we remove an over-generalization that obscures the Dionysian in jazz singing.

In the dream world of American popular music, the most enduring of culturally embedded songs are called *standards*. A standard, like "Blue Skies" or "Blue Moon," usually attains a certain familiarity with generation after generation of performers, with new recordings of older tunes a common and continuing practice. We sometimes refer to the collective whole of standards, as when we speak of "The Great American Songbook." Standards stand the test of time. Concentrating on standards, Levinson makes a number of good points about their role in jazz. Standards are songs; that is, music with words, and the singers of standards, by virtue of the very act of singing, become their interpreters. That these songs are generally established and familiar adds to the interest a listener may have in their interpretation. Singers have options and listeners, especially those who know the lyrics by heart, may evaluate each singer's individual direction in performing a well-known song.

We propose that Levinson goes awry, however, when he makes use of the idea of the standard and its interpretation to mark the distinction between jazz and non-jazz singing. He holds that, "for a singer to interpret a song in a jazz context … is to do so in a particular way, with a range of freedoms to depart from the chart or score of the song."[58] We note that Levinson does not say that the jazz singer departs from a certain *performance* of a song, one that identifies as a standard approach or what he calls "the straight version," but rather that what is interpreted by the singer – the object of interpretation in the act of singing – is not itself a sound or sonic object, not itself music. For Levinson, the object of interpretation is a sound structure, as indicated by the notated music, the "chart or score." The next thing to note about the analysis is that a score can be most anything – with more or less information available for interpretation. A score that has very little information, such as a short chart or a set of written notes, may offer little direction to its performers. Hundreds of years ago this minimal information amounted to only a few temporally organized notes.

Compared to the classical tradition, the scores of standards are what we call minimal scores. From a broad historical perspective, the anomaly is the "classical" music practice of coordinating every instrument in the orchestra through multiple-stave notation, detailing every note that is to be played. There was a period when jazz orchestras such as Fletcher Henderson's and Duke Ellington's relied on charts, but this practice waned with the rise of bop and the return of collective improvisation.[59] Since the 1950s, many jazz performers have made use of so-called "fake books," designed to let them improvise collectively on a song in the absence of a multi-stave chart. For example, *The Real Jazz Standards Fake Book* provides nothing but the basic melody and, more importantly, the chord progression that a group of jazz musicians will follow in a given key – which may be reharmonized from the music as originally published.[60]

If jazz "freedom" is interpretation that departs from a minimal score, most anything would count as *departing* from a song's score, jazz and non-jazz singing alike. The score is "thinner" than any possible performance, that is, it is completely silent on the musical details that will occur in actual performance. Suppose a jazz trio pulls Irving Berlin's "Always" from a fake book when a patron requests it: the musicians will see that it's in ¾ time, but just what are the drummer and bass player supposed to do to support the piano? Anything they do will be more than the notation specifies. (We note that this absence of instrumental "prearrangement" is part of the attraction of Holiday's 1930s recordings with Teddy Wilson.[61]) So although Levinson suggests that interpretive "departures" from scores are characteristic of jazz singing, this characterization is uninformative. First, there are lots of departures, enactments of the kinds of freedom Levinson thinks apply only to jazz, that result in non-jazz singing as the singer interprets the score in a variety of ways. In addition, we can imagine a score with a plethora of information, the result of an interpretation, i.e., its performance, being both a standard *and* jazz by sticking closely to the information given in the score. Again, if the score is sufficiently detailed, an interpretation compliant with the score, that is, a relative non-departure from the score, may well turn out to be jazz, with a departure from the score ending up as a straight "standard" rendition. In fact, this is more or less the gimmick and attraction of vocalese, where jazz songs are written by combining lyrics with a melody that was generated as an improvised jazz solo. As we noted in Chapter 2, Joni Mitchell's version of "Twisted" is *less* jazzy than its model, not more; this is certainly due, in large part, because she cannot accurately mimic singer Annie Ross.

In noting that there is no such thing as a neutral score we are saying that any talk about freely departing from a score must be contingent upon an actual, specific score. Many standards are products of the Tin Pan Alley era, when music industry profits were mainly a function of the sale of sheet music. But not every jazz standard comes from that tradition, so in many cases there is no score. And of course a good deal of jazz singing is of something other than standards. A case of the former, for example, is Carmen McRae singing Thelonious Monk's "Straight

No Chaser," which is a jazz standard, if anything is. Yet Monk's composition was made known through his recordings of it, not through a score, and it was not originally a *song*, for the words came later. Or, in the case of Cassandra Wilson singing a Robert Johnson blues song, there is simply no *standard*, at least not in the jazz tradition. If Levinson were to counter our point by saying that his reference to the score is really a reference to the sound structure that would be indicated by a minimal score, the blues tradition undercuts that move. Johnson's blues songs are not "original" in the Tin Pan Alley sense. They are, instead, variations and assemblages of the oral tradition of the Mississippi Delta. We may say that Wilson is interpreting Johnson's "Come On in My Kitchen," but the song is really a set of borrowed words grafted to an existing blues tune popularized by the Mississippi Sheiks.[62] In drawing on this tradition, a jazz performance is more often an interpretation of a song family, not a fixed song.

Levinson also claims that the jazz singer has a high degree of freedoms relative to the "straight version." Here, Levinson seems to be imagining a specific case where the song, not the score, is already a non-jazz standard – that is, a song, somewhat standing the test of time – and the song's status as a standard chronologically precedes any attempt by a singer to interpret it as a jazz song. But, on this assumption, when the issue of interpretation is raised, the idea is that there is *one* entity called a song and that what happens in a performance is *the* song's interpretation. But this claim, we think, is unclear. Either he is claiming the jazz singer interprets a song, where the singer of non-jazz does not, or that all singing is interpreting but that the jazz singer interprets the song to a greater degree than the "straight" singer ever could. Regarding the latter claim, it seems to follow that when enough "freedoms" are exercised, the singer can be identified as a jazz singer. However, every vehicle of "freedom" named by Levinson also exists with respect to standards that are non-jazz. Changes in tempo, musical style, phrasing, vocal timbre, volume, "how the singer alters the song" and the like, vary with the song and singer even in the case of non-jazz standards. Suppose we consider a single recording, the amazing CD *Red, Hot + Blue* (1990), performed by twenty-one very different artists. The album is a tribute to Cole Porter, perhaps the most prolific composer of what are now standards. Here we can note the incredible diversity of interpretations of his work, an exercise in vocal freedoms if you will, yet only two of the vocals could be characterized as *jazz* interpretations. Take, as another example, the 1934 Rogers and Hart song "Blue Moon." At first the sung song reflected a kind of quiet sentimentality, a prayer to the moon for a rare (once in a blue moon) stroke of luck. "Blue Moon" was then recorded by a diversity of artists, including Fitzgerald and Sinatra, but also Elvis Presley and Bob Dylan. When The Marcels recorded it as a fast doo-wop number, it became a rousing celebration of good fortune.[63] Significantly different from each other though they are, none of the instances mentioned are jazz renditions. Our objection to Levinson's distinction then, is not that jazz singers don't utilize a variety of vocal techniques, but rather that other singers do, non-jazz artists as well as jazz singers.

We think Levinson raises other points in this article very much worth tending to – about the relationship between the person singing and the person *while singing*, by which he means "the performing personality," or what we would ordinarily call the *persona* of the singer, which shifts or changes depending upon the song. Levinson offers some examples of vocal jazz renditions by Anita O'Day and Sarah Vaughan and has an eye for nicely describing what goes on there, their mode of artistic expression, when they sing, or at least *sometimes* when they sing. The advantage of this reading of jazz singing is that it locates expression in the persona without buying into the strong version of expression theory. But then Levinson says:

> In many modes of art making it may be possible for the artist to more or less *hide* from his or her audience. That is, it may be possible for viewers or listeners to understand and appreciate what is offered artistically and yet form little idea of the personality, or at any rate the persona, of the artist. But jazz singing, I venture to suggest, is not one of these modes.[64]

We could say many things about this last claim regarding the jazz singer, and in Chapter 5, we do. Personality, Levinson *seems* to suggest, is different from persona, which is the public display of *a* personality. But persona may have little or no significant relationship with a singer's actual personality. The latter, but not the former, like a good role in acting, can change, perhaps ought to change, in some contexts with changes in songs sung – whether it is happy and about being in love or mourning a lost love. In contrast to what Levinson says, in the case of a persona, there is nothing hidden or rather the question of what may be hiding does not arise, because we know that the singer who sings of a lost love may not ever have had one in her life – an assumption few listeners would make. Personality would be different from persona, but "hidden" is not the correct word here since there is no contrast in that artistic mode of presentation. That is, no one would be able to draw conclusions from a jazz singer's rendition of a standard as to what they are like outside the song. The two are intimately related only if strong expression theory is correct – a theory we have already dismissed. From the song sung alone (as opposed to what may be rumored in the tabloids) we remain agnostic. We know someone, an artist actually, who claims he could tell Frank Sinatra's relationship to organized crime by listening to his singing. We are skeptical of that claim.

The relevant point here has to do with the persona and personality difference with respect to the jazz singer. We see no relevant difference with the non-jazz singer's mode of artistic presentation. In each case we may have a distinct style and in each case talents and innovations may occur without significant difference of degree. Gene Lees points to a case of mild controversy, when he says, "Occasionally through the years there has been a debate as to whether or not Ella Fitzgerald was a 'jazz singer.'" He notes that in the American songbook albums, of which there were many, "she sang the songs straight with minimal embellish-ment."[65] Perhaps "deadpan" is a good word here. And of Sinatra, Lees notes that while at a certain point in his career his singing took on a certain "hue of jazz," Sinatra never considered himself a jazz singer, referring to himself instead as a "saloon singer."[66] What is closer to the truth is that Fitzgerald and Sinatra, so prolific over so many years, clearly sang songs that would never be considered jazz, whatever else they did regarding scatting (Ella) or swinging (Frank). Yet each established some of the clearest personae in popular music ever to record any music. As an art, *singing* typically involves persona construction.[67]

There is, however, a deeper point regarding this discussion and it is a philo-sophical one about identity, or on a grander scale, about the separation of the arts from the artist. Is singing, jazz and otherwise, to be separated from the rest of our "normal" lives? Or, put more dramatically, is there a personality that dominates our normal lives in all situations such that singing hides it successfully, as Levinson seems to claim? We believe, by contrast, that there are many expressions of our personalities outside of performance (even those that include singing, such as singing in the shower) whereas it would be difficult to form criteria if it was necessary for us to choose some dominant one from which all others deviate, and then go on to use that as the standard from which jazz singing, but not other singing, would depart.

We applaud Levinson for raising several issues of philosophical note about songs and singing, but disagree that the issues he raises are jazz specific. If it is true that how a singer handles a song reflects the singer's personality, as Levinson says it does, *at least while singing*,[68] then it is true for a singer of any songs, not simply jazz. And, as mentioned earlier, some singers perform a sad song as if sad, a sexy one as if sexy, but it is unclear that this says anything about what they are really feeling or what they are like, when the song is over. Singing, we think, is a bit like acting – the script, like lyrics, can make you feel that a certain feeling should be conveyed, and that the melody and the lyrics may make you feel sad, but that it may well be finished and over when the act is finished and the song over. The actor or singer, for example when receiving applause, often reverts to a routine a good distance from the feeling conveyed in the performance. Then again, what does it mean to convey sadness? We can imagine lyrics that are about some personal trouble – sad lyrics. But we can imagine the lyrics themselves conveying the feeling, while a singer, perhaps having lost hope or in a kind of emotional shock, sings against the grain, with a certain indifference. Singers as different as Ella Fitzgerald and Bob Dylan sing songs just this way – sad songs with sad melodies and sad lyrics but with a vocality that borders on indifference. These renditions are nevertheless effective in conveying sadness, without getting sentimental. A brave front, we might think. To return briefly to the example of a lost love: just as one may daydream about love (losing at love, being in love, hoping for love), a song, jazz or otherwise, might offer the opportunity *to think* about love, certainly for the attentive listener, with the song casting a certain mood that can help those thoughts move along. However, these possibilities shed no light on *jazz* singing; again, nothing Levinson says about jazz singing is unique to jazz singing.

5. Scatting

Levinson says that one of the "freedoms" jazz singers optimize is scatting. However, he makes the misleading and hence troublesome claim that the jazz singer departs from the melody less than the jazz instrumentalist.[69] We are not sure how to measure this departure, or how to measure it throughout jazz's long history. Holiday set a high standard for jazz singing by routinely reworking established melodies. Green offers the personal anecdote that he did not know the standard melody of "Mean to Me" for many years. Familiar with Holiday's version, he was shocked by the banality of the "original" when he first encountered it while performing onstage in a jazz club.[70] In our view, the idea that singers take fewer liberties says less about the jazz singer than about jazz music generally. Improvisation by jazz instrumentalists is a departure from established melody, but so is scatting, a topic we now address. Where Levinson sees scatting as one tool of the jazz singer among many, we give it a more prominent place. Despite the fact that its use is relatively infrequent, scatting is a paradigm of improvisation and it is something unique to jazz. Above all, it is a vocal practice in which there is no division between the singing and the song, and therefore no standard of eloquence by which the singing can be judged. To borrow a phrase from Garry Hagberg, jazz scatting foregrounds "spontaneous human action."[71]

Scat singing has a history that is intimately related to jazz. However, it must be said that there are lots of non-jazz, non-semantic, wordless vocal displays of singing outside of jazz. Singers have made use of whistling (if that is vocal), humming, and "doo-be-doos" that are not scatting. Backup singers can repeat phrases that appear as nonsensical after so many vocalizations. What sets off scatting as uniquely jazz is the improvisational aspects of song performance, traditionally connected to the imitations of jazz instruments. Functionally, it is important that scatting is a black art. We do not mean this in a racially essentialist way, but if we ask what kind of activity scatting is, part of the answer is that it is a musical resource that is understood, after 1926, to be an African–American social practice.[72]

At the center of the history of scatting, most famously, is the 1926 Louis Armstrong recording of "Heebie Jeebies," where Armstrong was supposed to have dropped pages of lyrics and began singing with made up words: "when I dropped the paper I immediately turned back into the horn."[73] True or not, what is the case is that scatting began well before that recording session. As Gene Santoro reminds us:

> Armstrong sang before he picked up a horn. It was a fundamental part of who he was and what he had to say. Ultimately, his vocals would make him

a world-famous star. More immediately, they were another virtuosic tool he used to change jazz and in the process, American culture.[74]

However, it would be an error to think that Armstrong was as innovative with scatting as he was with his horn. According to Alyn Shipton, Armstrong "was not doing anything particularly novel – simply falling back on what was, within the world of vaudeville and theater, already a fairly well known manner of singing, employed by African-American and white musicians alike."[75] Shipton notes that Armstrong had already scatted on a recording when he appeared on Fletcher Henderson's "Everybody Loves My Baby" (1924). But he also observes that early scat singing was most often performed by women. A notable early recording is Edith Wilson performing "Dixie Blues" in 1922,[76] and a slightly later one features Adelaide Hall on Duke Ellington's 1927 recording of "Creole Love Call." Here, with Hall, was a successful attempt to imitate the instrumental style of Bubber Miley, what Shipton calls an abstraction, of Bessie Smith, with the words removed.[77]

Scat became an integral part of jazz singing with acts like the Rhythm Boys (Bing Crosby, Al Rinker, and Harry Barris), the Mills Brothers, and many of Duke Ellington's vocalists. Yet, above all, Armstrong and Ella Fitzgerald became widely known for their scatting. And there is, notably, Cab Calloway's 1931 "Minnie the Moocher" and his 1932 "The Scat Song," where a call and response dominates the wordless interaction, as the band and audience sing the nonsense, "Hi-de-hi-de-ho." Here, the division between performers and audience is dissolved, if only briefly, in joyous affirmation. But the division was restored whenever Calloway really cut loose and the audience could not follow – a prime example is the virtuosic scat interlude of "Nagasaki" (1935). Nonetheless, Armstrong was the pivotal figure. Santoro quotes Rudy Vallee, the singer famous for his megaphone in the days before the microphone. Vallee says of Armstrong, "No one in America sang the same after him."[78] Armstrong's vocal on "Heebie Jeebies" opened the floodgate of imitation and appropriation.

The aspect of scatting that became an early goal of many jazz singers was the imitation of instruments so that the vocals and instrumental music came close to being indiscernible. What must be sacrificed, of course, is concern for the song's words. For those who subscribe to an eloquence model of musical performance, unconstrained scatting is problematic. As we noted earlier, Green builds up Holiday by belittling scatting: "Gibberish vocals are the price the singer has to pay for this freedom to move about the realms of discord and resolution ... while abandoning its one great advantage, the achievement of catharsis through the use of familiar words."[79] The scatting of Fitzgerald and (Sarah) Vaughan is "amusing and skillful," but it is not a display of the "art" of singing.[80] At first, it seems that Levinson parts company with Green when he praises Fitzgerald with humor as capable of singing "a page from the phone book."[81] However, the criteria for performance success with a phone book would have to be very different from the criteria Levinson explicitly employs concerning the interpretation of jazz standards. A list of names and numbers provides no emotional cues, and success would be purely musical and therefore not a matter of expressive eloquence in *song* interpretation. (Yes, we know Levinson was joking to make a point.)

To this extent, we agree with Will Friedwald: the success criteria for jazz scatting are "completely different" from those of Holiday's construction of an expressive persona. We defer to a description by Friedwald:

> We need [scatting] to remind us that our great songwriters wrote music as well as words. Ella's success with "Memories of You" ... owes nothing to "waking skies at sunrise" but to the diatonic obstacle course that leads her away from and ultimately toward the resolving five-note figure that con-cludes the melodic payoff. Our pulses race when Fitzgerald starts to scat. Will she follow the melody? For how long? Will a fragment of another tune momentarily pop into her head? Will she slow down the tempo, double it, or suspend the beat altogether? Will she do her crowd-pleasing "bass solo"? Will she trade four with her accompanists, and will they be able to keep up with her endless inventiveness?[82]

Here, in the inventiveness of scatting, we have an indication of what a good deal of jazz singing is about: jazz singing is, like tap dancing, a seamless continuation of jazz music. Even with worded vocals in the conventional sense, jazz singing takes the form of another instrument, with the tones and timbres of how jazz is performed and recorded, whether bluesy or swinging, sweet or harsh.

We want to push beyond these evaluations by proposing that scatting is more than either "gibberish" or pure musical display. Functionally, it can permit the vocalist to take wing by "forgetting" speech, as Nietzsche says of the Dionysian aesthetic, and so to participate on exactly the same footing as the other jazz musicians. (From another point of view, if you were to isolate the sounds of scat and present them to the uninitiated, they may well sound like the purported "insanity" of Voodoo.) At the same time, there is an important difference between, say, Holiday's voice and Lester Young's saxophone in their celebrated "duets." Young is manipulating a musical instrument; Holiday *is* her musical instrument. Holiday's jazz singing is praised as instrumentality by other means, with lyrics adding a layer of meaning transporting a song into the personal lives of the audience. There is an additional factor, however: a vocal performance remains tethered to the body that sings. Take away the attempt to articulate meaningful words, and the sole focus of appreciation is the act of singing itself. Ella is performing when scatting, true enough, but she is not performing a persona. The performance is the creative act, but there is no mimetic gap between the person and what is presented. Consequently, it is a genuinely Dionysian activity: in singing, she herself has become the work of art. If the classic blues of the 1920s and 1930s are significant as "representational freedom,"[83] then scatting was, too, but untethered from representation.

6. Summary and Conclusion

This chapter has been about jazz singing and song. As in Nietzsche's exploration of Dionysian ritual and Michel Foucault's analysis of sex, madness or punishment, we have adopted the perspective of going back to origins. In doing so, we find stages in the history of jazz – most notably proto-jazz, especially the Ring Dances of *Place Congo* and the rituals of Voodoo, and then later in the Jazz Age – when the association of jazz with certain disreputable, if not irrational spheres, forged significant commonalities. In particular, we see that certain cultural practices were perceived as a threat to civilized life by its more conservative forces. In addition, we claimed that, in principle, there is no general distinction between jazz and non-jazz singing; the differences are there in practice, but they require us to look and see. Finally, a match-up in any given period may yield contingent differences of intensity and abandon; a fluctuation that is to be expected from the historical definition of jazz that we outlined in Chapter 3.

We will conclude by relating jazz singing and scatting to a pivotal claim in Paul Taylor's recent study of black aesthetics, *Black is Beautiful*. Although jazz was rapidly appropriated by mainstream white culture, jazz singing remained "blacker" than jazz generally. Asked to name the ten best jazz vocalists, many knowledgeable jazz fans will name only African-American artists – something much less likely if we asked about pianists or even trumpet players. Moreover, other than Armstrong, it is possible that the list of singers would be a list of black women.[84] Consider, in this context, Taylor's point that black music does more than knit together a "geographically dispersed" and marginalized culture. For someone who is labeled "black" in a race-conscious society, the music is a mode of "inhabiting" that culture, "giving the individuals in those cultures the resources to think of themselves as particular kinds of persons, as, in this case, as black persons."[85] In carving out a space in popular music that remains racially exclusive – where non-black jazz singers remain rare and "more an exception than a rule"[86] – jazz singing has been a resource for a public activity that cannot be captured by a theory of eloquent expression.

Pursuing Taylor's proposal, we propose that jazz singing allows the singer, while singing, to inhabit, or possess, a cultural space. Read in this way, the singer is not to be understood as constructing a persona or making a statement of any kind. We do not deny that the performances of Holiday and other jazz vocalists "bear witness to the phenomenon of living as a Black woman."[87] Nor do we mean to diminish Angela Davis's argument that much of the value of jazz is due to the way it "expresses the hope and struggle for freedom" in the African-American community.[88] These are things that anyone, hearing jazz as a cultural space, might recognize even in a "white" performance of jazz – in, say, Sophie Tucker's "Some of these Days."[89] Where Melanie Bratcher praises women blues and jazz vocalists for commenting on the struggle of African-American women in the face of their alienation and social invisibility, we think that the singing, apart from the words, is the more significant activity.[90] What we have in mind is encapsulated in a remark made by Nina Simone in the course of an interview: "I've had a couple of times onstage when I really felt free. And that's something else! ... No fear. I mean really no fear!"[91] If we return to Sartre and the issue of creative freedom articulated by Nina Simone, we find a significant analogy with her relationship to her audience in what Sartre says about the writer and his or her reader:

> [S]ince the one who writes recognizes, by the very fact that he takes the trouble to write, the freedom of his readers, and since the one who reads, by the mere fact of his opening the book, recognizes the freedom of the writer, the work of art, from whichever side you approach it, is an act of confidence in the freedom of men. And since readers, like the author, recognize this freedom only to demand that it manifest itself, the work can be defined as an imaginary presentation of the world in so far as it demands human freedom.[92]

Rather than express ideas and feelings about freedom, the jazz performance sometimes aspires to be a place of freedom, and to inhabit that space is, sometimes, to be free. In the context of the interview, Simone implies that she has never had this experience at any other time in her life. When Ella takes flight in scatting, the song is left behind and there is no longer any pretense of portrayal, depiction, or representation: the singer visibly closes the gap between person and persona. In later chapters we will take a closer look at the degree and kinds of creative freedom present in jazz improvisation. For now, we merely propose that jazz singing is the most significant repository of the Dionysian impulse within jazz, most notably in scatting.

Notes

1 Jean-Paul Sartre, *La nausée* (Paris: Gallimard, 1938). Unfortunately, the novel does not offer enough details to confirm that Roquentin is listening to Sophie Tucker, but it is likely that Sartre is thinking of Tucker's 1926 million-selling recording for Columbia Records.
2 This theme is developed at length in another existentialist novel, Charles Wright's *The Messenger* (New York: Farrar, Straus, & Co. 1963).
3 Jean-Paul Sartre, *The Psychology of Imagination*, trans. Bernard Frechtman (New York: Philosophical Library, 1948), 281.
4 See James Donald, *Some of These Days: Black Stars, Jazz Aesthetics, and Modernist Culture* (Oxford: Oxford University Press, 2015), 1–3. Our thanks to John Carvalho for suggesting the richness of this example.
5 In Chapter 6, we respond to Theodor Adorno's notorious skepticism about this possibility. On the idea that improvised music is also a symbol of freedom in non-Western music, see Bruno Nettl, "Musical Values and Social Values: Symbols in Iran," *Asian Music* 12 (1980): 129–148.
6 Frank A. Salamone, *The Culture of Jazz: Jazz as Critical Culture* (Lanham: University Press of America, 2009), 51. Salamone notes that this view is especially common in France.

7 André Gide, *Journals 1914–1927*, trans. Justin O'Brien (Urbana: University of Illinois Press, 2000), 342.

8 Despite many philosophical differences, Sartre's *Nausea* is deeply influenced by Nietzsche; see John Duncan, "Sartre and Realism-All-the-Way-Down," *Sartre Studies International* 11:1–2 (2005): 91–113.

9 Friedrich Wilhelm Nietzsche, *The Birth of Tragedy and The Genealogy of Morals*, trans. Francis Golffing (New York: Random House, 1956), 25–26.

10 On the pernicious error of linking jazz with the savage and the primitive, see Ted Gioia, *The Imperfect Art: Reflections on Jazz and Modern Culture* (Oxford: Oxford University Press, 1988), chap. 2.

11 Perhaps the richest reading of jazz as Dionysian is Joachim-Ernst Berendt's discussion of jazz as dance music; see Andrew Wright Hurley, *The Return of Jazz: Joachim-Ernst Berendt and West German Cultural Change* (New York: Berghahn, 2009), 38–41.

12 Nietzsche, *Birth of Tragedy*, 23.

13 For analysis of what the song and its dance rhythm were like, see Armand D'Angour, "Music and Movement in the Dithyramb," in *Dithyramb in Context*, ed. Barbara Kowalzig and Peter Wilson (Oxford: Oxford University Press, 2012), 198–209.

14 See Gilbert Rouget, *Music and Trance: A Theory of the Relations between Music and Possession*, trans. Brunhilde Biebuyck (Chicago: University of Chicago Press, 1985), 79.

15 M. S. Silk and J. P. Stern, *Nietzsche on Tragedy* (Cambridge: Cambridge University Press, 1981), 39.

16 Grace Elizabeth King, *New Orleans; the Place and the People* (New York and London: Macmillan, 1896), 340. King's account plays an important role in Alyn Shipton's analysis of how the music of New Orleans differed from the rest of the South; *A New History of Jazz*, rev. and updated ed. (London: Bloomsbury, 2007), 18–22.

17 Henry A. Kmen, "The Roots of Jazz and the Dance in Place Congo: A Re-Appraisal," *Inter-American Musical Research Yearbook* 8 (1972), 5–16.

18 Kmen, "Roots of Jazz," 14. James Lincoln Collier makes the case that musical assimilation was reduced through fresh infusions of African-based music as Haitian immigrants continued to enter Louisiana throughout the nineteenth century; see his *Jazz: The American Theme Song* (Oxford: Oxford University Press, 1993), 194–197.

19 Ted Gioia, *The History of Jazz*, 2nd ed. (Oxford: Oxford University Press, 2011), 4.

20 Kmen, "Roots of Jazz," 14.

21 One history of the region reports that Voodoo rituals were held at Lake Pontchartrain and Bayou St. John on each St. John's Eve (23 June), and that the practice continued through the nineteenth century; see Edna B. Freiberg, *Bayou St. John in Colonial Louisiana, 1699–1803* (New Orleans: Harvey Press, 1980), 293–294. Exploring the connection between *Place Congo*, voodoo, and jazz, Susan Cavin makes a case for the central role that women played in the music making that led to jazz; see her "Missing Women: On the Voodoo Trail to Jazz," *Journal of Jazz Studies* 3:1 (1975): 6–27.

22 King, *New Orleans*, 341.

23 Marie B. Williams, "A Night with the Voudous," *Appleton's Journal*, March 27, 1875: 403–404, at 404.

24 Nietzsche, *Birth of Tragedy*, 8.

25 Silk and Stern, *Nietzsche on Tragedy*, 87.

26 Shipton, *New History*, 17.

27 Gioia, *History of Jazz*, 11.

28 Nietzsche, *Birth of Tragedy*, 47. There was, as Silk and Stern put it, "originally no spectacle for it to be spectator of" (*Nietzsche on Tragedy*, 86).

29 Nietzsche, *Birth of Tragedy*, 7, emphasis in original.

30 Gioia, *Imperfect Art*, 66. We return to this idea in Chapter 10.

31 Nietzsche, *Birth of Tragedy*, 7, and Friedrich Nietzsche, *On the Genealogy of Morals and Ecce Homo*, trans. Walter Kaufmann (New York: Random House, 1967), 305–306.

32 See John Carvalho, "Improvisations, on Nietzsche, on Jazz," in *Nietzsche, Philosophy and the Arts*, ed. Salim Kemal, Ivan Gaskell, and Daniel W. Conway (Cambridge: Cambridge University Press, 1998), 187–211, at 194.

33 Friedrich Wilhelm Nietzsche, *The Birth of Tragedy and The Case of Wagner*, trans. Walter Kaufmann (New York: Random House,1967), 157–158. We might note that *Carmen*'s display of immorality and lawlessness caused a scandal at the time of its initial performance in 1875. In addition to the 1954 film *Carmen Jones* (20th Century Fox), with an African-American cast, we note the existence of a straightforwardly jazz version of *Carmen* in 1961: Cozy Cole, *A Cozy Conception of Carmen* (Charlie Parker Records PLP-403).

34 Carvalho, "Improvisations," 201–203. Without citing Nietzsche, David Toop makes similar claims about free improvisation; he cites Alan Davie on "the marvelous abandon" that can arise in improvisation, and usefully observes that standard practices generate muscle memory that inhibits abandonment. See Toop, *Into the Maelstrom: Music, Improvisation and the Dream of Freedom: Before 1970* (New York: Bloomsbury, 2016), at 264 and 46, respectively.

35 Jerrold Levinson, "Jazz Vocal Interpretation: A Philosophical Analysis," *Journal of Aesthetics and Art Criticism* 71:1 (2013): 35–43, at 38.

36 Holiday's ironic stance is explained by Stacy Linn Holman Jones, *Torch Singing: Performing Resistance and Desire from Billie Holiday to Edith Piaf* (Lanham: Rowman & Littlefield, 2007), 87–88.

37 Theodore Gracyk, "Fakin' It: Is There Authenticity in Commercial Music?" in *Aesthetics: A Reader in Philosophy of the Arts*, 4th ed., ed. David Goldblatt, Lee B. Brown, and Stephanie Patridge (New York: Routledge, 2017), 244–249, and "The Song Remains the Same, But Not Always," in *Led Zeppelin and Philosophy*, ed. Scott Calef (Chicago: Open Court, 2009), 31–45. See also Jeanette Bicknell, *A Philosophy of Song and Singing: An Introduction* (New York: Routledge, 2015), 63–64, 68.

38 John Szwed, *Billie Holiday: The Musician and the Myth* (New York: Penguin, 2015), 107.

39 Szwed, *Billie Holiday*, 104.

40 Levinson, "Jazz Vocal," 38–39. See also Jeanette Bicknell, "Song," in *The Routledge Companion to the Philosophy of Music*, ed. Theodore Gracyk and Andrew Kania (New York: Routledge, 2011), 437–445, at 442. Angela Y. Davis notes that Holiday's voice and singing style "establishes its female persona as an equal participant," challenging female inequality; see *Blues Legacies and Black Feminism: Gertrude "Ma" Rainey, Bessie Smith, and Billie Holiday* (New York: Random House, 1998), 179–180.

41 See Szwed, *Billie Holiday*, 103.

42 Bicknell, *Philosophy of Song*, 31.

43 Quoted in Nat Shapiro and Nat Hentoff, *Hear Me Talkin' to Ya: The Story of Jazz as Told by the Men Who Made It* (New York: Rinehart, 1955), 405; see also the remarks of Jo Jones, 405–406, which are even more clearly an appeal to expression theory.

44 For refutation of strong expression theory, see Alex Neill, "Art and Emotion," in *The Oxford Handbook of Aesthetics*, ed. Jerrold Levinson (Oxford: Oxford University Press, 2003), 421–435; in relation to music, see Stephen Davies, "The Expression Theory Again," *Theoria* 52:3 (1986): 146–167. A modified and more plausible version of expression theory is defended by Jenefer Robinson, *Deeper than Reason: Emotion and its Role in Literature, Music, and Art* (Oxford: Clarendon Press, 2005).

45 Bicknell, *Philosophy of Song*, 32.

46 Natalie Kononenko, "When Traditional Improvisation Is Prohibited: Contemporary Ukrainian Funeral Laments," in *Musical Improvisation: Art, Education, and Society*, ed. Gabriel Solis and Bruno Nettl (Urbana: University of Illinois Press, 2009), 52–71, at 57–58.

47 Charles Batteux, *The Fine Arts Reduced to a Single Principle*, trans. James O. Young (Oxford: Oxford University Press, 2015), 10, 20.

48 Batteux, *Fine Arts*, 5–6.
49 Batteux, *Fine Arts*, 129, 137.
50 Batteux, *Fine Arts*, 7.
51 Benny Green, *The Reluctant Art: The Growth of Jazz* (London: MacGibbon and Kee, 1962), 158. Similarly, Davis writes that "Holiday's genius was to give her life experiences an aesthetic form that recast them as windows through which other women could peer critically at their own lives" (*Blues Legacies*, 140; see also 194). Billie Holiday says as much about her own performances: "Unless I feel something, I can't sing. ... Give me a song I can feel, and it's never work" (Billie Holiday with William Duffy, *Lady Sings the Blues* (New York: Doubleday, 1956), 138). Given Duffy's role in the book, however, nothing in it can be taken as the actual words of Holiday: see Robert G. O'Meally, *Lady Day: The Many Faces of Billie Holiday* (New York: Arcade, 1991), 21.
52 Green, *Reluctant Art*, 156–157. Bicknell also emphasizes the ongoing tension between purely musical expression and the intelligibility of a song's words; "Songs," 441–442.
53 Peter Kivy, "How Did Mozart Do It?: Living Conditions in the World of Opera," *The Fine Art of Repetition: Essays in the Philosophy of Music* (Cambridge: Cambridge University Press, 1993), 160–177, at 174.
54 Green, *Reluctant Art*, 136–137, 154–158.
55 Nietzsche, *Birth of Tragedy* (1956), 23–24, emphasis added.
56 Nietzsche, *Birth of Tragedy* (1956), 27.
57 Levinson, "Jazz Vocal," 38.
58 Levinson, "Jazz Vocal," 35.
59 There is some question of whether Louis Armstrong was a competent sight reader of notation before his residency with Fletcher Henderson required it; for a famous anecdote of his lack of skill, see Gioia, *Imperfect Art*, 3.
60 E.g., both "My Funny Valentine" and Miles Davis's "All Blues" are recast in C major in *The Hal Leonard Real Jazz Standards Fake Book: C Edition*, 2nd ed. (Milwaukee: Hal Leonard, 2001), 362 and 560, respectively.
61 Green, *Reluctant Art*, 129.
62 Steve Sullivan, *Encyclopedia of Great Popular Song Recordings, Volume 1* (Lanham: Scarecrow, 2013), 280.
63 David Goldblatt, "Nonsense in Public Places: Songs of Black Vocal Rhythm and Blues or Doo-Wop," *Journal of Aesthetics and Art Criticism* 71:1 (2013): 101–110, at 106.
64 Levinson, "Jazz Vocal," 42.
65 Gene Lees, *Singers and the Song* (Oxford: Oxford University Press, 1987), 150.
66 Lees, *Singers*, 101
67 See Bicknell, *Philosophy of Song*, 43–47.
68 Levinson, "Jazz Vocal," 38.
69 Levinson, "Jazz Vocal," 36.
70 Green, *Reluctant Art*, 123.
71 Garry L. Hagberg, "Jazz Improvisation and Ethical Interaction: A Sketch of the Connections," in *Art and Ethical Criticism*, ed. Garry L. Hagberg (Malden, MA: Blackwell, 2008), 261–285, at 261.
72 The importance of this point is explained by Paul C. Taylor, *Black is Beautiful: A Philosophy of Black Aesthetics* (Malden, MA: Wiley Blackwell, 2016), chap. 6.
73 Quoted in Shipton, *New History*, 421.
74 Gene Santoro, *Highway 61 Revisited: The Tangled Roots of American Jazz, Blues, Rock, & Country Music* (Oxford: Oxford University Press, 2004), 11.
75 Shipton, *New History*, 421.
76 Shipton, *New History*, 419.
77 Shipton, *New History*, 422.
78 Santoro, *Highway 61*, 12.
79 Green, *Reluctant Art*, 156.

80 Green, *Reluctant Art*, 157.
81 Levinson, "Jazz Vocal," 36.
82 Will Friedwald, *Jazz Singing: America's Great Voices from Bessie Smith to Bebop and Beyond* (New York: Scribner's, 1990), 153.
83 Davis, *Blues Legacies*, 3.
84 Others have noted that emphasis on instrumental innovators at the expense of vocalists minimizes the contribution of women to jazz. For example, see Lara Pellegrinelli, "Separated at 'Birth': Singing and the History of Jazz," in *Big Ears: Listening for Gender in Jazz Studies*, ed. Nichole T. Rustin and Sherrie Tucker (Durham, NC: Duke University Press, 2008), 31–47.
85 Taylor, *Black is Beautiful*, 174.
86 Taylor, *Black is Beautiful*, 176.
87 Melanie E. Bratcher, *Words and Songs of Bessie Smith, Billie Holiday, and Nina Simone: Sound Motion, Blues Spirit, and African Memory* (New York: Routledge, 2007), 86; see also p. 55.
88 Davis, *Blues Legacies*, 167.
89 On "honorary" black singers, see Taylor, *Black is Beautiful*, 177.
90 Bratcher, *Words and Songs*, 57.
91 *What Happened, Miss Simone?*, directed by Liz Garbus, Netflix, 2015.
92 Jean-Paul Sartre, *What is Literature?*, trans. Steven Ungar (Cambridge, MA: Harvard University Press, 1988), 67.

References

Batteux, Charles. *The Fine Arts Reduced to a Single Principle*, trans. James O. Young. Oxford: Oxford University Press, 2015.
Bicknell, Jeanette. *A Philosophy of Song and Singing: An Introduction*. New York: Routledge, 2015.
Bicknell, Jeanette. "Song." In *The Routledge Companion to the Philosophy of Music*, ed. Theodore Gracyk and Andrew Kania, 437–445. New York: Routledge, 2011.
Bratcher, Melanie E. *Words and Songs of Bessie Smith, Billie Holiday, and Nina Simone: Sound Motion, Blues Spirit, and African Memory*. New York: Routledge, 2007.
Carvalho, John. "Improvisations, on Nietzsche, on Jazz." In *Nietzsche, Philosophy and the Arts*, ed. Salim Kemal, Ivan Gaskell, and Daniel W. Conway, 187–211. Cambridge: Cambridge University Press, 1998.
Cavin, Susan. "Missing Women: On the Voodoo Trail to Jazz." *Journal of Jazz Studies* 3:1 (1975): 6–27.
Collier, James Lincoln. *Jazz: The American Theme Song*. Oxford: Oxford University Press, 1993.
Crowther, Bruce, and Mike Pinfold. *Singing Jazz: The Singers and Their Styles*. London: Blandford, 1997.
D'Angour, Armand. "Music and Movement in the Dithyramb." In *Dithyramb in Context*, ed. Barbara Kowalzig and Peter Wilson, 198–209. Oxford: Oxford University Press, 2012.
Davies, Stephen. "The Expression Theory Again." *Theoria* 52:3 (1986): 146–167.
Davis, Angela Y. *Blues Legacies and Black Feminism: Gertrude "Ma" Rainey, Bessie Smith, and Billie Holiday*. New York: Random House, 1998.
Donald, James. *Some of These Days: Black Stars, Jazz Aesthetics, and Modernist Culture*. Oxford: Oxford University Press, 2015.
Duncan, John. "Sartre and Realism-All-the-Way-Down." *Sartre Studies International* 11:1–2 (2005): 91–113.

Freiberg, Edna B. *Bayou St. John in Colonial Louisiana, 1699–1803*. New Orleans: Harvey Press, 1980.

Friedwald, Will. *Jazz Singing: America's Great Voices from Bessie Smith to Bebop and Beyond*. New York: Scribner's, 1990.

Gide, André. *Journals 1914–1927*, trans. Justin O'Brien. Urbana: University of Illinois Press, 2000.

Gioia, Ted. *The History of Jazz*, 2nd ed. Oxford: Oxford University Press, 2011.

Gioia, Ted. *The Imperfect Art: Reflections on Jazz and Modern Culture*. Oxford: Oxford University Press, 1988.

Goldblatt, David. "Nonsense in Public Places: Songs of Black Vocal Rhythm and Blues or Doo-Wop." *Journal of Aesthetics and Art Criticism* 71:1 (2013): 101–110.

Gracyk, Theodore. "Fakin' It: Is There Authenticity in Commercial Music?" In *Aesthetics: A Reader in Philosophy of the Arts*, 4th ed., ed. David Goldblatt, Lee B. Brown, and Stephanie Patridge, 244–249. New York: Routledge, 2017.

Gracyk, Theodore. "The Song Remains the Same, But Not Always." In *Led Zeppelin and Philosophy*, ed. Scott Calef, 31–45. Chicago: Open Court, 2009.

Green, Benny. *The Reluctant Art: The Growth of Jazz*. London: MacGibbon and Kee, 1962.

Hagberg, Garry L. "Jazz Improvisation and Ethical Interaction: A Sketch of the Connections." In *Art and Ethical Criticism*, ed. Garry L. Hagberg, 261–285. Malden, MA: Blackwell. 2008.

The Hal Leonard Real Jazz Standards Fake Book: C Edition, 2nd ed. Milwaukee: Hal Leonard, 2001.

Holiday, Billie, with William Duffy. *Lady Sings the Blues*. New York: Doubleday, 1956.

Hurley, Andrew Wright. *The Return of Jazz: Joachim-Ernst Berendt and West German Cultural Change*. New York: Berghahn, 2009.

Jones, Stacy Linn Holman. *Torch Singing: Performing Resistance and Desire from Billie Holiday to Edith Piaf*. Lanham: Rowman & Littlefield, 2007.

King, Grace Elizabeth. *New Orleans; the Place and the People*. New York and London: Macmillan, 1896.

Kivy, Peter. "How Did Mozart Do It?: Living Conditions in the World of Opera." In *The Fine Art of Repetition: Essays in the Philosophy of Music*, 160–177. Cambridge: Cambridge University Press, 1993.

Kmen, Henry A. "The Roots of Jazz and the Dance in Place Congo: A Re-Appraisal." *Inter-American Musical Research Yearbook* 8 (1972): 5–16.

Kononenko, Natalie. "When Traditional Improvisation Is Prohibited: Contemporary Ukrainian Funeral Laments." In *Musical Improvisation: Art, Education, and Society*, ed. Gabriel Solis and Bruno Nettl, 52–71. Urbana: University of Illinois Press, 2009.

Lees, Gene. *Singers and the Song*. Oxford: Oxford University Press, 1987.

Levinson, Jerrold. "Jazz Vocal Interpretation: A Philosophical Analysis." *Journal of Aesthetics and Art Criticism* 71:1 (2013): 35–43.

Neill, Alex. "Art and Emotion." In *The Oxford Handbook of Aesthetics*, ed. Jerrold Levinson, 421–435. Oxford: Oxford University Press, 2003.

Nettl, Bruno. "Musical Values and Social Values: Symbols in Iran." *Asian Music* 12:1 (1980): 129–148.

Nietzsche, Friedrich Wilhelm. *On the Genealogy of Morals* and *Ecce Homo*, trans. Walter Kaufmann. New York: Random House, 1967.

Nietzsche, Friedrich Wilhelm. *The Birth of Tragedy* and *The Case of Wagner*, trans. Walter Kaufmann. New York: Random House, 1967.

Nietzsche, Friedrich Wilhelm. *The Birth of Tragedy* and *The Genealogy of Morals*, trans. Francis Golffing. New York: Random House, 1956.

O'Meally, Robert G. *Lady Day: The Many Faces of Billie Holiday*. New York: Arcade, 1991.

Pellegrinelli, Lara. 2008. "Separated at 'Birth': Singing and the History of Jazz." In *Big Ears: Listening for Gender in Jazz Studies*, ed. Nichole T. Rustin and Sherrie Tucker, 31–47. Durham, NC: Duke University Press, 2008.

Robinson, Jenefer. *Deeper than Reason: Emotion and its Role in Literature, Music, and Art*. Oxford: Clarendon Press, 2005.

Rouget, Gilbert. *Music and Trance: A Theory of the Relations Between Music and Possession*, trans. Brunhilde Biebuyck. Chicago: University of Chicago Press, 1985.

Salamone, Frank A. *The Culture of Jazz: Jazz as Critical Culture*. Lanham: University Press of America, 2009.

Santoro, Gene. *Highway 61 Revisited: The Tangled Roots of American Jazz, Blues, Rock, & Country Music*. Oxford: Oxford University Press, 2004.

Sartre, Jean-Paul. *La nausée*. Paris: Gallimard, 1938.

Sartre, Jean-Paul. *The Psychology of Imagination*, trans. Bernard Frechtman. New York: Philosophical Library, 1948.

Sartre, Jean-Paul. *What is Literature?*, trans. Steven Ungar. Cambridge, MA: Harvard University Press, 1988.

Shapiro, Nat, and Nat Hentoff. *Hear Me Talkin' to Ya: The Story of Jazz as Told by the Men Who Made It*. New York: Rinehart, 1955.

Shipton, Alyn. *A New History of Jazz*, rev. and updated ed. London: Bloomsbury, 2007.

Silk, M. S., and J. P. Stern. *Nietzsche on Tragedy*. Cambridge: Cambridge University Press, 1981.

Sullivan, Steve. *Encyclopedia of Great Popular Song Recordings*, vol. 1. Lanham: Scarecrow, 2013.

Szwed, John. *Billie Holiday: The Musician and the Myth*. New York: Penguin, 2015.

Taylor, Paul C. *Black is Beautiful: A Philosophy of Black Aesthetics*. Malden, MA: Wiley Blackwell, 2016.

Toop, David. *Into the Maelstrom: Music, Improvisation and the Dream of Freedom: Before 1970*. New York: Bloomsbury, 2016.

Williams, Marie B. "A Night with the Voudous." *Appleton's Journal* (March 27, 1875): 403–404.

Wright, Charles. *The Messenger*. New York: Farrar, Straus, & Co., 1963.

5

RACE, JAZZ, AND POPULAR MUSIC
The Legacy of Blackface Minstrelsy

She went over to the gramophone and picked up a disc. "Do you like jazz?" she said, changing the subject. "Oh, it's all right, it's not negro jazz. I love it, don't you?" Only non-negro jazz is permitted in Germany now, but I often wonder how they can tell the difference.

— *Philip Kerr*, March Violets, *The Berlin Noir Trilogy*

The station I turned to was playing an old number by the Paul Whiteman band, hot music made safely cool for the masses. It beats me how a guy with the name Whiteman ever got up the nerve to play jazz.

— *Benjamin Black*, The Black–Eyed Blonde

1. Appropriation and the Minstrel Hypothesis

When it comes to music, philosophers pay due attention to general considerations regarding the nature of certain sounds, live or recorded, or to the creation of those sounds, perhaps through inscribed notations, which surely constitute the data of their inquiries.

However, we take the view that it is also important to pay attention to those *persons* who create or perform music just as one might attend to painters of murals or directors of movies: persons who are part of the social fabric that forms the context of the arts in which they perform. Questions about the authenticity of social engagement have to be addressed, not merely questions about the authenticity of musical sound. For jazz, as with hockey or basketball, the numbers that signify obvious racial imbalances can lead us to ask questions spotlighting issues of origin, authenticity, ability, and even rights.

For example, when Jed Rasula says, "Jazz music *is* black history," the point of view is obvious.[1] Or, in André Hodeir's now classic *Jazz: Evolution and Essence*, writing in 1954 he says, "By now it has become evident that jazz is the Negro's art, and that all the great jazz musicians are Negroes."[2] This is the context that gave us Norman Mailer's 1957 essay for *Dissent*, "The White Negro." A shocker at the time, Mailer describes *hipsters*, a term he borrowed from Caroline Bird's recent "Born 1930: The Unlost Generation," an article in *Harper's Bazaar*.[3] Hipsters were whites who for decades had taken on black cultural traits, including language and dress, but especially music. For Mailer's generation, that music was jazz.[4] Mailer being Mailer says:

> For jazz is orgasm, it is the music of orgasm, good orgasm and bad, and so it spoke across a nation, it had the communication of art even where it was watered, perverted, corrupted, and almost killed, it spoke in no matter what laundered popular way of instantaneous existential states to which some whites could respond, it was indeed a communication by art because it said, "I feel this, and now you do too."[5]

Like many of his generation, Mailer proposes that jazz has an intrinsic power to communicate strong emotion. He also claims that the lived experience of African-Americans imparts it with an anti-authoritarian, existentialist philosophy, going well beyond the emotion of music into a style of living. Unlike many, Mailer here insists that both the emotion and the philosophy endure even in "watered," "laundered," and "popular" versions (that is, even following its appropriation and commercialization by whites). The implications of jazz, from its early forms onward, became embedded in both the music and the cultures of white and black America by its invitation to a newer, looser rhythm of life. Mailer's particular reading of jazz is not the primary point here. What he recognizes, rightly, is that disinterested aesthetic appreciation is largely a myth: aesthetic response to music is – and should be – informed by consideration of its social-historical context. With American music, that context is frequently racial.

Perhaps the strangest case of the aesthetic relevance of race in American music is black minstrelsy, itself a performance of race by whites persisting throughout a hundred years of a rapidly changing American culture. Unlike the hipster, who wanted in some sense to *be* black (or what he imagined being black was like) via the mechanisms of imitation, minstrelsy was parody and stereotyping, efficacious in its imagery of blacks in America. Its popularity was testament to its unconscious perpetuation of racial presentation through music. Minstrel shows were musical theater – the embedded music moved from plantations (or so it was claimed) and urban streets to the white and black stage. Although minstrelsy originated as a theatrical tradition by whites, for whites, minstrelsy by blacks morphed into general black theatre where thousands of black entertainers took on elements of minstrel shows and performed in clubs and auditoriums throughout the United States. "What distinguished minstrelsy," Elijah Wald observes, "was the blackface makeup and comic stage business more than any particular music, which is why the form was able to survive through a hundred years of shifting musical styles." Minstrel shows were more than their music and their music covered lots of territory, not simply the kind that we can think of as jazz.[6] These shows – music, singing, dancing, and talking – left an impression that was later posed on the long-running radio (then television) show *Amos 'n' Andy*, among others. In these disrespectful displays of African-Americans for the sake of comedy, audiences were made to feel superior to the simpleton characters portrayed. Sometimes, minstrelsy took an even more bizarre turn as African-Americans used burnt cork to blacken themselves, with lips painted red or white, looking like whites in blackface who were attempting to look like them. African-Americans performing in blackface was a case of blacks imitating whites imitating black stereotypes for white audiences. The result was a disastrous perpetuation of white racism against African-Americans by the performance of African-Americans. Perhaps only Michael Jackson's "whiteface" is comparable in its odd racial overtones.

Blackface entertainment raises the issue of imitation and origin in American music generally: that whites "took" black music and made it their own: that music that is somehow essentially black was co-opted by whites.[7] It was imitation, which leads us to a jazz hypothesis worth considering, one we will call the minstrel hypothesis: that American white popular music is pervasively indebted to minstrel theater and thereby perpetuates racism. As Robert Christgau puts it, minstrelsy "tells a story about the white-from-black 'appropriation' not just of minstrelsy but of all American popular music."[8] This relatively new line of interpretation was articulated by Eric Lott in a 1992 essay and then immediately expanded into the book *Love and Theft: Blackface Minstrelsy and the American Working Class*.[9] The minstrel hypothesis claims that the influence of minstrelsy is so pervasive that it serves as the model of the "white Imaginary" that informs "popular white racial feeling in the United States."[10] To some extent, "its legacy is all around us."[11] Again, it must be stressed that minstrel shows were primarily music-focused theater shows, with music that borrowed from (and often purported to be authentic presentations of) African-American music. For Lott, minstrelsy informs all subsequent appropriation in popular music by providing an "articulation of racial difference" that combines "cross-racial desire" with "a self-protective derision with respect to black people and their cultural practices."[12] In short, the enduring cultural pattern of white expropriation of African-American culture encodes a particular form of racial consciousness. Here we would be remiss not to mention the recent fraternity blackface Halloween scandals disseminated through social media.[13] In the wake of minstrelsy, white appropriation is never politically innocent. Because jazz arose in a culture of entertainment where white appropriations of black music were routinely accompanied by a fantasy "blackness," elements of minstrelsy entered jazz, and did so from the start, with the clowning and faked primitivism of The Original Dixieland Jazz Band. However, as we argued in Chapter 1, we should be aware as well that the pioneering African-American jazz musicians were frequently entertainers, not just musicians, and also that many of the jazz greats, like Louis Armstrong, played lots of kinds of music for different kinds of occasions, not just the jazz for which they are primarily known.

The question, then, is how to apply the minstrel hypothesis to jazz. Unfortunately, we see a tendency to use it to paint all American popular music with a single broad brush: white participation in the jazz tradition is always controversial. But we are skeptical of a "one size fits all" approach and intend to sketch an interpretive framework that requires us to examine, case by case, whether this or that particular borrowing is tainted.

2. Innovation and Imitation in Jazz Vocals

The minstrel hypothesis will be our point of departure for a number of issues and insights into a period of jazz in which a white Bing Crosby and a black Louis Armstrong played important roles. It might seem odd to bring together two such different American vocal icons as Armstrong and Crosby. Crosby's voice was best known as he sounded later in his career – a velvety crooning baritone heard every year on his recording of Irving Berlin's "White Christmas." Listeners who came to know Crosby through his film appearances and his later recordings will generally hear no trace of blackness in his singing. However, he was an important early figure among jazz vocalists. His early, less well-known sound on his classic recordings was lighter in timbre, higher in range, and more agile. Armstrong's voice, particularly as he aged, sounded more and more like a cement mixer tossing gravel. His younger voice, though, was lighter, often quite beautiful, and also more agile. In spite of the obvious differences between the pair in maturity, they were born only two years apart at the beginning of the twentieth century, and their performances in the late '20s and early '30s betray strikingly common features. Crosby, with his musical partner Al Rinker, was cutting his second record, "Wistful and Blue," with Paul Whiteman in Chicago, in 1926 when he first heard Armstrong playing with King Oliver's band at the Sunset Cafe.

F. Scott Fitzgerald's *Tales of the Jazz Age* (1922) indelibly associated one decade with jazz, but it is important to remember that the musical category was understood quite broadly. It included any recent popular dance music performed by an orchestra with a prominent horn section. At that point, the featured instrumental solo was still several years away from emerging as an aesthetic focal point of the dawning instrumental jazz. There was not yet a distinctive jazz vocal style. The situation was different at the decade's end, thanks to Armstrong and Crosby – the two main sources of inspiration for decades of American popular male vocal art.[14]

Zealous historians are always in the wings to refute claims of "firsts" in popular music. But few would now disagree that Armstrong's rhythmic inflections established much of the foundation, not only of jazz, but consequently of the popular music that fed on it.[15] To sum it up, Armstrong taught the world the meaning of *swing*. His vocal performances were an extension of his horn playing, as is famously illustrated by his riveting 1928 vocalese on the recording of "West End Blues." Armstrong is the one customarily credited for the wordless improvising known as "scat," supposedly invented when he lost track of the words to "Heebie Jeebies" in 1926. Crosby, singing with the Rhythm Boys, was also known for his scatting. As we noted in Chapter 4, Armstrong was not the first,[16] but he certainly opened the floodgate of "wordless" lyrics constructed of nonsense syllables: we have The Beatles' joyous full verse of repeated "Sha la la la la la la la" in their early cover of "Baby It's You," the menacing full chorus of repeated "la-la-la" in Iggy Pop's "The Passenger," Clare Torry's wordless vocal obbligato for Pink Floyd's "The Great Gig in the Sky," and The Police's goofy hit "De Do Do Do, De Da Da Da." And then there is doo–wop, where non–improvised nonsense sounds provided the musical engine *backing* the lead. But scat is *improvised* "nonsense." Scatting is difficult to do. It is not simply the repetition of some melodic nonsense sounds. It is rather the improvised creation of a multiple set of sounds that could well be language from another planet. The occasional wordless vocalizing in pop hits almost never rises to the level of genuine scatting.

What interested Armstrong and Crosby were various ways of manipulating a musical line rhythmically. As we noted in Chapter 2, some twenty measures of the solo Louis Armstrong plays on the Hot Five recording of "Muggles" either orbit around or play nothing but the tone C. The only inflections we hear are those of the beat. Heard as mere melody, one can hardly get the point of the effort. Heard as swinging music, the solo is enthralling. Put otherwise, a soloist's musical line will be felt as moving independently of the underlying pulse and then, strategically, as being recaptured by it. What is felt is a need to reconcile partly synchronous, partly asynchronous rhythmic lines.

Among Crosby's specialties was the strategy of holding notes at the end of a line in order to play with time, as on his 1928 recording of "'Taint so, Honey, 'Taint So."[17] Another device he used for breaking up time – so essential to jazz inflection – was the use of little trills or grace notes. The year 1932, when he recorded "Sweet Georgia Brown," "Some of These Days," and (with Duke Ellington) "St. Louis Blues," was the high point of Crosby's early career.[18] His influence was vast. Even black jazz singers, like Billy Eckstine, Johnny Hartman, and Ellington's vocalist Herb Jeffries, would be unimaginable without Crosby's conversational approach. Frank Sinatra and Tony Bennett both modeled their singing on Crosby, and strong echoes can be heard in "Love Me Tender" and other ballads that Elvis Presley sang along with his country rock.[19]

A second factor in the new vocal revolution is easy to overlook since it is a function of the medium by which popular singing was produced after 1925. Before that time, a male vocalist recording on primitive so-called "acoustic" technology, the megaphone for example, tended to shout, as if trying to force his voice through the recording horn up to a balcony of an imaginary theater from which he could project himself heroically. With Crosby, all this changed. He saw the potential of the microphone, made possible by the new electrical amplification. The breakthrough would forever after affect our perception of the human voice. Henceforth, singers could be heard from a literal or figurative distance and yet be intimate, conversational, and rife with subtleties. No one understood this better than Crosby. Armstrong and others quickly exploited the secret.

By the mid '30s, both Crosby and Armstrong were recording for (American) Decca's infamous Jack Kapp, whose anti-jazz philistinism had them recording, along with some good releases, an annoying mix of everything from hillbilly to Hawaiian to hymns, often accompanied by sickly sweet choirs. Crosby later returned occasionally to his jazz roots. Armstrong – who became known during the Cold War as America's "musical ambassador" – always kept his jazz chops reasonably well honed and left us with vocal recordings that have become classics, including his vocal duets with Ella Fitzgerald in the late 1950s.

According to a widely accepted narrative about the bearing of race on popular culture, no one should be surprised to learn that Crosby's style borrowed from black sources as white America has routinely appropriated black culture on a massive scale, particularly in popular music.[20] Black musical styles have been continually caught in an enormous whirlpool, sucked down into white repositories, repackaged there, and then piped out again, for profit, of course – or so goes the claim. The surprise, if there is one, is that the process has been going on for so long. Lott argues that "the heedless ... appropriation of 'black' culture by whites" originated in the minstrel shows of the 1840s, and it "was little more than cultural robbery, a form of what Karl Marx called expropriation."[21] Anyone who tends to agree would be likely to conclude in advance that – given any stylistic interplay between our two icons – the white man, Crosby, must have been the one who appropriated his style from the other, that is, from Armstrong, the black man. "Afro-America makes, Euro-America takes," in Christgua's pithy summary.[22]

However, what we know about the interaction of Crosby and Armstrong challenges this picture of one-way raids by whites of black material.[23] There's no doubt from Crosby's singing that he had listened to Armstrong. And he obviously applied the scat technique that he learned from Armstrong's recordings. Crosby could not have been possible without Armstrong. However, Crosby thoroughly personalized what he acquired. More importantly, the influence and personalization ran both ways. For instance, Crosby was ahead of Armstrong in applying the vocabulary and rhythm of jazz to commercial Tin Pan Alley music. But Armstrong soon followed suit. An Armstrong recording that reflects Crosby's influence is his 1930 version of "I'm Confessin'," which features Crosby-ish trills and extended line endings, along with Armstrong's characteristic phrase repetitions and interjections. Armstrong's 1932 recording of "Stardust" includes verbalized add-ons to the lyric, very much in Crosby style.[24]

So, if we say that Bing Crosby identified with Louis Armstrong – or was at least strongly influenced by him – do we not have to grant that the relationship also runs the other way? The general point is that, if the Armstrong–Crosby relationship is more than a rare exception, the supposed one-way drain by whites of black resources is more complicated than typically assumed nowadays. In the American context, it requires us to face the question of whether there could be *American* culture if it were genuinely the case that white and black cultures were unambiguously distinct. Could we speak of jazz as *American music* if mainstream popular music is unmitigated cultural robbery from the African-American minority, other than by granting that American music is a racist project? The intellectual cost of this idea is frequently associated with some form of racial and cultural essentialism. However, Lott's version of the minstrel hypothesis sidesteps essentialism by emphasizing that race is a complex social construct. Contextualized in this way, the minstrel hypothesis challenges the idea that recognition of mutual influences between black and white jazz musicians validates some of the cultural exchange and mitigates the charge of cultural robbery.

3. Minstrel History and Theory

Although remnants of blackface theatre could be found well into the twentieth century, it is hard to believe that at one time it was the most popular entertainment available to American audiences. Mark Twain and Abraham Lincoln loved it. According to legend, the earliest white man to perform in blackface was Thomas D. ("Daddy") Rice. In 1830, or thereabouts, Rice noticed a black laborer dubbed "Cuff" (by some accounts, a stevedore, by others a stable hand) who was known for a curious dance he would now and then break into. On one occasion, so the story goes, Rice grabbed Cuff's clothing more or less off his back, jumped onto a local stage, and did a caricature of the dance, accompanied by the song that later became a synonym for racism, namely, "Jump Jim Crow."[25]

A typical minstrel show was quite complex in form, and combined music, dance, joke-telling, and theatrical skits.[26] Besides the obvious black face that white people put on in minstrel theatre with the help of burnt cork, the tropes of the genre include stylizations or parodies of black music, dance, speech, and character.

Actual blackface theatre was already in decline toward the end of the nineteenth century, but here and there it survived much later. One well-documented tradition survived in the foothills of the Adirondacks well into the 1950s.[27] For example, the American Federation of Labor, the AFL, regularly performed minstrel entertainment at its conventions throughout World War II while largely excluding blacks from its membership.

In his influential work, Lott organizes perspectives on minstrelsy into three types, more or less succeeding each other historically.[28] The first approach, which Lott terms *populist*, treats the minstrel tradition as a "public forum for slave culture that might have liberating effects." He cites anthropologists such as Franz Boas and Ruth Benedict, as well as the poet Walt Whitman, holding this kind of view. Illustrating a second approach – which Lott terms *revisionism* – are writers such as

Ralph Ellison, Amiri Baraka (aka LeRoi Jones), and Nathan Huggins.[29] By comparison with populism, revisionism was harsh in its judgments about minstrelsy. Many of us nowadays probably share some version of revisionism. Anticipations of it, however, could be found as long ago as the first half of the nineteenth century. In 1848, Frederick Douglass scornfully branded blackface minstrels as "the filthy scum of white society, who have stolen from us a complexion denied to them by nature."[30] This should remind us that in the years when blackface theatre was most popular, slavery was still an American fact of life in Southern states. As one historian put the matter, for a "half-century" these entertainments represented "inurement to the uses of white supremacy."[31]

Lott rightly observes that revisionism, based too much on what he calls "the essential black subject," is simplistically idealistic. He defends a third approach, which pop music guru Robert Christgau dubs *postmodernist*.[32] It is mainly from this perspective that the minstrel hypothesis has been propounded.

Postmodernism is recognizable by the stress it puts on the density of conceptual meanings and on the highly contextualized, socially constructed, even unconscious, pressures that impinge upon our concepts and practices. Thus, Lott describes the blackface mask as "a distorted mirror, reflecting displacements and condensations and discontinuities between which and the social field there exist lags, unevennesses, multiple determinations."[33] Postmodernist theory takes pains to show how minstrel masks often conceal other masks, which can even contain messages at odds with surface significations. For our purposes, it is significant that the postmodernist interpretation is being applied to cultural forms that predate the rise of postmodern society (which is usually recognized as arising in industrialized nations in the latter half of the twentieth century). Cultural bastardization and contradictory messages did not suddenly arise in late capitalism, but can be expected to arise wherever we find exchanges between dominant and subordinate groups. The United States Supreme Court did not turn to postmodern theory to justify their conclusion that the rap group 2 Live Crew made fair use of Roy Orbison's song "Oh, Pretty Woman" by constructing a parody version; in the processes of encoding meanings, African-American appropriations are not inherently different from white appropriations.[34] In one case, *Billboard* reviews a 1934 performance by the black Washboard Serenaders, an instrumental novelty and comedy act at the Loew's State Theater in New York City:

> The thing that gets the boys over is their terrific energy. They pound out the queer hotcha 'music' and then pep it up with occasional warbling and comedy bits at the mike. One boy stands out with a comedy impersonation of Crosby (Bing). Stopped the show here and encored with a hot 'St. Louis Blues.'[35]

In fact, such inversions of meaning were recognized by audiences before recent theorizing. For example, mixed with the condescending white representations of black people in minstrel theatre, one could find coded mockery. A typical segment of a minstrel show was a conversation between an "interlocutor" and two "end men," usually named "Bones" and "Tambo" because of the instruments they played. In this interplay, the apparently uncomprehending responses of the end men were easily seen to be making fun of the interlocutor's pompous English. These semiotic twists and turns could be surprising. W. T. Lhamon argues that early American minstrel theatre inherited a form of solidarity among poor people, black *and* white, a phenomenon he traces back to the activities documented in the Catherine Market of New York City's seventh ward. There he discerns what he terms a "mingling of disdained equals."[36]

A postmodernist view of minstrelsy makes it easier, perhaps, to discern the phenomenon of contradictory messages in unsuspected forms and places. We might be somewhat more willing to admit, of a Rolling Stones concert, that it contains vestiges of blackface minstrelsy.[37] However, among its adherents the hypothesis has taken on the trappings of uninformative dogma. According to criteria used in key applications of the minstrel hypothesis to pop music, the minstrel connection is taken for granted and applied in the absence of any particular historical connection between recent actions and the minstrel era. For example, Lhamon accuses white rappers like Vanilla Ice of trying "to haul back from beyond the pale some of that fancied black energy that Cool White, one of the earliest minstrel performers, was after over a hundred and fifty years ago."[38] Although Lhamon does not explicitly universalize the example, the context suggests that this is his intention. But this move begs the question: if the energy is merely "fancied" (and so in the mind of the appropriating white rapper), what is the actual connection back to Cool White (as opposed to models close at hand, historically and geographically)? But the minstrel hypothesis denies that we need to make the connection because, as Barry Shank puts it, "there is no escaping the legacy of blackface minstrelsy in [American] popular music."[39]

The question, then, is how, according to the minstrel hypothesis, *all* of American popular music came to find itself in anything like this plight? After all, given generally shared criteria of minstrelsy, to be told that American pop music is soaked in it is, well, a bit shocking. Elvis Presley's best-selling single "It's Now or Never" is clearly an appropriation of the nineteenth-century Neapolitan song "O Sole Mio." The Weavers' bestselling "Wimoweh" and The Tokens' reworking, "The Lion Sleeps Tonight," were very close copies of an African (not African-American) song, "Mbube." Appropriations, certainly, but minstrelsy? Perhaps an analogy might help. Perhaps minstrelsy permeates the social fabric the way carbon monoxide can permeate the atmosphere without being recognized as such. As Lott suggests, "Every time you hear an expansive white man drop into his version of black English, you are in the presence of blackface's unconscious return."[40] But the hypothesis does not have to depend only upon pointedly racist illustrations. Minstrelsy was, above all, a form of imitation. But so is American white culture in general, from the dreadlocks of the skateboard subculture to the apotheosis of Texas cuisine, barbecue. Is the analogy with carbon monoxide compelling? Maybe, maybe not.

In the carbon monoxide case, we would obviously have something like what Lott, speaking of minstrelsy, terms "unevennesses." Carbon monoxide might be lurking dangerously in *this* apartment building, but not necessarily all over town, and not necessarily for years to come. There exists such a thing as an American "gun culture." However, it by no means thrives everywhere in the same strength. Indeed, it is scorned in many quarters. Why should the same not be true of minstrelsy? Little more than a half-century ago, people were apparently unfazed by the fact that customers of the Coon Chicken Inn restaurants in Salt Lake City and Seattle would enter through the mouth of an enormous black face, grinning in minstrel style. Nowadays, such an image would be regarded as outrageous.[41]

But our topic here is not culture in general, but jazz and American popular music. As already hinted, to address the minstrel hypothesis about that matter, minstrel theorists suggest we need another piece of theory, namely, a hypothesis that supplements appropriation with *identification*.

4. Identification

No doubt, the skills of blackface entertainers in minstrel theatre reached very high levels, and were often appreciated as such. Current theorizing, however, goes further and claims to discern in minstrel art a white impulse to *identify* with the cultural "other." Reflecting an assumed white admiration of superior black athleticism, musicality, and sexuality, John Strausbaugh describes a phenomenon he refers to as "displaying blackness."[42] It helps here to realize that the artists in many minstrel troupes were actually black, not white. In such a context, black negritude was on display literally, not merely in proxy form. Note also that the focus in the theory is on the presumed fixation on blacks by the white *male*. Lott cites the early fascination with the minstrel dandy known as "Long Tail Blue," who, Lott suggests, represents the white man's obsession with the "rampageous black penis."[43] The image of Zip Coon was another example of the type.

This focus on men, it seems clear, derives from the influence of the psycho-analytic tradition, with its fixation on men and their supposed sexually rooted anxieties. However, it is also true that with some exceptions, the artists in actual blackface theatre were men. The appearance in the twentieth century of women, like Judy Garland, on the screen in blackface is presumably a meaningful but adapted comic phenomenon. The foregoing may help explain how rarely female jazz and pop vocalists are the focus of trendy minstrel studies. The theoretical sources about the theme of male identification are often dense, and are made more so by batteries of further perspectives that are typically invoked to support them.

Suppose we focus on one reasonably tractable version of the view, namely, that offered by Shank in which a thesis about Bob Dylan's identification with black musicians is the centerpiece.[44] Let us pause to say that Shank's essay is full of brilliant aperçus about both his subject and the period. Indeed, it is stunningly imaginative. And there, perhaps, lies a problem – as shall be explained in due course.

Shank begins with the simple thought that Dylan was influenced early in his career by black musicians such as Little Richard and Blind Lemon Jefferson.[45] However, he quickly converts this fact into a striking generality, namely, that "personal transformation, whereby a young white male attempts to remake himself through performing black music, is the *classic trope* of the great American tradition of blackface minstrelsy."[46] The thrust of this bold statement would seem to be that the *essence* of minstrelsy is identification with black people – in particular, of white men with black men.

Now, first, one might suggest that a little healthy skepticism about the concept of *identification* might be appropriate. The concept is a modern one with roots in the fuzzy realm of psychoanalytic theory. Although it has slipped into casual everyday usage, it is worth asking, particularly when the concept is employed now as part of what is in effect a sociological theory, by what criteria we might recognize it. There may be a difference between a white musician identifying with a black musician and simply borrowing tricks of the trade from him. But what marks the difference?

Suppose, however, we just grant that there exists a widespread white impulse to identify with black people – as if Mailer's hipster can be made into a general phenomenon. Even then, the bare, abstract concept of identification with black men could not tell us everything we need to know about minstrelsy in order to understand how the theory works. The ideal candidate for identification would be Huckleberry Finn (*vis à vis* Jim, the runaway slave), in Mark Twain's novel. But is this really a *blackface minstrel* story?

In other words, without deploying at least some markers of minstrelsy other than abstract identification, this central concept cannot do any real work. Unfortunately, Shank does not make it easy to flesh out the concept in any useful way. Dylan, he says, sought a "union through an imaginary identification with that culture – *through blackface*."[47] To say that identification is sought *through* blackface gives the impression that the latter is explaining the former. But if the basic claim really is that *identification* is what minstrelsy centrally is, then the *explanans* adds nothing.[48]

5. Expansion of the Minstrel Hypothesis

Readers who bear in mind typical markers of blackface might be struck by how little the standard negative features of minstrelsy make themselves felt in these postmodernist treatments. Black features as typically imagined through minstrelsy are coins with two sides, after all. On the one side we find sketches of the potently energetic kind of black male figure of which Lott speaks. On the other side are painted the familiar demeaning images of stupid people, replete with rolling eyeballs and a shuffling gait. In fact, though, Shank tells little about the imagined features portrayed on either side of the coin. What then does he give us?

Shank makes fleeting references to the concept of a *mask*, in a mainly figurative sense.[49] He states clearly that his analysis has nothing to do with the fact that

Dylan, in the mid-1990s, made recordings featuring minstrel songs.[50] What then about the stylistic features of Dylan's voice, which obviously don't derive from his Minnesota background? (Dylan pointedly slurs words and scoops into notes rather than landing on their center.) However, Shank is not interested in working this data into a marker of minstrelsy. In fact, he makes it difficult to do so by noting that Dylan was also "entranced" by the singing of Woody Guthrie – indeed, by much of the material on the Folkways multi-album collection *The Anthology of American Folk*. Dylan's white sources, according to Shank himself, include Hank Williams, the Stoneman Family, Elvis Presley, and Gid Tanner and the Skillet Lickers.[51] Thus, it might be difficult to decide whether Dylan's style is black or something more general – something generally Southern and rural, so to say, but his presentation to mostly white, young audiences, certainly appeared as something quite different: folk perhaps, but leaving behind its black roots. Dylan imitates (and pokes fun at) audience understanding of his early performance persona in a line on his 1962 debut album: "You sound like a hillbilly. We want folk singers here."

However, Shank does want to connect one feature of Dylan's voice to minstrelsy, namely, the way he shifts the pitch of his voice up from that of his formative influences, e.g., Little Richard. Citing a theory worked up by Ronald Radano, Shank claims that this shift is a blackface minstrel characteristic reflecting a "white urge to supplement the losses believed to have been induced by civilization into the purity and wholeness of black music."[52] What this means or why it is a mark of minstrelsy is, alas, just not clear.

So far, then, what Shank gives us for enriching the concept of minstrelsy is marginal, obscure, or unconvincing. Beyond that, we have commentaries on two Dylan recorded performances. The text to Dylan's recorded song "Subterranean Homesick Blues" is a stew of allusions to politics, police, civil rights, the drug scene, and the contrast between straight and "beat" life styles. However, Shank obscurely focuses on its stomping bass line and wailing harmonica. These elements "render explicit," he claims, "the power of blackface minstrelsy."[53] The rhythmic treatment and the timbre may indeed have black origins, but what tips off Shank that they have been channeled through minstrelsy – unless the assumption is that *any* music betraying black roots is blackface? Or should we read the claim as an idiosyncratic stipulative redefinition of the term "blackface?"

On the surface, the song "Like a Rolling Stone" addresses a privileged young woman now living on the streets who is therefore (unhappily) free of her illusions. As Shank reads the song, however, Dylan is actually addressing *himself* agonizing over "the painful contradictions" he feels about "late-modern America" and "the simultaneous incorporation and denial of blackness that is the minstrelsy of rock."[54]

Dylan is, after all, a Nobel prizewinning poet, with all rights and privileges that a poet can reasonably claim. However, you get chaos when you try to hitch poetic figures of speech to factual theses about how minstrelsy – its actual tradition, that is – plays out its historical line in American popular music.

In fact, though, it may be that neither Shank's readings of these songs *nor* his thesis about minstrelsy and popular music are intended to say anything about any matters of fact. Buried in a footnote, Shank casually remarks that he is, in this essay, "working with a less literal understanding of Dylan's relationship with blackface."[55]

None of this would matter were it not that Shank, like other contemporary theorists, is determined to apply his analysis of Dylan to popular music in general. As he puts it, to say that Dylan is in the minstrel tradition is "equivalent simply to saying that Dylan was making American music."[56] Now it would be hard to blame a reader for not taking this remarkable statement as making reference to generally shared criteria of the concept of *blackface minstrelsy*. Read this way, though, counterexamples tumble out. Consider, for instance, the popular '50s singer, Julius La Rosa, who favored Italianesque songs like "Eh, Cumpari." Defenders of the hypothesis might sneer at this singer as having no serious cultural significance. But in the present argument, such cases cannot be discounted. After all, La Rosa was as American as pizza pie (as it would have been called in those days). What about Tejano music of central and south Texas, with its marriage of Mexican music with the music of Czech and German settlers? And what of the strong tradition of Polka music in the American Midwest? We may sneer at Lawrence Welk and the "Pennsylvania Polka," but no one has ever accused Welk of perpetuating minstrelsy. However, there may be no point in testing Shank's claim about American popular music in general with the help of counterexamples. After all, citing cases for or against a theory that has only a figurative status seems idle. But so too would be bringing a merely figurative story to bear on a question about minstrelsy's actual historical record.

But perhaps we can extract a reasonable point from Shank's thesis. Grant again for the sake of argument the tendency of many well-meaning white people to identify with the plight of black people. Is this identification doomed to failure just because the white person will never get it – that is, get what it is like to be black in America, if there is one thing to being black in America? Perhaps. However, this flaw would affect only those cases of *white* musicians who have such an agenda. As already noted, there are countless cases to the contrary. Worse yet is that Shank provides the means for undermining his own generalization. The identification that serves as the cornerstone of his analysis is specific to white investment in the civil rights movement. As completed, his idea runs as follows: The leftist white movement of the civil rights era displaced its sense of *political solidarity* "onto black culture" and then reabsorbed "the possibility of the union through an imaginary identification with that culture" (through blackface, of course).[57] In short, Dylan's early career was, on Shank's own terms, a fairly special case, contextualized as it was by his specific interests and the civil rights era.

As an account of Dylan and his early career, Shank's picture might be true. From within the culture of the civil rights movement, Dylan might indeed have come to believe that he felt a special solidarity with black people. It is explicit in songs like "The Lonesome Death of Hattie Carroll," "The Death of Emmett Till," and "Oxford Town."[58] However, the historical point of Shank's examination of Dylan, as contextualized, can be encapsulated in a far more direct, less theory-laden way. Consider, for instance, the song, "Folk Singer's Blues," as composed and sung by Shel Silverstein. In it, Silverstein tries to imagine himself toting cotton bales on the levee, working on a chain gang, or swinging twelve-pound hammers. But reality punctures the fantasy:

> What do you do if you're young and white and Jewish?
> And the only levee you know is
> the Levy who lives on the block?

Silverstein is referencing roughly the same social context that frames the early Bob Dylan. No doubt, as the civil rights movement was beginning to make a dent in America's complacency, mid-twentieth-century white singers could very easily have regarded themselves as standing in some imagined solidarity with black people.[59] The humor of Silverstein's song does not reflect recognition of some supposed universal American condition, let alone one deriving from minstrel theatre. It arises from the acknowledgment of the naïveté of the sentiment, at that specific time, when a particular genre of pop music was in vogue. To generalize then, even if Shank's analysis of Dylan's early career is apt, to project the peculiarities of that time and those musicians onto the entire history of American popular music is implausible.

6. Minstrel Theatre: The Other Tradition

William Henry Lane, aka Master Juba (ca. 1825–ca. 1852), traveled as far as London with a minstrel group, the Ethiopian Serenaders, part of a tradition parallel to white minstrel theatre, featuring entertainments of the same kind – but practiced by *black* people who, in an imitation of an imitation, also blacked their faces.[60] Frederick Douglass acknowledged minstrelsy by black people in a curiously positive statement. It is "something gained," he wrote, "when the colored man in any form can appear before a white audience."[61] However, having gone to see Gavitt's Original Ethiopian Serenaders, his attitude took a different turn. "Douglass watched the spectacle with dismay and made a gloomy conclusion: 'they will make themselves ridiculous wherever they go.'"[62]

Whether specific popular American musicians might have been influenced specifically by this tradition is not always easy to tell. Black American singers have often exploited minstrel tropes, whatever their source. Recall Fats Waller's dialect-tinged song "Your Feets Too Big," with its pointedly pedantic English ("your pedal extremities are colossal"), which surely harks back to the pomposity of the interlocutor's exchanges with the end men in standard minstrel skits. The idea that latter day black musicians in some degree imitated this parallel tradition makes some kind of sense on the assumption that black artistry might be regarded, rightly or wrongly, as somehow closer to "the real thing." However weak such a case might be made about Fats Waller, Wynton Marsalis suggests that he can cite a case that can be traced back to *black* blackface minstrelsy.

The title track of Marsalis's album, *Plantation to the Penitentiary*, sung by Jennifer Sanon, includes these lines: "From the plantation to the penitentiary / from the yassuh boss to the ghetto minstrelsy." As Marsalis explains the text, it appears to suggest a link between modern male black ghetto youth culture and the "Tomin' and Jessin'" of minstrel shows and then to use this link in a polemic against gangsta rap.[63] In his commentary, Marsalis addresses these rappers in the following terms:

> You might be callin' yourself a nigger for some money [and] calling your woman a bitch shufflin'. You got the gold grill, but you're just Uncle Tomin' … [From] Stepin' Fetchit to Flavor Flav, it's the same. From Zip Coon to the guy from the ghetto who's going to threaten you.[64]

As Marsalis makes clear by his tacit reference to William Henry Lane, the tradition he has in mind is minstrel theatre as played by black people. As we stressed at the outset of this chapter, the accusation of minstrelsy may turn largely on non-musical factors. Now, in this context, there are two ways of thinking about cases like that of Flavor Flav. Until he provided the vocal on Public Enemy's 1990 rap hit "911 is a Joke," Flavor Flav was mainly known as the group's comic foil, and for his goofy visual identity, which included oversized hats and sunglasses and clocks worn as pendants.

On the one hand, one might reflect on the roots of this musician's behavior. Is it not reasonable that rappers like him acquired their style from some earlier source? (Recall Strausbaugh's concept of *presenting blackness*.) Certainly. But we would be skating out onto thin ice if we were to insist that this pattern of dress and behavior had been learned from some version of the minstrel tradition. However, Marsalis adopts a very different way of thinking about the matter from the accounts discussed earlier and he has no interest in searching out a historical source of the stance adopted by musicians like Flavor Flav.

Warming to his theme, Marsalis makes it clear that he is concerned with the way that black musicians present themselves to the dominant culture. He analogizes white gangsta rap fans with safari seekers: "'Wow, that was a real lion we saw on safari.' You know, it's like 'Let's go in the ghetto and see what the natives are doing.'" He caps off his polemic by recalling an ad for an early popular *black* blackface minstrel show, which read, "Real Coons from the Real Plantation."[65] The cynical message in the ancient promo is "why go for the fake stuff (*white* minstrelsy) when you can have the real thing?" Marsalis undoubtedly assumes that the "real" here is phony and that alternative representations of black life before emancipation would tell quite a different story about it.[66]

The efficacy of alternative representation, however, is a function of the receptivity of the audience. One African-American attempt to counter the tide of negative stereotyping by minstrel theater was Duke Ellington's all-black musical revue *Jump for Joy*, which opened in July of 1941 in Los Angeles and ran for 122 performances. The review was funded in part and otherwise supported by whites as well as blacks and included a cast of Dorothy Dandridge and Big Joe Turner. The musical comedy attempted to upend "every demeaning Hollywood stereotype of African Americans and lampooned Jim Crow and other relics of white racism."[67] But when it tried to perform songs such as "I've Got a Passport from Georgia," "I'm Sailing for the U. S. A.," and "Uncle Tom's Cabin is a Drive-In Now," it was met with death threats and violence and those particular songs were removed. The show never made it to Broadway.

However, the important point here is that Marsalis's polemic has nothing to do with a thesis about the genesis or historical root of rap music behavior. *A fortiori*, he avoids the overreach of claiming that *all* American popular music, black or white, remains rooted in minstrelsy, or even that it is rooted in the general phenomenon of "presenting blackness." So, in what sense does Marsalis think Flavor Flav presents a species of latter day black minstrelsy? In fact, in no sense. He is simply moralizing on the basis of an analogy: the old time black minstrel theater gave people a phony, offensive picture of black life. If it would be reasonable to object to that, why would you not feel the same way about your gangsta rap as likewise presenting a phony, offensive picture of black life?[68] Where the minstrel hypothesis assumes that minstrelsy confers an indelible illocutionary force on all American music, Marsalis's concern is the tendency of ill-chosen stage presentation and lyrics to generate undesirable perlocutionary effects in audience reception.[69] And Marsalis would seem to be right: the persistent racism within American society is itself sufficient to generate an unintended minstrelsy effect in African-American performance whenever the stage persona plays into racist conceptions of black culture and behavior.

Given his lack of interest in the genesis of the music to which he objects, proponents of the minstrel hypothesis will consider Marsalis's response to be superficial. They might be right. However, it can be said in his favor that Marsalis's ruminations do at least avoid the kind of freewheeling speculations and non-literal interpretations that typify defenses of the minstrel hypothesis. One might quarrel with Marsalis's analogy between rap music and minstrelsy and with his amusing but rather sour use of it. But it is at least clear what his point is.

7. Armstrong and Crosby: Their Obvious Debt to Minstrelsy

Early in the twentieth century – and for several decades on – popular white singers such as Al Jolson and Eddie Cantor routinely performed in blackface. Consider the crucial year of 1927. Armstrong's Hot Five recordings had met with commercial success and in May 1927, he organized the Hot Seven sessions, resulting in his "two most compelling" recorded solos to that date.[70] A few weeks earlier, Bessie Smith recorded "Alexander's Ragtime Band," written by the great Irving Berlin, a Jewish immigrant, when he was twenty-three years old. It was also the year of the first feature-length film with synchronized sound. *The Jazz Singer* starred Al Jolson who played a white son of a cantor but who left the fold to be a performer and sang on stage in blackface. (He also sings Berlin's then recent hit, "Blue Skies.") In that landmark movie Jolson shot to the top of the entertainment business, which led to his blackface performances, and blackface became his signature. But his role was different and more complex than earlier parodies, bringing serious, if sentimental songs to white America; musicians were now to be praised for the roots from which they came. And his influence on future jazz singers cannot be overestimated. Jolson was once part of Lew Dock-stader's *The Possum Hunt Club*, a fifty-man show playing the lively music and dance of blackface minstrelsy. But nothing can bring the face of Jolson in black-face closer to an audience than the magic of the camera, where the so-called "mask" of blackface up-close, was never intended to obscure the white face beneath the makeup.[71]

One hardly needs a reminder of the general context of race relations into which jazz was embedded. But it is worth a mention that on October 5, 1923, Armstrong was playing with King Oliver's band recording at Gennett Records in Richmond, Indiana. That same night, the Ku Klux Klan had their largest march through that city to date, some reporting 6,000 marchers with almost 24,000 watching.

It is hard to know what Jolson's and Cantor's appreciation of American negritude amounted to, given the stereotypical minstrel conventions in which their perfor-mances were packaged. Some have explained their use of blackface as a metaphor for Jewish empathy with the suffering of black people.[72] If so, would this not be a case where literal blackface and identificationism come neatly together? Our guess is that defenders of the minstrel hypothesis would not appreciate this bit of help. Consider Al Jolson's sentimentalization of Southern life in his best-known per-formance, "Swanee." Maybe this counts as an example of the kind of sexually nervous white male concern about black male potency profiled in the minstrel hypothesis, or as an example of the kind of politicized bonding that Dylan might have represented. But it seems like a stretch to say so.

As for Armstrong and Crosby, it is pretty clear that neither of them entirely shook off the styles of the tradition. They certainly hadn't done so during their rich early vocal careers. Music critic Will Friedwald goes too far when he writes, about Crosby, that in this period he removed "all traces of the minstrel show."[73] The degree to which Crosby shed minstrel influence depended, in part, on the material he was given to sing. Crosby's 1929 vocal on Reginald Foresythe's "Southern Melody" with the Paul Whiteman Orchestra is firmly in the tradition that we expect with Stephen Foster's minstrel songs, as the instrumental interlude goes into Foster's "My Old Kentucky Home." Although Armstrong could put his mugging and vocal exaggerations to remarkable use, he made little attempt to conceal their minstrel origins. And he was capable of recording pure "mammy" songs, like "Little Joe" (1931). But neither singer had reason to eradicate minstrel effects and themes. Minstrel shows were losing popularity in the 1920s, but there was still an audience for blackface minstrelsy, and demeaning stereotypes remained standard fare.

A pair of recordings of the 1910 Tin Pan Alley song "Shine" by both Armstrong and Crosby encapsulates the problem. Armstrong can be seen singing it (while wearing a leopard skin and standing knee-deep in frothy bubbles) in the short film, *A Rhapsody in Black and Blue* (1932). He also recorded it for OKeh in 1931. Crosby recorded it in 1932. The fictional narrator in the song describes himself as a curly haired "chocolate drop" with pearly teeth, who takes his "troubles all with a smile." Despite the condescending lyrics and film staging, Armstrong turns in a stunning performance. He might even be winking at his audience as he delivers the song's message. Crosby's performance cannot quite match Armstrong's, but it is very strong. Given the lyrics, it too cannot avoid the minstrel signification. Ironically, then, Armstrong's success as a mainstream entertainer may have had an unintended consequence of reinforcing negative stereotypes. The historian Brian Roberts, writing about Armstrong, puts it this way:

> He became one of the favorites in Harlem, one of the very few to parlay his early fame into a career of mainstream show business. His well-known act, playing trumpet, scatting and making bug-eyed grimaces while singing in characteristic tones that made every song unforgettable, made him a prime example of the minstrel perception.[74]

Today, appreciative listeners run into real conflicts about these performances. Could the current lively philosophical debate about moralism versus aestheticism – or qualified versions of these options – be brought to bear here?[75] There are doubts about working out any algorithm for determining what a rational response to such cases ought to be. Reasonable, reflective listeners who agree on ethical generalities can have conflicting intuitions about the merits of minstrel-derived jazz and pop vocal performances.

Consider Fred Astaire's 1936 blackface piece in the film *Swing Time*, intended to pay homage to the legendary black dancer, Bill "Bojangles" Robinson. It would be a stonehearted audience who could resist Astaire's talent as a tap dancer. (Astaire learned tap by taking lessons from John W. "Bubbles" Sublett, and his tap style pays homage to Sublett more than Robinson.) But who today does not feel at least somewhat uneasy about its susceptibility to the performance? And who does not wince watching Crosby in the 1942 film, *Holiday Inn*, singing the (admittedly meretricious) Irving Berlin song, "Abraham," in blackface?[76]

Would something like the following be helpful? One need not endorse a strong version of the minstrel hypothesis to grant that the history of a phenomenon makes a great difference to its character. In that spirit, one can acknowledge that the functions of the various familiar tropes of minstrelsy too have their own history. Is it not likely that even during the early Armstrong–Crosby years, the harsh reality behind the use of these tropes was beginning to lose some of its earlier charge? Perhaps the symbolisms of minstrelsy were gradually becoming little more than ingredients in the cultural soup from which American entertainers throughout the twentieth century drew. Similar ingredients came from the originally pre-judicial American discourse about various foreign immigrant groups. Entertainers always drew from such a world of stock figures, which they could depend upon audiences to recognize. As the musician and historian Terry Waldo puts it, "such characters have no reality … They become part of a cartoon world."[77] Their obnoxious meanings, derived from the very real context in which they were deployed, have been to some extent drained away.[78] (Today, how many viewers of Marx Brothers films are aware that the stage personae of Groucho, Harpo, and Chico were variations of established, ethnically demeaning stock figures of the Vaudeville circuit?) Of course, applying this wisdom, if it be such, has limits. At the moment, no one would get on board with the suggestion that restaurants in Coon-Chicken-Inn style should be reopened, replete with the original imagery. And Native Americans rightly protest the continuing use of stereotype Indians in American sports logos, advertising, and entertainment.

Whether some of the strongest of Armstrong's and Crosby's early vocal recordings are spoiled by their minstrel-derived characteristics is a question that listeners will answer for themselves. There will be those for whom the pleasures of these performances are at best forbidden fruit, at worst, just forbidden. Others will find that the morally offensive material leads them to engage in imaginative resistance, generating repugnance rather than engagement with the worldview it invites us to entertain.[79] Still others will find that a balanced appraisal leaves their quality undimmed. So we grant that aesthetic achievement is diminished by moral offense. But we can find no good reason to suppose that the sins of the fathers are inevitably passed along: the very real presence of the minstrel tradition in early jazz does not taint all subsequent jazz with the moral failings of the blackface tradition.

8. Armstrong and Beiderbecke

In 2003, the music critic Thomas Hallett, in honor of Black History Month, posted his list of "Five Black Jazz Legends You Should Hear." Thing was, Bix Beiderbecke's name was on that list. Hallett got the notorious praise one would expect for listing a white musician, but having gone by his recordings alone, it was only an act of ignorance, the point of which takes us back to our epigraph for this chapter: sometimes it is hard to tell black from white. And, it is part of the theme of this chapter to write about black/white relationships in the world of jazz and so, paralleling Armstrong and Crosby, we would be remiss if we excluded Armstrong and Bix. Tellingly, this pairing moves us from the realm of early jazz vocal performances, so often saturated with minstrel influences, to that of the jazz instrumental solo.

What Hallett has right is that Bix was, or did become, a legend. And because he was, the distinction Brendan Wolfe makes, between "Bix and What Bix Means," becomes relevant.[80] What he means is something like Bix the legendary white genius, an exception in a world of black music, but as ordinary Bix, a slob and a drunkard who may have sold out. He died young, at twenty-nine, as befitting a legend. (One view is that his employment by Paul Whiteman was the sell-out that eventually did him in.) He was, as Ted Gioia says, "an outsider among outsiders," "cool personified," and the "progenitor" of all the cool white hipsters of the jazz world.[81]

The story of the real Leon Beiderbecke, not even attempted here, is a bit "In a Mist," as Bix's most famous original composition is titled. One of the most repeated stories is that Armstrong met Beiderbecke, a white young man of eighteen on a Streckfus steamboat.[82] Louis was two years older than Bix. Louis headed north when the notorious Storyville was shut up just after World War I. Eventually, each played the cornet aboard the S. S. Capitol. In Chapter 1 we emphasized the importance of *place* for the permissions given to music, and steamboats were notorious places for what was inappropriate or illegal on Midwestern land, not the least of which was gambling and the vulgar music of jazz – the latter exiled to the river. Satisfying as it may be, this romantic tale of the early meeting of the two young men is almost certainly a fiction.[83]

But we are confident that we know some things when it comes to Beiderbecke's relationship with Armstrong. First, that they met up in 1923, in Chicago. Their origins were from different ends of the economic spectrum: Louis was poor and Bix the product of a comfortable middle-class home. Louis grew up in the heart of New Orleans jazz, sang and played in Storyville, while Bix first heard the music that influenced him by listening to records. Each played the cornet and neither could read music well: both succeeded musically through their superior listening skills. There are many accounts of Armstrong praising Beiderbecke's music, although influence is pretty much absent here. Armstrong's first book, a memoir, was dedicated to Bix and his second, written in 1954, remembers Bix as "the great cornet genius" and "almighty Bix Beiderbecke" whom all the world respected and admired.[84] On at least one occasion, Armstrong praised Beiderbecke as the "superior" cornet player.[85]

It is telling that, if Beiderbecke ever engaged in minstrelsy, it was through the legacy of his initial exposure to jazz: the recordings of the (white) Original Dixieland Jazz Band. Minstrelsy, as we've noted, was a matter of blacks and whites imitating absurd black stereotypes in the name of entertainment for whites. Brendan Wolfe, in his 2017 book *Finding Bix*, draws a parallel between this inauthentic aspect of minstrelsy, and the bizarre feigning of the white Paul Whiteman Orchestra, home to Beiderbecke in his final years. His musicians pretended to play like downhome blacks in many of their New Orleans jazz numbers. Wolfe says when Whiteman's band performed 'Livery Stable Blues,' it participated in this same tradition [minstrelsy], with classically trained symphony players pretending to be unschooled New Orleans white men pretending ... to be the music's black originators who, in turn, copied, learned from, and goofed on all sorts of high European idioms. In the end, what's vulgar and what isn't gets lost ... No wonder Whiteman panicked.[86]

Whiteman aimed at condescension toward the music's sources, but when the playing was hot, the difference between imitation and legitimate playing was blurred beyond recognition.

In Chapter 1, we approvingly cited Albert Murray's *Stomping the Blues* for his insights into central relationships between jazz, blues, and African-American culture. It is telling, in the present context, to note his disdain for Beiderbecke's "intrusion" into jazz.[87] The intrusion, in brief, was that Beiderbecke offered a compelling alternative to Armstrong's approach to solo improvisation. Once he located a sympathetic partner in Frank Trumbauer, Bix developed a mature style that "veers less toward the flattened tones of the African-American blues scale than to whole-tone scales or ninth and thirteenth intervals"; in place of the vocalizing timbres favored by black players, Bix favored "a clear, bell-like cornet tone"; in contrast to the ubiquitous "hot" approach, he "adopted an unhurried timing that frequently placed key notes or accents slightly behind the beat."[88] In other words, Beiderbecke demonstrated that musicians could replace African-American musical techniques with ones that were more overtly European or "white" and yet still play jazz – and that this could be done without succumbing to either the slick, bland sound of the Whiteman orchestra in their "serious" mode or the outrageous gestures of minstrelsy.

Murray, then, is correct to regard Beiderbecke as an intrusion into an African-American art. But it is also, therefore, an intrusion into the legacy of minstrelsy. If one adopts Murray's basic dichotomy, according to which jazz is either the blues (shorthand for authentically African-American) or white minstrelsy, then Beiderbecke's most original solos should be read as a decisive breaking of that mold. If Len Lyons is correct and Beiderbecke's performance on "Singin' the Blues" (1927) was "the most imitated solo of the 1920s, save for Armstrong's 'West End Blues'" (1928), then Beiderbecke taught a generation how to play a new kind of jazz: the cool approach, which owed nothing to minstrelsy. Given the social and musical constraints of the jazz scene of the 1920s, it may be correct to call Beiderbecke "the most original talent jazz ever produced."[89] Finally, Beiderbecke deserves some credit for moving jazz vocals away from minstrelsy. His late cornet solos directly influenced the vocal phrasing of Bing Crosby after they became bandmates in Whiteman's orchestra.[90]

9. A Final Word

Beiderbecke's trajectory away from minstrelsy is not unique in American popular music. Elijah Wald offers the illuminating comment that, in hindsight, "one could think of Elvis [Presley] as a 1950s equivalent of Bing Crosby." Both careers were jumpstarted through appropriation of black music and then, once established, each singer favored "more sedate styles" and became yet more mainstream after crossing over to film.[91]

According to Albert Goldman, Sam Phillips asked Elvis to perform something by black vocalist Arthur "Big Boy" Crudup. After some clowning around, Presley recorded "That's All Right (Mama)." It was July 1954, in the recording studio of Sun Records, Elvis was nineteen years old, and it was his first professional recording session. Goldman describes the comparison this way:

> The record so modestly described by one of its makers was, in fact, a remarkable feat of breathing in one cultural atmosphere and breathing out another. When you play the Presley side immediately after hearing the Crudup cut, you can hardly believe that both singers are doing the same tune ... Crudup's old recording summons up the atmosphere of the South Chicago blues bars during the days of go-man-go jump jazz. The tempo is fast, the rhythm is tense, the vocal delivery is as hard and straight as a hard black bowling ball rolling down a polished alley. Elvis' performance by contrast, suggests a farm boy lying up in a fragrant hayloft daydreaming of what he'd like to do with that little mama who is giving him such a run-around. The rhythm is relaxed and rural, the guitar chimes like a bell, the atmosphere is vernal – a hillbilly *Fruhlingstimmen*.[92]

What are we to make of these two versions of "That's All Right (Mama)?" We think we have here a case of failed appropriation – an attempt at imitation that resulted in so great a difference, that the same song was nearly unrecognizable in each recording. Nor can we say that Presley identified with Crudup, even if his manager, a key element in Presley's production, intended the similarity and identification of one kind of music with another: white sounding black – Sam Philips said as much. Nevertheless, Presley was indebted, to whatever extent, to Crudup since without his hearing Crudup, the style or manner of presenting his own song would probably never have been made.

Suppose we return now to the Crosby/Armstrong relationship. Armstrong became a paradigm of jazz artistry, especially during the early and middle years of his career. Crosby nearly had us forget his jazz talents when he became a star crooner in one of the most successful radio careers ever, but the merits of his performances as a jazz singer are indisputable. (Later on, Crosby's son Gary toured with Armstrong all over the States and the mutual admiration between Bing and Louis was publicly declared.) Nevertheless, as with the Crudup/Presley example, comparing two recordings of the same song by Crosby and Armstrong reveals differences too great to think of either of them as appropriations or imitations.

Returning to the minstrel hypothesis, all of jazz may have been impossible without the contributions of the widespread and accessible performances of minstrelsy blackface. A debt can be small or large, but in terms of indebtedness, we find sources of both Crosby's and Armstrong's work in minstrel singers and songs. The development of American popular music in the twentieth century is characterized by an increasingly complex cultural interplay between white and African-American musicians – leaving the minstrel hypothesis provocative and controversial. But as for the differences and distances of all or most white popular American music, the amount of the debt owed to minstrelsy becomes seriously in doubt.

Notes

1 Jed Rasula, "The Seductive Menace of Records in Jazz History," in *Jazz Among the Discourses*, ed. Krin Gabbard (Durham: Duke University Press, 1995), 134–162, at 156.
2 André Hodeir, *Jazz: Its Evolution and Essence*, trans. David Noakes (New York: Grove, 1956), 7.
3 Caroline Bird, "Born 1930: The Unlost Generation," *Harper's Bazaar* 2943 (February 1957), 104–107, 174–175.
4 Concerning the rise of the hipster in the 1940s, see Paul Lopes, *The Rise of a Jazz Art World* (Cambridge: Cambridge University Press, 2002), 209–212.
5 Norman Mailer, "The White Negro," in *Advertisements for Myself* (Cambridge, MA: Harvard University Press, 1985), 337–358, at 341. A prominent (but unnamed) model for Mailer's "white negro" is Mezz Mezzrow (born Milton Mesirow), whose 1946 autobiography documents his immersion in jazz and black culture; Mezzrow (with Bernard Wolf), *Really the Blues* (Garden City, NY: Doubleday, 1972).
6 Elijah Wald, *How the Beatles Destroyed Rock and Roll: An Alternative History of American Popular Music* (Oxford: Oxford University Press, 2009), 25.
7 "It's the American Negro's tradition, it's his music," wrote Charles Mingus. "White people don't have a right to play it" (*Beneath the Underdog: His World as Composed by Mingus*, ed. Nel King (New York: Vintage, 1991), 351).
8 Robert Christgau, "In Search of Jim Crow: Why Postmodern Minstrelsy Studies Matter," in *Da Capo Best Music Writing 2005*, ed. J. T. Leroy (New York: DaCapo Press, 2005), 17–39, at 21.
9 Eric Lott, *Love and Theft: Blackface Minstrelsy and the American Working Class* (Oxford: Oxford University Press, 1993). We will not pursue this angle, but Lott's thesis has been extended to ragtime and jazz social dancing; see Danielle Robinson, *Modern Moves: Dancing Race during the Ragtime and Jazz Eras* (Oxford: Oxford University Press, 2015), chap. 2.
10 Lott, *Love and Theft*, 5.
11 Lott, *Love and Theft*, 11.
12 Lott, *Love and Theft*, 6.
13 E.g., at Auburn University in 2001, Northwestern University in 2009, and at the University of California, Irvine, in 2012; the last was an Asian-American fraternity.
14 The careers of both have been expertly detailed in Will Friedwald's history of jazz singing: *Jazz Singing: America's Great Voices from Bessie Smith to Bebop and Beyond* (New York: C. Scribner's Sons, 1990; reissued 1996 with revised discography by Da Capo Press, New York). An invaluable study is Gary Giddens, *Bing Crosby: A Pocket of Dreams – The Early Years, 1903–1940* (New York: Little Brown, 2001).
15 As Friedwald puts it, Armstrong launched the shifts in the music that "would enable [jazz] to become both a high-brow art form and an international pop entertainment" (*Jazz Singing*, 27).
16 Friedwald (*Jazz Singing*, 16) notes sporadic examples of "scat" before Armstrong. For instance, Cliff Edwards – later known for singing the part of Jiminy Cricket in the

Disney film, *Pinocchio* – used the technique in accompanying silent movies on the ukulele. (Edwards called it "eefin'.")

17 Friedwald, *Jazz Singing*, 31.

18 See Friedwald, *Jazz Singing*, 34, for a vivid run-through of the ins and outs of Crosby's recording of "Sweet Georgia Brown."

19 On Sinatra and Bennett, see Richard Grudens, *Bing Crosby: Crooner of the Century* (New York: Celebrity Profiles Publishing, 2003), xv–xvi.

20 For a useful discussion of the view that these appropriations are inherently wrong, see Joel Rudinow, "Race, Ethnicity, Expressive Authenticity: Can White People Sing the Blues?" *Journal of Aesthetics and Art Criticism* 52:1 (1994): 127–137; Paul C. Taylor, "… So Black and Blue: Response to Rudinow," *Journal of Aesthetics and Art Criticism* 53:3 (1995): 313–316; and Theodore Gracyk, *I Wanna be Me: Rock Music and the Politics of Identity* (Philadelphia: Temple University Press, 2001), chaps. 5 and 6.

21 Lott, *Love and Theft*, 8. Lott's purpose is not merely to accuse and dismiss, but to examine the political complexity of the appropriation.

22 Christgau, "In Search of Jim Crow," 21.

23 Another striking example is the degree of mutual influence between Paul Whiteman and Duke Ellington. Whiteman's development of "symphonic" jazz (e.g., commissioning "Rhapsody in Blue") led Duke Ellington to pursue his own concert-jazz compositions; see John Howland, *Ellington Uptown: Duke Ellington, James P. Johnson, and the Birth of Concert Jazz* (Ann Arbor: University of Michigan Press, 2009). For additional examples, see Burton W. Peretti, *The Creation of Jazz: Music, Race, and Culture in Urban America* (Urbana: University of Illinois Press, 1994), 199.

24 For instance, Crosby's "boo-boo-boo" that eventually became an easily mocked cliché.

25 Although sheet music of the song was published c. 1832, it may well have pre-existed Rice's use of it. Jim Crow was a real person, whose character was apparently quite free of the unflattering features that came to be associated with the name. Christgau summarizes the scholarship that suggests that Cuff did not exist ("In Search of Jim Crow").

26 Summarized by Lott, *Love and Theft*, 14. For details of a show's typical structure, together with theatrical and musical examples, see Dailey Paskman and Sigmund Spaeth, *"Gentlemen, Be Seated!" A Parade of the Old-Time Minstrels* (Garden City, New York: Doubleday, Doran & Company, Inc., 1928).

27 http://www.nyfolklore.org/pubs/voic30-3-4/blkface.html.

28 Lott, *Love and Theft*, 7–8.

29 Ralph Ellison, "Change the Joke and Slip the Yoke" [1958], in *Shadow and Act* (New York: Vintage, 1972), 45–69; Amiri Baraka [LeRoi Jones], *Blues People: Negro Music in White America* (New York: William Morrow, 1963); Nathan Irvin Huggins, *Harlem Renaissance* (Oxford: Oxford University Press, 1971).

30 Frederick Douglass, "Gavitt's Original Ethiopian Serenaders," *The North Star*, October 27, 1849; reprinted in *The Life and Writings of Frederick Douglass*, ed. Philip. S. Foner (New York: International Publishers, 1950–75), 5 vols., Vol. I, 141–142. Cited [without title] by Eric Lott in "Blackface and Blackness: The Minstrel Show in American Culture," in *Inside the Minstrel Mask*, ed. Annemarie Bean, James V. Hatch, and Brooks McNamara (Hanover and London: Wesleyan University Press, 1996), 3–32.

31 Alexander Saxton, "Blackface Minstrelsy and Jacksonian Ideology," *American Quarterly* 27:1 (1975): 3–28. Cited by Lott, *Love and Theft*, 3.

32 Christgau, "In Search of Jim Crow."

33 Lott, *Love and Theft*, 8.

34 Campbell v. Acuff-Rose Music, 510 U.S. 569 (1994).

35 Henry T. Sampson, *Blacks in Blackface: A Sourcebook on Early Black Musical Shows*, Vol. 1 (Lanham: Scarecrow Press, 2014), 553.

144 Jazz and American Culture

36 W. T. Lhamon, Jr., *Raising Cain: Blackface Performance from Jim Crow to Hip Hop* (Cambridge, MA: Harvard University Press, 1998), 17.

37 Lott, *Love and Theft*, 7.

38 See W. T. Lhamon, Jr., "'Every Time I Wheel about I Jump Jim Crow': Cycles of Minstrel Transgression from Cool White to Vanilla Ice," in *Inside the Minstrel Mask*, ed. Annemarie Bean, James V. Hatch, and Brooks McNamara, 275–284, at 282.

39 Barry Shank, personal correspondence with Lee Brown, August 22, 2010. He adds that "something close to that position is now common sense among younger ... popular music scholars."

40 Lott, *Love and Theft*, 5.

41 Along with the most obvious objections to the traditional tropes of blackface minstrelsy, we must acknowledge their negative potential for long-range social and economic consequences for African-Americans in a culture in which white people rule, even after emancipation. On this matter, see James O. Young, *Cultural Appropriation and the Arts* (Oxford: Blackwell, 2008), chap. 4, section 2.

42 John Strausbaugh, *Black Like You: Blackface, Whiteface, Insult and Imitation in Popular American Culture* (New York: Jeremy P. Tarcher / Penguin, 2006), 35–36.

43 Lott, *Love and Theft*, 26, quoting Victor Turner.

44 Barry Shank, "'That Wild Mercury Sound': Bob Dylan and the Illusion of American Culture," *Boundary 2* 29:1 (2002): 95–123. See also Lott, *Love and Theft*, 9.

45 In his Nobel Lecture on Literature, Dylan names Leadbelly (Huddie Ledbetter) as the decisive influence ("Bob Dylan – Nobel Lecture." Nobelprize.org. http://www. nobelprize.org/nobel_prizes/literature/laureates/2016/dylan-lecture.html).

46 Shank, "Wild Mercury Sound," 104, emphasis added.

47 Shank, "Wild Mercury Sound," 102–103, emphasis added.

48 What we get is that Dylan – and others – sought identification with black people through identifying with black people.

49 Shank, "Wild Mercury Sound," 98, 99, 114, 123. The significance of the mask is neutered by Jeanette Bicknell's account of the ubiquitous adoption of performance persona (in "Just a Song? Exploring the Aesthetics of Popular Song Performance," *Journal of Aesthetics and Art Criticism* 63:3 (2005): 261–270).

50 Shank, "Wild Mercury Sound," 104.

51 Shank, "Wild Mercury Sound," 104, 107, 119.

52 Shank, "Wild Mercury Sound," 109–110. He cites Ronald Radano, "Denoting Difference: The Writing of the Slave Spirituals," *Critical Inquiry* 22:3 (1996): 506–544. Addressing nineteenth-century difficulties in transcribing musical sources, Radano argues that white writers "invented new ways to suggest in writing this apparently essential difference between black and white vocalizing." But it seems a wild stretch to move from this technical problem to minstrelsy and from there to American pop music in general. Curiously, in the same pages, Shank also explains how Dylan tries (unsuccessfully) to sound *lower*, given the influence of Blind Lemon Jefferson, whose chest cavity apparently resonated with a lower set of overtones than Dylan's.

53 Shank, "Wild Mercury Sound," 120. He adds that the song is about the "tension between blackness and whiteness in American culture."

54 Shank, "Wild Mercury Sound," 121.The reference to "rock" and "minstrelsy," by the way, embeds a compressed generalization that Shank, at this point, apparently takes to be self-evident.

55 Shank, "Wild Mercury Sound," 101. It is hard to curb one's impatience here. It would have helped to have had this point made loudly and clearly somewhere in the main body of the text. Annoyance aside, one wonders how broadly to apply the non-literalist caveat. Is the claim about the centrality of *identification* also intended non-literally? If so, any worry about the minstrel theory's possible essentialism would be put to rest.

But so too would any hope for an explanation of why Dylan, or popular music in general, is *historically* indebted to blackface minstrelsy.

56 Shank, "Wild Mercury Sound," 111. He introduces the claim with "To a certain extent," which simply adds confusion, of course.

57 Shank, "Wild Mercury Sound," 102–103.

58 Yet, infamously, Dylan also gave a public speech in which he admitted to some degree of identification with Lee Harvey Oswald. The occasion was his receipt of the Tom Paine Award – for his work on behalf of civil rights – only three weeks after the assassination of President Kennedy.

59 The self-representation in the song may indeed be an example of a general type. Lee Brown observed a musician who routinely showed up at a Saint Louis jazz festival dressed and groomed to look like Bix Beiderbecke, the legendary white musician. The man would stay in a very down-market hotel because "that's what Bix would do." There is sad humor in the human susceptibility to this kind of thing. But it surely cannot be explained generally as something learned from blackface minstrel theatre.

60 Lott, "Blackface and Blackness," 25–26, cites Douglass, "Gavitt's Original Ethiopian Serenaders." See also Lott's *Love and Theft*, 36–37, and Marian Hannah Winter, "Juba and American Minstrelsy," *Inside the Minstrel Mask*, ed. Annemarie Bean, James V. Hatch, and Brooks McNamara, 223–241. Winter cites late nineteenth-century testimony that no "audience was able to resist the beauty of Negro music" (240).

61 Douglass, "Gavitt's Original Ethiopian Serenaders."

62 Brian Roberts, *Blackface Nation: Race, Reform, and Identity in American Popular Music, 1812–1925* (Chicago: University of Chicago Press, 2017), 273.

63 Marsalis, interviewed by Bill Milkowski in "Wynton Throws Down the Gauntlet," *JazzTimes* 37: 3 (2007): 44–50, 95; at 48.

64 "Stepin' Fetchit" was the stage name of Lincoln T. M. A. Perry, who played a stereotypical black role in a multitude of films. "Flavor Flav" is the professional name of William Jonathan Drayton, Jr.

65 Milkowski, "Wynton Throws Down," 48.

66 Like Marsalis, in his writings about the black minstrel tradition, Douglass suggests that there is something very problematic in the assumption that this form of minstrelsy did actually present some "real" as contrasted with the "fake" thing.

67 Janna Tull Steed, *Duke Ellington: A Spiritual Biography* (Ann Arbor: University of Michigan Press, 2010), 84.

68 Marsalis is not concerned with fine distinctions. Technically, Public Enemy were not a gangsta rap act, and their 1994 album *Muse Sick-N-Hour Mess Age* included lyrics highly critical of that genre.

69 The classic source of the distinction between locutionary, illocutionary, and perlocutionary strands of the same speech event is J. L. Austin, *How to Do Things with Words* (Oxford: Clarendon, 1962).

70 Thomas Brothers, *Louis Armstrong: Master of Modernism* (New York: W.W. Norton, 2014), 499n49.

71 Jolson is also featured in a much lengthier presentation of minstrelsy in 20th Century Fox's Technicolor biography of Stephen Foster, *Swanee River* (1939).

72 See Michael Alexander, *Jazz Age Jews* (Princeton: Princeton University Press, 2003).

73 Friedwald, *Jazz Singing*, 31.

74 Roberts, *Blackface Nation*, 291.

75 For example, see Berys Gaut, *Art, Emotion and Ethics* (Oxford: Oxford University Press, 2007).

76 The performance has often been cut from re-releases of the film.

77 In conversation with Lee Brown.

78 True, various symbolisms operate on different time scales of change, in this regard. The German use of the swastika has, for many, clung to its earliest usage. Sophisticated crowds, to

be sure, could withstand the unfurling of swastikas in the musical *The Producers*. But we know of one audience member whose family was embarrassed when he tried to get out from his middle-of-the-row theater seat and leave, yelling, "I don't do swastikas!"

79 An excellent introduction to this topic is Kendall L. Walton, "On the (So-Called) Puzzle of Imaginative Resistance," in *Marvelous Images: On Values and the Arts* (Oxford: Oxford University Press, 2008), 47–59.

80 Brendan Wolfe, *Finding Bix: The Life and Afterlife of a Jazz Legend* (Iowa City: University of Iowa Press, 2017), 99.

81 Ted Gioia, *The Birth (and Death) of the Cool* (Golden, CO: Speck, 2009), 60; quoted by Wolfe, *Finding Bix*, 100.

82 Louis Armstrong, *Satchmo: My Life in New Orleans* (New York: Prentice-Hall, 1954), 209.

83 James Lincoln Collier, *Louis Armstrong: An American Genius* (Oxford: Oxford University Press, 1983), 80–81.

84 Armstrong, *Satchmo*, 209.

85 Armstrong quoted in Digby Fairweather, "Bix Beiderbecke," in *The Oxford Companion to Jazz*, ed. Bill Kirchner (Oxford: Oxford University Press, 2000), 122–131, at 125.

86 Wolfe, *Finding Bix*, 97.

87 Albert Murray, *Stomping the Blues*, 2nd ed. (New York: Da Capo, 2000), 50.

88 Alyn Shipton, *A New History of Jazz*, rev. and updated ed. (London: Bloomsbury, 2007), 110.

89 Philip Larkin, *All What Jazz: A Record Diary 1961–1971* (London: Faber and Faber, 1985), 51.

90 Beiderbecke's influence on Crosby is noted by Ted Gioia, *The Imperfect Art: Reflections on Jazz and Modern Culture* (Oxford: Oxford University Press, 1992), 139, and Friedwald, *Jazz Singing*, 31.

91 Wald, *How the Beatles Destroyed Rock and Roll*, 7.

92 Albert Goldman, *Elvis* (New York: McGraw Hill, 1981), 114. In other accounts, Phillips does not initiate the singing of "That's All Right." See Peter Guralnick, *Last Train to Memphis: The Rise of Elvis Presley* (New York: Little, Brown, 1994), 94–95.

References

Alexander, Michael. *Jazz Age Jews*. Princeton: Princeton University Press, 2003.

Armstrong, Louis. *Satchmo: My Life in New Orleans*. New York: Prentice-Hall, 1954.

Austin, J. L. *How to Do Things with Words*. Oxford: Clarendon, 1962.

Bicknell, Jeanette. "Just a Song? Exploring the Aesthetics of Popular Song Performance." *Journal of Aesthetics and Art Criticism* 63:3 (2005): 261–270.

Bird, Caroline. "Born 1930: The Unlost Generation." *Harper's Bazaar* 2943 (February 1957): 104–107, 174–175.

Brothers, Thomas. *Louis Armstrong: Master of Modernism*. New York: W.W. Norton, 2014.

Christgau, Robert. ""In Search of Jim Crow: Why Postmodern Minstrelsy Studies Matter." In *Da Capo Best Music Writing 2005*, ed. J. T. Leroy, 17–39. New York: DaCapo Press, 2005.

Collier, James Lincoln. *Louis Armstrong: An American Genius*. Oxford: Oxford University Press, 1983.

Douglass, Frederick. "Gavitt's Original Ethiopian Serenaders." *The North Star* (October 27, 1849).

Dylan, Bob. "Nobel Lecture." *Nobelprize.org* (2017): http://www.nobelprize.org/nobel_prizes/literature/laureates/2016/dylan-lecture.html.

Ellison, Ralph. "Change the Joke and Slip the Yoke." In *Shadow and Act*, 45–69. New York: Vintage, 1972 [1958].

Fairweather, Digby. "Bix Beiderbecke." In *The Oxford Companion to Jazz*, ed. Bill Kirchner, 122–131. Oxford: Oxford University Press, 2000.

Friedwald, Will, *Jazz Singing: America's Great Voices from Bessie Smith to Bebop and Beyond*. New York: C. Scribner's Sons, 1990; rev. New York by Da Capo Press, 1996.

Gaut, Berys. *Art, Emotion and Ethics*. Oxford: Oxford University Press, 2007.

Giddens, Gary. *Bing Crosby: A Pocket of Dreams – The Early Years, 1903–1940*. New York: Little, Brown, 2001.

Gioia, Ted. *The Birth (and Death) of the Cool*. Golden, CO: Speck, 2009.

Gioia, Ted. *The Imperfect Art: Reflections on Jazz and Modern Culture*. Oxford: Oxford University Press, 1992.

Goldman, Albert. *Elvis*. New York: McGraw Hill, 1981.

Gracyk, Theodore. *I Wanna be Me: Rock Music and the Politics of Identity*. Philadelphia: Temple University Press, 2001.

Grudens, Richard. *Bing Crosby: Crooner of the Century*. New York: Celebrity Profiles Publishing, 2003.

Guralnick, Peter. *Last Train to Memphis: The Rise of Elvis Presley*. New York: Little, Brown, 1994.

Hodeir, André. *Jazz: Its Evolution and Essence*, trans. David Noakes. New York: Grove, 1956.

Howland, John. *Ellington Uptown: Duke Ellington, James P. Johnson, and the Birth of Concert Jazz*. Ann Arbor: University of Michigan Press, 2009.

Huggins, Nathan Irvin. *Harlem Renaissance*. Oxford: Oxford University Press, 1971.

Jones, LeRoi [Amiri Baraka]. *Blues People: Negro Music in White America*. New York: William Morrow, 1963.

Kerr, Philip. *March Violets*. London: Viking, 1989.

Larkin, Philip. *All What Jazz: A Record Diary 1961–1971*. London: Faber and Faber, 1985.

Lhamon, W. T., Jr., "'Every Time I Wheel about I Jump Jim Crow': Cycles of Minstrel Transgression from Cool White to Vanilla Ice." In *Inside the Minstrel Mask*, ed. Annemarie Bean, James V. Hatch, and Brooks McNamara, 275–284. Hanover and London: Wesleyan University Press, 1996.

Lhamon, W. T., Jr., *Raising Cain: Blackface Performance from Jim Crow to Hip Hop*. Cambridge, MA: Harvard University Press, 1998.

Lopes, Paul. *The Rise of a Jazz Art World*. Cambridge: Cambridge University Press, 2002.

Lott, Eric. "Blackface and Blackness: The Minstrel Show in American Culture." In *Inside the Minstrel Mask*, ed. Annemarie Bean, James V. Hatch, and Brooks McNamara, 3–32. Hanover and London: Wesleyan University Press, 1996.

Lott, Eric. *Love and Theft: Blackface Minstrelsy and the American Working Class*. Oxford: Oxford University Press, 1993.

Mailer, Norman. "The White Negro." In *Advertisements for Myself*, 337–358. Cambridge, MA: Harvard University Press, 1985.

Mezzrow, Mezz (with Bernard Wolf). *Really the Blues*. Garden City, NY: Doubleday, 1972.

Milkowski, Bill. "Wynton Throws Down the Gauntlet." *JazzTimes* 37:3 (2007): 44–50, 95.

Mingus, Charles. *Beneath the Underdog: His World as Composed by Mingus*, ed. Nel King. New York: Vintage, 1991.

Murray, Albert. *Stomping the Blues*, 2nd ed. New York: Da Capo, 2000.

Paskman, Dailey, and Sigmund Spaeth. *"Gentlemen, Be Seated!" A Parade of the Old-Time Minstrels*. Garden City, New York: Doubleday, Doran & Company, 1928.

148 Jazz and American Culture

Peretti, Burton W. *The Creation of Jazz: Music, Race, and Culture in Urban America*. Urbana: University of Illinois Press, 1994.

Radano, Ronald. "Denoting Difference: The Writing of the Slave Spirituals." *Critical Inquiry* 22:3 (1996): 506–544.

Rasula, Jed. "The Seductive Menace of Records in Jazz History." In *Jazz Among the Discourses*, ed. Krin Gabbard, 134–162. Durham: Duke University Press, 1995.

Roberts, Brian. *Blackface Nation: Race, Reform, and Identity in American Popular Music, 1812–1925*. Chicago: University of Chicago Press, 2017.

Robinson, Danielle. *Modern Moves: Dancing Race during the Ragtime and Jazz Eras*. Oxford: Oxford University Press, 2015.

Rudinow, Joel. "Race, Ethnicity, Expressive Authenticity: Can White People Sing the Blues?" *Journal of Aesthetics and Art Criticism* 52:1 (1994): 127–137.

Sampson, Henry T. *Blacks in Blackface: A Sourcebook on Early Black Musical Shows*, vol. 1. Lanham: Scarecrow Press, 2014.

Saxton, Alexander. "Blackface Minstrelsy and Jacksonian Ideology." *American Quarterly* 27:1 (1975): 3–28.

Shank, Barry. "'That Wild Mercury Sound': Bob Dylan and the Illusion of American Culture." *Boundary 2* 29:1 (2002): 95–123.

Shipton, Alyn. *A New History of Jazz*, rev. and updated ed. London: Bloomsbury, 2007.

Steed, Janna Tull. *Duke Ellington: A Spiritual Biography*. Ann Arbor: University of Michigan Press, 2010.

Strausbaugh, John. *Black Like You: Blackface, Whiteface, Insult and Imitation in Popular American Culture*. New York: Jeremy P. Tarcher/Penguin, 2006.

Taylor, Paul C. "… So Black and Blue: Response to Rudinow." *Journal of Aesthetics and Art Criticism* 53:3 (1995): 313–316.

Wald, Elijah. *How the Beatles Destroyed Rock and Roll: An Alternative History of American Popular Music*. Oxford: Oxford University Press, 2009.

Walton, Kendall L. "On the (So-Called) Puzzle of Imaginative Resistance." In *Marvelous Images: On Values and the Arts*, 47–59. Oxford: Oxford University Press, 2008.

Winter, Marian Hannah. "Juba and American Minstrelsy." In *Inside the Minstrel Mask*, ed. Annemarie Bean, James V. Hatch, and Brooks McNamara, 223–241. Hanover and London: Wesleyan University Press, 1996.

Wolfe, Brendan. *Finding Bix: The Life and Afterlife of a Jazz Legend*. Iowa City: University of Iowa Press, 2017.

Young, James O. *Cultural Appropriation and the Arts*. Oxford: Blackwell, 2008.

6

JAZZ AND THE CULTURE INDUSTRY

No music has the slightest aesthetic worth if it is not socially true.
— *Theodor W. Adorno*

And here, I believe, is the truth in Adorno's complaint against mass culture, or at least a certain kind of mass culture — that its pleasures are too easily obtained and obtained without effort.
— *Roger Scruton*

Theodor Adorno was one of the first philosophers to theorize about jazz. His initial essay on the topic, "Farewell to Jazz" (1933), describes a musical movement that is no longer "authentic Negro music" and in such decline that it "will soon die away."[1] If remembered at all, this prediction would be a mere curiosity were it not for the fact that Adorno continued to write about jazz, as if trying to drive a stake through the heart of a patient who refused to succumb to a terminal condition. His many volumes of writings on music, philosophy and culture are divided between dense philosophical theory and a relatively more accessible body of musical and literary criticism. The result is one of the most sustained engagements with jazz and popular music in Western philosophy. His main complaint? Jazz is "bad art," for "immediate consumption."[2] It is not that immediacy is bad, but rather that the immediacy of entertainment is bad in the context of modern culture. In this context, "bad" means "bad for": bad for the reception of art, and bad for the people of a democracy. He draws the same conclusion again when he returns to jazz in the 1960s: "Within pop music jazz has its unquestioned merits," yet it was and is a "captive of the culture industry."[3] Jazz merits special attention within popular culture because its supporters wrongly and pretentiously "misconceive" it as modern or, worse, as avant-garde.[4] Modern jazz *seems* progressive, but it is not really different from 1930s swing in the way that matters most: jazz is just another tool of social conformity.[5] The aim of this chapter is to explain and evaluate this infamous denouncement of jazz.

We stress that there is much more to Adorno's critique of jazz than is captured in the stereotypical response that he was an elitist who thought that jazz could not measure up to the standards of art music. Adorno rejects all simple dualisms. Granted, he frequently frames an issue in terms of some extreme contrast: emphasizing the differences between, say, an avant-garde work like Arnold Schönberg's *Sechs kleine Klavierstücke* (Op. 19) and a pop trifle like Irving Berlin's "Mr. Jazz Himself" (1917). However, these framing contrasts are offered as "exaggerations of what was almost universal below the surface,"[6] and they are generally a prelude to Adorno's examination of the tensions and contradictions that arise from these oppositions, frequently yielding counterintuitive results. For this, and for the originality and influence of his analysis of the place of jazz in contemporary life, Adorno's account is well worth our attention.

The central issue, for Adorno, is the degree to which jazz can stimulate critical consciousness.[7] What we show in this chapter is how Adorno's view that the popular arts are simply entertainment – part of the realm of apparition only – applies to popular music and to jazz in particular. All of which depends on the plausibility of his concept of culture, central to his disparaging phrase, "the culture industry." When we see what Adorno has to say regarding the culture industry and the commodification of the popular arts, we will better understand his doubts about jazz and we can counter them with an account of how jazz resists his criticisms.

1. Fireworks and Functionality

Adorno's overwhelming concern is the development of modernism in art, philosophy, and the general culture. Adorno denies that art and music have static essences.[8] They can only be understood and objectively evaluated by contrast with "art as past history," so that we see what is new and so will not be misled into thinking music is valuable when it is merely an "echo" of the past.[9] Although understanding the past is essential for understanding the present, origins do not fully determine the later stages of any cultural phenomenon. Their social functions are subject to historical change. (Compare modern symphonic concert music with music in its earliest forms – when it was bound up with the fabric of human activities such as birth, death, war, marriage, and work.) Consequently, art and music cannot be understood by unpacking static concepts. If we want to understand – much less evaluate – the standard view that jazz is an important art form, we must engage with complex and contradictory historical developments. And, as we have emphasized throughout this book, we must also understand changes within jazz, both as music and as social activity.

Adorno's *Aesthetic Theory* frames these issues in a surprising way. He shows an interest in fireworks, which he views as a *prototype* of art.[10] Fireworks make no claims about their own significance – they neither want to endure nor mimic any other phenomenon. He says:

> Fireworks are apparitions *par excellence*. They are an empirical appearance free of the burden of empirical being in general, [however, fireworks have no duration]: they are a sign of heaven and yet artifactual; they are both a writing on the wall, rising and fading away in short order, and yet not a writing with any meaning we can make sense of.[11]

When it comes to fireworks, Adorno is an enthusiast, but of course, simply put, fireworks are not serious. They are, to borrow a familiar phrase, sound and fury signifying nothing.

Yet, as "simple entertainment," fireworks illuminate, through contrast, Adorno's general critique of the popular arts.[12] In their aesthetic segregation, in their brilliance and expressiveness, in their status as mere empirical appearance, fireworks are, in those respects, very like works of art. Indeed, fireworks, in their state of momentary apparition – not in their pre-explosiveness, where they can be purchased across state lines – have no commodity value, as their appearance, an evanescent disappearing act, cannot be bought and sold. Like artworks, they are segregated in an aesthetic sphere and share the afunctionality of artworks.

Reading Adorno, one can almost forget that the aesthetic dimension, coupled with afunctionality, strongly recalls Immanuel Kant's doctrine that a pure aesthetic judgment involves disinterested recognition of apparent purposeful form apart from recognition of any definite purpose or end that accounts for that form.[13] And, it recalls Friedrich Nietzsche's requirement of the dropping of will in §V of *The Birth of Tragedy*.[14] So, here, while we can only mention these resemblances to Kant and Nietzsche, it is worth noting that we believe that these echoes are intentional: Adorno's aesthetic theory is offered as a self-conscious culmination of the German tradition that begins with Kant. Although we are minimizing this strand of his thinking in examining his views about jazz, it is important to flag it, because it raises the issue of the extent to which jazz, America's main form of popular music as he sees it, is the cultural product of European culture and so an appropriate target of Adorno's philosophy of music. We confront this issue more directly at the end of this chapter.

Picking up on Ernst Schoen's suggestion that fireworks are "the only art that does not want to endure but is content to sparkle and then fade away," Adorno comments that fireworks might serve as a model for critically interpreting temporal arts such as drama and music, whose reification only degrades them.[15] The apparitional quality of fireworks defies "the ruling principle of [modern] reality," namely that all things are fungible and "can be exchanged for other things."[16]

However, for Adorno, fireworks differ from artworks in being occasions for aesthetic stimulation, but *nothing more*. Ghostlike, fireworks remind us of a pre-artistic period in the history of artworks. Unlike artworks, fireworks lack *duration* and *mimesis*: they mimic nothing, they present no illusion, and they are without content. The pleasure of fireworks is completely independent of the gestural or expressive function that characterizes art. But then it might be tempting to suppose that this aligns them with absolute or pure music, which is music that exists solely for the sake of our aesthetic gratification and rarely representative of anything. And we might further suppose that some jazz falls into this category, especially jazz that is not designed to support dancing. Some jazz writers have claimed that, with bebop, instrumental jazz became just such pure music.[17] From Adorno's perspective, this music remains closer to fireworks, but with the additional problem of having been commodified.

In the context of Adorno's philosophy, "pure" instrumental music is central to aesthetic theory. Its relative autonomy demonstrates that the absence of utilitarian functionality and overt representational content is insufficient to distinguish works of art from fireworks and other "pre-artistic" phenomena (including many circus acts and other non-narrative entertainments).[18] Artworks, while apparitional, are never merely or only that, not even in the case of pure music. If we want to endorse Dizzy Gillespie's claim that, with bebop "jazz [became] strictly an art form … a creative art form," we need to show that it contains something more than an aesthetically interesting surface.[19] Successful artworks possess something that entertainments – in such forms as fireworks and circus high wire acts – do not have. The key element, Adorno sometimes says, is that artworks are more than apparitions in being *promises*: potentials that contain something hidden, something not directly perceived, something spiritual that is presented as a *cipher*.[20] For Adorno, art conceals a Nietzschean veil of irrationality: "art is the truth about society in the sense that in its most authentic creations the hidden irrationality of a seemingly rational world is brought to light."[21] In short, if popular music is to rise above the pre-artistic status of fireworks, it will have to do more than tickle our ears and move our feet: it must offer something more than the sensuality of a fleeting apparition.

Adorno's critique, or rather accusation, that jazz is akin to fireworks as apparition only, has consequences outside the artworld – that is, external to the history of art to which it purports to be a part. One of Adorno's overarching themes is that we are social beings, inescapably shaped by language, economic relations, and historical forces beyond our direct control. The value or legitimacy of any music is to be measured by how it affects those who are subject to its presence in the culture of the times. This, in turn, returns us to one of Adorno's major insights: capitalism reduces culture to the fungibility of cultural elements, which Adorno baptizes with the powerful epithet "culture industry."

As we explain in the next two sections, Adorno identifies the culture industry as the greatest threat to the survival of art. In offering us the lie that jazz is "America's classical music," the culture industry offers us pseudo-art, a hollow doppelgänger of art.[22]

More precisely, Adorno's criterion for the genuine or authentic in music – popular or otherwise – has to do with its capacity to resist the culture industry and to support those breathing the air of that culture in being *persons* who resist the culture industry. He concludes that jazz, as he knew it, does not – does in fact the very opposite, by lubricating uncritical participation in modern, "rational" culture. Jazz is like other popular entertainment in providing its consumers a path of least resistance, falling into response without effort. Even if it does not always deliver, it is also marked by the additional temptation of just having fun, in settings both lowbrow (dancing the Charleston in a dance hall in the 1920s) and highbrow (having cocktails in the afternoon at the Plaza Hotel, watching Miles Davis and Bill Evans play "My Funny Valentine").[23] One of Davis's albums is even called *Relaxin' with the Miles Davis Quintet* (1958) and another bears the title *Big Fun* (1974). So, what's so wrong with music that offers an opportunity for relaxation and fun? Does having fun preclude being serious? Does relaxation contradict focus and intensity?

2. Autonomous Art and Resistance to Conformity

Adorno underpins his examination of the arts with a general critical theory of culture. With the rise of capitalism, he maintains, the things humans produce have lost touch with their original value for the sake of a secondary value, their *exchange value*. Putting an exchange value on art undermines the status of genuine art as an autonomous praxis. Put briefly, the capitalist system attempts to treat every effort of human productivity – including the arts – as a marketable commodity. Indeed, what has more recently come to be called the artworld includes a network of commercial institutions such as galleries, auction houses and, yes, museums, where sales can make newspaper headlines with prices that rival penthouse real estate in urban hotspots.[24] In Chapter 1, we emphasized major shifts in performance locations and associated uses of pre-jazz and then jazz, from Congo Square to the Savoy Ballroom to the modern concert hall and, correspondingly, from communal ritual to social dance and then to performed "art" music. We noted that these changes also reflected – and were to some extent driven by – changes in the manner and degree to which promoters and others in the "culture industry" profit from jazz.[25] Adorno insists that these issues must take center stage when we think about the arts, by asking whether they have neutralized the music by reducing it to a product for consumption.

In response to the commodification and standardization that characterizes the modern condition, art cultivated a sphere – both literal and symbolic – unto itself.[26] To offer two small symptoms of this phenomenon in relation to jazz: beginning in the 1920s, classical music was not issued on the same record labels as "race" or other popular music. And Carnegie Hall was so closely associated with "art" music that when Benny Goodman had the nerve to stage a jazz concert there in 1938, trumpeter Harry James voiced the misgivings of many of the assembled musicians when he was heard to say, as the concert started, "I feel like a whore in church."[27] Corresponding with this impulse toward autonomy, art has cultivated the philosophical stance commonly labeled "purist" or "formalist." However, we must be careful here. Adorno explains that there are several levels of form in a musical composition and its performance, and it is the tension between these which makes possible the "mystery" or "cipher" that facilitates genuine resistance.

The key move in Adorno's theory is his thesis that modern artworks simultaneously reflect and transcend their socio-historical origins. Every successful artwork is both a recycling of the past and a unique formal structure, permitting them to be content-laden and yet autonomous. To the degree that music reflects established patterns of music making, it can be meaningful; to the extent that its design includes some uniquely disruptive "negation" of those formal patterns, it is autonomous, resistive, and authentic. Adorno summarizes this positive achievement with the phrase "truth content."[28] To the extent that artworks are autonomous through the absence of direct social utility, resisting their own commodification, they retain the possibility of being socially transformative, preserving the Enlightenment's promise of human freedom in the face of our collectively imposed standardization and alienation. However, this promise must be continually renewed by fresh art. If cultural conformity and standardization prevail, there is a real possibility that art will die out. To count as an authentic and non-trivial contribution to culture, a jazz performance would have to possess a new truth content that resists its utility as a commodity of the culture industry.[29] Music's authenticity, truth content, and value arise as social facts based on context.[30]

Adorno is hardly alone in holding that *originality* is a necessary condition of the artworld, whether it be in form or content, style, or technique and in some cases – Christo's *Floating Piers* (2016) or in the huge towers in the world of architecture – quantity. If we take but one example, the work of Roy Lichtenstein, we can note that his popular paintings brought about new aesthetic ideas in style, including some nearly precise copying of comic book content but enlarged and glorified with dynamic color while emphasizing simplicity and pop. Often his characters "spoke" to us and to each other through comic book bubbles. His work claimed to have original content by virtue of utilizing the ordinary. However, the outstanding feature of Lichtenstein's work, as well as other pop artists like Andy Warhol and Robert Rauschenberg, was that it was fun. And it was easily accessible in the most unintimidating way possible, while still acknowledged as important new art. Needless to say, while the popularity of pop was vast, its commodification was confined to a much smaller population, who could afford its prices. Unlike jazz.

When Adorno advocates newness that comes from spurning repetition, he is not specifically foregrounding art with political content. Instead, he plays upon a concept at the center of Aristotle's ethics and more recently revised by Alasdair MacIntyre, namely habit, but in an entirely different, non-Aristotelian way.[31] Or so it seems to us. The musical avant-garde requires new challenges, ever new attitudes towards it, that break from established listening habits in order to instill the habit of being continuously open to thinking hard thoughts and seeing in new ways. We should expect music and musicians to extend their domains with each new work or performance. Any work with the capacity to challenge would present auditors with a kind of cipher, the promised mystery, which *they* can *work* to unveil.[32] These new modes of habitual thinking can then be transferred to the exercise of thinking politically, in the way Adorno imagines would usurp the culture industry and its mantra of the exchange value of all objects.

The kind of artistic resistance that Adorno takes seriously is exemplified by the modernist music of composers like Schönberg or Alban Berg. The almost painful abstractness of such music, he believes, is the truly serious means by which we can hold out against the superficial pleasures of popular culture. By these means, art resists the invasive effects of commodification on other aspects of life, and serves as a standard against which actual life can be measured. The downside is that in its isolated autonomy, art can all too easily become a plaything of bourgeois culture passed down to the working or middle classes. So compromised, it becomes a source of escapism, or a purveyor of easy, falsely reassuring views of our lives. It would be difficult to overlook a certain irony between a "newness" requirement in art and the continuous innovation of capitalist corporations where, like Apple, there is a need to reinvent itself or die, offering new products of questionable necessity to a public for consumption, well beyond its original breakthrough utility. The life of high art under capitalism is thus a precarious one. Suffering from virtually contradictory pressures, genuine art must hold out against the socio-economic forces that rule our lives. By contrast, the popular arts – particularly those we nowadays term "mass" arts – thrive contentedly within the commodity system.[33] Indeed, they are commodities *par excellence*. Later in this chapter, we directly address the charge that all jazz is subject to this constraint.

3. The Realm of the Popular

Nothing captures Adorno's killjoy attitude toward popular music as well as his 1940 radio broadcasts from New York City, where he was living as a refugee. First there was a series of Adorno-penned critiques against the current government-sponsored radio program, the *Music Appreciation Hour*. These were followed by his own radio broadcasts, criticizing jazz and presenting the proper way to learn to appreciate serious, authentic music.[34] The United States had not entered World War II, and the terrible saga of the holocaust had not yet reached the ears of an American public. In this context, the *Music Appreciation Hour* was just another form of entertainment, teaching the appreciation of music by attempting to make listening to classical music a kind of game – to identify the "master" composer of this piece or that and hence be educated into the world of authentic music. Worse yet, from Adorno's perspective, the music's conductor was marketed as the star attraction.[35] Two things were wrong here: the first was a methodical attempt to deify composers and conductors and hence, he thought, inculcate authoritarianism while learning nothing about the music itself. Classical music has taken on the marketing of the Hollywood dream factory: just as jazz band leaders got more attention and credit than the music's arrangers, conductors became the "stars" of the classical music world, deflecting attention away from the historically based challenges of the music itself.[36] The second failing was that such identification, music with master, was putting serious, authentic music into the realm of having fun and hence making it into a commodity, as one would expect of capitalism in any case. Adorno says:

> the *Music Appreciation Hour* destroys respect for the work, its meaning, and its achievement by transposing it into the effect it has upon the listener and inculcating in him composer-fetishes, which become virtually identical with the 'fun' he derives from watching a World Series baseball game.[37]

Adorno was clear about serious, authentic music not being a fun activity. That should be left to entertainment – the kind of fun that would have exchange value and hence could be bought and sold. Rather, Adorno imagined a kind of dialogue with members of a non-authoritarian, egalitarian democracy, where questions could be asked about the music (through letters), some of which would be critical inquiries into what would be considered serious music.[38] In the radiocasts and related material we see Adorno revealing his faith in democracy and his anti-capitalist stance, but unfortunately also emphasizing that musical value and having fun are mutually exclusive. We return to this point in the concluding section of this chapter.

Adorno takes it for granted that *standardization* and *individualization* are at odds. Since popularity is founded on a high degree of standardization, popular music lacks a hallmark of genuine art, which always speaks with an individualized voice. For Adorno, therefore, popular music does not speak with *anyone's* voice, any more than a sewing machine does. Instead, popular music makes use of what Adorno calls *pseudo-individualization*. A good example is what is known in the industry as a "hook" – a simple but distinctive chordal pattern, beat, or theme, by means of which record producers try to grab our attention.

Through pseudo-individualism, the industry creates music that *sounds* like a genuinely personal expression, even though it really isn't. (Compare the insincere formulae with which we pretend to express genuine feelings to each other in countless social situations.) Likewise, institutions such as "Top Forty" ratings and the "Grammies" only create a pretense that competing pop groups are highly individualized, perhaps through hairstyles or attire rather than their music. Adorno believes the comparisons are largely bogus, and that the differences between various pop groups are superficial. The *DownBeat* Jazz Hall of Fame is more of the same. He characterizes these institutions as examples of "plugging the whole field."[39] In the narrow sense, song "plugging" on American radio and TV, or through social media, is simply the familiar process by which new recordings are marketed by being aired over and over again. By "plugging the field," Adorno is talking about the way a complex system of practices, such as the Grammies, gives the products of the industry *as a whole* an undeserved sense of importance.

Adorno's views on popular music are expressed in many writings, but nowhere more accessibly than in his long essay, "On Popular Music" (1941). The examples Adorno uses there are obviously dated. (His reference to "the King" is not to Elvis Presley or Michael Jackson but to Benny Goodman, the so-called "King of Swing.") However, if Adorno were still alive, he would no doubt argue that in a hyper-mediatized twenty-first century environment, his position is even more relevant.[40] The culture industry that formerly offered us cartoons and horoscopes has now morphed our mobile telephones into platforms for games, "networking," and other entertainment, all the while narrowing the range of thinking we encounter while simultaneously tracking our movements – the loss of genuine autonomy is more insidious than anything Adorno imagines. And the wheels keep turning, coming up with new ways to target consumer markets through our mobile devices. Yet it conforms to the cultural logic he discovered in the fox-trot and in television programming. So although Adorno died in 1969, we offer no apologies that our discussion introduces more recent examples as extensions of Adorno's arguments.

The basic concepts of Adorno's analysis are the interrelated ones of *commodification, simplicity,* and *standardization.* The tunes, rhythms, and harmonies of popular music, he asserts, are built out of simple, repeatable parts. What cannot be standardized cannot be commodified, and therefore simplicity and standardization are increasingly present in music within a capitalistic culture industry.

Consider, first, the character and effect of the well-known rhythmic pulse of most American and American-influenced popular music. Nowadays, most fans of rock, jazz, punk, electronic dance music, and country music are unaware of the shared historical source of this metronomic feature of their favored music. In fact, if one traces back through rock and rhythm 'n' blues, to swing and jazz, and before that to ragtime, one comes to the ancestor of them all – the military marching band, à la Sousa and others. What, Adorno, asks, is the point of a military marching band – except to *regiment* people? The rigid beat of popular music has a similarly regimenting effect, he believes. Elsewhere, Adorno offers a psychoanalytic analysis, diagnosing the dancing that accompanied swing music as mere "convulsive" or "reflex" actions in which he claims to perceive thinly concealed states of rage and self-hatred.[41] At the same time, the mechanical character of the omnipresent beat of American popular music illustrates Adorno's view of it as an industrial product, like things made on assembly lines, like ordinary appliances. The division of labor essential to the assembly line is tied to a simple, repeatable task, making those who work it expendable and alienated from the very means of production necessary for their existence.

Next, we must bear in mind that, for the past century, most American popular music has been embedded in one of two typical forms. The first basic form for pop music – and, because form is the key to truth content, the chief focus of Adorno's discussion – is the thirty-two-measure show tune. Such a piece is distributed across four 8-bar segments, in which two tunes are organized according to the pattern AABA. This is the basic model for the composers of Broadway music, such as Irving Berlin and George Gershwin, as well as many rock era tunes by such groups as The Beatles. It is the model for thousands of pop standards such as "Body and Soul" and "Stormy Weather," classics of jazz instrumentally and vocally. Although he didn't do so, Adorno could have further supported his case by citing the other fundamental pop music form – the blues. The standard blues is twelve measures long and moves predictably through a standard progression of chords. Each verse of a blues song involves two lines, the first sung twice, the second once, as in the following: "I woke up this morning with an awful aching head / [Repeat] / Because my man had left me with nothin' but an empty bed." Much of jazz, rock, and, of course, "rhythm and blues" derives musical patterns from the blues. And the blues is so generic, so standardized, that when Led Zeppelin took writer's credit for a song they called "Whole Lotta Love," Willie Dixon was only able to sue for plagiarism because they had taken chunks of his lyrics, too. Jazz musicians, endlessly recycling blues progressions and appropriating the changes of Gershwin's "I Got Rhythm" and Ray Noble's "Cherokee," faced no such problem when they produced instrumental versions. Without lyrics, the copyright system regarded their retitled repackaging as protected creativity.

Such repetition, with one song being *musically* like so many other songs, is hidden by the culture industry: minor differences are touted as new and different. If not explicitly designed to, this repetition has the effect of making listeners passive and uncritical, non-thinking and superficial. This is what Adorno describes as the "predigested" quality of popular music and jazz.[42] It is no surprise, given the foregoing, that Adorno regards popular music – both in form and content – as appealing mainly to immature impulses. He terms the desire for sheer repetition "regressive," a psychoanalytic term connoting an infantile fixation. He regards such obsessive pleasures as masochistic ones – like biting your nails. The activity is partly painful, and you never get full satisfaction from it, but you can't stop doing it. This infantilism is also registered in the music's vocabulary. (Consider how often lovers are addressed as "baby," "mama," or "papa.") No doubt, we can all name popular musicians whose work is grittier or more advanced than the popular music Adorno heard. But he would be struck by the way pop music still celebrates adolescent values and attitudes.

Because of the endless reuse of these two musical forms, we can think of the creation of popular songs after the analogy of a cookie cutter. But Adorno's favored analogy is an appliance, such as a washing machine, or an industrial product, such as an automobile, with their replaceable parts. If one part is broken or doesn't work well, another can replace it. For example, when Broadway composers found that the B section of a song did not work, they often simply borrowed one from another song. When the Beatles recorded "I Me Mine" as a song of less than ninety seconds, legendary producer Phil Spector extended it to a more standard length by simply copying the taped performance from the second verse to the end, then pasting the copy at the end, repeating one minute of the performance a second time.[43] No one seems to have noticed the literal repetition at the time of release. In the subsequent age of sampling, a few seconds of recorded rhythm are endlessly repeated as the foundation of a new song – it's estimated that a few seconds of a drum break from The Winstons' "Amen, Brother" (1969) has served as the basis of more than two thousand hip-hop recordings.

The subject matter of popular music is equally simplistic. The perennial topics, the content of popular music, are the standard sentimental ones – fantasy narratives of love, in which all the real trials of life are magically resolved. Even the dark shadows in pop songs, Adorno would probably say, are formulaic. The singer Lyle Lovett has wittily boiled down the love content of country music as "Boy meets girl, boy shoots girl."[44]

Repetition, however, is not always a simple matter. It is the subject of Søren Kierkegaard's short novel, *Repetition*, as aspects of life appear to repeat and take on an aesthetic character. More recently, it is the subject of Peter Kivy's book, *The Fine Art of Repetition: Essays in the Philosophy of Music*, which contains an essay by that name. Kivy argues that repeated material in instrumental music is not redundant, because what is apparently repeated comes after and is perceived differently than its first occurrence – largely because the repetition plays a role in generating a musical pattern of one kind rather than another. More importantly, Kivy borrows a point from musicologist Edward T. Cone, putting it this way:

> we do, or should, hear music differently when it appears the second or third (or whatever) time from the way we did the first, and that the performer should play it differently. With that, any sensitive … listener or musician must agree.[45]

It is like, in baseball, ball one is not the same as ball two or three. Repetition changes the context of each instance and so alters its significance. Consequently, musical repetition is not always *meaningless* repetition. Jazz uses repetition in both of those ways. Additionally, jazz improvisations often "quote" briefly from familiar music in order to generate new ideas (or to correct errors in phrasing). In his 1963 instrumental recording of "How About You," pianist Bill Evans clearly articulates the melodic phrase that goes with the words, "I like New York in June, how about you?" He then breaks from the pattern of "how about you" by inserting a short phrase from the song "Autumn in New York," wittily answering the question with a musically encoded response. So repetition, whether literal or slightly altered, can introduce intertextualities that resonate within and across traditions.[46]

Furthermore, if there were *no* repetition, there would be no continuity of culture: a piece of music would be no more meaningful to us than bird song.[47]

Every cultural product betrays a practical making of something out of materials. Material "is all that the artist is confronted by, all that he must make a decision about," Adorno explains, "and that includes forms as well."[48] So "material" has a broad meaning for Adorno. The materiality of each particular work includes the formal rules and stylistic practices that directed and limited its production process. Both the 12-bar blues form and the tonal and timbre parameters of the modern piano are materials incorporated into Thelonious Monk's "Ba-lue Bolivar Ba-lues-Are" (1956). Understood in this way, materiality has an inescapable historical dimension. Every product of modern culture displays some degree of capitulation to society and its dominant economic structure. Yet every production is a fresh chance to resist the material that is employed. Where a cultural product displays resistance, it is authentic art. Close analysis is needed to reveal which particular cases of music, painting, literature and theater are authentically self-resisting.

Because of its simplicity in form and content, however, popular music seldom rises to the status of art. Granted, "classic" jazz is more challenging than the average pop song, but it steadily lost popularity in the post-swing era. By the 1990s, many jazz radio stations switched to the "smooth jazz" format, and the dominant sound of "jazz" was a style of background music. Adorno likes to say that popular music hears *for* the listener, by which he means that it leaves no mental work for us to do for ourselves.[49] This fits his view that modern listeners are deficient in real musical literacy. Consider the degree to which stereos replaced pianos as the chief source of music in the home; more recently, music has migrated to digital storage, and if it is played through a shared sound system, it is most often through the speakers of a home theater. As a result, our relationship to music is nowadays more a matter of passive consumption than of music making, rendering our responses superficial, at best.

To illustrate his point that repetition is a problem in popular music, Adorno makes pointed comparisons between examples of "classical" and popular music.[50] A work such as Beethoven's Fifth Symphony does not – like a piece of popular music – consist of a few simple parts revolving repetitiously for our passive reception. First, as a totality, it constitutes an elaborate design, within which its subsidiary parts – or "movements" – have complex and subtle relationships to each other. Second, each movement is an elaborate structure involving complex relationships between the parts. Third, the symphony effects elaborate transformations of its musical sources. For instance, the scherzo movement of the Fifth Symphony is a form derivative from a relatively simple dance form. But in Beethoven's hands, the simple elements have been transformed almost beyond recognition. Instead of consisting of polite tunes repeated monotonously, Beethoven's scherzo is wonderfully complex. Adorno takes pains to explain how it makes use of a powerful thematic duality, involving – in his words – a "creeping" theme in the strings, contrasted with a "stone-like" response in the woodwinds. As these interact, a tremendous sense of tension and foreboding is set up, which serves, in turn, as a dramatic introduction to the triumphant music of the last movement.

In such "serious" music, what would otherwise be simple is made complex, developmental, and dramatic. We are challenged to track what is happening and to understand the relationships among new and repeating parts. Further, we could not replace bits of the music of Beethoven's Fifth with alternatives without ruining its overall sense. Comparatively, the placement of the bits in a piece of popular music is fortuitous, devoid of the "logic" of musical progression.[51] In contrast, the order of the soloists in a jazz performance makes little or no difference. Against this charge, jazz fans are likely to point to an example like Gunther Schuller's demonstration that the improvisations of saxophonist Sonny Rollins display a complex melodic coherence in the form of motivic development.[52] Adorno would not be swayed: producing a limited set of counterexamples from within jazz does not really defuse his arguments if he is accurate about the general tendencies of popular music and jazz. Drawing any line between (artistic) jazz and (non-artistic) popular music is an endorsement of Adorno's general point: it simply transposes dubious hierarchical distinctions from classical music to jazz and so makes us feel secure about our own listening, and so reinforces the logic of the culture industry.[53]

Many writers point to improvisation as the essence of jazz. When it is present, improvisation makes a performance unique and autonomous. For Adorno, this is the advertiser's hook. Jazz too is a commodity. When Miles Davis was their best-selling jazz artist, music industry giant Columbia Records created the advertising slogan "The Man Can't Bust Our Music." The truth is otherwise. In the jazz world of that era, Columbia *was* "the man." When Charles Mingus entered the studio to record "Fables of Faubus," it included lyrics that ridiculed the governor of Arkansas, Orval Faubus, who had recently resisted integration of the public schools. Columbia would not permit him to use the lyrics on the 1959 album *Mingus Ah Um*, so the piece appears as an instrumental. In subsequent live performances, "Fables" remained an instrumental, but Mingus sometimes stretched it to thirty minutes and incorporated snatches of "When Johnny Comes Marching Home" and "God Bless America" to ironic effect. Yet Adorno dismisses even this practice of jazz adaptation and improvisation, central to Mingus's jazz workshops, as mere pseudo-individuation. Contrary to the idea that the jazz improviser is freely expressing himself, Adorno believes that the possibilities of anything really unique – and therefore transgressive – happening in such music are extremely limited. The music, he insists, is always framed within the context of a musical prison, the walls of which include the ongoing beat, the rigid forms, and the narrow confines of the music's harmonic potentialities. The individualism is superficial.

Going hand in hand with the standardization of the music itself, Adorno believes, is the process by which the audience's *reactions* are standardized. Just as we are programmed to expect the standardized food at McDonald's franchises, we are programmed to *expect* the music we get. Adorno would reject the widely repeated claim that the commodity industry "only gives people what they want." Yet he does not suppose that McDonald's is what everyone will buy; some people flock to slightly more upscale chains. The fast food and music industries must introduce just enough variation so that at least one of the available "brands" will appeal to each of several public tastes.[54] Generally, when the fan thinks the pleasure is a response to the objective value of the music they favor, the listener is instead identifying with others who are also bonding with that piece of music. As jazz developed beyond swing, it became the favored music of "resentment listeners" who believe their music is a pure, "germ-free art" and whose primary goal is identification with a specialized community of like-minded listeners.[55]

By offering us cheap pleasures and escapist fantasies of freedom and individuality, the commodity industry realizes several cooperating goals: above all, we become "reconciled," as Adorno puts it, to the capitalism in which we live, move, and have our being. One of the functions of popular music is to assimilate consumers to the system. The truth is that popular music, unlike serious classical music, is not able to resist the system. In the absence of learning music theory and adopting analytical listening skills, the process of becoming knowledgeable about favorite musicians and their careers reinforces our status as "culture consumers," capable of enjoying consumption but not attentive listening.[56]

4. Responding to Adorno: Initial Criticisms

What case can we make that jazz produces artworks that are able to resist the system from which they spring, a system in which everything is a commodity? In what other ways might jazz be valuable? We begin with several criticisms that may seem important, but which actually have limited force.

One might suppose that in making his contrast between popular and classical music, Adorno unfairly picks the worst examples of the former while focusing on the best examples of the latter. Surely, tedious and banal examples of classical music abound. Operas that were popular in the seventeenth century may please no one today.

Classical music and popular music seem to be on all fours in still one further respect. Consider the possibility that not even Beethoven's music can survive the endless replaying it receives on "good music" radio stations. Can even the finest music, by sheer repetition, not become a sophisticated form of Muzak? (How often do even dedicated listeners to "good music" stations actually sit down and *listen*?) However, these are not genuine objections to Adorno. If we look across the range of his writings, we see that he recognizes all of these points, and in particular emphasizes the destructive effect that mass communication has on art music, and its failure to have a lasting progressive impact: all art grows cold, and dies.[57] After all, major artworld institutions are capitalist enterprises, too.

Another obvious argument is that Adorno underestimates the degree to which popular music – like classical music – can transcend the pressures of the commodity industry and create music of enduring value. Who would deny, in all seriousness, that Duke Ellington, Charlie Parker, or Billie Holiday did not do so?

Another way of putting this point is to note how there can be vastly better and worse versions of a single song when it is performed by two different artists – artistically, we can have very different results. Thinking of the many recordings of "These Foolish Things" – from Sinatra and Bob Dylan, for example, to Ella Fitzgerald and Bryan Ferry, to Emmy Rossum and Sam Cooke – it would be problematic to think of them as repetitious of each other. More importantly, look how the dross and fluff of popular music is transformed by skilled jazz singers. Holiday's early recordings are primarily of "second-rate" songs that established singers had rejected; working with pianist Teddy Wilson and modifying the tunes to fit her voice and style, they created a series of "jazz classics."[58] Or, more recently, consider The Monkees' 1966 debut recording, "Last Train to Clarksville" – predictably, in the context of Adorno's theory, a simplified aping of The Beatles' "Paperback Writer." A lightweight pop hit about romantic separation, Cassandra Wilson transforms into a slow, surprisingly moving expression of loss and longing.

Against this form of counter example, however, Adorno simply acknowledges that jazz has considerable musical merits.[59] The argument against him misses the point. Among "good bad music," Wilson's version might actually be worse than the original, because at least the Monkees had no pretensions about their significance.[60] Wilson's jazz version, however, may mislead people into thinking they are having a culturally significant experience when, in fact, nothing transgressive is really happening.

Next, we might accuse Adorno of indifference to the kinds of discriminations that are requisite for making informed aesthetic judgments about jazz. Almost anyone can hear the stylistic differences between Stan Getz and John Coltrane – two tenor saxophonists. And that Coltrane is more transgressive than Getz, just as Charlie Parker's bebop is far more transgressive than Paul Whiteman's dance orchestra. It is symptomatic that even in the 1960s, Adorno ignores these differences. Furthermore, he continues to use "jazz" as a synonym for popular music generally, a usage that had not been correct since the late 1930s, when "swing" supplanted "jazz" as the general category term. He puts the best music of Cole Porter and George Gershwin on the same level as the most cynical products of the music industry. Against such observations, however, we recall Adorno's point that these various commercial products are tailored to please different segments of society. Again, engaging in a game of distinctions avoids Adorno's primary concern: none of it has emancipatory potential in relation to its audience. We might suppose that classic jazz of the post-swing era brings a certain seriousness to popular music, meeting the challenge of being a thinking person's music, akin to classical, even if (eventually) its auditors get no further than becoming listeners. But Adorno considered this idea in the early 1960s, and rejected it. The so-called "jazz expert" scorns the dominant culture: "seemingly nonconformist," their preference for a more "primal" and organic music is really an elitism within sanctioned popular culture.[61]

Coming nearer to the target, one might argue that popular music has often been a basis for protest. Despite its direct challenge to American racism, Billie

Holiday's popularization of "Strange Fruit" (1939) sold more than a million copies. The entire free jazz movement is routinely understood as a form of protest.[62] However, Adorno would likely point out, first, that the industry has a way of converting social protest into fashion, while leaving a merely superficial impression of resistance. Consider the way the industry found it easy to turn the revolutionary images of Mao Tse-Tung and Che Guevara into fashion chic. Then have a look at *Time* magazine's 1964 cover story on Thelonious Monk, which gave international fame to a jazz iconoclast by "selling" the man as a "shambling" genius who wears funny hats, all the while saying little about the music.[63] Second, although idealizing views of jazz celebrate it as an expression of rebellion, Adorno responds that jazz musicians live in a hostile but basically "compliant" relationship to the system that promotes their music, rendering it harmless.[64] He would not find it remarkable that the cult of pop stardom typically overtakes "edgier" musicians, especially those with a more tragic image: Holiday but not Sarah Vaughan, and Coltrane but not Herbie Hancock. (In the case of Coltrane, cult status is to be taken literally.) Commercial success is always the real agenda, and an untimely death is a marketing asset.

More to the point, Adorno repeatedly addresses and dismisses the resistive capacity of jazz and other popular music. Progressive content does not facilitate a progressive function, because "discursive" and "haranguing" artworks do not transform consciousness.[65] Almost no one is educated through "entertainment" that pursues serious themes or signals political resistance. The culture industry neutralizes it by selling it as a "classic," voiding any requirement to respond to its particularity.[66] To make the horrors of racism and war consumable, as in "Strange Fruit" and 1960s protest music directed against the Vietnam War, is to veil their horrors and thus to make them tolerable. (Today, he might point out that showing *Schindler's List* in schools has not reduced American anti-Semitism.) The concessions employed to attract a mass audience neutralize the message, and the passivity of consumption absolves consumers of any need to achieve the personal internalization required in any meaningful critique.

Contrary to Adorno's stance, "compliant" and "submissive" are hardly the labels we would apply to the art of Mingus, Ornette Coleman, or Sun Ra, artists not part of Adorno's vocabulary. The tragic tone of Coltrane's "Alabama" (1963) is surely as resistant as any music by Schönberg. To toss it into a heap with the most cynical products of the music industry is laughable. At this point, Adorno can launch a more theoretical argument. He makes a sharp distinction between truth content and mere expression. Expression is representational: Coltrane's "Alabama" expresses *his* feelings and, by association, those of his community. The expression of emotion in music is a mimetic act, an auditory gesture that generates an "image" of what it mimics.[67] However powerful this may be, the image is "blind" because it lacks the rational force of organized language, and therefore cannot provide thought and so cannot voice resistance.[68] Failing to drill down to the source of protest and resistance in art as understood by

Adorno, defensive replies that stress expression in music – however nihilistic or bleak – miss their target.[69]

Writing about jazz and the culture industry for nearly forty years, Adorno has anticipated most of the criticisms that we are likely to direct his way. To steer clear of his position, we must do more than employ the method of counterexample.

5. A Plurality of Values

Is Adorno right in claiming that popular music *never* resists the system or does so too seldom to make a difference? To launch a serious challenge against Adorno, we must either show that jazz musicians routinely employ structures that secure truth content or we must show that other values are equally important. We argue for both.

In the last section, we reviewed the more obvious objections to Adorno's critiques of jazz and the culture industry together with his responses. This survey suggests that a successful challenge to his positon must be directed against the basic philosophical framework that shapes his interpretation of art and music. In our view, his attack on jazz is an edifice built on a questionable foundation: it relies on a questionable model of historical and cultural development. As we explained in our first three chapters, there is no good reason to think that later stages of a cultural phenomenon represent progress. In order to make sense of art and music, we see no need to tell a story about its ongoing adaptations (an evolutionary model buried within Adorno's dialectical method). Nor does it help to read later stages as developments from nascent features moving towards a single goal (the teleological model). Yet Adorno's dismissal of the pseudo-art of the culture industry requires just such a story: through its negation of the materials it inherits, avant-garde art remains a progressive and resistive element within modern culture. Everything else must be a recycling, and so "popular music constitutes the dregs of musical history."[70]

When Adorno hears Ellington as deriving from Claude Debussy, the most obvious point of failure is that he fastens on the composing and arranging and thus its link to the "high" European tradition.[71] However, we reject the "Hegelian underpinning to all Adorno's thinking."[72] It provides a compelling story about musical progress, but this tidy unification carries too high a price: it cannot celebrate the delightfully messy pluralism of popular music and jazz. In our view, the supposed progress of "serious" music has no direct implications for the value of any jazz. Where it has any bearing, it will be because jazz musicians have chosen to make a connection between the two traditions, rather than the other way around.

We do not have to be anti-formalists to say that Adorno's view of music is fundamentally graphocentric. Adorno does not allow himself to hear – cannot hear? – the oral tradition behind and within jazz. We know, however, that the blues tradition that fed jazz is an offshoot of the West African griot tradition carried into the Americas in the middle passage of the slave trade.[73] In many important respects, it is a living relic – an oral "poetic" tradition of the sort that gave us the Homeric poems.[74] Those poems were themselves popular music – touring rhapsodes performing them – the stories better remembered when put to song. The Robert Fitzgerald translation of *The Odyssey* begins, "*Sing* in me, Muse, and through me tell the story of that man skilled in all ways of contending..."[75] The story contains two key songs: one, in Book VIII, occurs when Demodokos, blinded but given the gift of sweet singing, brings Odysseus to tears, which he hides, by his performance of three songs. The other, more famously, is the beautiful song of the Sirens in Book XII.

Ironically, the song of the Sirens is the part of *The Odyssey* that interests Adorno, who, with Max Horkheimer, writes about it in *The Dialectic of Enlightenment*, in the chapter "Odysseus and the Enlightenment." The essay is about some of the many aspects and themes of *The Odyssey*, where our protagonist is likened to a "bourgeois individual," once living in the confines of order and domesticity but now, as a veteran of lawless war, fated to wander into a past time of nature and mythology, somehow surviving their onslaughts and returning home a changed self (*autos*). His return brings additional challenges regarding his wife Penelope and the hundreds of suitors standing by to replace him. It is the well-known episode of the Sirens, however, that we want to juxtapose with Adorno's critique of popular music, especially "the untruth of artifice" as he sees it in that section.[76] The song of the Sirens, as wonderful as we are asked to imagine it, is the instantiation of temptation. It plays on the attraction of music generally, and while the Sirens' song is hardly "popular," it has the power of music to draw men even to their death. So, famously, Odysseus has his men tie him to the mast of his ship while their ears are made deaf by beeswax – Odysseus hearing the song but saving his ship and his life by his crafty resistance to this musical and dangerous phase of his journey. Adorno points out the dual advantage of Odysseus's mode of resistance: "Odysseus recognizes the archaic superior power of the song even when, as a technically enlightened man, he has himself bound. He listens to the song of pleasure and thwarts it as he thwarts death."[77] Adorno and Horkheimer make clear that the situation of Odysseus has relevance for contemporary music – as if the sounds of the culture industry have played the role of Sirens' tempting, even if the songs are less than beautiful. They say, "Since Odysseus' successful-unsuccessful encounter with the Sirens, all songs have been affected, and Western music as a whole suffers from the contradiction of song in civilization – song which nevertheless proclaims the emotional power of all art music."[78]

The contradiction here is between temptation and resistance. The case of Odysseus, we want to say, is similar to the situation of the citizens of a democracy when presented with popular music and jazz as Adorno sees them, affected and put in danger by their shallow charms. The citizenry is not tied to a mast and so, if this analogy is correct, would be drawn to the music, tempted by it, without the critical capacity to resist. The enlightened Odysseus understands the dominance of art over his unconscious mind, but elects to place his rationality at the mercy of song. Adorno does not attribute even this awareness to most citizens of modern society; he reserves the insight of Odysseus for an elite group of fully expert listeners.[79]

Adorno's analysis of Odysseus and the Sirens' song lays bare his commitment to a unifying history for all Western music and its heirs: "all songs have been affected." Adorno consequently refuses – or is unable – to hear jazz as we do, as the product of "polyglot origins."[80] Consider the matter of tonality, for example. Much of African-American music makes use of so-called "blue" notes that arise because certain notes of the standard European scale are, in the context of popular music, flatted or bent down in pitch. This practice gives much of our blues, jazz, and rock its distinctive sound. Adorno believes that when we listen to these "bent" notes, our ear struggles to correct them back to their "correct" pitch.[81] In other words, we hear them as artificial gimmicks, if not outright mistakes in European scales. On this matter, one might charge Adorno with tonal chauvinism. As Berthold Hoeckner replies, "a blue note sounds outside diatonic intonation" and does not call for correction with listeners who are at home in this tradition.[82] In other words, the notion of "right" notes becomes relative to a musical system in a world in which European tonality is only one alternative among many.

The complaint can be generalized. Adorno does not reckon with the fact that much of the music of the world is not governed by the hierarchies and compositional practices taken for granted in European classical music. In such music, for instance, harmonic development is paramount, whereas in African music – and much of the American popular music that derives from it – specialized modes of rhythmic elaboration are paramount. Indeed, on Adorno's own terms, one might flip the order of musical priority around in order to arrive at a conclusion opposite from his. Gauged by standards reflecting the practices of a Latin percussion ensemble, with its complicated polyrhythms, the music of Bach and Beethoven is simplistic. But even a piano is quite enough for a skilled jazz musician to demonstrate a non-European approach to rhythm. André Hodeir devotes a lengthy essay to Monk's radical innovations in musical time and musical space. Deploying an *unheard* metrical frame and "brilliant simplicity," Monk subjects insignificant blues clichés and Tin Pan Alley melodies to an "acid bath" that restores a "polyphonic fabric" to jazz: "asymmetry and discontinuity enhance one another [in] symbiotic significance."[83] Despite the formal standardizations that permit him to interact with other musicians, Hodeir notes that Monk's ideas about acousmatic space are indigenous to jazz and without precedent in serious music.

Adorno's failure to register such achievements is ironic, for he would be the first to fault listeners who are not able or willing to make similarly refined discriminations within the sphere of classical music. Adorno's thinking seems to be trapped within the false dilemma that jazz is either European or African, never considering the idea that African–American culture is neither of those, but instead a distinctive and independent musical culture. Despite his claim that jazz is a European tradition that has almost nothing to do with "genuine black music" after the 1920s, jazz dissonances do not derive from Debussy.[84] Likewise, the bulk of the audience for jazz has never been the "expert" who, knowledgeable about music theory, engages in analytical or "structural" listening.[85] Because the vast majority of listeners occupy relatively self-contained cultural zones, there is no substance to the worry that popular music is undesirable because it competes with genuine art music: the enduring pleasures of Dave Brubeck's *Take Five* (1959) are not turning anyone away from the benefits of the true avant-garde, whatever that may be.

This analysis brings us to a deeper issue. It should be apparent that Adorno's critique of popular music, or the popular arts generally, is intimately linked to reception theory. That is, he is a consequentialist in the sense that he is interested in what such music does to those *persons* who partake in that music in one form or another. The mere presence of artistic truth content is useless unless the audience has the philosophical perspective to grasp it.[86] Today, virtually everyone has superficial listening and viewing habits that neutralize any formal achievement. Adorno is therefore an extreme pessimist: even if avant-garde serious music succeeds in negating the culture industry, almost no one is going to be affected. Why, then, adopt this all-or-nothing approach? Why not applaud smaller victories where we can get them?

From the vantage point of reception, jazz presents us with an alternative way to avoid the Siren trap that Adorno assigns to jazz – the superficial pseudo-individualization, the lure of the mimicry of emotional expression, the trivial pleasure of recognition, and the hypnotic spell of pop music rhythms. Instead of burying truth content deep within the formal logic of the resistive composition, jazz places both the promise and the cipher on the surface, available to all. Here, we need only cite Robert Walser's discussion of the infamous 1964 performance of "My Funny Valentine" by the Miles Davis Quintet. Knowing that the audience knew the melody, Davis feels free to abandon it almost immediately, after which his soloing seems to be filled with both technical and rhythmic errors. However, we are not hearing a great trumpet player having an "off" night. Instead, we are hearing a foreshadowing of the more radical transgressions of Davis's "electric" period. With "My Funny Valentine," the standardization and familiarity of the tune allow him to construct musical ideas that are meant to be "heard up against the listeners' [prior] experiences" of the song.[87] He simultaneously plays against expectations about the sound of the trumpet, frequently half-valving to produce unexpected timbres.[88] Combine these "flaws" with dissonances and unexpected stretches of silence, and Davis's solo generates an ongoing effect of dashed expectations and dislocation. Much like Coltrane's deconstructions of "My Favorite Things" (1961) and "Chim Chim Cher-ee" (1965), Davis stages a dialogic engagement with the dominant culture by wrestling with and *negating* his source material, recycling but disassembling a musical triviality popularized by the culture industry. A strong element of irrationality is present, but never veiled.

6. Conclusion

If we return to the year of Adorno's radio broadcasts, 1941, we come across a Preston Sturges movie, *Sullivan's Travels*.[89] In that comedy, the protagonist movie director, John L. Sullivan, thinks much the way Adorno does, that Hollywood produces mindless movies that help to perpetuate a suffering working class and, instead, Sullivan wants to make movies that would be "realizing the potentialities of *Film* as the sociological and artistic medium that it is" – movies that would be like holding up a mirror to life.[90] In other words, Sullivan wants to make meaningful movies. But, disguised as a "hobo," his adventures take him to the very bottoms of society and he becomes a prisoner in a chain gang. But when Sunday movie night comes around and the misery of his new colleagues is temporarily relieved with hearty laughter, he comes to see that some fun in the midst of dire straits is better than the best thoughtful filmic tragedies. James Ursini describes that scene as follows:

> A cartoon flashes across an improvised screen. As Pluto dashes across a room, and falls, predictably flat on his face, laughter rocks the old building. Sullivan looks around in amazement. Gone is the pain from the faces of his cellmates; gone is the enmity between races; and gone is the brutality of the warden as faces light up with joy.[91]

There is an analogy with the Sullivan situation in thinking of the off-duty armies of World War II dancing to big band swing music as a manifestation of an Aristotelian catharsis – the purging of our worst stresses – the joy that comes with dancing to jazz. Dancing to the music of jazz certainly has a cathartic function even if jazz itself is to some degree segregated from an everyday empirical reality. It may even rise to the level of "existential escape."[92] As we've said in Chapter 1, when "straight jazz" replaced swing, this particular use of jazz became less common. What happened can be exaggerated as a Cartesian reversal. Rather than an instinctive body moving as a whole by dancing, jazz became something to follow from a stationary position. A matter of scrutinizing, a head thing, rather than a body thing – compromised only by the somaesthetic entrainment we also spoke of in Chapter 1. In arguing that jazz always falls short, Adorno endorses the Cartesian prioritization of the mental over the bodily, fails to see that jazz has shifted its own priorities, and then stubbornly denies that jazz falls on the valuable side of the divide. As we noted earlier, he thinks all music, however serious, is itself "mute" and is made complete through philosophically informed interpretation. We cannot accept this claim. If anything, we revert to Karl Marx's warning that conditions of estranged labor create a situation in which the alienated masses experience freedom in physical, rather than mental, activities.[93] Granted, Marx doesn't mention the arts in this context, but the power of the popular to invoke visceral response confers real value on the popular arts, if only as reminders of the possibility of greater freedom. As Mahalia Jackson says of the source of her blending of gospel and jazz, "we make a joyful noise sometimes when we feel that we are oppressed."[94]

In our view, Adorno underestimates the cathartic function that arts serve in purging us, if only temporarily, of some of our anxieties and stresses. Of course, Aristotle was concerned with the cathartic function of tragic art, and we are suggesting that there can also be cathartic release in laughter and in joyful art.[95] Jazz offers both. The tragedy of "Strange Fruit," Coltrane's "Alabama," and Davis's *A Tribute to Jack Johnson* (1971) is offset by the joy of "Swing, Swing, Swing" and Jason Moran's take on "This Joint is Jumpin'" (2014).

It is difficult, in reading Adorno, to estimate the stretch and range of his culture industry. In the aesthetic theorizing of the early 1940s, Adorno simply ignores the fact there is life outside the culture industry, external to an autonomous art history and within empirical reality. But in that functional world, there may be plenty of seriousness, perhaps more than is needed, of the kind required by Adorno. African-Americans who fled the South and poured into the assembly lines of Detroit and the shipyards of California could hardly have been expected to sit down and listen to the Second Viennese School when they got home from working the swing shift. "Okie" refugees from the dust bowl could hardly be expected to debate Gustav Mahler after a back-breaking day of harvesting lettuce or fruit. There is plenty of seriousness in family matters and paying bills, in local politics and staying out of trouble. And, there is little point in condemning more popular forms of jazz for their ease of absorption and the immediacy of our response. They are only one element in a broad society. We think that contextual place is overlooked by Adorno: despite our common social structures under capitalism, the United States was not fascist Germany, as obvious as this point is.[96] Jazz isn't Schönberg, and that's to its credit.

Notes

1 Theodor W. Adorno, "Farewell to Jazz," in *Essays on Music*, ed. Richard Leppert, trans. Jamie Owen Daniel, modified by Richard Leppert (Berkeley: University of California Press, 2002), 496–499, at 496.
2 Adorno, "Farewell," 497.
3 Theodor W. Adorno, *Introduction to the Sociology of Music*, trans. E. B. Ashton (New York: Seabury Press, 1962), 33. This position is endorsed by David W. Stowe, *Swing Changes: Big-band Jazz in New Deal America* (Cambridge, MA: Harvard University Press, 1994), 279n6.
4 Adorno, *Sociology of Music*, 33.
5 Adorno, *Sociology of Music*, 38.
6 Theodor W. Adorno, Else Frenkel-Brunswik, Daniel J. Levinson, and R. Nevitt Sanford, *The Authoritarian Personality* (New York: Harper & Brothers, 1950), 7.

7   One of the better introductions of the general topic of Adorno and popular music is Babette Babich, *The Hallelujah Effect: Philosophical Reflections on Music, Performance Practice, and Technology* (London: Routledge 2013); see also Robert W. Witkin, *Adorno on Music* (London: Routledge, 1998), chap. 9, and Alex Thomson, *Adorno: A Guide for the Perplexed* (London: Bloomsbury, 2006), chap. 2.

8   Theodor W. Adorno, *Aesthetic Theory*, trans. Christian Lenhardt (London: Routledge & Kegan Paul, 1984), 2–3.

9   Adorno, *Aesthetic Theory*, 4.

10 Adorno, *Aesthetic Theory*, 119.

11 Adorno, *Aesthetic Theory*, 120.

12 Adorno, *Aesthetic Theory*, 120.

13 Immanuel Kant, *Critique of the Power of Judgment*, ed. Paul Guyer, trans. Paul Guyer and Eric Matthews (Cambridge: Cambridge University Press, 2000), §15.

14 Friedrich Nietzsche, *The Birth of Tragedy and The Genealogy of Morals*, trans. Francis Golffing (New York: Doubleday, 1956), 45.

15 Adorno, *Aesthetic Theory*, 42.

16 Adorno, *Aesthetic Theory*, 122.

17 See, for example, Joe Goldberg, *Jazz Masters of the Fifties* (New York: Macmillan, 1965), 209; and Peter Tschmuck, *Creativity and Innovation in the Music Industry*, 2nd ed. (Heidelberg: Springer, 2012), 100.

18 Adorno, *Aesthetic Theory*, 120.

19 Dizzy Gillespie with Al Fraser, *To Be, Or Not … to Bop: Memoirs* (Minneapolis: University of Minnesota Press, 2009), 230. Sounding very much like Adorno, Gillespie accuses most jazz players of producing "pretty, manufactured meaningless tinsel rolling off an assembly line" (230).

20 E.g., Adorno, *Aesthetic Theory*, 122.

21 Adorno, *Aesthetic Theory*, 124; cf. Nietzsche, *Birth of Tragedy*, §I, 23.

22 Adorno ridicules the idea as presented in Wilder Hobson, *American Jazz Music* (New York: Norton, 1938). See Theodor W. Adorno, "Review of *American Jazz Music* by Wilder Hobson and of *Jazz: Hot and Hybrid* by Winthrop Sargeant," *Studies in Philosophy and Social Science* 7:9 (1941): 167–178. The phrase "America's classical music" has become closely associated with Wynton Marsalis; e.g., Leslie Gourse, *Wynton Marsalis: Skain's Domain: A Biography* (New York: Schirmer, 1999), 186, 199.

23 Theodor W. Adorno, *Current of Music: Elements of a Radio Theory*, ed. Robert Hullot-Kentor (Cambridge: Polity Press, 2008), 191–196. The examples are ours, not his.

24 The initial philosophical treatment was Arthur C. Danto, "The Artworld," *The Journal of Philosophy* 61:19 (1964): 571–584. Danto's idea was developed into a much-discussed institutional theory of art by George Dickie, *Art and the Aesthetic: An Institutional Analysis* (Ithaca, NY: Cornell University Press, 1974).

25 For a detailed study of jazz as a commodity, see Damon J. Phillips, *Shaping Jazz: Cities, Labels, and the Global Emergence of an Art Form* (Princeton: Princeton University Press, 2013).

26 One of the best studies of this process is Lawrence W. Levine, *Highbrow/Lowbrow: The Emergence of Cultural Hierarchy in America* (Cambridge, MA: Harvard University Press 1988).

27 Ross Firestone, *Swing, Swing, Swing: The Life and Times of Benny Goodman* (New York: Norton, 1993), 212.

28 Adorno, *Aesthetic Theory*, 186–189.

29 For discussion of some ways bebop was touted as anti-commercial revolt, and criticism of that marketing, see Scott DeVeaux, "'Nice Work if You Can Get It': Thelonious Monk and Popular Song," *Black Music Research Journal* 19:2 (1999): 41–58.

30 Adorno, *Aesthetic Theory*, 6–7.

31 Alasdair MacIntyre, *After Virtue: A Study in Moral Theory*, 3rd ed. (Notre Dame, IN: University of Notre Dame Press, 2007).

32 Adorno, *Aesthetic Theory*, 32, 186–187.

33 A useful overview of some of Adorno's key arguments is provided by Noël Carroll, *A Philosophy of Mass Art* (Oxford: Oxford University Press, 1998), 70–89, 103–109.

34 See Shannon L. Mariotti, *Adorno and Democracy: The American Years* (Lexington: University Press of Kentucky, 2016), 138–142. Adorno's plan for the radio series is outlined in *Current of Music*, chap. 5. It is unclear how many of Adorno's own broadcasts took place.

35 Adorno, *Current of Music*, 62, 89.

36 Adorno, *Current of Music*, 297–298, and "On Popular Music," (with George Simpson), in *Essays on Music*, ed. Richard Leppert, trans. Susan H. Gillespie (Berkeley: University of California Press, 2002), 437–469, at 452.

37 Adorno, *Current of Music*, 197. James M. Harding observes that this line of criticism brings Adorno into the company of the beboppers, who leveled the same charge at Louis Armstrong; see "Adorno, Ellison, and the Critique of Jazz," *Cultural Critique* 31:1 (1995), 129–158, at 149.

38 Adorno, *Current of Music*, 222.

39 Adorno, "On Popular Music," 451.

40 Not long before his death, Adorno was interviewed on German television, and a widely circulated excerpt includes his explanation of why recent popular music does not serve as an effective protest against the horrors of the war in Vietnam; "Theodor Adorno – Music and Protest," *Youtube*, https://youtu.be/-njxKF8CkoU.

41 Adorno, "On the Fetish-Character of Music and the Regression of Listening," in *Essays on Music*, ed. Richard Leppert, trans. Richard Leppert, 288–317, at 309.

42 Adorno, "On Popular Music," 443, 445.

43 Mark Lewisohn, *The Beatles Recording Sessions* (New York: Harmony Books, 1988), 199.

44 Scott Brodeur, "Lyle Lovett, Songwriter, At The Shubert," *The Philadelphia Inquirer* (March 18, 1989), http://articles.philly.com/1989-03-18/news/26130502_1_francine-reed-lyle-lovett-songs.

45 Peter Kivy, *The Fine Art of Repetition: Essays in the Philosophy of Music* (Cambridge: Cambridge University Press, 1993), 341.

46 See Theodore Gracyk, "Allusions and Intentions in Popular Art," in *Philosophy and the Interpretation of Pop Culture*, ed. William Irwin and Jorge J. E. Gracia (Lanham, MD: Rowman & Littlefield: 2007), 65–87.

47 A genuinely primitive artist, Kant notes, produces only "original nonsense" (*Critique*, §46, 186). Charles Mingus makes a similar point when he criticizes the attempt to form a jazz avant-garde (free jazz, evidently): "if I'm a surgeon, am I going to cut you open 'by heart,' just free-form it, you know?" There is no "ready-born doctor," and, by analogy, there is no jazz without study and structure. Quoted in John F. Goodman, *Mingus Speaks* (Berkeley: University of California Press, 2013), 2, 17.

48 Adorno, *Aesthetic Theory*, 213.

49 Adorno's general point is supported by Gamaliel Percino, Peter Klimek, and Stefan Thurner. "Instrumentational Complexity of Music Genres and Why Simplicity Sells," *PLoS ONE* 9:12 (2014).

50 E.g., Adorno, "On Popular Music," 439–441.

51 Adorno, "On Popular Music," 439–441.

52 Gunther Schuller, "Sonny Rollins and the Challenge of Thematic Improvisation," *Jazz Review* (November, 1958), 6–11.

53 Adorno, "Review of *American Jazz Music*." See also James Buhler, "Frankfurt School Blues: Rethinking Adorno's Critique of Jazz," in *Apparitions: Essays on Adorno and Twentieth-Century Music*, ed. Berthold Hoeckner (New York: Routledge, 2006), 103–130.

54 Adorno, *Sociology of Music*, 5–14.

55 Adorno, *Sociology of Music*, 11–12.

56 Adorno, *Sociology of Music*, 6–7. On the pernicious contrast between passive consumption and active listening, see Theodore Gracyk, *Listening to Popular Music Or, How I Learned to Stop Worrying and Love Led Zeppelin* (Ann Arbor: University of Michigan Press, 2007), chap. 5.
57 See Adorno, *Aesthetic Theory*, 6; see also Theodore W. Adorno, "The Aging of the New Music," in *Essays on Music*, ed. Richard Leppert, trans. Robert Hullot-Kentor and Frederic Will, 181–202.
58 Meg Greene, *Billie Holiday: A Biography* (Westport: Greenwood Press, 2007), 39. Making much the same point in 1994, Donald Clarke feels compelled to emphasize that these Tin Pan Alley products are superior to "today's rock hackwork." Donald Clarke, *Billie Holiday: Wishing on the Moon* (New York: Viking, 1994), 93.
59 Adorno, *Sociology of Music*, 33.
60 See Theodor W. Adorno, "Kitsch," in *Essays on Music*, ed. Richard Leppert, trans. Susan H. Gillespie, 501–505, at 502.
61 Adorno, *Sociology of Music*, 12–13.
62 See Philippe Carles and Jean-Louis Comolli, *Free Jazz/Black Power*, trans. Grégory Pierrot (Jackson: University of Mississippi Press, 2015).
63 Barry Farrell, "The Loneliest Monk," *Time* (February 28, 1964), 84–88.
64 Adorno, "Fetish Character of Music," 306.
65 Adorno, *Aesthetic Theory*, 344–345. See also Theodor W. Adorno, "Commitment," *New Left Review* 87/88 (1974): 75–89.
66 Theodor W. Adorno, "On Tradition," trans. E. Geulen, *Telos* 94 (1993): 75–82.
67 Max Horkheimer and Theodor W. Adorno, *The Dialectic of Enlightenment*, trans. John Cumming (New York: Continuum, 1982), 17–18.
68 Adorno, *Aesthetic Theory*, 167.
69 An example of this disconnect is Mathijs Peters, "Adorno Meets Welsh Alternative Rock Band Manic Street Preachers: Three Proposed Critical Models," *Journal of Popular Culture* 48:6 (2016): 1346–1373.
70 Adorno, *Sociology of Music*, 29.
71 Theodor W. Adorno, "On Jazz," in *Essays on Music*, ed. Richard Leppert, trans. Jamie Owen Daniel, modified by Richard Leppert, 470–495, at 484.
72 This phrase comes from Max Paddison in his excellent study, "Authenticity and Failure in Adorno's Aesthetics of Music," in *The Cambridge Companion to Adorno*, ed. Tom Huhn (Cambridge: Cambridge University Press, 2004), 198–221, at 200.
73 See Jean-Philippe Marcoux, *Jazz Griots: Music as History in the 1960s African American Poem* (Lanham, MD: Lexington Books, 2012), and Ted Gioia, *The History of Jazz*, 2nd ed. (Oxford: Oxford University Press, 2011), 15.
74 In the African-American tradition, song is the "primary recorder, the means of documentation of life and experience." Fahamisha Patricia Brown, *Performing the Word: African American Poetry as Vernacular Culture* (New Brunswick, NJ: Rutgers University Press, 1999), 82.
75 Homer, *The Odyssey*, trans. Robert Fitzgerald (New York: Vintage, 1961), 1.
76 Horkheimer and Adorno, *Dialectic of Enlightenment*, 56.
77 Horkheimer and Adorno, *Dialectic of Enlightenment*, 59.
78 Horkheimer and Adorno, *Dialectic of Enlightenment*, 59–60.
79 Adorno, *Sociology of Music*, 4–5.
80 Barry Ulanov, *A History of Jazz in America* (New York: Viking Press, 1952), 13.
81 Adorno, "On Jazz," 490.
82 Buhler, "Frankfurt School Blues," 126.
83 André Hodeir, *Toward Jazz*, trans. Noel Burch (New York: Grove Press, 1962), 166, 169, 171.
84 Adorno, "On Jazz," 477 and 484, respectively.
85 Adorno, *Sociology of Music*, 4–5.

86 Adorno is explicit about this point, e.g., *Aesthetic Theory*, 107, 189–190.
87 Robert Walser, "Out of Notes: Signification, Interpretation, and the Problem of Miles Davis," in *Jazz among the Discourses*, ed. Krin Gabbard (Durham: Duke University Press, 1995), 165–188, at 173.
88 Walser, "Out of Notes," 174–175. Walser also notes Davis's similarities to Monk in his use of space and fortuitous accidents. Although Walser does not mention Adorno, his reading of Davis is intended to sidestep the interpretive framework of modernism.
89 For other discussions of Adorno and *Sullivan's Travels*, see Stanley Cavell, *Philosophy the Day after Tomorrow* (Cambridge, MA: Harvard University Press, 2005), 88–90, and Anca Parvulescu, *Laughter: Notes on a Passion* (Cambridge, MA: MIT Press, 2010), 148–151.
90 James Ursini, *The Fabulous Life and Times of Preston Sturges: An American Dreamer* (New York: Curtis Books, 1973), 91.
91 Ursini, *Fabulous Life*, 95–96.
92 Joachim-Ernst Berendt, quoted in Andrew Wright Hurley, *The Return of Jazz: Joachim-Ernst Berendt and West German Cultural Change* (New York: Berghahn Books, 2009), 40.
93 Karl Marx, "Alienation," in *Karl Marx: Reader*, ed. Jon Elster (Cambridge: Cambridge University Press, 1986), 35–47, at 40.
94 Quoted in Laurraine Goreau, *Just Mahalia, Baby: The Mahalia Jackson Story* (Waco: Word Books, 1975), 559. For more on the positive value of laughter and humor in Adorno's critique of the culture industry, see Sheryl Tuttle Ross and Aaron Golec, "The Folly of Reason and Gravity of Reconciled Humor in Horkheimer and Adorno's *Dialectic of Enlightenment*," *Aesthetic Investigations* 1:2 (2016): 292–307.
95 See Eli Rozik, *Comedy: A Critical Introduction* (Eastbourne: Sussex Academic Press, 2011), chap. 2, and Lane Cooper, *An Aristotelian Theory of Comedy with an Adaptation of the* Poetics, *and a Translation of the* Tractatus Coislinianus (New York: Harcourt, 1922), 60–76.
96 Adorno continued to compare jazz fans and Germany's fascists. See Theodor W. Adorno, "Perennial Fashion – Jazz," in *Prisms*, trans. Samuel Webster and Shierry Webster (Cambridge, MA: MIT Press, 1983), 119–132, at 129.

References

Adorno, Theodor W. *Aesthetic Theory*, trans. Christian Lenhardt. London: Routledge & Kegan Paul, 1984.
Adorno, Theodor W. "The Aging of the New Music." In *Essays on Music*, ed. Richard Leppert, trans. Robert Hullot-Kentor and Frederic Will, 181–202. Berkeley: University of California Press, 2002.
Adorno, Theodor W. "Commitment." *New Left Review* 87/88 (1974): 75–89.
Adorno, Theodor W. *Current of Music: Elements of a Radio Theory*, ed. Robert Hullot-Kentor. Cambridge: Polity Press, 2008.
Adorno, Theodor W. *Essays on Music*, ed. Richard Leppert. Berkeley: University of California Press, 2002.
Adorno, Theodor W. "Farewell to Jazz." In *Essays on Music*, ed. Richard Leppert, trans. Jamie Owen Daniel, modified by Richard Leppert, 496–499. Berkeley: University of California Press, 2002.
Adorno, Theodor W. *Introduction to the Sociology of Music*, trans. E. B. Ashton. New York: Seabury Press, 1962.
Adorno, Theodor W. "Kitsch." In *Essays on Music*, ed. Richard Leppert, trans. Susan H. Gillespie, 501–505. Berkeley: University of California Press, 2002.
Adorno, Theodor W. (with George Simpson). "On Popular Music." In *Essays on Music*, ed. Richard Leppert, trans. Susan H. Gillespie, 437–469. Berkeley: University of California Press, 2002.

Adorno, Theodor W. "On the Fetish-Character of Music and the Regression of Listening." In *Essays on Music*, ed. Richard Leppert, trans. Richard Leppert, 288–317. Berkeley: University of California Press, 2002.

Adorno, Theodor W. "On Jazz." In *Essays on Music*, ed. Richard Leppert, trans. Jamie Owen Daniel, modified by Richard Leppert, 470–495. Berkeley: University of California Press, 2002.

Adorno, Theodor W. "On Tradition." trans. E. Geulen, *Telos* 94 (1993): 75–82.

Adorno, Theodor W. "Perennial Fashion – Jazz." In *Prisms*, trans. Samuel Webster and Shierry Webster, 119–132. Cambridge, MA: MIT Press, 1983.

Adorno, Theodor W. "Review of *American Jazz Music* by Wilder Hobson and of *Jazz: Hot and Hybrid* by Winthrop Sargeant." *Studies in Philosophy and Social Science* 7:9 (1941): 167–178.

Adorno, Theodor W., Else Frenkel-Brunswick, Daniel J. Levinson, and R. Nevitt Sanford. *The Authoritarian Personality*. New York: Harper & Brothers, 1950.

Babich, Babette. *The Hallelujah Effect: Philosophical Reflections on Music, Performance Practice, and Technology*. London: Routledge, 2013.

Brodeur, Scott. "Lyle Lovett, Songwriter, At The Shubert." *The Philadelphia Inquirer* (March 18, 1989): http://articles.philly.com/1989-03-18/news/26130502_1_francine-reed-lyle-lovett-songs.

Brown, Fahamisha Patricia. *Performing the Word: African American Poetry as Vernacular Culture*. New Brunswick, NJ: Rutgers University Press, 1999.

Buhler, James. "Frankfurt School Blues: Rethinking Adorno's Critique of Jazz." In *Apparitions: Essays on Adorno and Twentieth-Century Music*, ed. Berthold Hoeckner, 103–130. New York: Routledge, 2006.

Carles, Philippe, and Jean-Louis Comolli. *Free Jazz/Black Power*, trans. Grégory Pierrot. Jackson: University of Mississippi Press, 2015.

Carroll, Noël. *A Philosophy of Mass Art*. Oxford: Oxford University Press, 1998.

Cavell, Stanley. *Philosophy the Day after Tomorrow*. Cambridge, MA: Harvard University Press, 2005.

Clarke, Donald. *Billie Holiday: Wishing on the Moon*. New York: Viking, 1994.

Cooper, Lane. *An Aristotelian Theory of Comedy with an Adaptation of the* Poetics, *and a Translation of the* Tractatus Coislinianus. New York: Harcourt, 1922.

Danto, Arthur C. "The Artworld." *Journal of Philosophy* 61:19 (1964): 571–584.

DeVeaux, Scott. "'Nice Work if You Can Get It': Thelonious Monk and Popular Song." *Black Music Research Journal* 19:2 (1999): 41–58.

Dickie, George. *Art and the Aesthetic: An Institutional Analysis*. Ithaca, NY: Cornell University Press, 1974.

Farrell, Barry. "The Loneliest Monk." *Time* (February 28, 1964): 84–88.

Firestone, Ross. *Swing, Swing, Swing: The Life and Times of Benny Goodman*. New York: Norton, 1993.

Gillespie, Dizzy, with Al Fraser. *To Be, Or Not ... to Bop*. Minneapolis: University of Minnesota Press, 2009 [1979].

Gioia, Ted. *The History of Jazz*, 2nd ed. Oxford: Oxford University Press, 2011.

Goldberg, Joe. *Jazz Masters of the Fifties*. New York: Macmillan, 1965.

Goodman, John F. *Mingus Speaks*. Berkeley: University of California Press, 2013.

Goreau, Laurraine. *Just Mahalia, Baby: The Mahalia Jackson Story*. Waco: Word Books, 1975.

Gourse, Leslie. *Wynton Marsalis: Skain's Domain: A Biography*. New York: Schirmer, 1999.

Gracyk, Theodore. "Allusions and Intentions in Popular Art." In *Philosophy and the Interpretation of Pop Culture*, eds. William Irwin and Jorge J. E. Gracia, 65–87. Lanham, MD: Rowman & Littlefield: 2007.

Gracyk, Theodore. *Listening to Popular Music Or, How I Learned to Stop Worrying and Love Led Zeppelin.* Ann Arbor: University of Michigan Press, 2007.

Greene, Meg. *Billie Holiday: A Biography.* Westport: Greenwood Press, 2007.

Harding, James M. "Adorno, Ellison, and the Critique of Jazz." *Cultural Critique* 31:1 (1995), 129–158.

Hobson, Wilder. *American Jazz Music.* New York: Norton, 1938.

Hodeir, André. *Toward Jazz*, trans. Noel Burch. New York: Grove Press, 1962.

Homer, *The Odyssey*, trans. Robert Fitzgerald. New York: Vintage, 1961.

Horkheimer, Max, and Theodor W. Adorno. *The Dialectic of Enlightenment*, trans. John Cumming. New York: Continuum, 1982.

Hurley, Andrew Wright. *The Return of Jazz: Joachim-Ernst Berendt and West German Cultural Change.* New York: Berghahn Books, 2009.

Kant, Immanuel. *Critique of the Power of Judgment*, ed. Paul Guyer, trans. Paul Guyer and Eric Matthews. Cambridge: Cambridge University Press, 2000.

Kivy, Peter. *The Fine Art of Repetition: Essays in the Philosophy of Music.* Cambridge: Cambridge University Press, 1993.

Levine, Lawrence W. *Highbrow/Lowbrow: The Emergence of Cultural Hierarchy in America.* Cambridge, MA: Harvard University Press 1988.

Lewisohn, Mark. *The Beatles Recording Sessions.* New York: Harmony Books, 1988.

MacIntyre, Alasdair. *After Virtue: A Study in Moral Theory*, 3rd ed. Notre Dame, IN: University of Notre Dame Press, 2007.

Marcoux, Jean-Philippe. *Jazz Griots: Music as History in the 1960s African American Poem.* Lanham: Lexington Books, 2012.

Mariotti, Shannon L. *Adorno and Democracy: The American Years.* Lexington: University Press of Kentucky, 2016.

Marx, Karl. "Alienation." In *Karl Marx: Reader*, ed. Jon Elster, 35–47. Cambridge: Cambridge University Press, 1986.

Nietzsche, Friedrich. *The Birth of Tragedy* and *The Genealogy of Morals*, trans. Francis Golffing. New York: Doubleday, 1956.

Paddison, Max. "Authenticity and Failure in Adorno's Aesthetics of Music." In *The Cambridge Companion to Adorno*, ed., Tom Huhn, 198–221. Cambridge: Cambridge University Press, 2004.

Parvulescu, Anca. *Laughter: Notes on a Passion.* Cambridge, MA: MIT Press, 2010.

Percino, Gamaliel, Peter Klimek, and Stefan Thurner. "Instrumentational Complexity of Music Genres and Why Simplicity Sells." *PLoS ONE* 9:12 (2014).

Peters, Mathijs. "Adorno Meets Welsh Alternative Rock Band Manic Street Preachers: Three Proposed Critical Models." *Journal of Popular Culture* 48:6 (2016): 1346–1373.

Phillips, Damon J. *Shaping Jazz: Cities, Labels, and the Global Emergence of an Art Form.* Princeton: Princeton University Press, 2013.

Ross, Sheryl Tuttle, and Aaron Golec. "The Folly of Reason and Gravity of Reconciled Humor in Horkheimer and Adorno's Dialectic of Enlightenment." *Aesthetic Investigations* 1:2 (2016): 292–307.

Rozik, Eli. *Comedy: A Critical Introduction.* Eastbourne: Sussex Academic Press, 2011.

Schuller, Gunther. "Sonny Rollins and the Challenge of Thematic Improvisation." *Jazz Review* (November 1958), 6–11.

Scruton, Roger. *Understanding Music: Philosophy and Interpretation*. London: Continuum, 2009.

Stowe, David W. *Swing Changes: Big-band Jazz in New Deal America*. Cambridge, MA: Harvard University Press, 1994.

Thomson, Alex. *Adorno: A Guide for the Perplexed*. London: Bloomsbury, 2006.

Tschmuck, Peter. *Creativity and Innovation in the Music Industry*, 2nd ed. Heidelberg: Springer, 2012.

Ulanov, Barry. *A History of Jazz in America*. New York: Viking Press, 1952.

Ursini, James. *The Fabulous Life and Times of Preston Sturges: An American Dreamer*. New York: Curtis Books, 1973.

Walser, Robert. "Out of Notes: Signification, Interpretation, and the Problem of Miles Davis." In *Jazz Among the Discourses*, ed. Krin Gabbard, 165–188. Durham: Duke University Press, 1995.

Witkin, Robert W. *Adorno on Music*. London: Routledge, 1998.

PART III

Music Ontology

7

IMPROVISATIONS AND SPONTANEITY

The improvisational nature of jazz musicianship is such that a truly competent performer must be prepared to function as an on-the-spot composer who is expected to contribute to the orchestration in progress, not simply to execute the score as it is written and rehearsed.

– Albert Murray

I joined and we opened at the Hollywood Bowl playing *Joshua*. And we had no rehearsal. Miles had said in the dressing room, "Do you know my music?" And I said, "Yeah." He said, "oh-oh." Then we went on. For six years.

– Wayne Shorter on joining Miles Davis

Conceptually, improvisation is associated with creative spontaneity.[1] There are periods in the history of jazz where jazz and improvisation are intimately linked. Since bebop, especially, an audience would expect a jazz soloist to improvise, either in a free jazz rendition or in a musical interpretation of an old standard. And while it might be thought that musical improvisation is the specialty of some forms of jazz, it has long been a common – indeed, perhaps basic – feature of music throughout the world. Arab, Indian, Iranian, and African musicians have all long been avid practitioners of it. From the Middle Ages through the Renaissance in European music, it was standard practice to improvise a line in counterpoint over a *cantus firmus*. In the classical era, keyboardists often competed with each other in improvisational contests – Mozart, for instance, against Muzio Clementi, or Beethoven against rivals such as Johann Nepomuck Hummel. Performances *extempore* are still standard features of organ recitals. However, improvisation in Western concert music declined in the nineteenth and twentieth centuries. Consequently, for many listeners in the Western tradition, the paradigm example of improvisation is jazz.

At the same time, we have emphasized that improvisation is not essential to any definition of jazz.[2] To think that it is essential would be to ignore a good deal of the history of jazz. The role of improvisation is often of negligible importance in the big band practices of Ellington, Whiteman, Dorsey, and Goodman. Another complication is that not every occasion for improvisation is actually an improvised performance. Because improvisation is often a challenge for musicians who may play night after night, it may come with a certain degree of pressure. But inspiration does not always coincide with the practical demand to solo. It should be noted, then, that there are times when a soloist plays something partly or even wholly remembered, either consciously or by body recall. It happens to almost everyone who performs.[3] However, what we discuss in this chapter is not the musical techniques and challenges of improvisation but rather the core concept of musical improvisation, leading us to distinguish between several kinds of idealized improvisation, including pure improvisation. If there is a distinction to be made between improvisation as it is practiced – and hence not always as spontaneous as audiences might expect – and improvisation in principle, then this chapter, for the most part, deals with the latter. We say this merely to begin with a clarification and to set the stage for what follows.

Here's how improvisation often works in mainstream jazz: A "head" – usually based on a 32-bar jazz "standard," such as "Body and Soul," or 12-bar blues pattern – is played over once, or perhaps twice, framing improvised solos. Typically, the improvised melodies are played on the harmonic and rhythmic foundation provided by the head. Alternative chords are often allowed, depending upon style. After a sequence of solos, the performance will normally end with a reprise of the head. There are many variations to the basic pattern. Several musicians may trade off with each other. Or, as in classic New Orleans jazz, many musicians can improvise collectively, individually augmenting and varying their contribution to the shared performance of a familiar tune. The basic pattern was challenged by the rise of so-called "modal" jazz in which, instead of improvising on melodies that fit a set of chords, soloists would create wide-ranging variations within a single scale. The free improvisations of the "New Thing" of the 1960s and the ensuing avant-garde movement pushed the envelope of collective improvisation. Meter, line length, duration of solos, and every other structural "given" are up to each musician. The crucial point is that there is no one practice that counts as jazz improvisation, and the amount and degree of improvisation that we can ascribe to different jazz styles and periods will depend on the description of improvisation that is adopted from several contending definitions. And because improvisation is regarded as an important musical value within jazz, the degree to which it *is* present is also relevant to jazz practice and to informed responses to it.

1. Two Ideologies of Improvisation

Neither of two extreme points of view about improvisation can be sustained. Unfortunately, both have had adherents, so it is best to begin with them before we go any further. One of these might be termed the *Romantic perspective*, according to which improvisation is utterly rule-free music making – music created "without previous preparation," as one work on piano instruction puts it.[4] Too often, though, the *ex nihilo* view is based on an equation of the improvised with the primitive or unschooled. Such a view, as applied to jazz, was popular in mid-twentieth century among certain French journalists – for example Robert Goffin, who often extolled the most untrained, most "frenzied," versions of jazz as the most authentic.[5] Ted Gioia rightly points out that this common equation of jazz spontaneity with musical primitivism is condescending and reflects racist stereotypes.[6]

This Romantic perspective reflects naïveté about the basic resources that improvisational performances inevitably presume. Experts on Iranian instrumental music, for instance, explain that improvisers in that tradition must learn several hundred elements that make up the repertoires of what is called the *radif*.[7] Analogous considerations apply to jazz improvisation, as demonstrated by Paul Berliner's massive ethnographic study of the topic.[8] Jazz musicians too internalize a cache of musical forms – e.g., meters, bar lengths, chord progressions, even phrase patterns – as frameworks and as material for improvised solos: Charlie Christian routinely returned to five or six melodic formulas in order to improvise his tightly structured guitar solos.[9] As we noted in Chapter 3, untold numbers of bop saxophonists honed their improvisation skills by practicing Charlie Parker's "licks" and even complete solos.[10] Dexter Gordon initially questioned Ornette Coleman's musical competence, but he reversed course when they were booked together at a jazz festival where he got to hear Coleman's pre-performance warmup: "a devastatingly accurate representation of Charlie Parker's playing."[11] Even Keith Jarrett's famously "free" piano improvisations were typically built upon a vamp of familiar chords.[12]

The freedom of the improviser is also limited by what she must not do. In Ghanaian drum music, for instance, only certain instruments are allowed to improvise and they can do so only within prescribed limits.[13] Unwitting musicians who beat out novel pulses without regard to customary practice could easily confuse the dancers and other musicians. In jazz, too, the most daring soloist realizes that there are any number of things she is not supposed to do. Even in a "free jazz" context, a keyboardist is not normally allowed to interpolate Frederick Chopin's *Ballade in G Minor*, or to beat the piano keys with a baseball bat.[14] Further, there are contextual stylistic constraints. As Stan Godlovitch puts it, "one isn't free to make musical nonsense" when improvising.[15] Finally, it might seem that while playing with Charles Mingus, Eric Dolphy had as much freedom as could be imagined. In fact, Mingus encouraged those specific qualities in Dolphy's playing that fit the conception of the music he wanted to realize. Mingus sought an "equalization of instrumental voices" in collective improvisation, facilitating "an extraordinarily high amount of group interaction."[16] Dolphy was expected to play in support of the other musicians to the same degree that they supported him, a notable departure from his role as a "front line" soloist as a member of John Coltrane's 1961 quintet.

Part of the explanation for the mystificationist perspective on improvisation is that most of us are mere auditors of the activity rather than participants. A partial antidote is the useful analogy some have suggested between musical improvisation and linguistic activity, in which we all participate. For instance, the highly interactive playing of jazz musicians has been framed as a musical conversation, which "is undeniably improvisational in nature." As in a spoken conversation between two people, jazz soloing often begins in one place and then the participants choose "where to go" as they go along.[17] Many jazz musicians think that art-as-language is more than a mere metaphor. They think that jazz *is* a language, and a jazz performance *is* a meaningful conversation.[18] However, there is little support for this stronger position among philosophers of art, because the most salient hallmarks of natural language are clearly lacking. The intelligibility of natural language is rooted in its capacity to refer to objects in our environment; all natural languages allow participants to state truths about the world, as well as to state lies (i.e., a semantic component); finally, natural languages possess translatability, permitting bilingual speakers to independently produce translations that closely match those produced by other bilingual speakers.[19] However, these features are notably lacking in the "language" of jazz. Two speakers who are competent in both French and English will independently translate "Normalement, le ciel est orange" as "Normally, the sky is orange" and will regard it as false. Asked to "translate" the 8-bar theme that constitutes the composed music of Wayne Shorter's "Limbo," any two jazz fans are likely to offer two very different descriptions (if any). Furthermore, while there are many ways that a jazz solo can go wrong, we are hard pressed to identify a jazz solo that makes a false statement, even assuming that jazz can make any statement at all. Jazz may be symbolically rich, but there are ways to be symbolically rich that are distinct from language use.

Equally extreme, of course, is the view that, once the materials that go into the process are understood, improvisation can, in effect, be explained away. According to this perspective, what we call "improvising" – unless it be mere noodling – always follows a preconceived plan. However, even if a performance were to consist of a dreary pastiche of learned material, there is no reason not to regard it as genuinely improvisational – unless all of the sequencing had also been worked out in advance.

Whether resemblances between collective jazz and language are strong or weak, it is obvious that improvisation plays a major role in both everyday linguistic activity and in jazz. It is an important feature of other performing contexts, including comedy clubs. Again, the analogy between collective improvisation and linguistic conversation is a good one, even if the core of the analogy between jazz and natural language seems to fall through. Finally, improvisation is also a major factor in other, non-spoken activities from cooking to sports and these have certain obvious resemblances to aspects of jazz performance.

2. What is Improvisation?

2A. Improvisation and Composition

It is striking that a principled analysis of the concept of the improvisational has been so elusive. Many writers have approached the concept by relating it to another supposedly less daunting one – composition, for instance.[20] Here, two opposite strategies open up. One is to illuminate improvisation by contrasting it with composition. The other is to try to demonstrate affinities between improvisation and composition.

Borrowing words from the jazz pianist Bill Evans, Gioia states that improvisational jazz differs from many other artistic practices, including musical composition, by its dependence upon a "retrospective" rather than a "blueprint," or "prospective," model. In the prospective model, artists make decisions about what is to come next in light of an overall conception. With the retrospective model, "the artist can start his work with an almost random maneuver – a brush stroke on canvas, an opening line, a musical motif – and then adapt his later moves to this gambit." The jazz improviser may proceed from his opening move in any number of directions.[21] However, there is no reason a composer too might not begin with a random maneuver and adapt later moves to the initial one.[22] Furthermore, there is no reason why improvising musicians need to play in the absence of an overall conception of what they are doing. Whatever Coleman Hawkins was creating in his famous 1939 recording of "Body and Soul," it was not the harmonic motion instanced by that song. He simply accepted it as a pattern for his solo. An overall conception can also govern a particular case of free improvisation. "Intuition," by the Lennie Tristano Quintet (1949), is thought to be one of the first free improvisations recorded. Although jazz fans had great difficulty comprehending music played "without a fixed chord progression; without a time signature; without a specific tempo,"[23] it betrays the plan that made it work: Tristano started it off with an improvised piano gesture, developed it, and then the other four musicians entered in a predetermined order, picking up and developing a musical idea already introduced by another player. The result is a dense "contrapuntal interaction."[24] Tristano's musical input may have been "random" but the other musicians' inputs, also improvised, certainly were not. They were handed a certain motif and their free play was partially determined by what came before them. Any "randomness" of improvised jazz needs at least serious qualification.

A novel way of contrasting improvisation and composition was articulated by the composer Ferruccio Busoni. Taking a stand against the common modern platitude voiced by Arnold Schönberg and others that the performer of a composed work is only the servant of it, Busoni claimed that improvisation is historically, and perhaps logically, more fundamental than composition. Compositional notation, he states, "is to improvisation as the portrait is to the living model." It is only "an ingenious expedient for catching an inspiration, with the purpose of exploiting it later." An interpreter of a notated work thus has the obligation to do his best to "restore" what "the composer's inspiration necessarily loses through notation."[25]

Of course, it is difficult to sustain the thesis. First, Busoni appears to assume mistakenly that all musical works for performance are tied to scores. However, as we explain in Chapter 4 in our response to Jerrold Levinson, the folk tradition offers no end of repeatable works that were handed down without notation or scores.[26] Second, even if the concept of a musical work has only developed in relatively recent music history, it does not follow that full-fledged musical works are awkward attempts at catching something more basic, fundamental, or original. Third, as Stephen Davies has explained, works for performance necessarily have some degree of thinness – that is, some degree to which the work's instructions, whether through a score or otherwise, leave some performance decisions to be determined by the performer.[27] To add that these decisions should be guided by some more fundamental model lying, so to say, behind the scored work is hardly helpful.

2B. Improvisation as Composition

An opposing approach is to stress affinities between improvisation and composition. Gunther Schuller, in one of his exhaustive historical studies of jazz, recommends that we should see a jazz soloist's recorded performance as a "work in progress."[28] If the similarity of Charlie Parker's recorded solos to compositions seems less than obvious, consider that when he recorded his music, the final product issued to the public would typically be picked as the best of several recording "takes." (And we must stress that Parker's case is not unique.) So, there is some correspondence between this practice and the kind of trial-and-error methods of composers. An example not limited to the territory of recorded music comes from the life of J. S. Bach. While at Potsdam, it is said, Bach improvised a three-part *ricercare* for Frederick the Great, but wrote the music down only later when he returned to Leipzig. According to Peter Kivy, "the composing was already done" when Bach improvised the piece.[29] Can we generalize from this kind of case? Performance of a work in progress implies that whatever is being performed is meant to be performed again, in some refined form, in the future. But with a Parker saxophone solo, each solo begins again, and it is irrelevant whether it ever leads to something else. In contrast, when a work in progress is performed but never performed again, it is an abandoned and unfinished work. We do not, however, think that a highly unique jazz solo is equivalent to an abandoned work.

In what might have been the first extended philosophical treatment of improvisation in English, Philip Alperson attempts to make the connection between improvisation and composition by means of a rather complex argument. He first establishes a reciprocal relationship between composition and work-performance.[30] In narrower senses of these concepts, it is customary to distinguish the two. However, in a broad sense, Alperson urges, composing always involves performance, e.g., running over music in one's mind if not actually playing it aloud. In a broad sense, too, the converse holds, given that, as already noted, there is always some degree to which the instructions for a work leave some decisions to the performer.

Now, when Alperson turns to improvisation, he says that we have an activity in which the improviser "practices simultaneously the interdependent functions of composition and performance in both the broad and narrow senses of the term."[31] By these moves, the gap between improvisation and composition is gradually closed so as to yield the wanted analysis: improvisation is the composition of a musical work as it is being performed.[32]

Alperson has been challenged on the grounds that he makes his case only by using the concepts of both composition and performance too loosely.[33] When arguing for the necessity of (improvisational) performance to composition, he sticks pretty closely to our standard concept of composition. However, when he turns to the converse point, Alperson uses "composition" in a much looser sense, where it now means something like "determining the sonic properties of a performance." Analogously, Alperson sometimes uses "performance" in a standard sense – roughly, the tokening of a pre-existing work-type. However, when arguing that composition requires performance, he shifts to a loose or "persuasive" sense of "performance," where the mere generation of some musical sounds qualifies. However, a composition that is never performed, despite intent, is nevertheless a composition. The grain of truth in Alperson's view might simply be that both improvisation and composition are creative activities.

If we compare improvisation and composition as practices, we can discern general reasons why the one cannot be assimilated to the other. Let us profile them briefly.

The French existentialists were fascinated by the idea of forced choice, according to which every moment in life – for those living authentically – is latent with an anxiety-charged choice among alternatives. This may be an exaggerated picture of human life in general, but the thought might have some application to improvisation. By contrast with the improviser, the composer can take time out in her project – indeed, set it aside for years. The improviser must plunge ahead and do something. Stretches of silence can be musically functional in all music, whether composed or not. However, a pause in the process of composing a work does not become a potentially unfortunate feature of the work. With improvisation, time-outs resulting from fatigue or a lack of inspiration carry costs. Indeed, these costs underlie one of the values of improvising during performance. (We will return to this topic in Chapter 10.) Alperson, whose overall theory seems to neglect it, notes a related difference between improvisation and composition.[34] At any point, the composer can alter what has so far been laid down. Not only can compositional projects be revised up to the point of publication; they can perhaps even be revised beyond that point, as when Carla Bley republished her short composition "Ictus" (1961) without bar lines in 1976. We normally call these revisions "versions," distinguishing them from other derivative forms, such as parodies and variations.[35] Alperson's useful observation is that subsequent effort by an *improviser* might be superior to a previous one, but it cannot count as a *revision* of an earlier one or as a preface to new music.

Finally, the improviser's choices ramify, in the sense that she must produce on-the-spot responses to something already laid down. An extended improvisation is a continuous feedback loop, such that later phrases are responses to previous ones. Sometimes, as we noted in our discussion of Tristano's "Intuition," this is the central organizing principle: later entrants into the improvisation took part by repeating and modifying earlier phrases. In improvisation, but not composition, there is no going back.

Now, none of the foregoing rules out that Bach, on the occasion cited earlier, was composing as he improvised, although we can see now how that is less clear than it might sound. Some jazz players may occasionally do so, too.[36] However, to generalize from that case to composition as a general practice is implausible. It is part of the *practice* of composing that composers do avail themselves of the conventions that allow the sorts of revisions and time-outs that are not allowed in genuine improvisational performances. (Imagine the riskiness of composition were it otherwise.) This is not to deny, however, that in non-performances (e.g., rehearsals) improvisations can share the stop and go qualities, even the abandonment of certain musical ideas, with composition. So the emphasis here is on context – improvisation in the spotlight is our standard case of improvisation and that is what we will consider next.

2C. Improvisation and Work-Performance

Another way to explicate improvisation is as part of the very concept of work-performance. Perhaps, as some have maintained, improvisation is not a curiously separate and distinctive form of performance, but an inevitable dimension of any music-making whatsoever.[37] For instance, Carol S. Gould and Kenneth Keaton argue that "all musical performance, no matter how meticulously interpreted and no matter how specific the inscribed score, requires improvisation."[38] Basic to the argument is the now familiar view – which the theory shares with Alperson's – that musical works underdetermine their performances. The authors go on to claim that such work-performances count as improvisation, for improvisation is "a relation between the score and the performance event."[39]

In order to support this broadening of the concept of improvisation, note, the authors must interpret improvisation in such a way that an improvisation need be neither spontaneous nor occur during performance.[40] So, a specific thickening of the instructions for Charles Mingus's *Epitaph* that conductor Gunther Schuller worked out in advance of sharing it with his musicians (e.g., the addition of a few dynamics) would, on this theory, qualify as improvisatory. However, this would surely be stretching the concept of *jazz* improvisation to the breaking point.[41] At the very least, a necessary condition on a jazz improvisation is that it involves spontaneity (i.e., extemporaneous decision-making) in performance. However, even if the Gould/Keaton point regarding the divide between score and performance was correct, one would still need to begin a discourse about degrees and kinds of score independence. Such a discussion will help mark the gap between improvisation in jazz and in the Gould/Keaton examples from classical music. We develop this idea below, in section 4.

2D. Improvisation and Spontaneous Creation

In a later essay, Alperson wrote, to "improvise is to do or produce something on the spur of the moment."[42] There must be something to this idea. But can the matter be that simple? Of course not, as Alperson is well aware.[43]

To improvise, let us say, is to make decisions about the music one is playing as one plays. Free improvisations such as Tristano's "Intuition" demonstrate that we must avoid equating "music" here with "a musical composition." But the formula faces other more serious difficulties of clarification. First, what should we make of the implicit temporal marker in the phrase, "as one plays?" Surely an improviser's decision to go one way rather than another must have been made at least a nanosecond before following through. In fact, though, we may not know enough about the mechanics of mental activity to decide the issue one way or another, so let us leave the matter open. An improvisational move is one made at the time of or slightly before the move itself – where we shall assume that either formulation would make the addition of "spontaneity" in the formulation unnecessary.[44] However, we cannot avoid fuzzy cases here. If Sonny Rollins lays out a second chorus while playing the first, should we regard the second as improvised?

Further, what is it to make "decisions about the music?" Given what we saw about the inevitable resources that are drawn upon in improvisational performance, it is not clear what this concept means, or how it applies. As already suggested, even very free improvisations have some structural guidance. In Ornette Coleman's early forays into free jazz, the overall structure of each performance was indeterminate, and many of the performances sound ramshackle and chaotic. Nonetheless, we can hear that the individual musicians are attending to each other as the music progresses, and both their individual contributions and their interactions betray considerable local coherence. Mingus called it "organized disorganization."[45] Decision-making is often tied to deliberation, and while spontaneous actions may retroactively be called decisions, it is a different kind of animal entirely than where forethought is involved.

This suggests a need to spell out the difference between mere noodling and decisions that are substantive. The keyboard improvisations of Cecil Taylor have struck many unappreciative listeners as noise, but no one has accused him of simply noodling. James O. Young and Carl Matheson have suggested that, in jazz, "an improvised performance is one in which the structural properties of a performance are not completely determined by decisions made prior to the time of performance," where "structural properties" include melody, harmony, and length as opposed to "expressive properties" like "tempo, the use of vibrato, dynamic, and so on."[46] Still, the concept of a structural property remains unclear. By what criterion would we distinguish between structural properties and others? More generally, it is difficult to see why the musical properties that can be improvised should be restricted at all – except to those over which the improviser has control. A case in point is "Nefertiti," a Wayne Shorter composition performed by the Miles Davis Quintet. As "structure" is understood by Young and Matheson, it appears to have been *completely* worked out in advance:

> [I]t contains no solos in any conventional sense. Instead, Davis and Shorter repeat the mournful theme over and over again through the long track (almost eight minutes). Yet [it] remains rich in spontaneity; improvisation is in a sense constant, not only in the play of the rhythm section but even in the theme statements by the horns, which repeat the same basic scale again and again with different nuances each time.[47]

Indeed, the piece strongly illustrates Ralph J. Gleason's remark that some of the Quintet's music can be heard as "a concerto for drums."[48] Once the "Nefertiti" performance is underway, Tony Williams's inventive percussion is the primary evidence of spontaneous decision-making, inventively filling the silences between repetitions of the 16-bar theme.

2E. A Matter of Degree or of Kind?

Let us grant then that an element of spontaneity is involved in any performance we term "improvisational." With that assumption, can we then say that improvisation and work-performance "differ more in degree than in kind?"[49] One might try to illustrate the view with a thought-experiment: imagine a stretch of music consisting of, say, one hundred notes, such that some are specified by a score, with the others to be filled in spontaneously by the performer. Now, imagine many such sets in a spectrum, ranging from ones where very few notes are to be filled in to the other extreme, where more and more are. The array might be thought to illustrate how the supposed difference between the two kinds of performance is only a matter of degree.

However, the thought-experiment at best illustrates the banality that in such a situation we have potential vagueness, since we cannot indicate a precise point at which a performance is no longer a work-performance but an original, full-blown improvisation. To conclude from that fact that there is no difference between the two kinds would involve a version of the so-called slippery slope fallacy. After all, it is easy to specify the intermediate case, which is neither of those two. In fact, this third category is completely familiar in jazz. A fixed work is played, and then its melody and "changes" become the basis for improvisation. Further, the thought experiment has left out of consideration what the performer intends to do – that is, what she thinks of herself as doing. Does she think of herself as spontaneously fleshing out a work while remaining faithful to its composer's intentions? Or does she think of herself as exploring, and hence exploiting, a given musical structure as a point of departure for music of her own?[50]

The difference – in kind – between the case where a performer thickens a relatively thin work while performing and the case where she improvises ought surely to go something like this: in the former kind of case, the performer fleshes out a pre-existing structure rather than using it as a springboard for what Stephen Davies terms a "gravity defying" departure from such a structure.[51] In the best cases of improvisation, the performer can turn a shallow work into one with depth and complexity, sometimes deepening its intensity as well.

But there are two grains of truth in the no–performance–without–improvisation view. First, we can envision cases on the boundary between the two types of performance. In jazz pianist Uri Caine's swinging performance of the first movement of Mozart's *Sonata in C Major* (2006), the "wrong" notes throughout can be assumed to have improvisational intention. But the performance does on the whole follow the general structure of the written music. Second, even within the class of improvisational performances, some may be more so than others. A typical solo by Louis Armstrong is less improvisational, for instance, than one by Charlie Parker. In fact, some of Armstrong's famous Hot Five and Hot Seven solos were merely close paraphrases of the basic material, and some of the more adventuresome solos were developed and practiced in advance of the recording sessions.[52] However, comparisons across musical genres will be difficult – if possible at all – for it is not clear how to enumerate the available options in one context by a measure that would apply in the other. How could we determine whether a bop solo by Charlie Parker is more or less improvisational than a classical Iranian performance on the 'ūd? A stopwatch alone won't do the trick.

3. The Ontology of Improvisation

Ontology is often understood in the context of metaphysics, but it is also used as a way of presenting the question "What is an X?" where X is some candidate for what distinguishes X from its pretenders: "What is the real X?" However, debates about the ontology of music have often centered on the concept of a work and in jazz, as we have seen elsewhere in this book and in this chapter in particular, the music is intimately connected with improvisation. Sometimes the concept *work* as in the question "What is an artwork?" simply draws attention to what we consider the most important aspect of the presentation of an art species. So, a claim about performance would be a relative one, that performance is more important than composition, say, or recording when it comes to jazz and how improvisation problematizes or complicates an ontological claim about jazz. In Chapter 2 we saw how ontology relates to the numerical existence of work – the number of instances that can still be called that work. If a real-time music performance is the fundamental focal point of appreciation in jazz, then it would seem obvious that, in jazz, the work is identical with the performance, and there is one and only one instance of each work. However, the intuitive appeal of this idea may be at odds with what we normally mean by a "musical work."

The inclusion of stretches of improvisation in a performance does not rule out that such a performance may still count, ontologically, as being *of* a work. (Consider a piano concerto containing an improvised cadenza; likewise, consider a Duke Ellington composition that leaves space for an improvised cadenza.) So should we simply borrow our ontology for improvisational performances from the best available view about musical works?[53] Such a view would be hard to generalize because it would leave certain cases homeless – free jazz performances, for instance, that are not of any antecedent work. Is it possible that the concept of workhood simply does not apply to such cases?[54] Upon what does the question turn?

First, let us assume that by "work" we mean something that can be *reidentified* – revisited, as it were, on multiple occasions. Obviously, a Keith Jarrett free improvisation cannot be revisited in the way that we can revisit the *Las Meninas* of Diego Velázquez, which can be found on a wall in the Prado, where we can go and see it anytime if we can afford to do so. But how could we possibly revisit an improvisation that is, so to say, entirely in-the-moment but now in the past? As we mentioned in Chapter 2, Jarrett's Cologne improvisations were transcribed and published. However, a performance of one of them from the sheet music, or indeed, a performed copy of it by any means, whether by Jarrett or by anyone else, would surely lack an essential feature of the original, namely that – with the necessary qualifications – the music was created as Jarrett performed it. Given its once-only character, must we conclude that a Jarrett improvisation is not a work at all? But now consider a visual work of performance art, such as those organized by Allan Kaprow, which, given their presumed spontaneity, could not be copied without loss of authenticity. In spite of this, such once-only events in visual art are documented and discussed just like artworks in general. Being an artwork is not incompatible with being ephemeral. To sum up, revisitation is not an essential requirement for being a work of art.

Perhaps a musical improvisation is not an artwork because an artwork is something worked on over time.[55] The wrapped buildings and environment-specific projects of Christo and Jeanne-Claude are temporary, but they involve years of planning. True, we can cite examples of artworks that were in fact not worked on over time – Samuel Taylor Coleridge's poem, *Kubla Khan*, for instance, if we accept the poet's story about its spontaneous genesis. The reply, however, is that Coleridge *could have* worked on it over time. In principle, he could have revised what he wrote, so that the poem encountered by his readers would be different from the familiar one he did offer them. The same cannot be said about Jarrett's improvisation at the Cologne Opera House on January 24, 1975. Jarrett might have stopped the improvisation. He might have played something other than he played. But he could not, in principle, *revise* the music that he provided to the audience. Here, "the music" does not refer to the same sort of thing that is referred to in a phrase like "the music of the second movement of Beethoven's 'Moonlight' sonata," where "the music" refers to an abstract structure in the same way that "the poem" refers to a complex linguistic object when we speak of *Kubla Khan*.

Another reasonable criterion of workhood is that an artwork is the focus of critical attention. By this criterion, Jarrett's performances presumably could be works in their own right – if we are untroubled by the thought that it seems conceptually impossible for these musical works to have more than a single instance. Writing about theater, James Hamilton is not troubled by this view and he explains and defends the resulting "ingredients model" of performance.[56] According to this approach, it is not the performer's task to respect the intentions of playwrights and composers. Their works may "inform" performances, but performances need not be an execution *of* a pre-existing work. If there is no goal of work-fidelity in performance, then the identity of the individual performance is the only identity condition that governs the performance. (The identity of "Intuition" is nothing but the music-making of the Tristano Quintet during a three-minute period on May 16, 1949.) Thus, not every artwork is an enduring thing.[57] But even where there *is* a relationship to a pre-existing work, it is never more than a source of *some* of the information that performers utilize when performing. A familiar case is the long-running Broadway play or musical. Hopefully, it is somewhat different each night of its performance, while following the same script.

Although we endorse the idea that there are free improvisations that are neither (1) performances *of* an existing work nor (2) an activity of *composing* a new work, we do not follow Hamilton in holding that this idea applies generally to theatrical and musical performances. As Brian Soucek warns, this approach is unnecessarily revisionary, for it requires us to say that someone who appreciates the *song* "My Funny Valentine" while listening to Chet Baker's 1952 performance with the Gerry Mulligan Quartet is misunderstanding what is really going on there.[58] Recognizing that many jazz performances are not faithful renditions of works is not a reason to endorse Hamilton's extreme position that performances are "never a performance *of* some other work."[59] At best, the ingredients model is a good analysis of what *sometimes* happens in jazz.

So with different criteria of workhood we get various problematic results. And sooner or later, we will find ourselves asking whether it is relevant that ECM recorded Jarrett's performances, and that we can listen to them as often as we wish. And would this be relevant because recordings do magically allow us to revisit an ephemeral event even though it has slipped into the past? Or is it because the Jarrett recording itself takes on the status of an artwork? An ontology for improvised jazz performances remains unfinished business.

4. Five Types of Jazz Improvisation

It would be nice if we could simply draw a line between spontaneous improvi-sation and performance of *pre-existent* musical works. However, we cannot do so, for two reasons.

First, the kinds and degrees of spontaneous deformations of musical materials that we can expect from jazz improvisers vary almost in a continuum as we move from jazz sub-category to sub-category. In some cases, as with the rhapsodic kind of jazz sometimes played by Keith Jarrett, players are expected to exhibit a range and kind of freedom that would be utterly out of place in contexts where players aim to hew to musical material more closely. Within the latter sphere, in turn, judgments we might make about Henry Threadgill dismantling a Scott Joplin rag could not be carried over to Ralph Sutton playing the same piece. And between these two, we can find further shades of categorial difference. (We provide a general typology at the end of this section.) If we reflect on this wide range of performance-types, we see that some of them are work-performances or lie very close to work-performances. There is a view of jazz according to which these performances are in the minority. However, this is incorrect – which leads to the second point.

The plain fact is that jazz improvisers are typically very clear that they *are*, after all, playing a given work – whether composed for the occasion or borrowed from a stock of standard jazz sources. It might be more accurate, however, to say that jazz improvisers playfully engage *with* a given work. Informed listeners know it too. Jazz listeners do not doubt that they are listening to, e.g., "Straight No Chaser," "Shreveport Stomp," or "Freddie Freeloader." There is a related sense in which Charlie Parker is playing, for example, a blues, or the changes to "I Got Rhythm." He is, in some sense, *performing* a pre-existing musical structure, even if it is not specific enough to qualify as a named work.[60] Such performances hew closely to Hamilton's ingredients model of performance. However, this does not entail that in jazz performance two distinct musical practices – work performance and free improvisation – simply happen to find themselves together. This needs explaining.

To generalize historically, the improvisational impulse and the compositional motive have continued to lie uneasily side-by-side throughout the history of jazz. For instance, Duke Ellington and Jelly Roll Morton – just to name two – composed music that, even in ensemble form, often kept free improvisation to a minimum. Works by Charles Mingus encourage more freedom, but still place limits on soloists. Not any solo by any soloist would fit a piece such as "Fables of Faubus." Pianist Art Tatum usually took his point of departure from "traditional" material (i.e., folk, light classical, or show tunes). He used his prodigious technique and understanding of harmony to break such pieces down into their motives. These, he then reharmonized, sometimes to the limit of recognition – while adding numerous counter-melodies – augmenting the results with rhythmically and harmonically elaborate variants on the basic "stride" bass pattern. Thelonious Monk's treatment of such material – as in his performance of "Smoke Gets in your Eyes" (1954) – is similar to Tatum's approach. However, he concentrates on varying the thematic line itself, rather than simply playing notes on the chords. Unlike Tatum, too, Monk's solos effect continual revisions of themes more by accentual displacement than by elaborate harmonic variation. Nonetheless, these alterations cannot be regarded as errors or inaccuracies in Monk's performance of the work composed by Jerome Kern. Monk did not *intend* to produce an "accurate" or score-compliant rendition of "Smoke Gets in your Eyes." Consequently, he might be judged not to have produced a version of it, but he cannot be judged to have failed in an attempt to perform it, for there was no such attempt.[61]

Neither Monk's nor Tatum's elaborate abstraction and rearrangement of the components of the tunes upon which their playing is based could be understood, except by reference to these works prior to their deconstruction of them. Even in the jazz context, they remain moored to identifiable entities. So, while there is certainly a reason to distinguish between free improvisation and work performance, the tune that is the basis of typical jazz improvisation is not always mere musical fodder. Far from undermining the spontaneous invention of jazz players, the use of pre-existent works underscores it. The wild spontaneity of George Russell's and Don Cherry's assault on "You Are My Sunshine," as played one evening in the Stuttgart Beethoven Hall,[62] would be meaningless in abstraction from the tune that is the basis of the performance. Only on the implausible assumption that genuinely spontaneous jazz music would have to be music completely without any framework – music coming from nowhere – would the work-performance in the jazz context be regarded as an inevitable limitation.[63]

Reflecting on the need for improvisers to draw on musical precedence, Bruce Ellis Benson offers an ambitious typology of improvisation that identifies fifteen distinct kinds of improvisation. Intriguing as it is, it is offered as a general theory of all the different ways that musicians can alter and modify pre-existing musical materials. Its application to jazz would require a determination of which of the fifteen categories are salient, and which are not. However, we immediately notice that none of them seems to cover free improvisation. When Benson does address that possibility, he does not place it squarely in any of his categories. Instead, he points to the example of pianist Marian McPartland and says, of her free improvisations, "While she is clearly not following a set tune, her 'free' improvisations tend to have a similar sort of form and utilize many of the same chords."[64] The implication is that McPartland is relying on a tacit, repeatable (albeit skeletal) composition. Hence, Benson puts "free" in scare quotes. However, this doesn't wash. Arguing that free jazz has boundaries and is less free than the name implies does not place it in any of Benson's categories in a principled manner. None of them seem to be a clear fit.

Another problem is that Benson regards *any* creative activity as "improvisation." At one point, he quotes Carla Bley's explanation of how her music works: "I write pieces that are like drawings in a crayon book and the musicians color them themselves."[65] Benson then denies that Bley has described anything special about jazz or her approach to it. In his view, every musical performance works this way, and the real issue is the degree of respect that a tradition has for the "lines" of the musical work, or the degree of respect that a group of musicians has for existing tradition. As such, the overall stylistic innovations of bebop are an improvisation, "modifying the tradition by augmentation and transformation."[66] We think that we have now moved beyond the usual domain of improvisation, which centers on creative extemporaneous action that is chosen to address a particular task on a particular occasion. Where Benson regards the difference between ornamenting a melody and co-inventing bebop as merely quantitative, we see it as qualitative. What the Ornette Coleman Quartet achieved on *The Shape of Jazz to Come* (1959) is qualitatively different from what Coleman and his group did to the jazz tradition with that high profile album. Their improvisations on "Lonely Woman" succeed if their intentions are fulfilled, but one can only alter a tradition if others imitate and incorporate your innovations.[67] Hence, the standards of successful "improvisation" are radically different in the two cases.

As an alternative to Benson's approach, we return to the idea that jazz improvisation involves choices about the music one is playing as one plays. Although they can be characterized as spontaneous, these choices are not random. They are shaped by musicians' shared knowledge, goals, and intentions. Consequently, we propose that the key to a typology of jazz improvisation will be found in musicians' performance intentions. Consider the worry of the jazz journalist who complained about hearing pianist Ray Bryant play "After Hours" in what sounded like a note-for-note copy of his famous recording of it on Verve Records.[68] In a commentary on the example, Andy Hamilton is perplexed to locate a relevant difference between the two, given that the subsequent performance was, like the original, "fine blues piano."[69] In fact, Hamilton has stumbled onto a perfect illustration of the fact that we tacitly appeal to a musician's intentions in order to mark an improvisation as such. Hamilton goes on to grant that there is an "improvised feel" in improvised music. But the observation fails to do any work. (What if Bryant's original performance had not, in spite of its "improvisational feel," actually been improvised – what if it had been written out, for instance, or was a copy of a previous improvisation?) We may not be able to say with certainty what Bryant was doing on either occasion – but whatever it was depends partly upon his intentions at the time. And it may also depend on what was *not* intended at the time. All other things being equal, a *group* improvisation should be appreciated and evaluated by reference to our understanding of what the ensemble intends – and does not intend – to accomplish during a specific performance.[70] Garry Hagberg contends that the relevant group intention is something more complex – and interesting – than mere attention to the activities of the other players, supplemented by the intention of each player to perform with, and in response to, the others. He proposes that, over and above the set of individual intentions, there is a distinct collective intention. In a good improvisation, we find something more than the interlocking and coordination of autonomous intentions.[71] A less radical proposal comes from Margaret Gilbert.[72] A group improvisation is a collective action, and so the players' intentions to perform collectively must be supplemented by their joint commitment to perform together. In electing to play together, jazz musicians enter into the performance with a tacit understanding that they are justified in having various expectations about what others will contribute – indeed, each player will be justified in demanding something of the other players, and be subject, in turn, to the demands of the others. Above all, we think that this is a joint commitment to interactive empathy.[73]

Without claiming that we have an exhaustive list, we think that five categories of performance-guiding intentions are the most salient in the jazz tradition.[74] Because the intentions differ in each, the differences should not be read as mere differences in degree. We mean to say, with André Hodeir, that different kinds of improvisation involve distinct "attitudes" toward musical source material.[75] Here are five that we see as fundamentally distinct.

1. Expressive Individualization of a Recognizable Work

Musicians perform a recognizable musical work (whether guided by musical notation or by working from memory) intending to allow one or more musicians to make extemporaneous interpretive decisions during the performance.[76] Besides liberties with rhythmic placement, these are primarily melodic embellishments and decisions about timbral effects.[77] However, the musicians intend to respect the work's "spare" or "thin" work–identifying elements.[78] Popular songs have "thin" work–identity conditions, so they are a fruitful basis for improvising in this category. Many of them can be rendered in different styles without violating their identity conditions. For example, because "St. James Infirmary Blues" took shape prior to being notated, the song underdetermines selection of instrumentation, length of performance, and many other features. Consequently, different performances can sound radically different while intending to be "true" to the work's minimal identity conditions – compare performances of "St. James Infirmary Blues" by Louis Armstrong and Cassandra Wilson. In contrast, James Booker's romp through Chopin's "Minute Waltz" does *not* belong in this category (because the syncopation is *contrary* to the score's work–determinative instructions). Given the popular music norm that a song is performed even if its lyrics are not, some instrumental performances of songs fall into this category. We should also note that some jazz performers do not count this form of improvisation as jazz improvisation. On this basis, jazz vocalists sometimes deny that Frank Sinatra and Tony Bennett are jazz singers.[79]

2. Improvisation Sanctioned Within a Score-Directed Performance

Musicians perform from scored parts and intend to execute their parts in a manner that respects the composer's intentions as they are embedded in the score.

There is some interpretive leeway due to the way that scores underdetermine the performance details, but the musicians intentionally deviate from the score with creative supplementation only where the score calls for it. Obvious examples include Duke Ellington's orchestra performing one of his scores. For example, Schuller points out that "Reminiscing in Tempo" (1935) runs three hundred measures, but leaves only two spots for unwritten solos: both go to alto saxophone.[80]

3. Improvisation Based on a Composed or Recognizable Work

Musicians intend to perform some parts of a recognizable work (whether guided by musical notation or by working from memory), but they also intend to deviate, sometimes significantly, from its established identity conditions while performing it.[81] In many cases, a recognizable work serves as the head, which provides the harmonic and rhythmic foundation for the improvised melodies. Paradigm examples are the Miles Davis Quintet's performances of "'Round Midnight," "All of You," and "Bye Bye Blackbird" on the album 'Round About Midnight (1956). Here, the musicians regard the composed music as an important and recognizable ingredient of the performance, but there is also a shared intention to engage in extemporaneous deviation from its identity conditions. Ralph Vaughan Williams's Tallis Fantasia derives from a melody by Thomas Tallis, but musicians performing the Fantasia are not attempting to play Tallis's music. In a parallel but more radical fashion, jazz musicians frequently derive their music from familiar music without intending to provide a performance of that source material. Examples are everywhere in mainstream jazz:

- Coleman Hawkins's 1939 transformation of "Body and Soul"
- Lester Young performing "These Foolish Things" (1944) but at no point delivering the melody as written – it is a mere reference point for his melodic line
- Coltrane performing "My Favorite Things," but from the outset, changing the time signature, simplifying the chord progression, and jettisoning some sections of the Broadway tune.

With a relatively "thick" work, the musicians may intend to extract a thinner structure from its recognized work–identity conditions; additionally, they intend to make extemporaneous decisions about the realization of the thin structure they have extracted. A nice example is Barney Kessel's performances of Georges Bizet's "Toreador Song." Song performances are an interesting case. When Billie Holiday first sang "Mean to Me" in the studio with Teddy Wilson and Lester Young (1937), she re-composed the melody. Returning to the revised melody as the template of her later performances, she does appear to have composed a new version of the song. In contrast, Ella Fitzgerald's scat sections of many of her performances do not amount to acts of composing.

4. Spontaneous Musical Development of Non-Work Ingredients

Musicians intend to make extemporaneous decisions about the course of a performance based on a recognizable musical idea or theme or framework that provides limited musical guidance for some or all of the musicians. There is no intention, however, to respect the work–identity conditions of any composed work with established identity conditions.[82] Nor is there any intention to extract a thin structure from another work. Instead, the shared intention is to make music out of ingredient material that so underdetermines the performance process that, without improvisational supplementation, there is no performance plan. Examples would include improvisation organized by any of the following: a blues progression (but not a particular blues composition), the bare "rhythm changes" that bebop players extracted from "I Got Rhythm," Coleman's "Lonely Woman" theme, Shorter's "Limbo" theme, and Carla Bley's "Ictus" (1976 version, which has no bar lines). Thus, Charlie Christian's "Blues in B" (1941) was launched during a jam session from the mere suggestion of doing a blues in that key, without preparation or guidance beyond the participants' joint familiarity with blues patterns and licks.

5. Free Improvisation

Musicians intend to draw on resources of the jazz tradition, but there is a collective intention to achieve spontaneous vertical and horizontal organization without reference to a recognizable or composed musical work, fixed form, or theme. As Ornette Coleman once put it, the intention is to proceed without the safety of *any* musical "map."[83] We have already mentioned the Tristano Quintet's "Intuition" and some of Jarrett's piano improvisations, but we might also note Julie Tippetts' *vocal* free improvisations with pianist Keith Tippett, such as "Blues 1" (1972). Notice that the difference between categories (4) and (5) is sometimes merely a matter of agreement about how the music begins. If a group performs Coleman's "Lonely Woman" as he intended, they will improvise "different changes as they take each [new] chorus" to produce "more variety," becoming a free improvisation after the initial statement of the theme.[84] Bley is even more explicit about her preference that "Ictus" should set up a free improvisation.[85]

We call attention to the way that only categories (1) and (2) include the intention to produce an instance of a composed or established musical work. In contrast, categories (3) and (4) involve an intention to use a composed work or some schematic but recognizable material as a *vehicle* for performing, but with no intention to produce an instance of any work.[86] Category (5) is distinguished by an intention to improvise without the guidance of any composed or recognizable work or fixed musical schema. We think it is obvious that many jazz performances are combinations of two or more of these categories. For example, Ellington's performances routinely combine (1) and (2). The celebrated Miles Davis Quintet of the 1950s is probably the paradigm example of an approach combining (3) and (4). In typical performances after the heyday of the jazz orchestras, jazz musicians intend to begin with individualization of a recognizable work, to extract some of the musical material (e.g., preserving the rhythm and the "changes"), then to engage in improvisation from this subtraction – which may, in turn, lead to spontaneous musical development that revises the intermediate structures.

In conclusion, improvising musicians draw on musical materials and practices in many ways. We reject the view that every jazz improvisation is either a species of work composition or a performance of a work. Yet the improvisation of music is never creation *ex nihilo*. As Mingus said, "You can't improvise on nothing, man."[87] When jazz improvisers draw on an existing musical work, the relationship of performance to work can be something other than a "loose" or divergent playing of that work. As evidenced by performances of medleys, the fact that a musical performance is launched with the intention to play one particular work does not imply a commitment to continue performing that work for the duration of that performance. Likewise, the fact that a jazz group begins with a recognizable presentation of "How High the Moon" does not imply that *that* song is still being performed when the melody is abandoned after one chorus. There are different *kinds* of improvisations, distinguished by performers' intentions about their playing. Consequently, a single jazz performance can display multiple relationships to musical works – or, at times, no relationship at all.

Notes

1 For an overview, see Aili Bresnahan, "Improvisation in the Arts," *Philosophy Compass* 10:9 (2015): 573–582.
2 For reasons explained in Chapter 2, we have already argued that improvisation is not a necessary condition for jazz.
3 See Andy Hamilton, *Aesthetics and Music* (London: Continuum, 2007), 202–203.
4 King Palmer, *The Piano (Teach Yourself)* (Chicago: NTC Publishing Group, 1992), 109.
5 Robert Goffin, *Jazz from the Congo to the Metropolitan* (New York: Doubleday, 1944), 124.
6 Ted Gioia, *The Imperfect Art: Reflections on Jazz and Modern Culture* (Oxford: Oxford University Press, 1992), 29–32. This point is developed at length in Patrick Burke, *Come in and Hear the Truth: Jazz and Race on 52nd Street* (Chicago: University of Chicago Press, 2008).
7 Bruno Nettl, *The Radif of Persian Music: Studies of Structure and Cultural Context*, rev. ed. (Champaign: University of Illinois Press, 1992).
8 Paul Berliner, *Thinking in Jazz: The Infinite Art of Improvisation* (Chicago: University of Chicago Press, 1994), chap. 4.
9 Howard Allen Spring, "The Use of Formulas in the Improvisations of Charlie Christian," *Jazzforschung/Jazz Research* 22 (1990): 11–51.
10 See, for example, Art Pepper and Laurie Pepper, *Straight Life: The Story of Art Pepper* (New York: Schirmer, 1979), 374.
11 Alyn Shipton, *A New History of Jazz*, rev. ed. (London: Bloomsbury, 2007), 570–571.
12 For technical analysis, see Peter Elsdon, *Keith Jarrett's* The Köln Concert (Oxford: Oxford University Press, 2013), chaps. 5 and 6.

13 John M. Chernoff, *African Rhythm and African Sensibility: Aesthetics and Social Action in African Musical Idioms* (Chicago: University of Chicago Press, 1979).

14 See the anecdote of the saxophonist who was instructed "not to bother to come back" after inserting a long passage of a popular song into a collective free improvisation; Ian Carr, "Freedom and Fish Soup," *Melody Maker* (May 22, 1971), 41.

15 Stan Godlovitch, *Musical Performance: A Philosophical Study* (London: Routledge, 1998), 84.

16 Mario Dunkel, *Aesthetics of Resistance: Charles Mingus and the Civil Rights Movement* (Zurich: Lit Verlag, 2012), 58.

17 Garry L. Hagberg, "Improvisation: Jazz Improvisation," in *Encyclopedia of Aesthetics*, 2nd ed., vol. 3, ed. Michael Kelly (New York: Oxford University Press, 2014), 441–448, at 443. See also R. Keith Sawyer, "Improvised Conversations: Music, Collaboration, and Development," *Psychology of Music* 27:2 (1999): 192–205, and Robert Kraut, *Artworld Metaphysics* (Oxford: Oxford University Press, 2007), 57–65, 177–182.

18 Kraut, *Artworld Metaphysics*, 18–19, 57–59.

19 This list is adapted from Saam Trivedi, "Artist-Audience Communication: Tolstoy Reclaimed," *Journal of Aesthetic Education* 38:2 (2004): 38–52, at 50. For additional discussion of "music as language," see Kofi Agawu, "The Challenge of Semiotics," in *Rethinking Music*, ed. Nicholas Cook and Mark Everist (New York: Oxford University Press, 2001), 138–160.

20 For a more radical approach, see Gary Peters, *The Philosophy of Improvisation* (Chicago: University of Chicago Press, 2009).

21 Gioia, *Imperfect Art*, 60.

22 See William Kinderman, "Improvisation in Beethoven's Creative Process," in *Musical Improvisation: Art, Education, and Society*, ed. Gabriel Solis and Bruno Nettl (Urbana: University of Illinois Press, 2009), 296–312.

23 Tristano, quoted in Eunmi Shim, *Lennie Tristano: His Life in Music* (Ann Arbor: University of Michigan Press, 2007), 51.

24 Shim, *Lennie Tristano*, 50; for details, see 178–180.

25 Ferruccio Busoni, "Sketch of a New Aesthetic of Music," in *Three Classics in the Aesthetic of Music*, trans. Theodore Baker (New York: Dover, 1962), 84.

26 For more on the distinction between musical works and scores, see Nicholas Wolterstorff, *Works and Worlds of Art* (Oxford: Clarendon, 1980), 38–39, and Stephen Davies, *Musical Works and Performances: A Philosophical Exploration* (Oxford: Clarendon Press, 2001), 100.

27 Davies, *Musical Works and Performances*, 3, 20.

28 Gunther Schuller, *Early Jazz: Its Roots and Musical Development* (Oxford: Oxford University Press, 1968), x.

29 Peter Kivy, "Platonism in Music: A Kind of Defense," *Grazer Philosophische Studien* 19:1 (1983): 109–129, at 124–125. See also David Davies, *Philosophy of the Performing Arts* (Malden: Wiley-Blackwell, 2011), 158–159.

30 Philip Alperson, "On Musical Improvisation," *Journal of Aesthetics and Art Criticism* 43:1 (1984): 17–29, at 19–20.

31 Alperson, "Musical Improvisation," 20.

32 Alperson, "Musical Improvisation," 20.

33 Paul Vincent Spade, "Do Composers Have To Be Performers Too?" *Journal of Aesthetics and Art Criticism* 49:4 (1991): 365–369.

34 Alperson, "Musical Improvisation," 23.

35 See Stephen Davies, "Versions of Musical Works and Literary Translations," in *Philosophers on Music: Experience, Meaning, and Work*, ed. Kathleen Stock (Oxford: Oxford University Press, 2007), 79–92. Through a process of localized revision over time, "folk" material often evolves into multiple versions, a phenomenon documented from the earliest days of folk song collecting; e.g. Francis James Child, *The English and Scottish Popular Ballads* (Boston and New York: Houghton, Mifflin and Company, 1882).

36 See Berliner, *Thinking in Jazz*, 240–241.
37 E.g., Godlovitch, *Musical Performance*, 83–90; Carol S. Gould and Kenneth Keaton, "The Essential Role of Improvisation in Musical Performance," *Journal of Aesthetics and Art Criticism* 58:2 (2000): 143–148; Bruce Ellis Benson, *The Improvisation of Musical Dialogue: A Phenomenology of Music* (Cambridge: Cambridge University Press, 2003).
38 Gould and Keaton, "Essential Role," 143.
39 Gould and Keaton, "Essential Role," 145. Throughout, it should be noted, the authors, like Busoni, assume what we deny – that all works are scored. However, there is no contradiction in saying that Child documented hundreds of existing works when he published the words in *The English and Scottish Popular Ballads*; we think the category of "work" applies equally well to those that had been published previously with their music and those that had not.
40 Gould and Keaton, "Essential Role," 144–145. For additional criticisms, see Davies, *Philosophy of the Performing Arts*, 151–154.
41 Benson endorses this result (*Improvisation*, 26), but as part of a larger argument to recommend one model of performance over others. However, we think this fails as a description of jazz improvisation – it is unjustifiably revisionary. As we said in Chapter 1, we are methodologically aligned with the pragmatic constraint that theorizing about art should be constrained by artistic practice; see David Davies, *Art as Performance* (Oxford: Blackwell, 2004), 16–20, and Amie L. Thomasson, "The Ontology of Art and Knowledge in Aesthetics," *Journal of Aesthetics and Art Criticism* 63:3 (2005): 221–229.
42 Philip Alperson, "Improvisation: Overview," in *Encyclopedia of Aesthetics*, 2nd ed., vol. 3, ed. Michael Kelly (New York: Oxford University Press, 2014), 439–441, at 439.
43 Philip Alperson, "Musical Improvisation and the Philosophy of Music," in *The Oxford Handbook of Critical Improvisation Studies*, vol. 1, ed. George E. Lewis and Benjamin Piekut (Oxford: Oxford University Press, 2016), 419–438.
44 Andrew Kania, "All Play and No Work: An Ontology of Jazz," *Journal of Aesthetics and Art Criticism* 69:4 (2011): 391–403.
45 Mingus quoted in Shipton, *New History*, 571.
46 James O. Young and Carl Matheson, "The Metaphysics of Jazz," *Journal of Aesthetics and Art Criticism* 58:2 (2000): 125–134, at 127.
47 Jack Chambers, *Milestones: The Music and Times of Miles Davis* (New York: Da Capo, 1998), 109.
48 Ralph J. Gleason, liner notes for Miles Davis, *Filles de Kilimanjaro* (Columbia Records, 1969).
49 Gould and Keaton, "Essential Role," 143.
50 However she sees it, there is evidence that the brain functions differently during improvisation and during the performance of a scored work, supporting the view that there is an underlying difference in the kind of activity that is taking place. See Charles J. Limb and Allen R. Braun, "Neural Substrates of Spontaneous Musical Performance: An fMRI Study of Jazz Improvisation," *PLoS ONE* 3:2 (2008): e1679.
51 Davies, *Musical Works*, 17. For a defense of the position that there is no relevant difference in kind between fleshing out a thin structure and improvising on selected elements of a thin structure, see Julian Dodd, "Upholding Standards: A Realist Ontology of Standard Form Jazz," *Journal of Aesthetics and Art Criticism* 72:3 (2014): 277–290. The crux of Dodd's defense is that jazz is a tradition in which performers license themselves to perform works *inauthentically*, where an authentic performance is one with a highly accurate presentation of the work's melodic and harmonic structure.
52 See Brian Harker, *Louis Armstrong's Hot Five and Hot Seven Recordings* (Oxford: Oxford University Press, 2011), 52, 69–70.
53 Such an approach is explicitly defended by Julian Dodd, *Works of Music: An Essay in Ontology* (Oxford: Oxford University Press, 2007). We critique it at length in Chapter 8.

54 Kania's "All Play and No Work" supports this conclusion, not just for free jazz, but for almost all jazz performance. The typology we advance in this chapter aligns closely – but not completely – with Kania's position.

55 Andrew Kania, "Works, Recordings, Performances: Classical, Rock, Jazz," in *Recorded Music: Philosophical and Critical Reflections*, ed. Mine Dogantan-Dack (Middlesex: Middlesex University Press, 2008), 3–21, at 6–7.

56 James R. Hamilton, *The Art of Theater* (New York: Blackwell, 2007), 30–32; see the response in Davies, *Art as Performance*, 113–119.

57 We return to the implications of this point at some length in Chapter 8.

58 Brian Soucek, Review of James R. Hamilton *The Art of Theater, Notre Dame Philosophical Reviews*, June 15, 2008, http://ndpr.nd.edu/news/the-art-of-theater/.

59 Hamilton, *Art of Theater*, 32.

60 When, on a second or third "take" in a Charlie Parker recording session, Bird did not simply try some other random improvisation. Rather, he tried to make a better recording of, e.g, "Chasin' the Bird" (a brief theme for generating improvisation using the changes of "I Got Rhythm"). Compare the alternative takes of this and other improvisations on Charlie Parker, *The Complete Savoy and Dial Studio Recordings 1944–1948* (Savoy Jazz, 2002).

61 See Christy Mag Uidhir, *Art and Art-Attempts* (Oxford: Oxford University Press, 2013), chap. 1.

62 As recorded at a live performance of *George Russell Sextet at Beethoven Hall* (BASF recording MC ZS125).

63 Curiously this is one assumption underlying Adorno's elitist critique of jazz. See Lee B. Brown, "Adorno's Critique of Popular Culture: The Case of Jazz Music," *Journal of Aesthetic Education* 26:1 (1992): 17–31.

64 Benson, *Improvisation*, 136.

65 Benson, *Improvisation*, 135.

66 Benson, *Improvisation*, 29.

67 For arguments that intentions cannot be eliminated from an informed account of performance, see Godlovitch, *Musical Performance*, 16–18. A central tenet of action theory is that actions involve action-guiding intentions. Hence, the position that jazz improvisations are actions, rather than things, commits us to some version of this view. See the essays collected in Jonathan Dancy and Constantine Sandis, eds., *Philosophy of Action: An Anthology* (Malden: Wiley-Blackwell, 2015), Part III.

68 Gioia, *Imperfect Art*, 52–53.

69 Hamilton, *Aesthetics and Music*, 201–202.

70 To return to the Hamilton/Bryant example, it may be possible for the musicians alone to know whether or not some music is improvised, and so leaving an audience in the dark in that respect. The position that intentions play a necessary role does not imply that all intentions will be transparent to the audience.

71 Garry L. Hagberg, "Ensemble Improvisation, Collective Intention, and Group Attention," in *The Oxford Handbook of Critical Improvisation Studies*, vol. 1, ed. George E. Lewis and Benjamin Piekut (Oxford: Oxford University Press, 2016), 481–499.

72 Margaret Gilbert, "Collective Action," in *A Companion to the Philosophy of Action*, ed. Timothy O'Connor and Constantine Sandis (Malden: Wiley-Blackwell, 2010), 67–73.

73 Hamilton, *Aesthetics and Music*, 213.

74 Suggestions pointing in the direction of our proposal are to be found in Davies, *Philosophy of the Performing Arts*, 156–157. For the sake of simplicity, we have treated categories (1) through (4) as involving composed or recognizable music with a single composer. Benson claims that jazz performances of Gershwin tunes respect George's but not Ira's intentions (*Improvisation*, 94–95).

75 André Hodeir, *Jazz: Its Evolution and Essence*, trans. David Noakes (New York: Grove Press, 1956), 161.

76 Philip Alperson describes this as "minor ornamental embellishments to a composed work": "A Topography of Improvisation," *Journal of Aesthetics and Art Criticism* 68:3 (2010): 273–280, at 275. Barry Kernfeld calls it "paraphrase improvisation"; *What to Listen For in Jazz* (New Haven: Yale University Press, 1995), 131.

77 See Berliner, *Thinking in Jazz*, 69–70, 124–125.

78 See Davies, *Musical Works*, 20–21, and "Versions of Musical Works," 85–86.

79 See the interviews with Sheila Jordan and Carol Sloane in Wayne Enstice and Janis Stockhouse, *Jazzwomen: Conversations with Twenty-One Musicians* (Bloomington: Indiana University Press, 2004), 173, 313.

80 For extended analysis of this piece, see Gunther Schuller, *The Swing Era: The Development of Jazz, 1930–1945* (Oxford: Oxford University Press, 1989), 75–83.

81 Kernfeld explains that the *method* employed here is generally some combination of formulaic, motivic, and modal improvisation (*What to Listen For*, 137–151). However, we are categorizing types, not methods, of jazz improvisation.

82 Here, we agree with Stephen Davies that there is too little musical guidance to say that there is a performance of a work (*Works and Performances*, 16–17). See also Stefan Caris Love, "The Jazz Solo as Virtuous Act," *Journal of Aesthetics and Art Criticism* 74:1 (2016): 61–74. In contrast, Dodd contends that these minimal musical resources count as an "especially thin kind of work" (Dodd, "Upholding Standards," 285), while David Davies thinks it is a "performable work" that "constrains performance in a looser way than traditional scores" (Davies, *Philosophy of the Performing Arts*, 157). However, these approaches have the unacceptable consequence that the phrase "twelve-bar blues in C major" is the name of a musical work. Therefore Leiber's and Stoller's "Hound Dog" is the same work as The Beatles' "Flying," which the former supplements with lyrics; any instrumental improvisation in C major that employs the blues framework would therefore be an instrumental performance of "Flying." We deny this and say that not every musical schema has sufficient specificity to count as a *work*.

83 Coleman quoted in Shipton, *New History*, 577.

84 Coleman quoted in Shipton, *New History*, 565.

85 Amy C. Beal, *Carla Bley* (Champaign: University of Illinois Press, 2011), 17.

86 Although not explicitly differentiated, we think that these categories are recognizably present in Berliner, *Thinking in Jazz*, chap. 3.

87 Quoted in Gene Santoro, *Myself When I Am Real: The Life and Music of Charles Mingus* (New York: Oxford University Press, 2000), 271.

References

Agawu, Kofi. "The Challenge of Semiotics." In *Rethinking Music*, ed. Nicholas Cook and Mark Everist, 138–160. New York: Oxford University Press, 2001.

Alperson, Philip A. "A Topography of Improvisation." *Journal of Aesthetics and Art Criticism* 68:3 (2010): 273–280.

Alperson, Philip A. "Improvisation: Overview." In *Encyclopedia of Aesthetics*, 2nd ed., vol. 3, ed. Michael Kelly, 439–441. New York: Oxford University Press, 2014.

Alperson, Philip A. "Musical Improvisation and the Philosophy of Music." In *The Oxford Handbook of Critical Improvisation Studies*, vol. 1, ed. George E. Lewis and Benjamin Piekut, 419–438. Oxford: Oxford University Press, 2016.

Alperson, Philip A. "On Musical Improvisation." *Journal of Aesthetics and Art Criticism* 43:1 (1984): 17–29.

Beal, Amy C. *Carla Bley*. Champaign: University of Illinois Press, 2011.

Benson, Bruce Ellis. *The Improvisation of Musical Dialogue: A Phenomenology of Music*. Cambridge: Cambridge University Press, 2003.

Berliner, Paul. *Thinking in Jazz: The Infinite Art of Improvisation*. Chicago: University of Chicago Press, 1994.

Bresnahan, Aili. "Improvisation in the Arts." *Philosophy Compass* 10:9 (2015): 573–582.

Brown, Lee B. "Adorno's Critique of Popular Culture: The Case of Jazz Music." *Journal of Aesthetic Education* 26:1 (1992): 17–31.

Brown, Lee B. "'Feeling My Way': Jazz Improvisation and its Vicissitudes – A Plea for Imperfection." *Journal of Aesthetics and Art Criticism* 58:2 (2000): 112–123.

Brown, Lee B. "Musical Works, Improvisation, and the Principle of Continuity." *Journal of Aesthetics and Art Criticism* 54:4 (1996): 353–569.

Burke, Patrick. *Come in and Hear the Truth: Jazz and Race on 52nd Street*. Chicago: University of Chicago Press, 2008.

Busoni, Ferruccio. "Sketch of a New Aesthetic of Music." In *Three Classics in the Aesthetic of Music*, trans. Theodore Baker. New York: Dover, 1962.

Carr, Ian. "Freedom and Fish Soup." *Melody Maker* (May 22, 1971): 41.

Chambers, Jack. *Milestones: The Music and Times of Miles Davis*. New York: Da Capo, 1998.

Chernoff, John Miller. *African Rhythm and African Sensibility: Aesthetics and Social Action in African Musical Idioms*. Chicago: University of Chicago Press, 1979.

Child, Francis James. *The English and Scottish Popular Ballads*. Boston and New York: Houghton, Mifflin and Company, 1882.

Dancy, Jonathan, and Constantine Sandis (eds.). *Philosophy of Action: An Anthology*. Malden: Wiley-Blackwell, 2015.

Davies, David. *Art as Performance*. Oxford: Blackwell, 2004.

Davies, David. *Philosophy of the Performing Arts*. Malden: Wiley-Blackwell, 2011.

Davies, Stephen. *Musical Works and Performances: A Philosophical Exploration*. Oxford: Clarendon Press, 2001.

Davies, Stephen. "Versions of Musical Works and Literary Translations." In *Philosophers on Music: Experience, Meaning, and Work*, ed. Kathleen Stock, 79–92. Oxford: Oxford University Press, 2007.

Dodd, Julian. "Upholding Standards: A Realist Ontology of Standard Form Jazz." *Journal of Aesthetics and Art Criticism* 72:3 (2014): 277–290.

Dodd, Julian. *Works of Music: An Essay in Ontology*. Oxford: Oxford University Press, 2007.

Dunkel, Mario. *Aesthetics of Resistance: Charles Mingus and the Civil Rights Movement*. Zurich: Lit Verlag, 2012.

Elsdon, Peter. *Keith Jarrett's* The Köln Concert. Oxford: Oxford University Press, 2013.

Enstice, Wayne, and Janis Stockhouse. *Jazzwomen: Conversations with Twenty-One Musicians*. Bloomington: Indiana University Press, 2004.

Gilbert, Margaret. "Collective Action." In *A Companion to the Philosophy of Action*, ed. Timothy O'Connor and Constantine Sandis, 67–73. Malden: Wiley-Blackwell, 2010.

Gioia, Ted. *The Imperfect Art: Reflections on Jazz and Modern Culture*. Oxford: Oxford University Press, 1992.

Gleason, Ralph J. Liner notes for Miles Davis, *Filles de Kilimanjaro*. Columbia Records, 1969.

Godlovitch, Stan. *Musical Performance: A Philosophical Study*. London: Routledge, 1998.

Goffin, Robert. *Jazz from the Congo to the Metropolitan*. New York: Doubleday. 1944.

Gould, Carol S., and Kenneth Keaton. "The Essential Role of Improvisation in Musical Performance." *Journal of Aesthetics and Art Criticism* 58:2 (2000): 143–148.

Hagberg, Garry L. "Ensemble Improvisation, Collective Intention, and Group Attention." In *The Oxford Handbook of Critical Improvisation Studies*, vol. 1, ed. George E. Lewis and Benjamin Piekut, 481–499. Oxford: Oxford University Press, 2016.

Hagberg, Garry L. "Improvisation: Jazz Improvisation." In *Encyclopedia of Aesthetics*, 2nd ed., vol. 3, ed. Michael Kelly, 441–448. New York: Oxford University Press, 2014.

Hamilton, Andy. *Aesthetics and Music*. London: Continuum, 2007.

Hamilton, Andy. "The Art of Improvisation and the Aesthetics of Imperfection." *British Journal of Aesthetics* 40:1 (2000): 168–185.

Hamilton, James R. *The Art of Theater*. New York: Blackwell, 2007.

Harker, Brian. *Louis Armstrong's Hot Five and Hot Seven Recordings*. Oxford: Oxford University Press, 2011.

Hodeir, André. *Jazz: Its Evolution and Essence*, trans. David Noakes. New York: Grove Press, 1956.

Kania, Andrew. "All Play and No Work: An Ontology of Jazz." *Journal of Aesthetics and Art Criticism* 69:4 (2011): 391–403.

Kania, Andrew. "Works, Recordings, Performances: Classical, Rock, Jazz." In *Recorded Music: Philosophical and Critical Reflections*, ed. Mine Dogantan-Dack, 3–21. Middlesex: Middlesex University Press, 2008.

Kernfeld, Barry. *What to Listen for in Jazz*. New Haven: Yale University Press, 1995.

Kinderman, William. "Improvisation in Beethoven's Creative Process." In *Musical Improvisation: Art, Education, and Society*, ed. Gabriel Solis and Bruno Nettl, 296–312. Urbana: University of Illinois Press, 2009.

Kivy, Peter. "Platonism in Music: A Kind of Defense." *Grazer Philosophische Studien* 19:1 (1983): 109–129.

Kraut, Robert. *Artworld Metaphysics*. Oxford: Oxford University Press, 2007.

Limb, Charles J., and Allen R. Braun. "Neural Substrates of Spontaneous Musical Performance: An fMRI Study of Jazz Improvisation." *PLoS ONE* 3:2 (2008): e1679.

Love, Stefan Caris. "The Jazz Solo as Virtuous Act." *Journal of Aesthetics and Art Criticism* 74:1 (2016): 61–74.

Mag Uidhir, Christy. *Art and Art-Attempts*. Oxford: Oxford University Press, 2013.

Murray, Albert. *Murray Talks: Albert Murray on Jazz and Blues*, ed. Paul Devlin. Minneapolis: University of Minnesota Press, 2016.

Nettl, Bruno. *The Radif of Persian Music: Studies of Structure and Cultural Context*, rev. ed. Champaign: University of Illinois Press, 1992.

Palmer, King. *The Piano (Teach Yourself)*. Chicago: NTC Publishing Group, 1992.

Pepper, Art, and Laurie Pepper. *Straight Life: The Story of Art Pepper*. New York: Schirmer, 1979.

Peters, Gary. *The Philosophy of Improvisation*. Chicago: University of Chicago Press, 2009.

Santoro, Gene. *Myself When I Am Real: The Life and Music of Charles Mingus*. New York: Oxford University Press, 2000.

Sawyer, R. Keith. "Improvised Conversations: Music, Collaboration, and Development." *Psychology of Music* 27:2 (1999): 192–205.

Schuller, Gunther. *Early Jazz: Its Roots and Musical Development*. New York: Oxford University Press, 1968.

Schuller, Gunther. *The Swing Era: The Development of Jazz, 1930–1945*. Oxford: Oxford University Press, 1989.

Shim, Eunmi. *Lennie Tristano: His Life in Music*. Ann Arbor: University of Michigan Press, 2007.

Shipton, Alyn. *A New History of Jazz*, rev. ed. London: Bloomsbury, 2007.

Soucek, Brian. Review of James R. Hamilton, *The Art of Theater*. *Notre Dame Philosophical Reviews* (June 15, 2008): http://ndpr.nd.edu/news/the-art-of-theater/.

Spade, Paul Vincent. "Do Composers Have To Be Performers Too?" *Journal of Aesthetics and Art Criticism* 49:4 (1991): 365–369.

Spring, Howard Allen. "The Use of Formulas in the Improvisations of Charlie Christian." *Jazzforschung/Jazz Research* 22 (1990): 11–51.

Thomasson, Amie L. "The Ontology of Art and Knowledge in Aesthetics." *Journal of Aesthetics and Art Criticism* 63:3 (2005): 221–229.

Trivedi, Saam. "Artist-Audience Communication: Tolstoy Reclaimed." *Journal of Aesthetic Education* 38:2 (2004): 38–52.

Wolterstorff, Nicholas. *Works and Worlds of Art.* Oxford: Clarendon Press, 1980.

Young, James O., and Carl Matheson. "The Metaphysics of Jazz." *Journal of Aesthetics and Art Criticism* 58:2 (2000): 125–134.

8

MUSICAL FORGERIES, IMPROVISATION, AND THE PRINCIPLE OF CONTINUITY

"One surely cannot play what is not."
"Oh yes, one can play what does not yet exist."

— *Thomas Mann*, Doctor Faustus

As should be apparent throughout this book, we regard jazz as an important musical art in which improvisation plays an important role. This chapter pursues certain provocations contained in Chapter 7, expanding on them by examining some central features of improvisational music that conflict with typical assumptions about art.[1] Specifically, we explain why it is impossible to find a place for some jazz performances within systems of aesthetics that treat artworks as obedient to what may be termed the *principle of continuity*, according to which, all art is presented as art *works*, and every work of art is subject to criteria of *reidentification*.[2] Accordingly, any music performance that possesses the status of art must be one in which there is a performance of a musical work or performable structure that can, in principle, be performed again at a later time.[3] However, the principle of continuity conflicts with the *principle of non-repeatability*, according to which some jazz improvisations do not generate works that can be performed again. Keith Jarrett's extended piano improvisation on January 24, 1975 (recorded and then released as *The Köln Concert*) is subject to our second principle. To say that others can play a work that Jarrett extemporaneously composed on that occasion is a misleading description of what takes place when a subsequent musician copies it.[4] Therefore a philosophy of jazz requires that at least one of these principles must give way. Any attempt to copy an improvised musical phrase would not, of course, be an improvisation, even if copying would not disqualify it as jazz.

We think that our understanding of jazz improvisation is enriched from considering exactly how the principle of continuity marginalizes it — primarily, by holding that every jazz improvisation is, in principle, repeatable. Admittedly, the conflict may not always be so obvious.[5] Either way, the main aim of this chapter is not to attack any particular version of the principle. However, there will be some discussion of Nelson Goodman's nicely articulated system of music and notation as a way to capture what is special about musical improvisations. While jazz improvisational performance is the immediate issue, the argument has implications for improvised material of all kinds – dance improvisations, dramatic pieces, "performance" art, or even improvised poetry and song, a form of which Giorgio Vasari tells us Leonardo da Vinci "sang divinely without any preparation."[6]

As will become clear, the underlying issue is the relevance of contextual considerations to our understanding of artistic phenomena. It seems clear to us that two identical literary texts should not be counted as instances of the same poem if one was composed in the sixteenth century, the other in the twentieth.[7] Analogous examples can be framed for musical works and paintings.[8] Among these considerations are those we shall term *contextual*. Based on the artistic norms of certain traditions, some appreciative response is properly directed at artistic processes, as contrasted with products. It may also focus on the *manner* in which these processes take place, e.g., *in accordance with a score, spontaneously*, and so on. The relevance of such considerations to our topic seems natural, given the distinctive manner in which improvisational music is generated. The degree of relevance is, however, contextual. Philosophers have suggested, quite independently of any concern with improvisation, that Goodman's categorizations of the "standard" arts need to be amplified in order to take account of these and other contextual factors.[9] However, we shall see that even if we were to augment Goodman's system along these lines, it will still be hard to find a place for improvisational art in it.

The argument will be developed in the following stages, corresponding to the sections of this chapter: (1) After a short characterization of improvisatory music and (2) a review of Goodman's division of the arts into the categories of the *allographic* and *autographic*, (3) we shall consider why improvisatory music will not fit in the former category. (4) We shall then consider an obstacle, reflecting the transitory nature of acoustic phenomena, about the placement of improvisational music within the category of the autographic. Taking some pains to understand the exact nature of this problem, (5) we shall then summarize the argument about the placement of improvisational music in Goodman's system. Finally, (6) an amplification of the contrast between work-performance (a music performance that aims to accurately perform an existing musical work) and improvisational performance will prompt (7) a closer consideration of the special features of improvisational *activity*. It will be important to bear in mind that for the purposes of this discussion, we shall assume that recording technology does not exist – or at least we shall try to do so, and will reserve a more detailed discussion for another chapter. Finally, a point about terminology: the term "work," as well as the related term "artwork," has connotations we sometimes wish to avoid. Therefore we shall now and then use the slightly more neutral expression "aesthetic object" when the occasion allows.

1. Improvisation

We begin with the central idea that an improviser makes substantive decisions about what music to play *while* playing it.[10] Throughout this chapter, we set aside improvisations – if they are to be counted as such – that consist merely of the addition of expressive nuance or "minor ornamental embellishments to a composed work."[11] These are clearly work-performances, i.e., performances that only interpret but do not recompose an existing work. Given that clarification, Ella Fitzgerald's 1956 studio performance of "Miss Otis Regrets" is a work-performance rather than an improvisation. In contrast, Lester Young's 1944 treatment of "These Foolish Things" is an improvisation, in the sense that he consistently and extemporaneously deviates from the standard melody. As we noted in Chapter 7, many jazz performances are a mixture of work-performance and improvisation. Finally, the emphasis here is improvisational performances as such, and not – except incidentally – transcriptions or arrangements of them for later performance, or musical works that have an improvisational origin.

An improviser (a) presents music intended to be worth hearing, by (b) creating it *as* she plays. Given conditions (a) and (b), risk is latent in improvisational performance. Still, it is a regulative ideal that an improviser attempts to satisfy the normative aim embedded in (a) while satisfying (b).[12] While in this chapter we shall generally speak of the improviser as someone acting alone, a consideration of collective improvisation underscores the character of improvisation by its resemblance to the flow of unscripted conversation. The difference is that the solitary improviser must often answer questions she poses to herself, so to say – where her answers typically lead to new questions. Collective improvisation, however, may be the greater wonder, as its complexity and creative communication distinguish it from improvisation that is solo.

As our reference to "These Foolish Things" indicates, improvisers do not create *ex nihilo* – a fact that is sometimes trotted out in a mistaken effort to debunk the improvisational enterprise.[13] Jazz improvisers do not take up instruments and improvise out of nothing, but take for granted a repertory of musical forms, e.g., the standard 12-bar I-IV-I-V-I blues chord progression distinctive of the blues, or the chord progressions of pre-existent tunes. Beginning conservatively, players master a repertoire of musical phrases, out of which they gradually learn to construct music of their own.[14] On-the-spot musical invention, however daring, invariably leaves something intact. In short, we want our conceptualization to be a modest one. While, for the sake of economy, we shall often speak of improvisers as creating music spontaneously, the hyperbole is not intended to rule out that an improviser's decisions while playing are often guided by a larger conception of where he or she is going. Odds are, the improvising musician is not doing so for the very first time. Nor should we require that every authentic performance meet stringent standards in regard to musical novelty, or that it stake out utterly new stylistic territory. However, one can resist the cynical conclusion that "improvisers" never really improvise. Even if all improvisatory music were made up entirely of formulaic musical atoms – a generous admission – we could still describe genuine improvisers as players who make on-the-spot decisions about how to sequence them as well as other variations on them.

Of course, improvisers have aims beyond the modest ones we have described. With many genres of improvised music, there is a tacit assumption that players will try, if they can, to surprise us. This *secondary* regulative ideal governs classical Iranian music, for example, where it is those "parts of the *radif* that lend themselves to far-flung improvisation [that] are valued; those that have predictability ... are lower ... The exceptional and unexpected is valued."[15] In the same spirit, every jazz improviser acknowledges an obligation to break out of the hand-me-down repertoire of materials he has internalized. All players have heard the kind of advice Charles Mingus gave beginners, namely to reach "beyond their formulas."[16] Indeed, what counts as a significant transmutation of musical materials varies widely as we move from jazz sub-category to sub-category. The rhapsodic kind of piano music Keith Jarrett plays would not reasonably be judged by the same criteria we would apply to mainstream "stride" playing by Teddy Wilson.

Although these secondary aims raise the ante on the risk that is inherent in improvisation, it would be too extreme to disqualify a performance as improvisational because it does not realize them. We shall later offer some remarks about differences between improvisation and work-performance in regard to musical expectation and fulfillment.

2. Autographic and Allographic

Goodman treats his central categories of the arts as exhaustive and mutually exclusive. He states, concerning the classification of music, that it is "nonautographic, or allographic."[17] What we have called *the principle of continuity* underlies Goodman's assumption that his two categories jointly exhaust the sphere of art. This claim deserves explanation.

A systematization of art would be simpler than it is if all art came packaged in the form of relatively enduring things. In that case, the concept of the *same* artwork would be exemplified only by works that have *physical continuity*. All art would then be *autographic*. A "work of art is autographic," Goodman says, "if and only if the distinction between original and forgery" is significant.[18] Forgeries, we should note, are not simply good likenesses of originals, nor are they merely attempts to work in the style of someone else, but are attempts at misrepresenting one for the other. Therefore, forgery lies in the arena of human intentions. An art student who copies a famous painting in order to hone her skills is not forging anything. The status of forgery might, however, accrue after any process of likeness is complete, by now offering the copy as the original. With painting and the other autographic arts, the central identity-question about particular enduring entities is whether they can be traced back to the moment when it came "from the artist's hand."[19] It takes only a slight adaptation of the idea to fit multiple-instanced autographic works, e.g., etchings. They are physical descendants, so to speak, of a common physical ancestor, the etched plate. However, there is no corresponding *material* continuity in some arts: poems and songs can survive simply by being remembered and passed on. Where physical continuity breaks down, proponents of work-continuity fall back upon the next best thing for explaining continuity: *structural continuity*. It gives us the category of *allographic* art. In spite of the transitory character of performances of musical works, their identity – and degree of accuracy of performance – can be measured by compliance with the strictly notational characters of a score.[20] As a result, a musical work manifested by one performance can be manifested by another, in spite of their physical discontinuity. The idea is not that the performances all derive from identical scores, but rather that the music is essentially notational (as a structure that is "amenable to notation") and the performances agree in all and only those features that are subject to notational specification.[21] There are any number of transcriptions of what Coleman Hawkins actually played when he recorded "Body and Soul" on October 11, 1939. These scores are radically noncompliant with any score that is normally associated with "Body and Soul." Using score compliance as our standard, Hawkins was playing a different but structurally related work; one that he spontaneously composed on that date.

The complementary application of the two categories to art in general would insure that it exhibits one kind of continuity or the other. (And what other sort of continuity could one imagine?) So, it is understandable why Goodman treats his central categories as exhaustive. It is a tidy system. But where should we place musical improvisation in a system of the arts that says all music is allographic?

3. A Thought-Experiment

A problem we run into immediately is a consequence of the fact that the theory of the allographic is – for our purposes here – the theory of musical works. More importantly, in principle, every musical work can be multiple-instanced. Improvisations, however, being unique, are not multiple-instanced. While this contrast is undoubtedly correct, it isn't enlightening. Let's press the point with the help of a counter-conjecture: perhaps multiple instantiation is a feature of the improvisational world, but not a very common one – or one which we just don't take much notice of. Suppose that an improvisation by Corman Hackins (H_1) just happens to be perceptually indistinguishable from the famous "Body and Soul" solo of Coleman Hawkins (H_2). The two form what we might term a *perfect pair*.[22] Now why couldn't H_1 and H_2 be regarded as compliants of some single set of notational characters? The type theory of musical works is more tolerant of such a proposal than one might suspect – indeed, probably too tolerant, as we shall see. An acoustic clone of an authentic performance of a given work, whether intentionally copied from the former or not, counts as a genuine instance of that work. After all, they will both conform to the same notated sound structure. Consider, in this light, a pianist who plays music by copying another performance – playing it by ear, in other words. As long as the copy complies with a work-score that notates the earlier performance, it qualifies as a genuine instance of that work. Indeed, the acoustic output of a performance would qualify as a genuine instance of a musical work, *however it originated*. In this view, should a long burst of radio static happen to comply with the score of Beethoven's "Moonlight Sonata" (Op. 27, No. 2), it counts as an authentic instance of that work.

Again, we are stressing that it makes no difference whether there is an existing common score with which H_1 and H_2 are compliant. It does not matter: folk songs came into existence before they got notated. Even if an improvisation is not actually notated, it will be to some degree *notatable*. Transcriptions of jazz solos are routinely published for pedagogical purposes. In Chapter 2, we noted that transcriptions are frequently performed, most notably of Miles Davis's *Kind of Blue* and Keith Jarrett's *Köln Concert*. Nothing in Goodman's analysis of musical works, it should be noted, entitles us to rule some scores out of court on the grounds of their origins, because origins are relevant to autographic works, but never to allographic ones.

Now a host of interesting technical issues arise about the applicability of Goodman's theory to this class of cases. First, we have to reckon with the fact that his theory of notationality is an idealization of a European musical tradition. No other culture, he says, "has developed any comparably effective musical notation over the centuries."[23] Surely, however, the applicability of the methodology to the wider range of musical practices found around the world is problematic. Many of these practices, it should be noted, make themselves felt in profound ways in American jazz. Both tonally and rhythmically, jazz is a sort of vectorial resultant of European and African practice, each of which, considered in itself, is a stranger to the other. Consequently, jazz contains a huge class of notes that are, from the point of view of European practice, systematically skewed from a tonal point of view – the so-called blue notes. Another example is the class of "swinging" eighth notes that are represented inaccurately in transcriptions of them – as, e.g., dotted eighth notes plus sixteenths. We would have to consider how such notes are to be represented by a Goodmanian notation.

One possibility is that such features might be represented by what Goodman calls *supplementary* instructions.[24] Such instructions include non-notational marks, e.g., diminuendo "hair pins," words written over the bar-line, traditions handed down verbally, and performance agreements made on the spot. So, perhaps we could include the tacit agreements that enable jazz players to interpret the inevitable misrepresentations of jazz music that lurk in European transcriptions of it as belonging to these supplemental instructions. For example, trained players will know how to interpret the standard scored *mis*representations of "swinging eighths" and make appropriate adjustments in order to get the required effects.

The problem is that the compliance of a performance with supplemental instructions does not play any role in identifying it as an instance of a musical work when the work is identified with an abstract structure. These are instructions about the way that the work should be performed, but the work is one thing, the performances another. Thus, Goodman thinks that such instructions account for the expressive features of *performances* of standard musical works. However, these features are, for identificational purposes, non-functional.[25] Even if this were a plausible approach to many of the salient features of work-performance, would we want to advance an analogous position about the wide range of "eccentric" sound-events that pervade a typical jazz improvisation? It would be absurd, surely, to treat them all as elaborately nuanced compliants of the ordinary European note-heads that make up the imaginary score that supposedly defines the hypothetical work in question.[26] Nor do we want to adopt the outlandish view that such sound-events must be regarded as failures to comply with given European note-heads – as *errors*, in short.[27] The problem, in sum, is that features of a jazz improvisation that play identifying roles fall into limbo on Goodman's account. This is understandable, given that some of them, e.g., blue notes, exist only in the cracks between the keys of a tempered keyboard.

While these are interesting theoretical questions, we do not want to become absorbed by them. For two related reasons, the real problems lie elsewhere. First, all readers should find themselves wondering if this idealization of the power of notation provides conditions that are either necessary or sufficient for the identification of instances of *ordinary* musical works in *ordinary* musical practice. Even in this sphere, Goodman is forced to admit that, for example, tempo specifications, being non-notational, "cannot be accounted integral parts of the defining score."[28] (Again, they belong to the supplemental instructions.) However, we think it is obvious that following a notated score of Miles Davis's "All Blues" (1959) while playing it at a tempo of one beat per minute does *not* generate a performance of "All Blues."

Keep in mind that our goal is to see why improvisational music is *peculiarly* resistant to allographic analysis, for our intuition is that work-performances and improvisations really are different in kind. For the sake of argument, then, we shall table the issue about the problems Goodman faces applying his idealized picture of notationality to music – whether of an improvised sort or not. We shall assume one of two possibilities: Either a notation-centered methodology for identifying pieces of music – including that of improvisational origin – is workable; or some other method of identifying a common structure or work-type in its various tokens is feasible.[29] In favor of something *like* Goodman's idealized approach is the fact that standard musical practice does have it that being true to a work *customarily* involves being true to its score. We want to explain why, however this matter be resolved, there would *still* be a gulf between improvisational music and work-performance. At this point, however, we need a more plausible account of work-performance before we can articulate an account of that gulf.

So, in order to continue with our thought-experiment, we must augment its application to ordinary work-performances. Revising Goodman, Jerrold Levinson defines one concept of the autographic (autographic(1) art, we might term it) as "art such that the question of the authenticity of works of that type is not determined at all by compliance with the characters of a notation." He further defines a concept of the allographic – allographic(1) art – as "art such that the identification of instances is *partly* determined by notational compliance."[30] On this analysis, genuine instances of a given work must not only token a given type, but also stand in "intentional and/or causal relatedness" to the composer's "dated act of indication."[31] (Scores, obviously, are the typical repository of such "indications.") A bonus is that these re-definitions stand a better chance of being coextensive with an alternative pair of definitions that Goodman also employs: Autographic(2) art is "art such that even the most exact duplicate of such a work cannot, under any conditions, 'count as genuine,' since it would not be the one that came from 'the artist's hand.'"[32] Correspondingly, allographic(2) art would be "art in which both one sound-event and its clone could, *under certain conditions*, serve in place of each other." Most importantly, Goodman's categories, with their revised definitions, now exhaust the artistic field. Or so Levinson claims.[33]

Levinson is concerned, as are we, that Goodman's general approach is insufficiently sensitive to the relevance of contextual contingencies. We shall evaluate Levinson's larger claim later. We now have enough of the pieces to make a comparison between improvisational music and notationally compliant allographic art.

The most obvious effect of Levinson's emendations on our comparison is that performances of improvised and score-compliant music proceed according to different intentions. A piece of improvised music is not generated the way that the augmented theory tells us work-performances are generated, that is, as an action that aims at structural compliance. Let's return to Hankins and Hawkins and their sonically indistinguishable renditions of "Body and Soul." True, H_1 and H_2 share a *general* aim, namely, to improvise some music. However, two performances of a common work W are bound together not merely by the shared aim to play some work or other. They are bound by a specific common aim, namely, to token the antecedently identified type W. It is no accident that scores for H_1 or H_2 would be merely hypothetical ones – or, if actual ones, written down *after* the fact. The hypothetical unity of H_1 and H_2 is just an artifact of the thought-experiment. Any structural agreement is a cosmic coincidence.

One might be tempted to endorse the work-continuity of H_1 and H_2 anyway, if we begin by thinking of the pair as composed of sheer acoustic events. However, any criterion of reidentification that might apply to improvisation would have to range over *actions*, not over acoustic events independent of those actions.[34] On Levinson's amended version of allographic art, no less than on the original account, criteria of authenticity range over "sequence[s] of sounds."[35] Obviously, the typical way of satisfying the "intentional and / or causal" conditions is by means of a standard type of intentional action, namely, musical *performance*. However, there is nothing in Levinson's revision that requires that actual performance play an intermediary role here. In the days of player-pianos, some piano rolls were constructed without the intermediary agency of any performer at all. Holes were simply punched in the paper corresponding with the details of the score of that musical work. Despite the absence of anything that would count as a *performance*, nothing in Levinson's account clearly rules out that a pair of sound-sequences produced by such a piano roll would qualify as two instances of that work. (And perhaps nothing should rule it out either.) With a pair of jazz improvisations, however, an analogous indifference to the fact that they arise as two *performances* would be incoherent. With improvisational music, the performance *process* gnaws into the very essence of the aesthetic object, so to say. We will expand on this point in section 7.

An improvisational action is an aesthetic singularity. If H_1 and H_2 really are improvisational in character, then each harbors its own generative act. Essential to H_1 is its being *this* spontaneous action; essential to H_2 is its being *that* one. H_1 and H_2 each possess a kind of *aesthetic indexicality*, so to say. Even if H_1 and H_2 did eventually follow the same course, they would still count as distinct aesthetic objects, not as tokens of a single aesthetic object-type.

All in all, then, the thought-experiment is surprisingly distortive. It invites us to take a decontextualized point of view of the matter that is framed, so to say, *sub specie aeternitatis*. From that point of view, H_1 and H_2 seem to be composed of a set of acoustic events, which are, furthermore, determinate in character. From a perspective on H_1 and H_2 as the *processes* they really are – a point of view *in media res*, so to say – there is no determinate pair to match up in the way we have supposed they are matched up. Each member of the pair hangs in the balance as long as the performance lasts. When each becomes determinate – and if, by a fluke, they were to do so in qualitatively indistinguishable ways – a moment essential to it has passed. With improvisational music, the performance *process* is an essential aspect of the aesthetic object.[36]

The foregoing considerations all fit the character of an informed interest in improvised music. They all reflect the fact that the *point* or *telos* of such performance is to create music in the course of playing it. In section 7 we will return to the contrast between reception of work-performance activity and our reception of musical improvisation. Already, though, it should be clear that someone who approaches improvisational music as if it were merely a string of sounds – or such a string *as* exemplifying a musical structure or pattern – would not be in a position to respond to it in an informed way. Further comparison between improvisations and work-performance will be made in section 6.

4. Ephemerality and Autographic Art

Returning to the allographic/autographic distinction, there is a *prima facie* reason for locating improvisations in the sphere of autographic art. The directness of our experience of improvised music seems to parallel that of our experience of painting. If we are visiting the *Musée d'Orsay* and gaze upon *Arrangement in Grey and Black No.1* ("Whistler's Mother"), we are gazing upon the very object that James McNeill Whistler has made. Similarly, when we are in a concert hall and listen to Keith Jarrett improvise, we are hearing the very sounds that constitute the improvisation. However, recall that it is definitional that autographic arts are subject to forgery. We immediately run into the difficulty that music, considered as an acoustic phenomenon, is ephemeral.[37] As a result, something curious happens when we try to impose the category of forgery onto improvisational performance. Given that the forgery of paintings is our standard example of the misrepresentation of authorship, the forgery of a musical work would require a very different narrative.

The issue here is about what Levinson describes as "referential forgery," that is, the forgery of specific works, as contrasted with "inventive forgeries," which are forgeries of works of a given *kind*.[38] To reproduce *Arrangement in Grey and Black* and then offer to sell it as the original *Arrangement in Grey and Black* is a case of referential forgery. To produce an original painting in the style of Picasso's Blue Period and offer to sell it as a "lost" Picasso is an inventive forgery. The problem is that when we try to apply notions of work-forgery to a pair of improvisations, we do not seem to be able to do so. (Musical scores and recordings are certainly subject to forgery, but we are not concerned with those phenomena here.)

A pair of performances such as H_1 and H_2 of our thought-experiment in the previous section could confuse a listener in the way perfect pairs of paintings might confuse, only if the listener could bear in mind the original with which the copy is liable to be confused. This excludes superficially similar kinds of error. Ceremonial recreations of improvisations are common, of course, and unobjectionable – although such copies obviously do not play the *improvisational* role of the original. An uninformed person listening to Coleman Hawkins ceremonially recreate his "Body and Soul" solo might believe he had been hearing Hawkins improvise the music on the spot. However, this mistake has nothing to do with confusing the performance with an earlier original. The problem is that if we try to revise the story so as to introduce the right kind of confusion, the situation provides the evidence that would expose the deception before it gets off the ground. Any cue that would suggest the possibility of forgery, e.g., the recognition of the similarity itself, would give the game away. Imagine a faker, Corman Hackins, playing notes very close to those of Hawkins's performance some fifty years earlier.[39] A listener would know that *if* fakery were involved, the original would have to be a performance that took place *prior* to the one the listener is hearing. While a painting can survive the ravages of time and confuse a viewer by turning up side-by-side with a clever forgery, it is otherwise with an improvisation. Of course, this problem would not prevent Hackins from *plagiarizing* Hawkins's performance. Plagiarism, however, is not the issue here. Plagiarism is a reversal of referential forgery, and involves the issue of which of two instances came first – an issue that does not arise with inventive forgery. So while plagiarists claim to be the authors of work that is not their own, forgers claim their work is really the work of someone else.

Supposing we have identified a problem about fitting improvisations into the category of the autographic, we have not yet shown it to be a problem that attaches to improvisations *qua* improvisations. The same problem could be raised about a broad sphere of aesthetic events that are *not* improvised. Consider other ephemeral aesthetic displays: preconceived but non-notated dance performances, for instance, or fireworks displays. Even assuming a practice of attribution to identifiable pyro-technicians, forgery projects for fireworks could not get off the ground. Now, a conspicuous difference between the two kinds of case is the different ways they are generated – a contextual difference, in short.[40] One guesses that, because of the way improvisational music is generated, projects of forgery would run into difficulty in that sphere even if acoustic phenomena *weren't* ephemeral. However, we will not get at the suspected difference unless we think about the matter in the right way.

Consider a hypothetical sub-class of paintings that are improvised.[41] Unlike musical improvisations, these works nevertheless involve relatively enduring material objects. Now the way such works are made is surely relevant to certain questions of authenticity we might raise about them. Imagine a project by Jones of making a copy of Smith's piece, *Blue Flash*, and presenting it as Smith's. Think of our player-piano example mentioned earlier. Unlike improvisations, no problem of ephemerality would interfere with Jones's plan. Applying standard reasoning about forgeries of ordinary paintings, we would say that Jones's copy – a referential forgery – would not serve in place of Smith's original. As objects of appreciative attention, one autographic work cannot substitute for another. However, whatever we think of this intuition, contextual considerations probably provide an additional reason for the negative reply as well. For suppose we hypothetically isolate and set aside the actual and possible perceptual differences between the two by pretending that there are none. It is arguable that Jones's copy would still not serve in place of Smith's because of the difference between the ways the two graphics were made.[42] Some philosophers would urge that contextual considerations probably affect informed responses to ordinary works of autographic art as well. Whatever other reasons might be given why a forged or plagiarized painting will not serve in place of the original – some would say – the *way* it is made, the process leading to its existence, is also relevant.[43]

However, as described, it seems that Jones *can* forge *Blue Flash*. As a work, it is subject to forgery. So far, then, we haven't turned up any special problem about classifying improvisational music as autographic, beyond the problem posed by its ephemerality. If the way improvisations are made provides a more *specific* reason why they are not autographic, the contextual factor must figure in those cases in some special way. We observed earlier that improvisational and autographic art both feature a kind of *directness*. However, there is a difference in this respect between the two. We shall term the kind of directness that typifies improvised music *presence*. Compare the following three conditions for an informed response:

a   A condition of one's informed response to *Arrangement in Grey and Black* is that one takes its lines and colors as being applied x-ly as one watches.
b   A condition of one's informed response to an improvisation is that one takes its sounds as being created spontaneously as one listens.
c   A condition of one's informed response to *Blue Flash* is that one takes its lines and colors as being applied spontaneously as one watches.

Never mind how to fill the place-holder in (a). (It isn't easy to give a general recipe for how to do so, except negatively, with a locution such as "non-forgedly." Ted Gioia says "spontaneously," but then points to many ways it is not spontaneous.[44]) The point is that whatever contextual conditions are relevant to our understanding of *Arrangement in Grey and Black*, they obviously do not dictate that we are supposed to *watch* the painting being made.[45] In spite of their relevance to an informed response to the work, they are not constitutive of the work. However, (b) seems exactly right. With improvisations, we *are* supposed to understand the music we hear as being created before our very ears. Again, this is a point about a difference of *presence*.

So, the problem we first identified about the transitory character of acoustic phenomena was an artificially abstracted aspect of a more fundamental feature of improvisation. The feature of the music we have called *presence* suggests that it is over *processes* that an autographic principle of continuity would have to range, if we are to apply it at all. Improvisations are not excluded from the sphere of the autographic simply because their effects are ephemeral *results* of processes. They are excluded because improvisations *are* transient processes. Indeed, they are *actions*, as we argued in the previous section. The *way* the acoustic material is generated in these cases is an essential component of the genuine article. This does not entail the absurdity that we are expected to respond to improvisational processes in abstraction from the sounds generated. An improvisation consists neither of disembodied sounds nor of an activity abstracted from the sounds. It consists of the whole activity of creating a sound-sequence in the course of playing it, for evaluation/appreciation *as* music created in that way.[46] Here, our position about improvisation dovetails with Goodman's interest in the possibility of forgery in the autographic arts. For Goodman, "The hardheaded question why there is any *aesthetic* difference between a deceptive forgery and an original work challenges a basic premiss upon which the very function of [art appreciation] depends."[47] That premise, in brief, is that knowledge of the true conditions of production "informs the very character" of our looking and our listening.[48]

Now what about (c)? While the *way* a copy of *Blue Flash* is made may well be relevant to certain critical questions we might pose about it, (c) is no more plausible than (a). However, if we alter the terms of the thought-experiment and reconceive *Blue Flash* as a type of improvisational *performance*, analogous to musical improvisations – an *improvigraphic*, as one might term it, then (c) would hold for it. The analogy between *Blue Flash* and an improvisational performance of music would be much closer. On its original interpretation, though, both *Blue Flash* and ordinary works of autographic art have a feature we might call *temporal indifference*. Any contextual condition relevant to an informed response to an example of either kind of work could be fulfilled at any temporal distance from the response itself. We would be in a position to respond no less appropriately to *Blue Flash* if we engaged it a hundred years after its creation than if we apprehended it hot off the easel. It might be replied that fireworks displays, by contrast with *Blue Flash*, are not temporally indifferent any more than musical improvisations are. However, their indifference has nothing to do with the process by which they are generated, but with the fact that fireworks probably *are* nothing more than the ephemeral products of those processes. (We discuss fireworks at greater length in our Chapter 6 discussion of Adorno's critique of popular music.)

We might ask why, given the similarity between autographic art and improvisatory music, we could not simply loosen up the concept of the autographic and place them there anyway. The argument of the last section in effect profiled the peculiarly singular character of improvisational performance. But is this not a feature of paintings as well? The difficulty with this attempt at rapprochement is that paintings are singly instanced simply because of the physical process by which they are made. There is nothing inherent about autographic art that requires works of that kind to be either singly or multiply "instanced," as Goodman puts it.[49] As we noted earlier, etchings illustrate that the category of the autographic embraces multiple-instanced works. But improvisations don't just *happen* to be singularities. If we are right, they could not be otherwise. Furthermore, even if we were to classify improvisational music as autographic, they would still be anomalous members of that group, given the presumed linkage between the autographic and the relatively endurable. After all, Goodman states that the "ephemeral character of performances" is a reason to think that some art is allographic.[50] He might have good reason to think so, as we have seen. However, as we know, the alternative doesn't work either.[51] So the two categories do not exhaust the field of possibilities. There must be a third category: music that we appreciate without appreciating a *work* that is subject to a principle of continuity.

If forgery does not threaten improvisational practice, what kind of inauthenticity does? Plagiarism, of course (including self-plagiarism[52]). We restrict ourselves to two comments about the matter. First, while a plagiarized "improvisation" really isn't the genuine article at all, one could hardly say anything analogous about either a plagiarized or a forged painting *except* with the help of a theory about work identity. Second, plagiarism in an improvisational context is a distinctively vexatious matter, because it betrays the goal that is so obviously foregrounded in this kind of art. The problem is compounded by the fact that such fakery is nevertheless endemic to improvisational practice. At least, this fact is conspicuous in the case of jazz. Given the demand to stand up and deliver whether ready to do so or not, soloists will understandably fall back on stretches of imitative material. (In fact, it was common practice in the 1920s for a soloist to do so: it was more important for a soloist to play "hot" than to improvise.[53]) Correlatively, jazz people keep their ears open to detect such lapses in each other's playing – even if otherwise harsh judgments about them will, under the circumstances, often be softened.

5. Preliminary Conclusions

In sum, improvisations are not subject to either kind of Goodmanian reidentifiability. The comparison of them with standard examples of autographic art shows an improvisation to be a certain kind of ephemeral process, namely, an action in which the artist must be present to the portion of the work created. The comparison of them with allographic art amplifies our description of them by profiling their singularity. They lack either autographic or allographic continuity. So, it seems that we cannot follow Levinson in his solidarity with Goodman's opinion that – given amendments of the sort he suggested – the allographic/autographic duality exhausts the artistic field. The larger moral for any aesthetic system that treats art as coming packaged in reidentifable *works* is that there simply is no entity with which an improvisation can be reidentified – nor any entity with which an improvisation might be mistakenly reidentified. The argument does not imply that we have no means of picking improvisations out, of course. Scholars of recorded jazz do it quite naturally, by referring to, e.g., Miles Davis's solo when the Quintet performed "My Funny Valentine" on June 12, 1959. If we are right, identifications of improvisations begin and end with such characterizations. If we jettison the linkage between forgery and the concept of autographic art, we might have a category of the autographic that would have application even in a world in which no "ill intent" to practice forgery could be found.[54] In that case, a "spontaneous invention having nothing to do with variation" could only be specified by reference to who played the music at a specified time and place.[55]

At this point, there seem to be two options available to us. We might hold that the categories of the autographic and allographic are exhaustive only for the category of art *works*; but then there are some arts that do not center on works.[56] Or we might hold that the distinction applies to all art without exception. In a passage of speculative history, Goodman proposes that originally all the arts might have been autographic, but that notation was devised "to transcend the limitations" of time, i.e., the ephemeral, and "the individual."[57] This is striking, because these "limitations" are, of course, typical features of improvisational music. However, we would reject any suggestion that such music is a vestige of an undeveloped stage in art's history. We conclude that, unless we set aside the assumption that the autographic concerns the relatively endurable – and hence the forgeable – we will have the same kind of trouble applying the label to ancient ephemeral art as we have had applying it to improvisatory music of our own time.

6. Contrasting Work-Performance and Improvisation

Comparing improvisations with work-performances, rather than with works themselves, seems awkward; but it seems just as awkward to make the comparison the other way. Perhaps improvisation is composing in the *course* of performing – as has been suggested by Philip Alperson and Gioia.[58] However, this won't do either, for it begs the question by incorporating the idea that something is being composed. Of course an improvisation is a process of creation; and it does eventually generate a determinate result – which *could* be transformed into a full-fledged work. However, while musical works are subject to reidentification, this isn't the case with improvisations *qua* improvisations. Could an improvisation be treated as a work-type that just happens to have a single performance-token?[59] Not likely. We can imagine the "Moonlight Sonata" having been played once, just after its composition, but then the autograph score is lost during shipment to the music publisher, and a busy Beethoven declines to reconstruct the score. So it is only performed once. However, it is inherent in the concept of it as a work that it *could* be instanced any number of times. But it would not have made sense to ask Charlie Parker to improvise a *given* solo a second time.

It has to be granted, though, that considerations relevant to the sphere of works and their performance and those pertinent to the territory of improvisatory music do blur into each other – or seem to. The matter can be considered by examining two complications that seem to reduce the difference between improvisation and work-performance.

The first complication is that improvisations are often performed in the course of playing modest works. The jazz field, for instance, contains a broad spectrum of musical material, jazz standards, along with specialized jazz compositions. We can only sketch one or two points about this practice. Many cases are full-fledged musical works containing improvisational components similar to both modern "serious" works and older ones, e.g., concertos, as played when their cadenzas were not yet fully written out. However, much mainstream jazz consists of *improvisations on* X – where "X" denotes a familiar tune.[60] They seem to be work-performances and improvisations at the same time. However, saying so is not like saying that someone at the same time improvises and plays the "Moonlight Sonata."

First, the sense in which improvisers perform *works* is much looser than the sense in which Serkin plays the "Moonlight Sonata." George Russell's deconstruction of the pop tune "You Are My Sunshine" and John Coltrane's assault on "Chim Chim Cher-ee" (both 1965) are obvious examples. A listener who said of one of the former performances, "That's just not 'You Are my Sunshine,'" because it didn't conform to a scored representation of it, would misunderstand the point of the performance. Second, for many jazz ears, what identifies a "work" is its pattern of harmonic motion.[61] For example, the strains of the AABA tune "Koko" that became the basis for a series of Charlie Parker improvisations do not have the same notes as the strains of the tune "Cherokee." So, from one point of view, a player who has performed one of these tunes would not have played the other.[62] However, since the two have – not by accident – basically similar patterns of harmonic motion, we might say that a performance of one *is* a performance of the other. The same point goes for the blues. There is a sense in which every 12-bar blues performance in B flat is an instance of a common, very "thin" work for which there are relatively few constitutive, work-defining features.

The problem is not just that we lack any theory about how to recover the improvisations themselves – the problem emphasized in section 3 – but that we lack clear antecedent guidelines for individuating the items that are the bases of the improvisations. Certainly, jazz players pay little attention to the simplistic representations of them in published sheet music. Unlike the situation with full-fledged musical works, there is no rigorous practice that theory *ought* to reflect. (Certainly, it would make no sense to detail ways in which any such item succeeds or fails to conform to strict criteria of allographic authenticity.) Given the built-in lack of precision about what counts as playing *the* work either in the improvisational or the non-improvisational context, it seems harmless to say, with this kind of jazz at any rate, that an improvisation on such a work does two things at once. The criteria for its being a work-performance *simpliciter* are too loose to get in the way. Jazz practice lives with this lack of precision. Indeed, it thrives on it. Jazz players continually reshape existing musical materials for new musical purposes.

Let us turn to a second complication. Given a focus on the *manner* in which a work is performed, as contrasted with an interest in the performed work *per se*, might our earlier argument not be turned against us? Consider an example of a perfect pair again, but this time composed of two performances of the "Moonlight Sonata" that equally qualify as performances of that work *and* are coincidentally nuanced the same way and with the same degree of spontaneity. One pianist is consistently successful in having the performance sound just as she intends, while the second is consistently failing to do so. Following the same reasoning as used earlier, we might conclude that neither performance could serve for the other.[63] But if that can be true of two performances of a scored piano sonata in the classical tradition, the difference between a work-performance and an improvisation seems diminished.

About this new thought-experiment, one might say, first, that identifying and evaluating work-performances in this way would be a very specialized project, as compared with identifying them as, e.g., Sviatoslav Richter's "highly idiosyncratic" reading of Franz Schubert's piano sonata in A major (D664).[64] Either way, though, we are still operating with the distinction between work-performances and improvisational performances. A performance by Richter could not meaningfully be called "idiosyncratic," construed simply as a bit of piano playing. It is idiosyncratic *as* a way of playing a definable, multiply-instanced work, e.g., that particular sonata. So, the specificity that we won on behalf of such performances is compromised by the fact that a description of one of them would still be predicated upon its ordinary identification *as* a performance of a given work. This fits the fact that when such personalized performances go so far as to intentionally depart from scores, the gesture begs for an explanation. This could hardly be said of a jazz improvisation. Miles Davis's selection of the pop tune "Time After Time" was seen as an idiosyncratic choice, but his improvisations when playing it cannot be so described.

We must avoid a possible misunderstanding about the difference between the two kinds of case. News about a high degree of acoustic similarity between two performances of the "Moonlight Sonata" would hardly come as a big surprise to the two pianists. By contrast, should Hawkins, for example, make such a discovery about the perfect pair described in section 3, he would probably be puzzled. (Indeed, he might wonder if there wasn't something fishy about the situation.[65]) However, this contrast can be misleading. The difference between the two types is not simply a function of the degree of sheer acoustic difference between a pair of improvisations – where each is based on the same tune, as in jazz, for instance – and the degree of acoustic difference between a pair of full-fledged performances of the same music score. Even if pairs of ordinary improvisational performances of the sort just described did as a rule diverge more from each other acoustically than pairs of performances of a given work do, we would certainly not assign the pairs to different kinds on that basis alone. Rather, acoustic differences are profiled in different ways in the two types of case because the two are antecedently assigned to distinct categories. We might reasonably believe that, by contrast with a pair of up-coming improvisations, both an afternoon and an evening performance of the "Moonlight Sonata" will generate much the same music. But that expectation would be a partial function of the fact that we antecedently categorize the pair *as* performances of a given work. Regarding them in that light, we might be inclined to overlook the multitude of acoustic differences that could differentiate the two. Admittedly, those differences would loom large, of course, should we consider the pair in altered terms – in light of their liveliness, or their idiosyncrasies, *as* work-performances. However, this fact does not erode the boundary between the two types of music. Consider the different ways – and responses to those ways – in which our expectations can be *unfulfilled* in the two cases.

Listening to a stretch of a work-performance, a listener might take a modulation as a cue for the recapitulation. Instead, suppose, the listener is surprised to hear some entirely new material. In some respects, this registry of the unexpected in this case is not utterly different from a confrontation with the unexpected in the sphere of jazz improvisation, as any eccentric modulation in such a performance illustrates.[66] However, the differences between the two categories in this respect are still overriding. At leisure, we can go back again – and again – and examine the unexpected twists and turns in a musical work. Soon, of course, we will learn to expect them. Further, the fulfillment of these expectations does not, on the whole, contribute negatively to aesthetic response. Indeed, the satisfaction of them is, quite often, a positive thing. In a fictional commentary – on a Beethoven sonata (Opus 111) – one of Thomas Mann's characters describes the "here it comes again" feature of listening, as we might describe it.[67]

With improvised music, things are different. True, some improvisations may *seem* predictable just because they unfold with such striking musical "rightness." That they do so may seem uncanny, indeed, surprising – surprising *for* an improvisation, that is. By contrast, it would be strange to describe a piece of music as sounding surprisingly "right" *for* a piece of composed music. Furthermore, consider the difference between responses to performances of the two kinds that are predictable because they sound *familiar*. Such a feeling about an improvisation will naturally cast a shadow over it, since it will suggest the possibility that the performance might be more borrowed than an authentic improvisation ought to be. True, a sense of familiarity with a musical work can also be a tip-off that it *might* be plagiarized, or perhaps composed in the style of another work. But in the latter case, an alternative explanation is always available that is not available in the former case. A work can sound familiar because we really *have* heard it before, by means of earlier performances of it. By contrast, if an improvisation is genuine, we could not have heard *it* before.

There may have been a time, even in Western music, when the distinction between the two kinds of performance would have made little sense. Theodor Adorno tried to identify underlying social reasons why, in the eighteenth century, musical practice became increasingly bound by the ever stricter authority of scores, with correspondingly less and less space for improvisation. He also noted that, alongside modern work-based practice, relics of a freer, more improvisational tradition continue to play a subsidiary role in later work-performance practice.[68] Nowadays, if we are looking for echoes of a time before the distinction hardened as much as it has, we might well consider jazz.[69] However, history did make its difference. That the dichotomy is not just an artifact of exaggerated zeal in border patrolling we can see by the way we describe the mixed cases – namely, *as* mixed. However, such cases also illustrate the fact that goals central to the one kind of performance can play relevant if subsidiary roles in the other.

7. Improvisation as Activity

The difference between the two categories of performance can be further profiled by reflecting on the way we regard performance *activity* in cases of each type. Activity may turn up in a work-performance as an aesthetic *quality* of the work itself – as exemplified by passages of music possessing a "running" character, for instance, or as a musical *image* of musical activity, e.g., the sound-picture of piano playing in Camille Saint-Saëns's *Carnival of the Animals* and Strauss's *Burlesque*. (Such examples are not unknown in improvisational music, e.g., the vocal sounds that could be heard in Eric Dolphy's sax playing.) However, with some music – if not with all – we are expected to take an interest in the *actual* activity involved in the performance. One's recognition of the brilliance of a performance of the Mephisto Waltz (No. 1) is partly a function of one's sense of the difficulties posed by the piece.[70] However, as already suggested in sections 3 and 4, informed responses to improvisational music involve a distinctive kind of registry of performance activity.

With improvisational performance, one's concern is about how a player's on-the-spot decisive actions create the very music unfolding as one listens. This focus is evidenced by the interest we take in collective improvisation in jazz, where players often try to unhorse fellow players by throwing them off balance.[71] However, such cases are only striking instances of a general feature of improvisational performance. In typical jazz improvisations, players can be heard probing and testing possibilities latent in the music they are making.[72] (The jazz pianist and composer George Russell refers to this self-monitoring feature of a typical improvisation as its *intuitive* quality.[73]) Correlatively, we take a special kind of interest in this activity – in how a performer is faring, so to say. If things are going well, we wonder if the player can sustain the level. If he seems to be getting into trouble, we worry about how he will address the problem. Gunther Schuller notes how Louis Armstrong's "fertile imagination" frequently generated potential breakdowns in the performance.[74] In the Hot Seven recording of "Potato Head Blues" (1927), "there is a feeling of 'is he going to make it?,' especially from measure seventeen on [where] Armstrong is just barely keeping up with the changes." We can hear moments of hesitation and uneasiness. Fortunately, "the band adjusts" and Armstrong brings the solo home with a relaxing conclusion in the final two bars.

As noted earlier, some improvisers manage to create well-organized musical material that sounds relatively free of the qualities we have just described. Bach's improvisations were said to come off as smoothly as if composed.[75] It would be odd, in contrast, to describe a Chopin Ballade as *sounding* composed; it *is* composed. Smooth as some genuine improvisations are, knowing listeners will not regard them in the same way as they would regard a work–performance.

It should be obvious, finally, that given an understanding of the kind of performance involved, we will not *evaluate* acoustic strings generated by improvisations and performances of works in all the same terms. Heard in a work-performance, the kind of notes played at various points in the Armstrong solo (and the metric adjustment that occurs) might strike a listener as a gaffe it would be best to overlook or forget. Heard as the improvisation it is, the performance has strikingly positive features.

8. Epilogue

This chapter has explained how complex issues generated by improvisation challenge the recent philosophical distinction between autographic and allographic arts – a distinction that assumes a principle of continuity, according to which musical performances are performances of works that can be performed multiple times. Consequently, one of the contributions that philosophy of art makes to our understanding of music is to articulate our criteria of reidentification. We have argued that a philosophy of jazz improvisation challenges the value of the principle of continuity as applied to some jazz.

A phenomenology of the experience of improvised music would profile what we called (in section 4) *presence*. The sense that a unique, unscripted event is taking place as we listen gives an improvisatory performance a sense of moment. We have to be there at the right time to hear a specific improvisation; yet, we cannot plan to hear *that* one. Being there at the right time, we have a special sense of that music's birth, as we listen. A feeling of indeterminacy is built into the situation and cannot be dissolved by an alteration of my epistemic relationship to the music. The excitement the experience engenders is enhanced as secondary regulative ideals make themselves felt – as when players take risks that are conspicuous. We can find ourselves slipping back and forth between our hopes for the ultimate quality of the music and our fascination with the activity by which it is generated – even when those actions appear to threaten the quality of the resulting music. For reasons discussed in Chapter 10, the strain contributes to the music's interest rather than detracting from it.

Is presence merely a value that improvised music has? Not "merely," since it is a feature both of imaginative and uninspired performances. It is a reflection of the way informed listeners address the music – a way that guides our judgments about the comparative merits of given improvisations. However, it is undeniable that presence is a kind of overarching feature of the music that can be savored, even in mediocre performances. There is nothing incoherent here. One can savor the cinematic characteristics of movies in general without judging any one of them to be a superb film among films. The presence of an improvised musical string indicates its now-or-never quality for its reception, but it also points to the ontological singularity of improvisation.

We said at the outset that we would do our best to assume in the argument of this chapter that recording technology does not exist. We failed, of course, since, in order to avail ourselves of a common currency of examples we made unavoidable recourse to recorded examples. The situation is ironic. Our understanding and appreciation of the living music seems inextricably entangled with our understanding and appreciation of the canned version. Consider how much of our understanding of improvised jazz – indeed, jazz's evolving understanding of itself – is based upon its recorded history. Yet, once recorded, one of the most important groups of improvisations we know may become fodder for a species of artwork that *does* obey the principle of continuity. Once embedded in the grooves or bytes of recording media, improvised music is in danger of becoming seriously alienated from itself. It takes only one punch of the "repeat" button to bring home the fact that the effect of recording on improvisational "presence" is corrosive. These matters are complex and are the topics for our next chapter.

Notes

1 The question of whether jazz improvisations are genuinely art is not the relevant point here; see Julian Dodd, "Upholding Standards: A Realist Ontology of Standard Form Jazz," *Journal of Aesthetics and Art Criticism* 72:3 (2014): 277–290, at 287–288.

2 A paradigm example of such a system is that of Nelson Goodman, in *The Languages of Art: An Introduction to a Theory of Symbols*, 2nd ed. (Indianapolis: Hackett, 1976). Goodman's system has often been challenged in its details, for reasons that have nothing to do with the present issue. We are interested in it only as a paradigmatic instance of a *type* of theory, one that divides artworks into two kinds of entities, *physical objects* and non-physical *types*. Reference to a principle of continuity is diagnostic. Goodman nowhere uses the phrase. Other examples of this type of theory are Richard Wollheim, *Art and its Objects: With Six Supplementary Essays* (Cambridge: Cambridge University Press, 1980), and Julian Dodd, *Works of Music: An Essay in Ontology* (Oxford: Oxford University Press, 2007).

3 Stan Godlovitch refers to the result as the "subordination view," in which "performances are functionally and ontologically subordinate" to musical works; in *Musical Performance: A Philosophical Study* (London: Routledge, 1998), 81.

4 We return to other aspects of this topic in Chapters 9 and 10.

5 Philip Alperson, for one, suggests that Goodman's system might be congenial to improvisational music. His objection to the applicability of Goodman's system only goes so far as to say that the two "stages" involved in Goodman's view of allographic art are blurred in musical improvisation ("On Musical Improvisation," *Journal of Aesthetics and Art Criticism* 43:1 (1984): 17–29, at 18–19). Dodd's analysis of jazz performance upholds the continuity thesis by classifying mainstream jazz improvisations as inauthentic or inaccurate performances of works; "Upholding Standards," 280–281. He recognizes an exception only in the case of "pure improvisation," as with Jarrett's *Köln Concert* improvisation (*Works of Music*, 3).

6 Giorgio Vasari, *The Lives of the Artists*, trans. Julia Conaway Bondanella (Oxford: Oxford University Press, 1991), 284.

7 Arthur C. Danto, *The Transfiguration of the Commonplace: A Philosophy of Art* (Cambridge, MA: Harvard University Press, 1981), 33–36

8 The point is made in various writings of Arthur Danto and Richard Wollheim, for instance. See the latter's Essay II in *Art and its Objects*.

9 See, for instance, Jerrold Levinson's "Autographic and Allographic Art Revisited," in *Music, Art, and Metaphysics* (Ithaca: Cornell University Press, 1990), 89–106.

10 We should recall that certain acts can be decisive, that is, can count as decisions, without required deliberation or forethought.

11 Philip Alperson, "A Topography of Improvisation," *Journal of Aesthetics and Art Criticism* 68:3 (2010): 273–280, at 275. In other words, we are setting aside the first of the five categories of improvisation that we outlined at the end of Chapter 7 as fully compatible with the principle of continuity.

12 On the usefulness of regulative concepts in understanding the European musical tradition, see Lydia Goehr, *The Imaginary Museum of Musical Works: An Essay in the Philosophy of Music* (Oxford: Oxford University Press, 1992). For Goehr, the concept of a musical

work is a regulative idea, instanced both paradigmatically and derivatively. For a critical evaluation that is sensitive to jazz, see Michael Talbot, "The Work-Concept and Composer-Centredness," in *The Musical Work: Reality or Invention?*, ed. Michael Talbot (Liverpool: Liverpool University Press, 2000), 168–186.

13 As in the final chapter of the otherwise insightful work by Winthrop Sargeant, *Jazz, Hot, and Hybrid*, 3rd ed. (New York: Da Capo, 1975).

14 The process is documented in detail in Paul Berliner, *Thinking in Jazz: The Infinite Art of Improvisation* (Chicago: University of Chicago Press, 1994).

15 Bruno Nettl, "'Musical Thinking' and 'Thinking about Music,'" *Journal of Aesthetics and Art Criticism* 52:1 (1994): 139–148, at 142.

16 David H. Rosenthal, *Hard Bop* (Oxford: Oxford University Press, 1992).

17 Goodman, *Languages of Art*, 113.

18 Goodman, *Languages of Art*, 113.

19 Goodman, *Languages of Art*, 116.

20 See Goodman, *Languages of Art*, chapter III (section 4), chapter IV, and chapter V (section 2), in which the theories of notation, compliance, and their application to a theory of work-defining scores are explained.

21 Goodman, *Languages of Art*, 121.

22 Of course, considered as shaping our conception of his oeuvre, Hackins's solo might not play the same role as Hawkins's solo would play in shaping our conception of his career. So let's agree to bracket and set aside this consideration. Concerning its general relevance, see Stephen Davies, *Musical Works and Performances: A Philosophical Exploration* (Oxford: Clarendon Press, 2001), 72–86.

23 Goodman, *Languages of Art*, 179. One wonders what the criterion of "effectiveness" is here – beyond its usefulness for Goodman's theory. Against Goodman on this point, see Davies, *Musical Works and Performances*, Chapter 3.

24 Goodman, *Languages of Art*, 237–238.

25 Goodman, *Languages of Art*, 187–188.

26 We identified a similar error in Chapter 4 concerning Levinson's account of jazz vocal performance.

27 Theodor W. Adorno, "On Jazz," in *Essays on Music*, ed. Richard Leppert, trans. Jamie Owen Daniel, modified by Richard Leppert (Berkeley: University of California Press, 2002), 470–495, at 483.

28 Goodman, *Languages of Art*, 185.

29 We leave it open here how structure is to be measured. The matter is complex. Any piece of music – whether composed or improvised – possesses a multiplicity of structures, typically organized in hierarchies. Flint Shier has suggested that Goodman's theory about compliance with a notational scheme is just his suggested method of insuring the identity of a common structure or work-type in its various tokens (*Deeper into Pictures: An Essay on Pictorial Representation* (Cambridge: Cambridge University Press, 1986), 29). See also Kendall L. Walton, "The Presentation and Portrayal of Sound Patterns," in *Human Agency – Language, Duty, and Value*, ed. Jonathan Dancy, J. M. E. Moravcsik, and C. C. W. Taylor (Stanford: Stanford University Press, 1988). Here, we are conjuring with *structure* in a specialized sense – a *single* structure that can be regarded as the *real definition*, so to say, of a musical work.

30 Levinson, "Autographic and Allographic," 101–102. Levinson's exposition addresses a number of concerns not directly relevant to the present discussion, including the application of Goodman's concepts to the literary arts. Our summary and adaptation is a simplification of Levinson's many-faceted discussion. Without Levinson's restriction, this was the concept that was put in place in section 2 of this chapter.

31 Levinson works out his intentionalistic view in terms of "compliance with a structure-as-indicated-by-X-at-t" ("Autographic and Allographic," 98). While sharpening up Levinson's definition takes some doing, it could probably be construed so as to

accommodate the case of the performer who plays the piece by ear, while excluding objectionable cases, e.g., the astral static.

32 It was this concept that we employed in section 2 of this chapter.

33 Levinson, "Autographic and Allographic," 101–102.

34 Because he stresses the nature of improvisations as *activities*, we regard Alperson's recognition of the centrality of activity in improvisational music to be the special virtue of his treatment of this topic; Alperson, "On Musical Improvisation," 24n21. In contrast, Ted Gioia says that "Improvisation … is spontaneous composition," which aligns it with the treatment of all music as allographic art (*The Imperfect Art: Reflections on Jazz and Modern Culture* (Oxford: Oxford University Press, 1988), 60–61).

35 Levinson, "Autographic and Allographic," 97.

36 Gioia gets at this point to some degree by emphasizing "retrospective" composition (*Imperfect Art*, 60–61). We discuss this matter at greater length in Chapter 10.

37 For more on the relevance of ephemerality, see Andy Hamilton, "The Art of Improvisation and the Aesthetics of Imperfection," *British Journal of Aesthetics* 40:1 (2000):168–185.

38 Levinson, "Autographic and Allographic," 103. Goodman, of course, wants to apply the lesson of his argument about the former type to cases of the latter. See Goodman, *Languages of Art*, chapter III (section 2).

39 See Gioia's comments on "cheating" in jazz (*Imperfect Art*, 52–53).

40 There may be no particular modal story to tell about the fireworks. In that case, the difference is that with improvised music, there *is* such a story.

41 Some Asian works, in which a drawing is completed in a single spontaneous brush stroke, come close to fitting the description, as do some de Kooning paintings – at least on a certain view of them. This analogy seems to have arisen with Bill Evans's famous liner notes for Miles Davis, *Kind of Blue*; see also Gioia, *Imperfect Art*, 61–62.

42 Such considerations, it might be noted, would also help explain why plagiarisms of *Blue Flash* – including self-plagiarisms – would not serve in place of originals.

43 See Gioia's contrast of the "blueprint" and "retrospective" methods (*Imperfect Art*, 60–61). Levinson states that if confronted with a forgery of Giorgione's *The Tempest*, we would "acutely" feel the "absence of physical connection to Giorgione ("Autographic and Allographic," 106). With a slight modification, Levinson's nice description would seem to apply to plagiarisms of autographic art as well. Suppose we were to learn that the "original" *The Tempest*, although painted by Giorgione, was a deceptive copy of a work by Lorenzo Lotto. Then, although the direct connection with the Giorgione would remain, we would feel a kind of "absence" in such a case anyway – namely, an absence of the right *kind* of connection.

44 Gioia, *Imperfect Art*, 33.

45 Perhaps contextual conditions are relevant to questions of identity about *all* autographic art – *Blue Flash* as well as ordinary paintings, for example. We would argue that such conditions still impinge on improvised music in a distinctive way.

46 The position we defend is opposed by Roger Scruton, who argues that music perception relies not on "physical context, but on organization that can be perceived in sound itself, *without reference to context*" (*Understanding Music: Philosophy and Interpretation* (London: Continuum, 2009), 5, our emphasis). Although Scruton is no fan of music ontology, his remarks on jazz and improvisation align with the thesis that every music performance is a work-performance (11–12).

47 Goodman, *Languages of Art*, 99.

48 Goodman, *Languages of Art*, 104.

49 Goodman, *Languages of Art*, 114–115.

50 Goodman, *Languages of Art*, 49.

51 In the context of the foregoing argument, Goodman's remark (*Languages of Art*, 118) that *work-performances* could be forged should not be misunderstood. Although he

speaks of "forgery" here, he does mean that such fakery would make performances autographic. It's only a *category* of artworks that could be called either autographic or allographic, and it would be a misunderstanding of the theory to regard a category of works as allographic, but authentic instances of them as autographic. The quoted remark only draws attention to a case of fakery that we might confuse with the kind that is of real theoretical interest. Someone could *falsely represent* an authentic work-performance as, e.g., a *première*. But such a performance would still be a genuine instance of the work of which it is a performance *if* compliant with the notational features of its score.

52 See for example, David Goldblatt, "Self-Plagiarism," *Journal of Aesthetics and Art Criticism* 43:1 (1984): 71–77.

53 See Lawrence Gushee, "Improvisation and Related Terms in Middle-Period Jazz," in *Musical Improvisation: Art, Education, and Society*, ed. Gabriel Solis and Bruno Nettl (Urbana: University of Illinois Press, 2009), 263–280, especially 270–273.

54 Nelson Goodman, "Comments on Wollheim's Paper," *Ratio* 20 (1978): 49–51, at 49.

55 Nelson Goodman and Catherine Elgin, *Reconceptions in Philosophy and other Arts and Sciences* (Indianapolis: Hackett, 1988), 66, 73. Having recognized the topic, it is abandoned without further comment.

56 Levinson, "Autographic and Allographic," 101–102, says that his revised version of Goodman's dichotomy is exhaustive for the "paradigm" arts.

57 Goodman, *Languages of Art*, 121.

58 Alperson, "On Musical Improvisation"; Gioia, *Imperfect Art*, chap. 3. This way of putting it is a congenial attitude toward Goodman's autographic/allographic duality. If an improvisation really is a species of *composing*, then what is composed must be a musical *work* obedient to the principle of continuity.

59 If we understand it, this suggestion, a mistaken one we believe, is affirmed by Alperson ("On Musical Improvisation," 26).

60 The concept can be amplified, of course. Such performances typically involve several improvisational solos.

61 A position articulated by Dodd, "Upholding Standards," 280.

62 On thicker and thinner works, see Davies, *Musical Works*, 20–29.

63 Of course, a mannered work-performance by the likes of Vladimir de Pachman would not have played the same aesthetic role in his *oeuvre* as a perceptually identical one by Artur Schnabel would play in his. As with our perfect pair, we shall then discount contextual considerations of this sort.

64 A major music critic describes Richter's approach to Schubert in this way; see Harold C. Schonberg, *The Great Pianists: From Mozart to the Present*, rev. ed. (New York: Simon and Schuster, 1987), 471.

65 A listener might wonder if both performances might not have a common ancestor – that each was unwittingly plagiarizing a third performance. Hawkins might wonder if Hackins wasn't plagiarizing him.

66 Of course, jazz improvisations will almost certainly never seem unexpected because of the fact that they violate, or even test, the kind of large scale formal principles of European composition.

67 Thomas Mann, *Doctor Faustus*, trans. H. T. Lowe-Porter (New York: Alfred A. Knopf, 1948), 51–57.

68 E.g., Theodor W. Adorno, "On the Social Situation of Music," in *Essays on Music*, ed. Richard Leppert, trans. Wes Blomster, 391–436.

69 For reasons we explained in Chapter 6, Adorno wouldn't agree. See also Lee B. Brown, "Adorno's Critique of Popular Culture: The Case of Jazz Music," *Journal of Aesthetic Education* 26:1 (1992): 17–31.

70 See Kendall L. Walton, "Categories of Art," *Philosophical Review* 79:3 (1970): 334–367.

71 As noted by Alperson, "On Musical Improvisation," 28n21, and Berliner, *Thinking in Jazz*, 44.

72 Hence, the nice title given to a guitar solo recorded in 1923 by Eddie Lang: "Feeling My Way." As Francis Sparshott puts it, a jazz improviser will often be "trying to do two things at once, changing his mind about where he is going, starting more hares than he can chase at once, picking up where he thought he had left off but resuming what was not quite there in the first place, discovering and pursuing tendencies in what he has done that would have taken a rather different form if he had thought of them at the time." See Francis Sparshott, *The Theory of the Arts* (Princeton: Princeton University Press, 1982), 255.

73 Cited by Max Harrison, *A Jazz Retrospect* (Boston: Crescendo, 1976), 15–16.

74 Gunther Schuller, *Early Jazz: Its Roots and Musical Development* (Oxford: Oxford University Press, 1968), 108.

75 Goehr, *Imaginary Museum*, 189. Goehr is citing the testimony of Lorenz Mizler, as recorded by Hans David and Arthur Mendel, *The Bach Reader: A Life of Johann Sebastian Bach in Letters and Documents* (New York: Norton, 1966).

References

Adorno, Theodor W. "On Jazz." In *Essays on Music*, ed. Richard Leppert, trans. Jamie Owen Daniel, modified by Richard Leppert, 470–495. Berkeley: University of California Press, 2002.

Adorno, Theodor W. "On the Social Situation of Music." In *Essays on Music*, ed. Richard Leppert, trans. Wes Blomster, 391–436. Berkeley: University of California Press, 2002.

Alperson, Philip A. "On Musical Improvisation." *Journal of Aesthetics and Art Criticism* 43:1 (1984): 17–29.

Alperson, Philip A. "A Topography of Improvisation." *Journal of Aesthetics and Art Criticism* 68:3 (2010): 273–280.

Berliner, Paul. *Thinking in Jazz: The Infinite Art of Improvisation*. Chicago: University of Chicago Press, 1994.

Brown, Lee B. "Adorno's Critique of Popular Culture: The Case of Jazz Music." *Journal of Aesthetic Education* 26:1 (1992): 17–31.

Danto, Arthur C. *The Transfiguration of the Commonplace: A Philosophy of Art*. Cambridge, MA: Harvard University Press, 1981.

David, Hans, and Arthur Mendel. *The Bach Reader: A Life of Johann Sebastian Bach in Letters and Documents*. New York: Norton, 1966.

Davies, Stephen. *Musical Works and Performances: A Philosophical Exploration*. Oxford: Clarendon Press, 2001.

Dodd, Julian. "Upholding Standards: A Realist Ontology of Standard Form Jazz." *Journal of Aesthetics and Art Criticism* 72:3 (2014): 277–290.

Dodd, Julian. *Works of Music: An Essay in Ontology*. Oxford: Oxford University Press, 2007.

Gioia, Ted. *The Imperfect Art: Reflections on Jazz and Modern Culture*. Oxford: Oxford University Press, 1988.

Godlovitch, Stan. *Musical Performance: A Philosophical Study*. London: Routledge, 1998.

Goehr, Lydia. *The Imaginary Museum of Musical Works: An Essay in the Philosophy of Music*. Oxford: Oxford University Press, 1992.

Goldblatt, David. "Self-Plagiarism." *Journal of Aesthetics and Art Criticism* 43:1 (1984): 71–77.

Goodman, Nelson. "Comments on Wollheim's Paper." *Ratio* 20 (1978): 49–51.

Goodman, Nelson. *The Languages of Art: An Introduction to a Theory of Symbols*, 2nd ed. Indianapolis: Hackett, 1976.

Goodman, Nelson, and Catherine Elgin. *Reconceptions in Philosophy and other Arts and Sciences.* Indianapolis: Hackett, 1988.

Gushee, Lawrence. "Improvisation and Related Terms in Middle-Period Jazz." In *Musical Improvisation: Art, Education, and Society*, ed. Gabriel Solis and Bruno Nettl, 263–280. Urbana: University of Illinois Press, 2009.

Hamilton, Andy. "The Art of Improvisation and the Aesthetics of Imperfection." *British Journal of Aesthetics* 40:1 (2000): 168–185.

Harrison, Max. *A Jazz Retrospect.* Boston: Crescendo, 1976.

Levinson, Jerrold. "Autographic and Allographic Art Revisited." In *Music, Art, and Metaphysics*, 89–106. Ithaca: Cornell University Press, 1990.

Mann, Thomas. *Doctor Faustus*, trans. H. T. Lowe-Porter. New York: Alfred A. Knopf, 1948.

Nettl, Bruno. "'Musical Thinking' and 'Thinking about Music.'" *Journal of Aesthetics and Art Criticism* 52:1 (1994): 139–148.

Rosenthal, David H. *Hard Bop.* Oxford: Oxford University Press, 1992.

Sargeant, Winthrop. *Jazz, Hot, and Hybrid*, 3rd ed. New York: Da Capo, 1975.

Schonberg, Harold C. *The Great Pianists: From Mozart to the Present*, rev. ed. New York: Simon and Schuster, 1987.

Schuller, Gunther. *Early Jazz: It Roots and Musical Development.* Oxford: Oxford University Press, 1968.

Scruton, Roger. *Understanding Music: Philosophy and Interpretation.* London: Continuum, 2009.

Shier, Flint. *Deeper into Pictures: An Essay on Pictorial Representation.* Cambridge: Cambridge University Press, 1986.

Sparshott, Francis. *The Theory of the Arts.* Princeton: Princeton University Press, 1982.

Talbot, Michael. "The Work-Concept and Composer-Centredness." In *The Musical Work: Reality or Invention?*, ed. Michael Talbot, 168–186. Liverpool: Liverpool University Press, 2000.

Vasari, Giorgio. *The Lives of the Artists*, trans. Julia Conaway Bondanella. Oxford: Oxford University Press, 1991.

Walton, Kendall L. "Categories of Art." *Philosophical Review* 79:3 (1970): 334–367.

Walton, Kendall L. "The Presentation and Portrayal of Sound Patterns." In *Human Agency – Language, Duty, and Value*, ed. Jonathan Dancy, J. M. E. Moravcsik, and C. C. W. Taylor. Stanford: Stanford University Press, 1988.

Wollheim, Richard. *Art and its Objects: With Six Supplementary Essays.* Cambridge: Cambridge University Press, 1980.

9

PHONOGRAPHY, REPETITION, AND SPONTANEITY

One thing I like about jazz, kid, is that you don't know what happens next?
Do you?

— *Bix Beiderbecke to cornetist Jim McPartland*

It is the phonograph that makes it possible to preserve and thereby savor the fine
flavor of what is necessarily a lucky chance result.

— *Aaron Copland*

In 1906 John Philip Sousa went before the United States Congress warning about
the dangers of the new technology destroying live music. His concerns were
publicized more broadly in a magazine article he published that year, "The
Menace of Mechanical Music."[1] In contrast, Glenn Gould, in his essay, "The
Prospects of Recording," famously privileges studio recording and living room
speakers over the concert hall where an audience at home can be ideally posi-
tioned to enjoy recorded music.[2] Ted Gioia credits Thomas Alva Edison as the
one person having the most influence on the arts in the twentieth century — not
only for his invention of the motion picture camera, but for his invention of the
phonograph and the recording of musical ideas other than notation.[3] While
phonograph recordings helped change the culture of the middle-class from one of
amateur music making to one in which people are primarily consumers of the
music industry, later developments of recording technology solidified the idea
that some sound recordings are works in themselves — most notably studio sound-
constructs that are technological artifacts by virtue of electronic manipulation,
nuanced or on a grand scale. This chapter examines the role of this "mechanical
music" for jazz generally and for jazz improvisation in particular. It also serves as a
general example of the ways technology can affect forms of art and hence what
philosophers of art, among other cultural theorists, have to say about them.[4]

1. Repetition of the Ephemeral

Following the incorporation of the Edison Phonograph Company in 1887, the music industry has been an ever-improving machine for capturing acoustic events, cloning them, and scattering them through the world. More eloquently than any professional media scholar, the journalist Evan Eisenberg made people see – in his book, *The Recording Angel* – that among the uses of sound recording, convenience is only the most obvious.[5] In a chapter titled "Ceremonies of a Solitary," for instance, Eisenberg details how recording media help consumers organize individualized, music-infused rituals tailored to their schedules.[6] People can repeat musical experiences as often as they like, and under conditions that are theirs to arrange. Eisenberg coined a new term, *phonography*, to capture technology's tendency to cleave music listening from its traditional sites of performance and so also from the music's social-historical provenance.[7] As much as anything, phonography took jazz out of the dance halls and clubs and into the homes of the white American middle-class, severing the ties between musicians and the social rituals of African-American life that New Orleans natives termed "a natural livin.'"[8] We have already noted, at the beginning of Chapter 4, that, early on, phonography helped spread jazz to Europe. It was a gramophone record of "Some of These Days," a jazz vocal played in a provincial French city café, that transformed the moment for Sartre's *Nausea* protagonist Roquentin.

In a world without recording technology, we might never raise identity-questions about what constitutes a musical work. At the very least, we would raise different ones. And philosophical issues regarding improvisations might never have surfaced. But of course, we can barely imagine such a world. The problem is that, as recorded, the experience of music may have an entirely different phenomenology from that of the living thing. Indeed, it may have a different ontology. And we must also consider the likelihood that recording technology has made possible a type of musical art hitherto unknown, deserving of its own aesthetic analysis, obeying its own principle of continuity. As musical works, recordings seem to be a species of multiple-instanced artworks with interesting similarities to etchings.[9] It is of a certain irony that this radical change of perspective regarding music is a product of non-musicians – producers and engineers who work their magic in the recording studio.

However, our present concern is with the effects of phonographic repetition on the audience's experience of jazz improvisation. In particular, how does "repeated" listening to recorded jazz alter the experience of the music even if the recording was "unmanipuated"? Clearly, there are many obvious positive benefits, including the chance to hear musicians who are no longer living and performances that are, by their very nature, ephemeral and gone.[10] There is also the opportunity to better understand music that does not conform neatly to our musical expectations – relistening to aspects of a musical string until we see just what the performer is doing. For the latter reason, the legendary New Orleans cornet player Freddie Keppard rejected the chance to appear on the very first jazz record when he spurned the opportunity to record for the Victor Talking Machine Company in 1915. He said he didn't want other musicians to analyze and then copy and so "steal" his music.[11] However, we want to explore a more pernicious issue with recorded music: the effect of repetition itself. There is good reason to worry that appreciative listening is undermined by the psychological effect of repeated exposure to the same improvisation. Anticipation of the details of the performance will mask and deaden its sense of presence and its dynamic impact.[12] Or so it would seem.

2. Nuance, Structure, Spontaneity

Leaving aside improvisation for the moment, we will begin with a question: Is not *all* music "deadened" once recorded? The composer Roger Sessions thought so. "Music," Sessions says,

> ceases to have interest for us, … the instant we become aware of the fact of literal repetition, of mechanical reproduction, when we know and can anticipate exactly how a given phrase is going to be modeled, exactly how long a given fermata is to be held, exactly what quality of accent or articulation, of acceleration, or retard, will occur at a given moment.[13]

Indeed, Sessions says, such "music" ceases even to be music. This last complaint, of course, stretches the point too far. His deadened metaphor makes the obvious point that recorded music is no longer "live," but it also emphasizes the stillness or frozen character of recorded music: it will no longer be changed by the musicians who made it. By extension, Sessions must also deny that there are musical works in the vast range of works that are nothing but artifacts of phonography – *works of phonography*, we term them.[14] Works of phonography are sound-constructs created by the use of recording technologies for an intrinsic aesthetic purpose, rather than for an extrinsic documentary one. As such, works of phonography are to be contrasted with documentary sound recordings, which are intended to function as transparent windows into the past.[15] In contrast, works of phonography are a species of representation: they are to any music they capture as da Vinci's *Mona Lisa* is to the flesh and blood Lisa Gherardini. Consider the taped compositions of Vladimir Ussachevsky, for instance, like "Underwater Waltz" – a piece generated by recording the lowest A on the piano at multiple tape speeds. The music exists only if, and because, the recording exists.

In popular music, consider the prominent passage for keyboard in the middle of The Beatles' "In My Life" (1965). What sounds like a harpsichord solo is a studio fabrication. It is actually an electronic manipulation of music performed on a Steinway piano at half speed and an octave lower. The eight-year recording career of The Beatles parallels significant technological and procedural changes in recording generally. Here, George Harrison remembers the early recording sessions:

> Right from the beginning when we started recording, we'd just record in one take. [T]hings like 'Twist and Shout' and 'I Saw Her Standing There,' which were all on our first album ... we just turned the recorder on ... So we never did any of this overdubbing or adding orchestras or anything like that.[16]

Harrison is describing the process for their debut album, in 1963, a documentary sound recording which they completed in a single day. Years later, in 1967, one year after their final tour, it took The Beatles 129 days to put *Sgt. Pepper's Lonely Hearts Club Band* into its final, marketable form as a work of phonography.

Jazz got its first *obvious* work of phonography soon after *Sgt. Pepper's*, with Miles Davis's *In A Silent Way* (1969), where it is apparent to any attentive listener that producer Teo Macero ends side one of the record with a tape "splice" of the same recorded music that opens the album. Where jazz fans expect a repeat of the musical head after the improvisations are concluded, Davis and Macero parody the practice with a mechanical repeat.[17]

However one may feel about works of phonography, surely it is objectionable to deny that such "music" really is music. Tabling Sessions's hyperbole, we want to reflect on his complaint with respect to three interacting dimensions of recordings of ordinary music performance: *nuance, structure,* and *spontaneity* in performance. Setting aside the question of whether some kind of cheat or fraud is involved when recordings are studio constructs of virtual performances, we pursue, for now, the question of whether "unvarnished documentations of independently existing musical performances" are necessarily such a bad thing, especially in a jazz context.[18] Furthermore, while Sessions draws our attention to "anticipation" in the experience of music, he fails to ask why such anticipation is a positive thing for many listeners who buy records with the intent of playing them more than once. This last point should make clear that the recorded music we are discussing – that Sessions may have been noting – is recorded music packaged and distributed, ready for listeners to consume, and not simply recorded throwaways, left on the cutting room floor.

2A. Nuance

Some phonophiles, agreeing that the best defense is a strong offense, reply that recording technology doesn't harm our understanding and appreciation of music – indeed, that it actually *helps*. Consider *nuances* of musical pitch, for instance. Diana Raffman, a philosopher of mind with expertise in cognitive psychology and music, has made a persuasive case that nuances of pitch are finer than the mental schemas with which we structure perception. Hence, they cannot be stored in memory.[19] If this is generally true of musical nuance, Sessions is off base in speaking of *exact* anticipation. Indeed, just because we can't *exactly* anticipate these nuances, recordings play a useful role in refreshing our experience and appreciation of them. We shall term it *the nuance argument*, namely that auditory memory of any particular sound is schematic and imprecise, and so *reheard* sounds are experientially richer than we can anticipate. An early use of the argument was articulated by Theodore Gracyk in a discussion of the appreciation of timbre in recorded rock music. Phonographic repetition is particularly useful for such music, given that rock is "music of very specific sound qualities and their combination."[20] The same argument has obvious relevance to jazz, where "subtleties of personal timbre" are regarded as an important aspect of a player's development of her own "voice."[21] Many other kinds of nuance are expressively potent in musical performance, especially in the areas of dynamic levels, melodic articulation and phrasing, and *rubato* (especially in the handling of phrase boundaries).[22] Because we cannot accurately memorize musical nuances, they can be just as much a focus of appreciative interest with recorded music as with live performance. While Sessions is hardly alone in valuing the ephemerality of live performance, he deploys a false assumption about the power of human memory to give a veneer of support to the idea that reheard music is not music.

But how far can we take the nuance argument? Even though we can't "replay" a familiar recording in memory in all its detail, maybe we can entertain an aural picture – an anticipatory image – of a specific musical passage in it *just before* it occurs.[23] Indeed, experience may suggest that we can do this. However, if we structure perceptions in memory the way the nuance argument says we do, we wouldn't really be able to know, simply by recollection, that our anticipatory aural image was an image of the *right* nuance. At best, one might *infer* that a second experience is a canned recap of an earlier one on the basis of other considerations about the situation, e.g., that the record one is playing is the same as the one played before. But a mere *judgment* of this sort is very different from an exact image of the passage one is about to hear. And of course we make all sorts of anticipatory judgments while listening to music in a familiar style: these anticipations are the cognitive backbone of music listening.

The real value of Sessions's emphasis on anticipation is that it brings to the fore an aspect of reception theory that is unique to improvisation. The concept of anticipation is not necessarily related to the excitement accompanying what comes next. Rather, it implies a kind of foreknowledge. Although Sessions has little to say about improvisation, his contrast of improvised and composed music suggests that knowing what comes next is anathema to improvisation.[24] Improvisation implies not knowing what comes next, so that the music is to some degree necessarily new to the listener. However, describing the typical response as one of excitement, surprise, or astonishment is far too strong and misleading. Think about this: hearing a jazz recording for the first time, all of it may well be anticipated in the first sense; looking forward to what comes next and being excited about what is about to take place. However, since we have not previously heard the recording, and thus can have no foreknowledge of what is to come, we cannot anticipate it in that second sense of knowing what the future will bring to our ears. The fact that we are about to listen to a *recording* is not what is at issue here though, because the same goes for any live performance of music. There, too, we don't know what is about to happen *and* this holds equally well for musical passages that are composed or improvised: for any music not heard previously, we can anticipate in the "looking forward/excitement" sense of anticipation, but not in the "foreknowledge" sense.

So, in the first hearing of any record, it may all bear the marks that make improvisation an interesting feature, not simply the parts that were improvised live. It is the second time, rehearing a recorded improvisation again, exactly repeated, that the listener would seem to lose the special virtues of improvisation. And yet, people do see movies like *Casablanca*, for example, many times without thinking of it as "dead" or without having the exact same experience. Few people buy records to hear them once only. Like returning to a painting many times, hearing an improvised section of a recording many times may well offer different experiences each time – the repetition (always a deceptive concept) being a factor in a valuable aesthetic experience. Whether returning to a favorite painting or a favorite record, the foreknowledge that one brings to it is never "exact" knowledge. Being highly "familiar with" a musical passage alters the *kind* of anticipation one has with respect to it, but it does not preclude novelty and new discoveries in the aural experience: there is always plenty of room for aspects unheard or forgotten.

2B. Structure

More fundamentally, a limitation in the nuance argument is that it *is* just about nuance. What should we say about the potentially negative effect of repetition on our reception of musical structure?

Perhaps the phonophile can once again take the offensive. One is reminded of a vivid passage in the novel *Doctor Faustus* in which Thomas Mann conjures up the pleasure of anticipating a well-remembered passage in Beethoven's Opus 111. One might put the point this way: it is inappropriate not to care about the structure of a piece of *composed* music. This aspect of our interest in a piece of music has nothing to do with our interest in a specific performance of it.[25] Indeed, to the extent that our concern is with structure, the less we should care whether music comes from recordings or not. From the perspective of structural listening, it does not even matter that the music is machine-generated rather than performed. *Switched on Bach* (1968), a pioneering synthesizer rendition of Bach compositions, reveals the structure of the third *Brandenburg Concerto* with the same accuracy as Trevor Pinnock's performances with a "period" orchestra. So, in regard to structure, it's hard to be an enemy of recorded music if one is trying to attend to the musical *work* (understood as an abstract type or repeatable structure). In fact, the repetition it affords ought to be an aid to the understanding and appreciation of musical structure and a criterion that can be used to test our purported memory. And so it will be a particular boon for understanding and appreciating jazz improvisations, especially those that do not instantiate composed works or, taking a work or standard song as a mere starting point, abandon work-instantiation in extemporaneous exploration of some of its features.

Fine. But we may still wonder why our enjoyment of a given musical structure – composed or improvised – still wouldn't pale with *repeated* auditions. If so, the benefits of repetition are at least compromised. At this point, however, we might consider the potential relevance of some interesting experiments about word-recognition done by the psychologist David Swinney.

In order to think about what these experiments suggest, it helps to conceive of the mind as the philosopher Jerry Fodor conceives it – a set of modules with a fair degree of independence from each other. Swinney experimented with subjects who listened to a stimulus sentence, such as "Because he was afraid of electronic surveillance, the spy carefully searched the room for ..." Now, in a context in which "microphones" and "bugs" are the options, the evidence is that either word will be just as easily selected as the other because both words fit the context of the mini-narrative. However, if the options are switched to "bugs" and "insects," it turns out that either of these *two* is just as likely to be selected as the other – in spite of the irrelevance of the word "insects" to the context provided by the mini-narrative.

The lesson, according to the experts, is that even when a person is primed to expect a certain word, that person's language module may still automatically and very briefly entertain other options that are really irrelevant to the context of the mini-narrative. What happens, in other words, is that, although a person may be aware of the context provided by the mini-narrative at a higher cognitive level, that person's lower-level mental processes may still briefly operate independently of the higher level. At the lower level, options are briefly considered, even though the context soon proves them to be out of place.[26] The *general* lesson here is that psychological processing is modular and what happens at a conscious level may be at odds with what takes place simultaneously at a pre-conscious level of mental processing. The effect that Swinney documented with language can be expected to reoccur in many other areas where humans respond to meaningful events in their environment.

How might this result be applied to the reception of music? It suggests that even though at a higher cognitive level, when we know where a stretch of music is going, we still entertain other options, if only briefly, even when these other options are soon closed off by the actual flow of the music.

The idea can be applied nicely to a classic view of music reception developed by Leonard Meyer.[27] Much of our interest in music, Meyer argues, depends upon the stimulation of tension and the eventual release of it. For instance, if harmonic ambiguity engenders mental tension, subsequent harmonic resolution will release the tension. In complex music, tension–release may be only provisional, because new states of tension will be set up as soon as prior tension is released. A rich example is the "Liebestod" of Wagner's *Tristan und Isolde*, in which complete tension–release is accomplished only with the final cadence. (We should note that Meyer was not trying to explain every response we have to music. He was investigating listeners' responses to the manipulation of musical "syntax" or structure, independent of musical reference to anything outside the musical experience and apart from the music's social functions.)

Meyer's is a powerfully suggestive view. But it faces a problem: once we learn how the music plays out, how can we *again* feel the tension when we hear the music on a subsequent occasion? And, if we cannot experience the tension a second time around, how can we experience the eventual release of it on the subsequent hearing? But if Swinney is right, maybe we can have our cake and eat it. This hope is strongly supported by recent studies of music processing and the psychology of expectation. David Huron points out that if we were *not* processing the music in two different ways, one "correcting" for the other, then musical surprises would be uniformly unsettling, weird, and unpleasant.[28] Yet, in fact, they are the source of a great deal of our musical pleasure. So although we may know at a higher cognitive level what's coming in the music, at a lower cognitive level, we continue to form expectations based on what we are hearing in the moment, and so we can still experience musical options as open ones and be surprised when anticipated events do not occur. Obviously, these effects depend on the direction the music actually takes as we listen. For an instant, however, we will be kept guessing, and sometimes be proved wrong – at the lower cognitive level, that is. We are able to savor both quasi-suspense and disruption, so to say.

Let us call this response to the puzzle about Meyer's view "the Swinney response." As with the nuance argument, there are limits to its use, however. We might wonder why, if we can use the Swinney response to explain why the "Liebestod" doesn't lose its freshness, can't we then use it to explain why a jazz standard such as "My Funny Valentine" does not lose *its* freshness either? If we bring Theodor Adorno back into the discussion, he would chime in with his familiar theme: given its structural simplicities, repetition will more quickly dull the pop tune.[29] However, overprinting Adorno's Manichean pop/classical music dualism is a larger question: why doesn't repetition have ultimately ravaging effects on *all* music? Why isn't the difference between the "Liebestod" and "My Funny Valentine" just that the learning curve toward boredom for the former is a little flatter? Indeed, aren't the phonograph and its technological cousins just machines for making the learning curve toward boredom steeper for *all* music? And *that*, unfortunately, is what experimental psychology predicts for all music that is heard repeatedly. There is good news, however. There are different kinds of surprises for music listeners – generating, for example, the distinct emotions of amusement, awe, and frisson – and "repeated listening seems to have different consequences for the various responses."[30]

In other words, the Swinney response might be a good one in the face of someone who wanted to argue that there is *never* a reason to listen to a piece of music with which we are already familiar. But the theory doesn't rule out the likelihood of boredom setting in for any music subjected to long-term repetition. It may take more repetitions before it happens with the music of Cecil Taylor and Albert Ayler than with Count Basie and Glenn Miller, but the problem remains that eventually the mechanism that kicks in to help make familiar music sound fresh would finally become stale. Given enough listenings, one would have learned the drill. This is not a matter of the predicate "boring" being attributed to the music with respect to one playing, live or recorded, but rather to the listener after repeated listening to music either live or recorded. And, of course, attributing boredom, to those with shorter spans of attention, can come quicker than to more patient listeners. Indeed, the variables regarding the attribution of boredom to persons vary greatly with circumstances, but that is an entirely other matter.

2C. Spontaneity

Let's complicate matters by bringing into the picture the family of highly inflected performances, ranging from expressive interpretation of composed works at one end of the spectrum to free improvisation at the other. (John Lewis's jazz versions of Bach would fall somewhere in the middle.) What happens to the spontaneous dimensions of musical performances once they are recorded? True, jazz improvisation was far from Sessions's mind. But his remarks seem to have application to this very different kind of music nevertheless. Let us consider that kind of case first.

Since improvised jazz leaves a broad trail of nuance, the virtue of recording for refreshing our experience of those nuances would seem to be obvious. The problem with this application of the nuance argument is that it isn't just the acoustic details that preoccupy us in jazz, but the performer's on-the-spot *choices and actions* that generate those nuanced details. The nuance argument seems to have no bearing on this dimension of the music.

How about the usefulness of the Swinney response to such cases? After all, since improvisational performances also exhibit sonic *structure* – or so it would seem – acousmatic isolation might help us better understand and appreciate this dimension of those performances. (In subsequent sections, we address the point that phonographic isolation is, after all, at the basis of jazz history.) The problem is that the Swinney response only has application to our experience of preformed structures to which we have been previously exposed. But some improvised music possesses no preformed structure that we could have learned and anticipated. With, for example, one of Cecil Taylor's free piano improvisations, we're not content with the quasi-suspense described earlier. Rather, we are always *on the alert* for real surprises.[31] Surely, our experience of the *spontaneous* aspects of a music performance would be negatively affected by a recording. With the repetition that recorded playback makes possible, we can clearly anticipate the choices Sonny Rollins will make eight minutes into his "Moritat" solo on *Saxophone Colossus* (1956).

One might put the problem this way: we can apply the Swinney response to explain how phonographic repetition contributes to our understanding and appreciation of the musical structure of improvised music if we don't mind treating the music the same way we regard recordings of fully composed music. But there is now a disconnection between our reception of live improvisatory music and the same thing canned. As listeners, we can hardly maintain the same appreciative stance toward recorded improvisations – if we know they are recorded and that we can rehear them – and a live improvisation heard while attending a performance. Furthermore, phonographic isolation may very well affect jazz performance itself. On at least one occasion, Miles Davis withheld the fact that he was recording an evening's performance, evidently to permit the other musicians to take more collective and individual chances onstage.[32]

Much of the foregoing would seem to apply to *non*-improvisational but nevertheless highly inflected *interpretations* of works of composed music. Further, the line between composed and improvised music can be subjected to further erosion. A bit of history helps see why. Musicologist Richard Taruskin has argued that the contemporary obsession with putatively true-to-the-work performances obscures the real facts about eighteenth-century performance. In that period, he argues, a soloist who would "fail to astonish, or surprise" an audience would have been the exception. Antonio Vivaldi, Taruskin tells us, would have been happy to add swells, tremolos, pizzicatos, and natural harmonics to the music as he himself played it. He would have looked for opportunities to bend, slide, and double his pitches. Taruskin cites a contemporary description of Vivaldi virtually improvising to his own scores.[33]

In sum, with all music performance, one is obviously interested in how the musical line will proceed. With a familiar work, one is interested in the nuances of the interpretation. However, with a broad spectrum of musical performance, we are also interested in a performer's on-the-spot decisions and actions that *generate* the sonic trail – *decisions* to go left, let us say, rather than right. But this interest is at odds with one of recorded music's chief "virtues," namely its capacity for repetition.

3. The New Phonophobes

Consider the following response to the argument in the previous section: if we *know* that options in a recorded jazz performance were taken in real-time, that knowledge ought to inform the way we respond to the recorded music. In that case, the appeal of such a performance is surely "not killed stone-dead," as one writer has put it.[34] The problem with this response is that its scope is too broad.

A lively but somewhat disorganized succession of notes is likely to be regarded more positively *if* it is understood as the product of improvisation than otherwise – whether the music is recorded or not.[35] And, more forgivingly, as we explain in Chapter 10. So, the response doesn't bear on the problem at hand, namely, the seemingly negative effect of *phonographic repetition* on improvised music.

However, let us reflect on the flow of knowledge from, rather than to, recorded performances. Consider this: never in the history of the world before phonographic repetition could *any* performance be revisited. Never before could the countless perfections and imperfections that flew by at countless concerts be savored, analyzed, or criticized at leisure. In particular, consider how difficult it would be to analyze jazz performance without recording technology. Obviously, next-day reviews of a jazz performance depend a great deal on impressions and imperfect and incomplete memories.

For instance, only because of sound recording is jazz historian Gunther Schuller able to analyze, in such fine-grained detail, a famous passage of music played by Louis Armstrong. In the early notes of Armstrong's famous *a cappella* introduction to his Okeh recording of "West End Blues," Armstrong brashly chooses a tempo too fast for what he wants to do later, and then spontaneously rectifies his mistake in mid-flight by slowing down just a little. Without unchanging reiteration in the repeated playbacks of the recording, Schuller would not have been able to put Armstrong's off-the-wall gambit and subsequent response to it under his analytical lens.[36] Without recourse to fixed reiteration of a large body of recorded work, we could not demonstrate that early complaints about Charlie Parker's dissonance are misrepresentations. In fact, "Parker [was] a musical conservative, a caretaker of the tonal tradition," with close analysis revealing that "there seems to be no times when Parker did not resolve extended chord-tones to more stable pitches."[37]

Detailed jazz analysis – supplemented with transcriptions of improvisations, by the likes of Schuller, André Hodeir, and Martin Williams, and more recently by Paul Berliner, Ingrid Monson, Peter Elsdon, and Henry Martin – depends upon the possibility of rehearing improvisational performances again and again.[38] Surely, here repetition isn't the enemy of improvised music, but rather an aid to our understanding and appreciation of it. But now, a problem arises from a new quarter.

In the eyes of many current thinkers, traditional jazz scholarship – of the kind just cited – is suspect. So too is the phonographic testimony upon which it is based. We might label such thinkers *revisionist phonophobes*.

Consider, for example, the hostility that Jed Rasula expresses toward what he regards as an obnoxious "phonocentrism," in the very title of an essay on the matter, "The Seductive Menace of Records in Jazz History."[39] Traditional critics, Rasula claims, unreasonably equated jazz history with the history of its recordings and, as a consequence, sponsored the "anti-jazz" concept of the "definitive" jazz performance, converting the extemporaneous into "scripture."[40] Similarly, jazz historian Scott DeVeaux, taking his theme from remarks by Sonny Rollins, declares jazz recordings to be little more than commercial advertisements for the living thing.[41] Indeed, we have returned to a market in which concert ticket sales regularly out-gross sales for recorded music.

As for traditional analyses based upon recordings, phonophobe critics pejoratively label them "formalist."[42] The musicologist, Robert Walser, for instance, blames traditional jazz scholarship for mistakenly applying "the vocabulary of academic musical analysis to jazz."[43] In effect, he accuses musicologists of the same error that we attributed to philosophers in Chapter 8. One could put the objection this way: traditional analysis approaches jazz performances as if they were *compositions*.

Sleuthing around for other targets of this kind of complaint, consider Hodeir's analysis of a famous Thelonious Monk recording of "Bag's Groove," in which Hodeir describes Monk as applying a principle about the "catalyzing effect asymmetrical structures can have on symmetrical ones." One might note, too, how Hodeir speaks of the music in the "Bag's Groove" recording as "renewing itself … as it goes along … from one transformation to the next."[44] What's striking about his description is the way it transforms an improvisatory *process* into a depersonalized, structured musical tissue.[45] As such, the position of musicologist is neither that of the performer nor the ordinary appreciative jazz fan.

And consider where Schuller takes his analysis of the Louis Armstrong performance cited earlier. He goes on to explain how, in order to deal with his musical problem, Armstrong alters his tempo in such a way as to place the following notes in an exact rhythmic relationship to the previous tempo, so that at least an underlying pattern is preserved through the change. In principle, this adds to Armstrong's brilliance as an improviser. However, Schuller cannot resist correlating the performance with a *compositional* strategy known as "metric modulation," practiced by composers such as Elliott Carter – namely, the exploitation of relationships common to diverse tempos.[46] Similarly, Martin cannot resist talk of Charlie Parker "composing" his three- to five-part polyphony.[47]

Of course, phonophobes see the compositional model of traditional jazz analysis as perfectly fitting the calcified subject matter of their analyses, namely, *recordings*. Indeed, one might argue that what is preserved in a recording has *more* fixity than a composition. Playbacks of recordings do not themselves require, indeed do not *allow*, a further step at which they are interpretively performed. The recording playback is the end of the line.

Phonophobe critics are certainly correct that traditional jazz scholarship treated recordings as its chief subject-matter. Hodeir, for example, refers to the topic of his musical analyses as musical "works," by which he clearly means "recordings." When he speaks of *versions* of such works, he is referring to recorded versions – e.g., the Brunswick, the Columbia, the Victor *recording* of Duke Ellington's "Mood Indigo" – in almost exactly the way we might speak of Stravinsky's different versions of *Firebird*.

Likewise, Schuller's two jazz histories are really histories of recordings. But his view is a twist on Hodeir's. He regards recordings as documents of

improvisations, which in turn are "works in progress," or trial runs at compositions.[48] Given a moment's thought, we ought to find this a strange view, surely.
In special cases, of course, improvisations *are* transformed into works performable
in accordance with scores. Adelaide Hall's extemporaneous vocalization of a secondary line above the main one in "Creole Love Call" did eventually become
part of a performable *work*. A "classical" piano recital by Alan Feinberg included
a performance of Thelonious Monk's tune "Ruby, My Dear" based not on a
published score of the work, but on one of Monk's recorded extemporaneous
versions of it.[49] However, these evolutions are special cases. To claim that *all*
improvisations are "works in progress" is to go too far by a mile. On this view,
Charlie Parker's recorded performances offer glimpses of mere discards, or trial
runs toward hypothetical artworks doomed never to be realized. Whether or not
something is a work in progress is irrelevant as to whether someone is there to
record it.

In evaluating the revisionist's critical perspective, we sympathize with their
attempts to profile dimensions of jazz that are resistant to formal musical analysis.
Traditional approaches, they say, tend to overprint or marginalize the rhetorical
aspects in jazz performance — the very aspects most likely to sound "unmusical"
to a formalist's ear. For example, what can a formalist make of Eric Dolphy's
pained, vocalized sax sounds on Charlie Mingus's "Fables of Faubus?" In fact,
such "unmusical," often quasi-linguistic features have pervaded jazz from its earliest
days, when instrumentalists learned how to push musical lines off course to
convey the effect of a sob, a laugh, or an expletive — when horns first learned to
"speak."

Such observations are compelling. However, they tend to mask the more basic
problem — the problem that concerns us in this chapter. The more fundamental
feature of improvised music that is likely to be marginalized in traditional jazz
analysis is the brute fact that some aspects of the music *are* improvised. Hodeir's
and Schuller's agendas are just instances of the critical prejudice. In general, traditional scholarship allows us to understand the music mainly in a psychologically
ossified version — namely, as recorded. If we seem to be putting too much
emphasis on Hodeir and Schuller, we can make the same case by picking up
almost any jazz history written in the past twenty years. Most notable among
these is *Jazz* by Gary Giddins and Scott DeVeaux.[50] Perhaps a quarter of the text
is devoted to moment-by-moment analyses of seminal jazz recordings.

4. The Phonophile's Dilemma

We seem to be faced with a double-bind: on the one hand, for jazz to be
analyzable — or teachable — it must be repeatable — the "teachee" in imitation of
the music heard. And it is repeatable not because it is precisely notatable — which
it isn't — but because it is recordable and subject to unchanging reiteration.[51] Of
course, this does rule out circumstances where teaching may involve face-to-face

repetition for the sake of improving a student's skill. Nevertheless, the history of jazz is unimaginable independent of the history of sound recording. (And, by the way, the phonophobes' analyses of the dimensions of the music they wish to profile are no less recording-based than the work of the "formalists" they despise. Walser's detailed analysis of Miles Davis's "signifyin'" is, after all, the analysis of a commercially released recording.[52]) But, from another point of view, the music stands in an adverse relationship with the calcifying medium by which we document it.

Indeed, the matter is even more complicated than the stark paradox just outlined indicates. In the beginning, phonography was designed to serve a fundamentally documentary role. Edison had set out to create a mechanical repeater that would replace the human hand in resending failing telegraph signals; he subsequently marketed the actual invention as an office dictation machine.[53] Soon adopted as an *entertainment* product, the music industry mass-marketed disc records with the promise that they were "a 'vanishing' mediator," faithfully reproducing the music "as if [they] were not there."[54] But it is important to acknowledge that this is a generalization about what was and is valued by the musicians and audiences. In practice, the ideal is frequently abandoned. Far more classic jazz recordings were artifacts of the recording studio than are acknowledged as such. Jazz "works," as Hodeir terms them, have always been geared to available recording formats, and have typically capitalized upon the special resources of the recording studio. Perhaps the most important examples of studio-manufactured jazz are Louis Armstrong's Hot Five recordings and Miles Davis's *Bitches Brew* sessions: both groups were created specifically for the purpose of recording new music, and the latter was, audibly, a constructed work of phonography.[55]

Documentary realism is particularly naive as a picture of late-century and twenty-first-century recorded jazz. As if in acknowledgment of the fate by which the recording process is bound to create its own world, more and more jazz recordings do not even *try* to represent real-time options. Even hard-core re-creations of classic jazz styles nowadays "benefit" from elaborate tape and digital surgery.[56] During the heyday of the "smooth jazz" radio format, the best-selling music in the jazz orbit was routinely constructed through meticulous overdubbing above programmed rhythm tracks, so that the impression of players reacting to each other's moves is sheer illusion. The technological medium has worked its way so deeply into the message that it has become, not merely a way of experiencing an object, but an object in its own right.

As a result, we listen to sound recordings as if they were documents of an art form that is more and more *constituted* by the medium of recorded sound. That is, our experience of the thing as it is documented is something very different from our experience of it in its live, never-to-be-repeated state. So, we seem to be faced with two possible stories about the relationship of phonographic isolation and repetition to jazz.

The first story is that, when jazz is accessed via recordings, the immediacy of the music just *is* mediated. It is always and already mediated. The more understanding that repeated playbacks of it provide – the kind of analytical understanding jazz scholars provide for jazz performance – the less direct our experience of it is. In this sense, then, recording does distort our experience of the real thing, understood as the live performance, even if unmanipulated to any further degree. One point, often overlooked, is that the "real thing" has a visual component as well as an auditory one and the visuality of what we hear, that alone, may make recording versus live a case of apples and oranges. That point aside, it is clear that the more manipulation a phonographic work has, the less there is any correspondence between the record and the live performance – the limiting case, as with *Sgt. Pepper's*, that there is no event that the record records.

The other story is that *the real thing* is a conceptual chimera. No live performance can compete with an over-dubbed fusion recording, not because it is a poorer version of the same thing, but for the opposite reason: the two lie in nearly distinct spheres. Indeed, no unrecorded performance yields the kind of detail for reflection and appreciation that recording does, manipulated or not. Since neither provides what the other does, the lesson is "so much for the concept of the *real thing*." We just can't make sense of the concept of a single real thing to which either approach does justice or fails to do justice.

These unhappy options are mirrored in the opposed perspectives we have characterized. Phonophiles tend to equate a jazz performer's artistic career with his or her recorded *oeuvre*, while phonophobes, especially the scholarly informed phonophobes, try to marginalize phonographic documentation. Sociologically, however, one suspects that the numbers of proponents of each side of the dilemma do not balance each other out. Given current trends, the number of phonophiles is likely to increase by contrast with the number committed to live music: major music festivals such as Coachella increasingly feature DJs, mixing pre-recorded dance tracks, as major attractions. "There's a generation that's used to flawless," explains Coachella founder Paul Tollett, and live music disappoints them because "it doesn't sound perfect."[57]

All of which is unfortunate, because a more moderate position than the ones framed above seems possible in principle. Consider that we are rarely in a position to even attempt comparisons between live and canned versions of the *same* performance. But it is quite easy to compare recorded and live music of the same generic kind, by the same performers, using the same musical material. So, with such cases in mind, why not grant that the detail made available by recordings can increase our understanding and appreciation of the living thing? Alas, this may not be the way of the listening world – if its addiction to canned music is as strong as it seems to be. Just as the loss of practical experience has led to a contemporary jazz culture in which almost no one hears the dance rhythms *as* dance rhythms, the ubiquity of recorded music yields a contemporary jazz scene in which some fans cannot hear improvisation *as* improvisation. However, we must not overlook the idea that many jazz enthusiasts hear a recording of a particular musician prior to going to *see* them live and in person. The recording, however approximate of what was recorded, can act as an inspiration to hear a performance live – the causal relation cannot be ignored aesthetically or commercially.

Let us pause to take stock. Improvisation is an action, and an action is not really a work of art or musical work, for *works* are standardly understood to be subject to criteria for reidentification. (There is not much point in engaging in the ontology of art except to pin down criteria for reidentification.) An improvisation is an ephemeral singularity that can be identified (by date and place) but not repeated.[58] Once a jazz improvisation moves beyond expressive embellishment, there simply is no entity or thing – abstract or concrete – with which the music can be reidentified. However, repeatability encourages us to hear jazz performances *as* composed entities: we come to reidentify more and more of what we hear each time we play the same record again, and the product of the action takes precedence over the action. Call this the *phonographic effect*.

We are now in a position to formulate the problem with precision:

1. Improvisation, the activity of extemporaneous musical performance, is a musical hallmark of jazz.
2. Informed appreciation of an improvisation requires appreciation of the singularity of the improvisational activity.
3. Except when one is present at a live jazz performance, access to the aesthetic properties of any specific improvisation requires listening to a recording of that improvisation. (We are setting aside the special case of hearing jazz during live radio and television broadcasts.)
4. Access to the aesthetic properties of any performance requires access to the full range of sonic properties that were originally present, which is possible by means of an "unvarnished" documentary recording with adequate transparency and fidelity, i.e., sound reproduction that provides access to the jazz performance as it sounded. (Granted, the ideal of complete sonic fidelity is merely an ideal.)
5. Historically, unvarnished documentary recording is coupled with repeatability.
6. Although an improvisation is a singularity, the experience of repeatedly listening to a documentary recording is antithetical to the experience of singularity.
7. Therefore, as a practical matter, the documentary access provided by a jazz recording is antithetical to something important about the music it presents.
8. Therefore, the mediated experience of recorded jazz is antithetical to jazz appreciation.
9. However, being an adequately knowledgeable appreciator of jazz requires the mediated experience of important milestones in jazz history.
10. Therefore, jazz is a self-alienating art form.

In short, the access to jazz provided by phonographic preservation is undermined by the material facts and psychological effects of phonographic repetition. The opportunity to hear an improvisation from the past is undermined by the repeatability of the technological process that lets us hear it.

5. Reproducibility as a Contextual Given

Having identified this dilemma, we might try to contain the problem in any of three ways. We can adopt the position of the phonophobes, we can adopt the position of the phonophiles, or we can see if we can locate an intermediate position. If our strategy is not yet obvious, we will develop the third option.

First, we could capitulate to the phonophobes and urge jazz fans to never listen to any recording more than once. The problem goes away. Well, good luck with that! One could "swear off" knowing jazz by means of recordings, but then one would not have sufficient knowledge of jazz history to make sufficiently informed judgments of it when listening to it. Hence, we introduced the premise that an adequately knowledgeable appreciator of jazz would know a certain amount of jazz history through recordings.[59] If we have nothing better to say than that, however, we are perilously close to endorsing the position that jazz has its own form of fixed musical works in its body of recordings – a different means than through musical notation, but with the same result.

The second route, which is that of the unapologetic phonophile, is no better. It is an unreflective endorsement of the flattening effects of phonographic isolation and repetition. Beyond the phonographic effects of repeated listening, phonography extracts music from its originating social contexts, encouraging an ahistorical, de-socialized perspective: "treated as autonomous, in that they are considered transcendent of time and space."[60] Jazz is just more grist for the mass art mill: a digitalized product that consumers buy and use, evaluating it only as it relates to their needs and pleasures.

Ironically, both the phonophobe and the phonophile are at risk of becoming stranded in a musical present, alienated from jazz history. For a historically reflexive art form, this result is deadening. Jazz phonophobes are vivaphiles. They hold that the lived moment is what matters – if you weren't there, the recording won't put you there, the practical result of which is that the musical past is relevant only to the degree that the listener personally experienced it. Jazz phonophiles hold that the recorded music is all they need – it doesn't matter when or where it was produced. If record sales confirm that jazz fans *enjoy* Miles Davis's *Kind of Blue* more than *Miles Smiles*, there is no reason for the phonophile to reflect on the line of development that carries jazz from the former to the latter. The musical past is irrelevant except as a treasure house of sonic resources.

We favor a middle position: recorded jazz is the lesser of evils, where the greater evil is ignorance of its past. Artworks aren't natural wonders that invite pure, aesthetic delight. They're products of human agency. As Immanuel Kant stressed, this is why roses and poems require different evaluative stances. Artworks should be evaluated as communicative acts, not as mere aesthetic effects.[61] As such, a formalist aesthetic theory – a theory that whatever is aesthetically important is completely determined by what we can perceive in the experience of it – is just about as wrong as a theory can be, at least when responding to art.[62] (We are speaking here of art, broadly construed, not fine art alone. It applies equally to jazz before and after the "modernist" turn of bebop.) In different ways, our rejection of aestheticism and formalism is defended by Kendall Walton, Arthur Danto, Denis Dutton, and more recently, David Davies.[63] As Dutton put it, "every work of art – every painting, statue, novel, symphony, ballet, as well as every interpretation or rendition of a piece of music, every reading of a poem or production of a play – involves the element of performance."[64] This performative element can be difficult to recognize with many art forms: most of us encounter "works" (artifacts) that are utterly isolated from their creative genesis. Strolling through an art gallery, we see watercolors, oil paintings, acrylics, bronze sculptures, marble sculptures, etchings, perhaps even tiger sharks preserved in formaldehyde. How many of the gallery's visitors appreciate the distinct challenges of these media – knowledge that often depends on having worked with them? As such, the unobserved creative act or performance can be difficult to appreciate or assess – the same danger that we have just identified with the phonophile's approach. Nonetheless, aesthetic evaluation of an artwork should always turn to the question of what the artist has done: what has the artist achieved? To answer that question, the audience must know *something* about the material processes and socio-historical circumstances that inform its production.

We are, in a word, contextualists. Coltrane's solos are not strings of notes with inherent expressive properties. To a large degree, they are products of *his* musical intelligence, his handling of his instrument, and of his interaction with his musical culture and his social-historical milieu. We have argued throughout this book that jazz is not simply a matter of what musicians do with instruments. In Chapter 1 we argued that tap dancers and social dancing were once as important to the understanding of jazz as cornet solos. There, too, we encouraged understanding the intimate relationship between music and place – the difference between the contexts of large dance halls like the Savoy Ballroom and the intimacy of smaller jazz clubs like the Blue Note in New York City or The A-Trane in Berlin. Now, we are extending that idea by saying that there is no *a priori* or universal rule that distinguishes what is relevant to jazz reception and what amounts to a distracting accident of history. In Chapter 5 we worried about the tendency to filter every jazz performance through specific doctrines about the formation of racial identity. But we also said that we have to look on a case by case basis, and there are times when attention to racial context is utterly important. "Strange Fruit" should be heard and interpreted in relation to many things, most obviously the horrors of lynching. (In her autobiography, Holiday pointedly ridicules a West Coast socialite who does not understand the lyrics.[65]) And so Milt Gabler's Commodore label, by recording "Strange Fruit," becomes part of the courageous context of the song. Some other jazz masterpieces, in contrast, tackle established racial boundaries from other angles. *A Love Supreme* should be understood in relation to Coltrane's relationship to his cultural moment, including his relationship to *both* Islamic and Asian religious practices, a rejection of his upbringing in the African Methodist Episcopal Zion Church.[66] To ignore the spiritual ethos of Coltrane's *A Love Supreme* is rather like admiring the Sistine Chapel while ignoring the meaning of Michelangelo's fresco of *The Last Judgment* – just as you can, perhaps, admire Billie Holiday's vocal on "Strange Fruit" while pretending that there has never been a race problem in the United States. But this level of disinterest would amount to a profound disrespect for performance in an action-based art. Just as it is an error to bifurcate form and content in Michelangelo's fresco in order to praise the form, it's an error to dismiss the message of *A Love Supreme* because we happen not to endorse that particular approach to the spiritual dimension of life. One can appreciate Coltrane's music without attending to his intended meanings, but that would be a partial – even shallow – appreciation.

Apart from its function as a communicator of ideas and values, jazz is important in Western culture because real-time human agency remains central to the creative process. And that is why the phonographic effect is troubling. One might counter that this is true of all the performing arts: jazz is not a special case. And here we see why matters of ontology cannot help but rear their head, and why we gave them so much attention in Chapters 7 and 8. Jazz remains remarkable, in large part, because the other modern performing arts still privilege the performance of recognizable works. They offer a steady diet of performances of notated works, or proceed under the direction of scripts or an established choreography. There have been attempts to break from the tyranny of the fixed work in the avant-garde wings of the fine arts, but the fact remains that the famous names in the visual arts, dance, and music in the past fifty years are artists who produce *works* for public consumption. Christo may be the most notable case among the handful of exceptions, but we wonder if his career would have suffered if each Christo project had been "staged" for the public for only a few hours, rather than, say, for days and weeks.

In contrast, it is understood that even when jazz musicians play shopworn standards, the audience has a legitimate expectation that they will witness some element of extemporaneous improvisation. It is not that there are no repeatable and re-identifiable artworks in jazz. There are frequently performances of recognizable musical works.[67] Rather, we are emphasizing that jazz fans understand that the activity of performing is the primary object of appreciative interest. Even if there is some overlap among the songs that are performed over the course of an evening at a jazz club, the second set will not be a carbon copy of the first set, and when Coltrane digs into "My Favorite Things," he will, in some degree, make it new.

6. Coming to Terms with Reproducibility

To return to the battle of the phonophobes and phonophiles, we stress that jazz recordings are *also* products of human agency, choice, and selection. They reflect changing technologies of sound reproduction, but they are also the product of business deals, contract restrictions, and calculations of sales potential. We are, therefore, apologetic phonophiles, aware that we are reliant on phonography, yet wary of the many ways that it transforms what it alleges to document.[68]

Jazz is, perversely, an art of live performance *and* an art of phonography. Informed, appreciative listening treats both "Strange Fruit" and *A Love Supreme* as products of commerce that often have their own significance in the development of jazz. "Strange Fruit" was a regular feature of Holiday's 1939 club performances but Columbia Records and ARC refused to let her record it.[69] Famously, she got permission to record it in a session for Commodore Records. As a result, her April 1939 session gave us "Strange Fruit," but it also allows us to hear Holiday perform four songs with the actual musicians she was working with, the Café Society band, rather than the "Teddy Wilson orchestra" or another ad hoc group assembled by Columbia.[70] Despite the inferior recorded sound at Commodore, Columbia's apprehension about the material resulted in a rare opportunity to hear Holiday performing arrangements she'd worked out with "her" musicians. In sharp contrast, Coltrane's *A Love Supreme* was not a by-product of antecedent live performances. It was actually composed for nine instruments, and then was simplified and took its familiar form when he made the decision to go ahead and record it with his standard quartet, and with a small amount of overdubbing.[71]

Thus, while there is a straightforward *documentary* function that recommends attention to a multitude of great jazz recordings, a contextualist perspective also asks how the process of documenting jazz contributes to jazz culture. Armstrong's Hot Five recordings are not Library of Congress field recordings of an otherwise pure and uncorrupted tradition. Commercial recordings are themselves elements of – not an intervention into – jazz practice.[72] They should always be interpreted in light of the co-dependence of jazz and the phonographic effect, which is itself the product of an evolving, socially embedded technology. To introduce an analogy, saying that phonography distorts jazz is rather like saying that cinematography distorts our view of Humphrey Bogart and Ingrid Bergman in *Casablanca*. Or, to paraphrase Socrates, it's like saying that we can have flute playing without flute players.[73] The objection misrepresents the basic relationship that we are attempting to describe. Historically, recording is an indispensable tool of jazz's dissemination and reception. A better description of jazz and its history will see recordings as essential to jazz culture, and will at the same time recognize them as a sphere of creative activity in jazz, rather than a mere documentation of music that somehow existed and developed apart from that documentation.

Are we simply putting a new wrapper on phonographic isolation, and accepting it? Or do we concede that the experience of improvisation is corrupted or harmed by hearing a recording of it? Both, if understood with appropriate qualification. Let's return to the argument we've reconstructed, especially step 4. Recording with complete transparency is an unreasonable goal; it's less an ideal for jazz preservation and recovery than a misleading fiction. The creative activity that can be recovered from listening to an undoctored recording of a jazz performance is not the only relevant human agency that should concern us. Returning to the argument laid out in section 4 above, the claim that improvisation is the aesthetic *sine qua non* of jazz should not be confused with the distinct proposal – which we have rejected – that improvisation is the *only* relevant activity to appreciate in a jazz performance or that it is an essential characteristic of all jazz. There is, after all, the swing feel of the drummer or vocalist and the propulsive groove of the ensemble; in a jazz context, it is a legitimate concern if the vocalist sings the melody too "straight." This is not, per se, an evaluation based on the presence or absence of improvisation. Appreciation of creative activity in jazz performance involves far more than attention to the quality of any improvisation. Also, we've noted how improvisation is a negligible factor in certain periods of jazz: the big band era, for example. And, as contextualists, we cannot draw a sharp boundary between what is internal to a performance and what is external to it. Lynchings and segregation might be classified as external to Holiday's performances and her recordings of "Strange Fruit," but they are relevant to any appreciative response to her creative artistry.[74]

In conclusion, rather than bemoan the way that phonographic isolation and repetition interferes with the appreciation of jazz improvisation, let's have our cake, and eat it, too. There appear to be psychological obstacles to attending to different aspects of a complex experience simultaneously, and this is a reason to *favor* repeatability. At the same time, we grant that there is a price additional to the way that repetition makes a jazz performance feel "canned": every recording introduces its own layer of additional human agency that may complicate our understanding of the music. When Rasula warns that records are a "seductive menace" in jazz history, we would warn that the failure to understand their essential contribution is the greater menace.

Notes

1 John Philip Sousa, "The Menace of Mechanical Music," *Appleton's Magazine* 8 (September 1906), 278–284.
2 Glenn Gould, "The Prospects of Recording," *High Fidelity* 16 (April 1966), 46–63.
3 Ted Gioia, *The Imperfect Art: Reflections on Jazz and Modern Culture* (Oxford: Oxford University Press, 1988), 63.
4 An excellent general overview is Alessandro Arbo, "Music and Technical Reproducibility: A Paradigm Shift," in *Musical Listening in the Age of Technological Reproduction*, ed. Gianmario Borio (New York: Routledge, 2015), 53–67.
5 Evan Eisenberg, *The Recording Angel: Explorations in Phonography* (New York: McGraw-Hill, 1987).

6 For a corrective to Eisenberg's over-emphasis on "solitary" listening, see William Howland Kenney, *Recorded Music in American Life: The Phonograph and Popular Memory, 1890–1945* (Oxford: Oxford University Press, 1999), chap. 1.

7 Eisenberg, *Recording Angel*, 35.

8 Tom Bethel, *George Lewis: A Jazzman from New Orleans* (Berkeley: University of California Press, 1977), 77.

9 Theodore Gracyk, *Rhythm and Noise: An Aesthetics of Rock* (Durham: Duke University Press, 1996), 31–35.

10 A range of benefits and costs is surveyed in Theodore Gracyk, "Listening to Music: Performances and Recordings," *Journal of Aesthetics and Art Criticism* 55:2 (1997): 139–150.

11 Scott Yanow, *Classic Jazz: The Essential Listening Companion* (San Francisco: Backbeat Books, 2001), 128.

12 Based on categories of musical anticipation developed by David Huron, the most insidious effect of repetition is that conscious veridical expectations of the invariant details will work against dynamic expectations that "arise from the immediately preceding experience"; *Sweet Anticipation: Music and the Psychology of Expectation* (Cambridge, MA: MIT Press, 2006), 363.

13 Roger Sessions, *The Musical Experience of Composer, Performer, Listener* (Princeton: Princeton University Press, 1950), 70. As this quotation should make clear, we begin by considering music's emotional effects when these arise from listener expectations; we are not yet discussing the expressive content that knowledgeable listeners may attribute to the music.

14 The first appearance of this phrase appears to be the 1997 publication of Lee B. Brown, "Phonography," currently in *Aesthetics: A Reader in Philosophy of the Arts*, 4th ed., ed. David Goldblatt, Lee B. Brown, and Stephanie Patridge (New York: Routledge, 2017), 207–212. See also the discussion in Lee B. Brown, "Phonography, Rock Records, and the Ontology of Recorded Music," *Journal of Aesthetics and Art Criticism* 58:4 (2000): 361–372.

15 A documentary recording will be one that is created and shared with the intention that listeners will not attend to, or will not seek aesthetic value in, the way the recording process represents the performance that it records. This way of framing the position derives from Catharine Abell, "Cinema as a Representational Art," *British Journal of Aesthetics* 50:3 (2010): 273–286, especially 278. Abell offers a plausible criterion for distinguishing between recordings as documentary depictions and as representational artworks.

16 Quoted in Jerry Zoltan, "The Beatles as Recording Artists," in *The Cambridge Companion to the Beatles*, ed. Kenneth Womack (Cambridge: Cambridge University Press, 2009), 33–61, at 38.

17 At the time, at least one major jazz critic thought that this was a production accident; see Martin Williams, "Jazz: Some Old Favorites are Back," *New York Times* (January 18, 1970), 112.

18 Noël Carroll, *A Philosophy of Mass Art* (Oxford: Oxford University Press, 1998), 218. We do not wish to minimize the distorting effects of inadvertent "varnish" in early recordings. See William Tallmadge, "Distortion in Acoustical Recording," *Journal of Jazz Studies* 5:2 (1979): 61–75.

19 Diana Raffman, *Language, Music and Mind* (Cambridge, MA: MIT Press, 1993), chaps. 4 and 5. We note that Raffman addresses only the dimension of pitch.

20 Gracyk, *Rhythm and Noise*, 52–53; see also 59–61.

21 Paul Berliner, *Thinking in Jazz: The Infinite Art of Improvisation* (Chicago: University of Chicago Press, 1994), 126.

22 Huron, *Sweet Anticipation*, 277, 315–316.

23 This is a thought suggested by Stephen Davies, *Musical Works and Performances: A Philosophical Exploration* (Oxford: Oxford University Press, 2001), chap. 7.

24 Sessions, *Musical Experience*, 4.
25 See Gracyk, "Listening to Music," 140. The context is an objection to the assumption that music doesn't *exist* until performed.
26 David Swinney, "Lexical Access during Sentence Comprehension: (Re)consideration of Context Effects," *Journal of Verbal Learning and Verbal Behavior* 18 (1979): 645–660.
27 As spelled out in Leonard B. Meyer, *Emotion and Meaning in Music* (Chicago: University of Chicago Press, 1956). For a treatment that revises Meyer's theory in light of more recent findings, see Eugene Narmour, *The Analysis and Cognition of Basic Melodic Structures: The Implication-Realization Model* (Chicago: University of Chicago Press, 1990).
28 Huron, *Sweet Anticipation*, 304. In fact, music psychology posits at least six distinctive mechanisms that generate emotional responses to music. See Patrik N. Juslin and Daniel Västfjäll, "Emotional Responses to Music: The Need to Consider Underlying Mechanisms," *Behavioral and Brain Sciences* 31:5 (2008): 559–621.
29 There is some empirical confirmation of this general principle, except that it has been most rigorously tested *within* popular music, e.g., Adrian C. North and David J. Hargreaves, "Subjective Complexity, Familiarity, and Liking for Popular Music," *Psychomusicology* 15 (1995): 77–93.
30 Huron, *Sweet Anticipation*, 304. Actually, Huron contends that some kinds of expectations will continue to occur, generating surprise, no matter how familiar the music (226).
31 Granted, surprise is always a matter of degree, and a jazz neophyte will experience more surprises listening, say, to Thelonious Monk than will a jazz fan who's heard Monk before. Still, it's not for noting that jazz critic Whitney Balliett named one of his essay collections *The Sound of Surprise: 46 Pieces on Jazz* (New York: Dutton, 1959).
32 See Michelle Mercer's liner notes to Miles Davis, *Miles in Berlin* (Columbia 519507 2, 2005).
33 See Richard Taruskin, "Early Music: Truly Old-Fashioned at Last?" *New York Times* (June 14, 1998), Arts and Leisure, 28.
34 As suggested by Davies, *Musical Works*, 303–305.
35 We examine this assumption in detail in Chapter 10.
36 Gunther Schuller, *Early Jazz* (New York: Oxford University Press, 1968), 116–118.
37 Henry Martin, *Charlie Parker and Thematic Improvisation* (Lanham, MD: Scarecrow Press, 2001), 113.
38 E.g., André Hodeir, *Toward Jazz*, trans. Noel Burch (New York: Grove Press, 1962); Martin Williams, *The Jazz Tradition*, 2nd ed. (New York: Oxford University Press, 1983); Berliner, *Thinking in Jazz*; Ingrid Monson, *Saying Something: Jazz Improvisation and Interaction* (Chicago: University of Chicago Press, 1996); Peter Elsdon, *Keith Jarrett's The Köln Concert* (Oxford: Oxford University Press, 2013); Martin, *Charlie Parker*.
39 Jed Rasula, "The Media of Memory: The Seductive Menace of Records in Jazz History," in *Jazz among the Discourses*, ed. Krin Gabbard (Durham: Duke University Press, 1995), 134–162.
40 Rasula, "Media of Memory," 144.
41 Scott DeVeaux, "This is What I Do," in *Art from Start to Finish: Jazz, Painting, Writing, and Other Improvisations*, ed. Howard S. Becker, Robert R. Faulkner, and Barbara Kirshenblatt-Gimblett (Chicago: University of Chicago Press, 2006), 119–125. See also Scott DeVeaux, *The Birth of Bebop: A Social and Musical History* (Berkeley: University of California Press, 1997), 365–366.
42 We explore the question of formalism in greater detail in Chapter 10.
43 Robert Walser, "Out of Notes: Signification, Interpretation, and the Problem of Miles Davis," in *Jazz among the Discourses*, ed. Krin Gabbard (Durham: Duke University Press, 1995), 165–188.
44 Hodeir, *Toward Jazz*, 175.

45 Hodeir, *Toward Jazz*, 175.
46 Schuller, *Early Jazz*, 117n16.
47 E.g., Martin, *Charlie Parker*, 54, 60, 79.
48 Schuller, *Early Jazz*, x.
49 Taped by WFMT Chicago and aired in April 1993 on WOSU-FM, Columbus, Ohio. The Monk performance is on his Columbia recording, *Solo Monk* (1965).
50 Gary Giddins and Scott DeVeaux, *Jazz* (New York: Norton, 2009).
51 Here, reiteration should be not be confused with Derrida's notion of iterability, in which each repetition modifies what is repeated. Jazz is an art of iteration; our concern is that reiteration interferes with iteration. See Jacques Derrida, "Signature Event Context," in *A Derrida Reader: Between the Blinds*, ed. Peggy Kamuf (New York: Harvester Wheatsheaf, 1991), 80–111.
52 Walser, "Out of Notes."
53 Michael Chanan, *Repeated Takes: A Short History of Recording and Its Effects on Music* (New York: Verso, 1995), 2.
54 Jonathan Sterne, *The Audible Past: Cultural Origins of Sound Reproduction* (Durham: Duke University Press, 2003), 218. See also Gracyk, *Rhythm and Noise*, 53.
55 See Brian Harker, *Louis Armstrong's Hot Five and Hot Seven Recordings* (Oxford: Oxford University Press, 2011), and George Grella, Jr., *Bitches Brew* (New York: Bloomsbury 2015), 68–70. For the three days of recording, Davis hired eight musicians to supplement the four who formed his working band.
56 A classic jazz band leader once explained to Lee Brown, in almost gruesome detail, how he tweaks the tapes to get "good music" out of them. For a short discussion of how *Mingus Ah Um* was improved through editing, see Grella, *Bitches Brew*, 48.
57 Quoted in John Seabrook, "The Immaculate Lineup: Music Festivals in the Instagram Age," *New Yorker* (April 17, 2017): 30–37, at 32.
58 A theory of artworks as action types is something altogether different. See David Davies, *Art as Performance* (Malden: Blackwell, 2004), chap. 6.
59 This premise is supported by our definition of jazz in Chapter 3. See also Eisenberg, *Recording Angel*, chap. 8; and Gioia, *Imperfect Art*, chap. 3, especially 66–67.
60 Tony Whyton, *Beyond A Love Supreme: John Coltrane and the Legacy of an Album* (Oxford: Oxford University Press, 2013), 22. One of the first jazz writers to make the point was Ronald M. Radano, *New Musical Figurations: Anthony Braxton's Cultural Critique* (Chicago: University of Chicago Press, 1993), 16.
61 Immanuel Kant, *Critique of the Power of Judgment*, ed. Paul Guyer, trans. Paul Guyer and Eric Matthews (Cambridge: Cambridge University Press, 2000), §43, 182; Immanuel Kant, *Gesammelte Schriften*, vol. 5, *Kritik der Urteilskraft*, Preußischen Akademie der Wissenschaften (Berlin: George Reimer, 1913), 303.
62 See Nick Zangwill, *The Metaphysics of Beauty* (Ithaca: Cornell University Press, 2001), chaps. 4 and 5. Zangwill defends a moderate formalism by conceding that representational properties are not formal. The significant features of jazz performance, such as syncopation, are formal qualities of the music (76n50).
63 Kendall L. Walton, "Categories of Art," *Philosophical Review* 79:3 (1970): 334–367; Arthur C. Danto, *The Transfiguration of the Commonplace: A Philosophy of Art* (Cambridge, MA: Harvard University Press, 1981); Denis Dutton, "Artistic Crimes: The Problem of Forgery in the Arts," *British Journal of Aesthetics* 19:4 (1979): 302–314; Davies, *Art as Performance*.
64 Dutton, "Artistic Crimes," 305.
65 Billie Holiday with William Duffy, *Lady Sings the Blues* (New York: Doubleday, 1956), 84.
66 See, for example, the essays in Leonard Brown, ed., *John Coltrane and Black America's Quest for Freedom: Spirituality and the Music* (Oxford: Oxford University Press, 2010).

67 An interesting exchange on this point can be found in Andrew Kania, "All Play and No Work: The Ontology of Jazz," *Journal of Aesthetics and Art Criticism* 69:4 (2011): 391–403, and Julian Dodd, "Upholding Standards: A Realist Ontology of Standard Form Jazz," *Journal of Aesthetics and Art Criticism* 72:3 (2014): 277–290.
68 The same point is made about jazz and photography in Benjamin Cawthra, *Blue Notes in Black and White: Photography and Jazz* (Chicago: University of Chicago Press, 2011).
69 On the role of institutional racism in the business practices of jazz, see Frank Kofsky, *Black Music, White Business: Illuminating the History and Political Economy of Jazz* (New York: Pathfinder, 1998); for other mistreatment of Holiday, see 29–31.
70 Meg Greene, *Billie Holiday: A Biography* (Westport: Greenwood Press, 2007), 61.
71 Whyton, *Beyond A Love Supreme*, 23.
72 See, for example, Dan Morgenstern, "Recorded Jazz," *The Oxford Companion to Jazz*, ed. Bill Kirchner (Oxford: Oxford University Press, 2000), 767–787.
73 Plato, *Apology*, 27b.
74 Therefore, it strikes us a false dilemma when Scott DeVeaux opposes "the ideology of jazz as aesthetic object" with appreciation of its "historical particularity." See Scott Deveaux, "Constructing the Jazz tradition: Jazz Historiography," *Black American Literature Forum* 25 (1991): 525–560, at 553.

References

Abell, Catharine. "Cinema as a Representational Art." *British Journal of Aesthetics* 50:3 (2010): 273–286.

Arbo, Alessandro. "Music and Technical Reproducibility: A Paradigm Shift." In *Musical Listening in the Age of Technological Reproduction*, ed. Gianmario Borio, 53–67. New York: Routledge, 2015.

Balliett, Whitney. *The Sound of Surprise: 46 Pieces on Jazz*. New York: Dutton, 1959.

Berliner, Paul. *Thinking in Jazz: The Infinite Art of Improvisation*. Chicago: University of Chicago Press, 1994.

Bethel, Tom. *George Lewis: A Jazzman from New Orleans*. Berkeley: University of California Press, 1977.

Brown, Lee B. "Phonography." In *Aesthetics: A Reader in Philosophy of the Arts*, 4th ed., ed. David Goldblatt, Lee B. Brown, and Stephanie Patridge, 207–212. New York: Routledge, 2017.

Brown, Lee B. "Phonography, Rock Records, and the Ontology of Recorded Music." *Journal of Aesthetics and Art Criticism* 58:4 (2000): 361–372.

Brown, Leonard, ed. *John Coltrane and Black America's Quest for Freedom: Spirituality and the Music*. Oxford: Oxford University Press, 2010.

Carroll, Noël. *A Philosophy of Mass Art*. Oxford: Oxford University Press, 1998.

Cawthra, Benjamin. *Blue Notes in Black and White: Photography and Jazz*. Chicago: University of Chicago Press, 2011.

Chanan, Michael. *Repeated Takes: A Short History of Recording and Its Effects on Music*. New York: Verso, 1995.

Copland, Aaron. *Music and Imagination*. Cambridge, MA: Harvard University Press, 1952.

Danto, Arthur C. *The Transfiguration of the Commonplace: A Philosophy of Art*. Cambridge, MA: Harvard University Press, 1981.

Davies, David. *Art as Performance*. Malden: Blackwell, 2004.

Davies, Stephen. *Musical Works and Performances: A Philosophical Exploration*. Oxford: Oxford University Press, 2001.

Derrida, Jacques. "Signature Event Context." In *A Derrida Reader: Between the Blinds*, ed. Peggy Kamuf, 80–111. New York: Harvester Wheatsheaf, 1991.

DeVeaux, Scott. *The Birth of Bebop: A Social and Musical History*. Berkeley: University of California Press, 1997.

DeVeaux, Scott. "Constructing the Jazz Tradition: Jazz Historiography." *Black American Literature Forum* 25:3 (1991): 525–560.

DeVeaux, Scott. "This is What I Do." In *Art from Start to Finish: Jazz, Painting, Writing and Other Improvisations*, ed. Howard S. Becker, Robert R. Faulkner, and Barbara Kirshenblatt-Gimblett, 119–125. Chicago: University of Chicago Press, 2006.

Dodd, Julian. "Upholding Standards: A Realist Ontology of Standard Form Jazz." *Journal of Aesthetics and Art Criticism* 72:3 (2014): 277–290.

Dutton, Denis. "Artistic Crimes: The Problem of Forgery in the Arts." *British Journal of Aesthetics* 19:4 (1979): 302–314.

Eisenberg, Evan. *The Recording Angel: Explorations in Phonography*. New York: McGraw-Hill, 1987.

Elsdon, Peter. *Keith Jarrett's The Köln Concert*. Oxford: Oxford University Press, 2013.

Fodor, Jerry A. *The Modularity of Mind: An Essay on Faculty Psychology*. Cambridge, MA: MIT Press, 1983.

Gabbard, Krin, ed. *Jazz among the Discourses*. Durham: Duke University Press, 1995.

Giddins, Gary, and Scott DeVeaux. *Jazz*. New York: Norton, 2009.

Gioia, Ted. *The Imperfect Art: Reflections on Jazz and Modern Culture*. Oxford: Oxford University Press, 1988.

Gould, Glenn. "The Prospects of Recording." *High Fidelity* 16:4 (April 1966): 46–63.

Gracyk, Theodore. "Listening to Music: Performances and Recordings." *Journal of Aesthetics and Art Criticism* 55:2 (1997): 139–150.

Gracyk, Theodore. *Rhythm and Noise: An Aesthetics of Rock*. Durham: Duke University Press, 1996.

Greene, Meg. *Billie Holiday: A Biography*. Westport: Greenwood Press, 2007.

Grella, George, Jr., *Bitches Brew*. New York: Bloomsbury, 2015.

Harker, Brian. *Louis Armstrong's Hot Five and Hot Seven Recordings*. Oxford: Oxford University Press, 2011.

Hodeir, André. *Toward Jazz*, trans. Noel Burch. New York: Grove Press, 1962.

Holiday, Billie, with William Duffy. *Lady Sings the Blues*. New York: Doubleday, 1956.

Huron, David. *Sweet Anticipation: Music and the Psychology of Expectation*. Cambridge, MA: MIT Press, 2006.

Juslin, Patrik N., and Daniel Västfjäll. "Emotional Responses to Music: The Need to Consider Underlying Mechanisms." *Behavioral and Brain Sciences* 31(2008): 559–621.

Kania, Andrew. "All Play and No Work: The Ontology of Jazz." *Journal of Aesthetics and Art Criticism* 69:4 (2011): 391–403.

Kant, Immanuel. *Critique of the Power of Judgment*, ed. Paul Guyer, trans. Paul Guyer and Eric Matthews. Cambridge: Cambridge University Press, 2000.

Kenney, William Howland. *Recorded Music in American Life: The Phonograph and Popular Memory, 1890–1945*. Oxford: Oxford University Press, 1999.

Kofsky, Frank. *Black Music, White Business: Illuminating the History and Political Economy of Jazz*. New York: Pathfinder, 1998.

Martin, Henry. *Charlie Parker and Thematic Improvisation*. Lanham, MD: Scarecrow Press, 2001.

Mercer, Michelle. Liner notes to Miles Davis, *Miles in Berlin*, Columbia 519507 2, 2005.

Meyer, Leonard B. *Emotion and Meaning in Music*. Chicago: University of Chicago Press, 1956.

Monson, Ingrid. *Saying Something: Jazz Improvisation and Interaction*. Chicago: University of Chicago Press, 1996.

Morgenstern, Dan. "Recorded Jazz." In *The Oxford Companion to Jazz*, ed. Bill Kirchner, 767–787. Oxford: Oxford University Press, 2000.

Narmour, Eugene. *The Analysis and Cognition of Basic Melodic Structures: The Implication-Realization Model*. Chicago: University of Chicago Press, 1990.

North, Adrian C., and David J. Hargreaves. "Subjective Complexity, Familiarity, and Liking for Popular Music." *Psychomusicology* 14:1 (1995): 77–93.

Plato. *Complete Works*, ed. John M. Cooper. Indianapolis: Hackett, 1997.

Radano, Ronald M. *New Musical Figurations: Anthony Braxton's Cultural Critique*. Chicago: University of Chicago Press, 1993.

Raffman, Diana. *Language, Music and Mind*. Cambridge, MA: MIT Press, 1993.

Rasula, Jed. "The Media of Memory: The Seductive Menace of Records in Jazz History." In *Jazz Among the Discourses*, ed. Krin Gabbard, 134–162. Durham: Duke University Press, 1995.

Schuller, Gunther. *Early Jazz*. New York: Oxford University Press, 1968.

Seabrook, John. "The Immaculate Lineup: Music Festivals in the Instagram Age." *New Yorker* (April 17, 2017): 30–37.

Sessions, Roger. *The Musical Experience of Composer, Performer, Listener*. Princeton: Princeton University Press, 1950.

Sousa, John Philip. "The Menace of Mechanical Music." *Appleton's Magazine* 8 (September 1906): 278–284.

Sterne, Jonathan. *The Audible Past: Cultural Origins of Sound Reproduction*. Durham: Duke University Press, 2003.

Swinney, David. "Lexical Access during Sentence Comprehension: (Re)consideration of Context Effects." *Journal of Verbal Learning and Verbal Behavior* 18 (1979): 645–660.

Tallmadge, William. "Distortion in Acoustical Recording." *Journal of Jazz Studies* 5:2 (1979): 61–75.

Taruskin, Richard. "Early Music: Truly Old-Fashioned at Last?" *New York Times* (June 14, 1998): Arts and Leisure, 28.

Walser, Robert. "Out of Notes: Signification, Interpretation, and the Problem of Miles Davis." In *Jazz Among the Discourses*, ed. Krin Gabbard, 165–188. Durham: Duke University Press, 1995.

Walton, Kendall L. "Categories of Art." *Philosophical Review* 79:3 (1970): 334–367.

Whyton, Tony. *Beyond A Love Supreme: John Coltrane and the Legacy of an Album*. Oxford: Oxford University Press, 2013.

Williams, Martin. "Jazz: Some Old Favorites are Back." *New York Times* (January 18, 1970): 112.

Williams, Martin. *The Jazz Tradition*, 2nd ed. New York: Oxford University Press, 1983.

Yanow, Scott. *Classic Jazz: The Essential Listening Companion*. San Francisco: Backbeat Books, 2001.

Zangwill, Nick. *The Metaphysics of Beauty*. Ithaca: Cornell University Press, 2001.

Zoltan, Jerry. "The Beatles as Recording Artists." In *The Cambridge Companion to the Beatles*, ed. Kenneth Womack, 33–61. Cambridge: Cambridge University Press, 2009.

10

JAZZ IMPROVISATION AND ITS VICISSITUDES

A Plea for Imperfection

> Whoever says 'work of art' says 'perfection.'
>
> — *Lucien Rudrauf*

> Part of the act of performing jazz is taking chances, and sometimes the chances you take don't work.
>
> — *Kenny Barron*

At the inception of modern philosophy, René Descartes explores his realization that by virtue of his own acts of doubting, he is an imperfect being. The contrast that concerns him in the *Meditations* is with the perfection of God.[1] Descartes offers his personal account as standing for all of humanity: he is often the victim of his own errors, as his will reaches beyond his capacities to know and to do the right thing.

In philosophy of art, the idea of imperfection applies not so much to persons, as with Descartes, as to artifacts and events. As Descartes founded modern philosophy, Immanuel Kant founded modern aesthetics. For Kant, beauty is not reducible to perfection. He says, "by beauty, as a formal subjective purposiveness, there is not conceived any perfection of the object."[2] Unlike the perception of beauty, a judgment of perfection posits an objective purposiveness, and identification of perfection requires that "the concept of *what sort of thing it is supposed to be* must come first," providing a standard of achievement.[3] Consider: a fragile vase is not an imperfect vase, but a fragile sledgehammer is an imperfect one. Since human creativity is always driven by some concept of what is to be achieved, artistic perfection consists of the completeness of anything after its kind. And yet this will not be an aesthetic judgment, a point generally overlooked by the formalists who took their inspiration from the Kantian text. This will interest us in this chapter, because when we ask what concept provides criteria of achievement for an improviser of a jazz musical passage, we need not grant that each jazz improviser has a clear idea of what sort of thing it is going to be. Furthermore, we offer a reminder that, as we explain in Chapter 7, not every jazz performance is equally improvisational, and there are several distinct kinds of improvisation. Consequently, different aspects of a single performance may have to be judged, retrospectively, under multiple, distinct criteria of achievement.

Pursuing Kant's insight, the perfection/imperfection binary is not coextensive with the good/bad distinction. Oddly, the attribution of "imperfect" to a work, say a painting or performance, is compatible with a work's being good and is hardly ever used when it is simply dismissed as bad. Being imperfect implies that something is off, but not a disaster. With individual works, we are familiar with the idea of the magnificent failure. In contrast, attribution of "imperfection" to a work generally involves a hypothetical: that those in the know have some idea of what would make this work better, if not perfect – or at least might correct its flaws. Professional jazz musicians frequently hear flaws in improvisations that are not apparent to younger players, and will point them out.[4] However, a parallel phenomenon can be found in all the arts, so it does nothing to advance the idea that jazz is an imperfect art.

Individual works aside, it would seem ludicrous to claim that painting, for example, is imperfect or that painting is an imperfect art. However, when it comes to jazz, with a focus on jazz that is improvised, that is exactly what some commentators claim – that jazz is an imperfect art. For example, jazz chronicler Ted Gioia used the phrase "imperfect art" as the title for his first book on jazz.[5] Barry Kernfeld independently argues that "jazz is an inherently imperfect music, and in significant ways a desire for perfection clashes with aesthetics peculiar to jazz."[6] In this chapter we explain our own reasons for thinking these descriptions to be apt, and why this inherent imperfection is nevertheless one of the music's most interesting features. In an improvisational art, especially jazz, imperfection is frequently present, yet it is not intrinsically a sign of something gone wrong. In jazz improvisation, imperfection frequently facilitates better performances.

1. The Formalist's Complaint

A newcomer to jazz, listening to a certain recorded performance of "My Funny Valentine" by Miles Davis, is likely to be shocked at its roughness.[7] As we mentioned in Chapter 6, Davis's performance features cracked notes not quite in tune, sloppy triplets, unaccountable pauses, arbitrary shifts of rhythm, and chaotic runs that go nowhere. Or consider the critical response to Davis's debut recording as a soloist, supporting Charlie Parker on "Now's the Time" (1945). A prominent critic has described Davis's contribution as "lugubrious, unswinging, no ideas."[8] And although it is not evident in that specific performance, subsequent release of the complete recording sessions for that day reveals Parker's willingness to attempt multiple takes with a broken, squeaky horn.[9] Knowing that performances of similar quality in "classical" music would never see the light of day, the neophyte will be puzzled to learn that many such jazz performances are recorded and issued to the public.

Strikingly, improvised jazz also exhibits a chronic defect of an almost opposite kind, namely, that much of the music seems – like Davis's first recorded solo – routine, predictable, formulaic. As we explained in Chapter 6, a main feature of Theodor Adorno's harsh critique of jazz turns on the charge that the jazz musician's spontaneity is a myth – indeed, that on the whole the music is monotonous.[10] In the same spirit, Winthrop Sargeant, whose classic study of jazz betrays a peculiar love–hate relationship with its subject, declares that "a sturdy repetition" of the music's basic elements always underlies "the apparent freedom of improvised" jazz.[11] More recently, Paul Berliner's monumental study of how jazz performers learn to improvise confirms that soloists construct a "storehouse" of both basic forms and favored phrase figures, which are then deployed and reworked in numerous solos.[12] "Certain formulas," notes Henry Martin, "can be traced from soloist to soloist and effectively position the player within substyles ... of the jazz tradition."[13] Blues improvisation is especially prone to this mode of repetition.[14] After hearing too many performances that merely shuffle through a sequence of orderly but tired clichés in "a stringing together of unrelated ideas,"[15] a listener may be tempted to conclude that Adorno and Sargeant are both basically correct.

One might pair the problems and dub them both *the formalist's complaints*. The reason for calling them both "formalist" should be clear. As Krin Gabbard says, "formalist" responses emphasize "internalist principles of unity and coherence" in jazz.[16] Music that is disordered, chaotic, and musically confused will lack "deep structural unity,"[17] where "structure" is a synonym for "form." Obviously, jazz will fail to satisfy formalist criteria of excellence. But the same failure holds for music that is formulaic, banal, and over-simple. Of course, jazz performances can be messy or routine or both at the same time for reasons that aren't very interesting, as when simple phrases are executed badly by beginners. We want to set such cases aside in order to address the deeper issue that the formalist's complaints jointly reflect. Our diagnosis is that the formalist focuses too narrowly on the sheer acoustic dimensions of the music at the expense of other considerations – in particular, those that concern (1) the cultural/historical context of the music and (2) the process by which it is generated.

After considering some resources for arguing against the grounds of the formalist's complaints, we make a case that one dimension of the music's imperfection remains that these strategies cannot rationalize. Our position, in brief, is that a jazz performance can be a successful performance despite the presence of genuine flaws – that is, despite the presence of flaws in the sense that the performance falls short of what the performers may hope to achieve with those performance flaws avoided. However, the deeper point for which we argue is that the residual imperfection in a jazz performance can be regarded as a vital aspect of jazz generally but of improvised jazz in particular, provided it is framed the right way.[18] In particular, how jazz improvisers recover midstream from those flaws is part of what we appreciate when listening. In order to make a case for this, however, we will articulate some very general parameters of jazz improvisation. To set the stage for the discussion, we first need to review some common ideas about the bases for evaluating jazz improvisation.

2. Improvisation and Artistic Quality

Judgments about the quality of improvisation have been made both from an extra- and an intra- point of view. The extramural perspective has been, naturally, Eurocentric, with a destructive tendency to regard improvisation as an exotic musical "other."[19] Building on his point that jazz solos rest on a repetitive foundation, Sargeant gives jazz a generally lower place in a scale of musical values, when compared with that of opera and concert music.[20] However well-informed his analysis, Sargeant's provocative discussion of jazz improvisation must be faulted for his tacit assumption that forms of music that privilege harmonic variety, at the expense of other values, are superior. André Hodeir and Roger Scruton are fellow travelers.[21] Similarly, Ingrid Monson points out that the evaluative standards articulated in Gunther Schuller's *Early Jazz* – "expressive fervor, artistic commitment, structural logic, virtuosity" (and, we might add, beauty) – are the standard criteria of Western art music as established to valorize "absolute and autonomous music and the artist as genius."[22] If we come at jazz from this angle, with Eurocentric aesthetic priorities, we are apt to overlook musical values that are prioritized in a particular musical and socio-political culture. For example, we are apt to place undue focus on two of five players in a jazz quintet, myopically privileging the skills of the "front line" over the equally important skills of the rhythm section. Seeking universal value, we will fail to hear its intertextual *signifying* and consequent richness of meaning.[23]

We will have something to say in section 4 about the extent to which the African-American sources of jazz make for an important difference when the music deploys quotation, repetition, and allusion. For now, we will note that the transformative potential of jazz repetition can be recognized extramurally, by drawing a lesson from European art music. As we observed in Chapter 6, Peter Kivy says that in absolute music (music sans words), "The importance of this question of the musical repeat is not to be underestimated."[24] Kivy turns to a position held by Edward T. Cone, that, "In general, there is no such thing as redundancy in music." So, while passages are frequently repeated, they are not redundant. Here's why: "It is part of Cone's point that we do, or should, hear music differently when it appears the second or third (or whatever) time from the way we did the first."[25] For Kivy, this makes repeated music not merely a difference in token, but one in type as well. Now, granted, Kivy is exploring the context of being at a classical concert and listening to a single work that contains repeats. Yet it aptly describes the standard approach, in jazz, of returning to the song's "head" following a set of improvised solos: what was introductory is now a conclusion, and what was open-ended is now formally balanced. We submit that the same force holds when the context is listening to "No Blues" performed by the Miles Davis Quintet on successive evenings in 1961, or even returning to the same recorded performance over a period of years.[26] New juxtapositions and new listening environments result in a different listening experience, despite the formalist's complaint that we have heard it all before.

There is a strain of philosophy that resists what we have just proposed. Defending musical empiricism, sonicists hold that every aesthetic merit and flaw in music can be recognized by style-knowledgeable listeners simply by attending to the music's sonic properties: "we need only use our ears."[27] The music's *aesthetic* value should not be confused with *artistic* value that is historically and contingently associated with it. On this view, the deep spirituality of John Coltrane's *A Love Supreme* is inherent in the music's structure. In contrast, neither Coltrane's technical expertise nor the performance's value as an expression of *Coltrane's* spirituality are aesthetic values; they are artistic values. For the sonicist, it would not subtract anything from the musical value of that recording if we uncovered indisputable evidence that he was insincere and that he composed the music only to mislead his deeply spiritual wife! Nor would the date or place of performance be a relevant matter. In other words, sonicism maintains that, in the same way that a high-quality forgery might be aesthetically successful and yet artistically derivative and second-rate, discovery of Coltrane's (hypothetical) deception would not be a reason for jazz fans to value the *music* any less.

However, we are not musical empiricists. We're contextualists.[28] There is no reason why the purely acoustic properties of *A Love Supreme* – sound patterns utterly divorced from all historical context – should be interpreted as spiritual, or why the decontextualized work possesses inherent "solemnity and depth."[29] Solemnity is a matter of comparison. While it is solemn compared to, say, Louis Armstrong's 1926 performance of "Heebie Jeebies," it is not especially solemn when compared to Haydn's string quartet version of *The Seven Last Words of Christ* (Opus 51). So why do we compare it to Armstrong rather than Haydn in determining its expressive character? As we argued in our opening chapters, there is simply no reason to group the recorded performances of Coltrane in the same comparison class as Armstrong – that is, as jazz – unless one recognizes a musico-historical relationship. Coming to New York from Chicago in the mid-1920s where George Gershwin and Paul Whiteman were busy polishing jazz, Armstrong was like the proverbial bull in the china shop. Additionally, there is no reason to understand its comparative solemnity as spiritual – as opposed, say, to reading it as an expression of a downswing in a bipolar disorder – unless we hear it as the offering of a musician who intends that it be heard as spiritual. Keep in mind that, as an ahistorical sonic phenomenon, Coltrane's title is not part of the work, and his chanting is just another sonic contribution, not a message in the English language.[30] The musical empiricist tells us that, had Coltrane named it

Aloe Supreme, in reference to the medicinal powers of aloe nectar, this would not have changed its expressive profile and aesthetic merits. Obviously, we disagree. Titles, as Arthur Danto has said, are often clues to the interpretation of a work.[31] Yet the formalist cannot appeal to titles for guidance.

However, we must beware of going to the other extreme, which is to suppose that every element of every jazz performance has a semiotic or quasi-linguistic function that accounts for its appearance in the performance. This would now involve us evaluating jazz improvisations according to another standard of perfection, the standard of aiming to achieve a perfect communication of emotional or other expression. As articulated in Romantic and late Romantic expression theories, expression theory will see imperfection wherever a performance decision fails to contribute to the expressive particularity of the performance.[32]

Given the need to view musical works and performances from a properly intramural perspective, issues of improvisational excellence are dauntingly complex. Generally, good improvisers will exhibit technical facility and display a resourceful and imaginative reach. They will engage in musical dialogue with the other players. Generally, this will be a respectful and mutually cooperative dialogue. In contemporary jazz, Cecil McBee explains:

> When the band begins to play, ... [y]ou as an individual must realize that I am here. You cannot control me; you can't come up here and ... [pre-determine] that you're going to play certain things. You're not going to play what you practiced.[33]

Bruce Ellis Benson plausibly contends that jazz musicians should also be evaluated under the responsibility of stewardship for the tradition they have inherited as a "gift."[34] But beyond these platitudes it is hard to generalize. Gambits appropriate to one period or setting would be inept or meaningless in another. However, the phenomenology of the knowledgeable listener's experience does suggest one additional but fairly constant norm of artistic quality in improvised music.

With any kind of unfamiliar music, one can be interested in how it will go. Where a work is familiar, a listener can also take an interest in the interpretive choices of the performer. However, with improvised music a knowledgeable listener's focus of interest is complex from the outset. One will be interested in how the musical line itself unfolds and whether it hangs together. At the same time one will be interested in aspects of the *activity itself*.[35] And this is where a peculiarly salient norm surfaces. Even when a performance is going well, a knowledgeable listener will be alert to the musician's "improvisational spirit"[36] – a willingness to take risks, at the peril of the quality of the musical line. And this possibility of failure arises even in the most extreme or "free" case: Ornette Coleman said that he knew he'd succeeded in his approach to free improvisation when he could hear mistakes in the playing.[37] If a performer's choices get her bogged down, or if she runs out of ideas, one worries about how she will deal with the problem. If she pulls the fat out of the fire, we will applaud.[38] One reason that Miles Davis was a great jazz artist, it has been argued, is that he "consistently put himself at risk in his trumpet playing. ... He played closer to the edge than anyone else."[39] However, his true greatness may not be in the risks *he* took, but rather in his encouragement of risk in his band members, and his ability to rescue them when they failed. Pianist Herbie Hancock recalls one such occasion:

> (W)e got to one chord and I played the chord too soon, way too soon; it clashed with everything that was going on. Miles played – it was during his solo – he played something on top of my chord to make it sound right. ... I'm sure he didn't think about it because it wasn't anything he could think about. He didn't hear it as a clash, he heard it as "this is what's happening right now so I'll make the most of it," and he did.[40]

Even here, we find a spectrum of degrees such that knowledgeable judgments will be highly contextualized. Given the style of music he played, we do not mind that Louis Armstrong worked out aspects of his performances in advance. By contrast, listeners have various expectations for music played by Charlie Parker. As alternative takes of his recording of "Embraceable You" for Dial records show, Parker would go in strikingly different directions with a given song, from one performance to an immediately successive one. Further, even more local circumstances make a difference. For instance, a solo in an Ellington concert would be expected to follow a prescribed melody more closely than a jazz jam using the same song.

3. Improvising Retroactively

At first glance, the spontaneity enjoyed by the jazz improviser seems obvious and unqualified. Borrowing words from the jazz pianist Bill Evans, Gioia states that jazz differs from many other arts by its dependence upon a "retrospective" rather than a "blueprint," or "prospective," model. In the prospective model, artists make decisions about what is to come next in light of an overall conception. With the retrospective model, "the artist can start his work with an almost random maneuver – a brush stroke on canvas, an opening line, a musical motif – and then adapt his later moves to this gambit."[41] The jazz improviser may proceed from his opening move in any number of directions.[42] However, we need to sharpen up Gioia's simple statement and make some of its formal parameters more explicit. We shall label these parameters: *situation, forced choice*, and *no script*. (For the time being, we are assuming that we are dealing with something more than mere expressive or ornamental embellishment of a composed tune.)

3A. Situation

We need the first of these three conditions in order to prevent Gioia's statement from collapsing into the blueprint perspective. After all, musical composition too can begin with a motif, chord, or interval and then adapt later moves to the gambit. True, a compositional practice where the composer is stuck with whatever he has laid down so far after his initial musical brush stroke would be analogous to the situation of the improviser. However, this is not what standard composition is like. As we argued in Chapter 7, a difference between ordinary compositional practice and improvisation is that while the composer can erase moves subsequent to the gambit and redo them, the jazz improviser cannot. He can only build upon the steps he has just taken. This is what we mean by referring to the improviser's *situation*. It is nicely captured in a description of jazz playing by drummer Max Roach:

> After you initiate the solo, one phrase determines what the next is going to be. From the first note that you hear, you are responding to what you've just played: you just said this on your instrument, *and now that's a constant.* What follows from that? … When I play, it's like having a conversation with myself.[43]

3B. Forced Choice

This condition draws our attention to another difference between composing and improvising. There is a popular myth that Mozart composed without going through a process of drafting and then revising his musical ideas, but we know that, in many cases, he did revise his compositions. Beethoven's sketchbooks provide a more typical model of the composer: the first ideas for the third symphony (the *Eroica*) were jotted down in 1802, but the symphony was not completed until 1804. The sketchbooks reveal that the symphony as we know it is the product of an initial, more conventional work, which the composer gradually expanded through the incorporation of musical ideas from an independently composed set of piano variations (Op. 35). Based on what appears on subsequent pages of the books, we can also see that he would begin to compose one movement, stop, work on another, stop, work on part of another movement, stop, and so on.[44] In other words, when inspiration failed in one area, Beethoven would set it aside until a later date. The sequence of composition is not reflected in the sequencing of the finished symphony, and a pause in the process of composing the work does not become part of it. In making movies, the filming hardly ever follows the linear narrative of the finished product and an overwhelming amount of it ends up on the cutting room floor. The situation is otherwise in improvisation. As with Beethoven, a jazz musician may find inspiration lacking after a certain point. Well, you might say, he can of course fall silent, can't he? In composed music, a stretch of silence can be part of the work, clearly, but this silence is not evidence of a failure of ideas. In jazz, the nearest parallel is found in the practice of one or more players who "lay out" in order to highlight – and challenge – other players.[45] In contrast, a pause in an improvisational performance, for whatever reason, goes down as part of the music. If the rhythm section creates a break for a soloist, who then fails to fill the break, everyone will understand it to be an error or mishap in the performance, but not what we are calling an imperfection. There is no taking time out, and there is no resequencing. At best, another player can rush in to fill the gap so that the ensemble can recover and continue.

3C. No Script

Finally, we have a negative condition. Like the improviser, the performer of a composed work is faced with many possible notes to play, many possible ways of inflecting them, and many possible ways of placing them rhythmically. However, the performer of a composed work is guided in the placement of those notes, which may be by highly specific antecedent instructions, e.g., scores. In dealing with his options, the improviser cannot, *qua* improviser, rely upon such directives.

Putting these together, the improviser is continuously faced with decisions that he is forced to make, not prescribed for him, and unrevisable once made. He finds himself in a feedback loop. He must produce on-the-spot responses to the music already laid down; and his responses continually force further choices. This becomes nicely complicated when players make on-the-spot responses to the actions of other players.

As it stands, our bald characterization might give a picture of the improviser as an existential hero taking irrational leaps into utter darkness.[46] This is a perspective to be avoided, not only because it is unwarranted, but also because its implausibility feeds the opposite, equally unwarranted, point of view – cynicism about the process.

Another qualification is in order: Following Evans, Gioia bifurcates musical creation into two mutually exclusive aspects, one retrospective, one prospective. However, there is no reason at all why an improvising musician cannot look forward as well. Almost all jazz improvisation is organized around precomposed ingredients. Jazz musicians typically have an overall conception of what they are doing, even if the conception does not dictate the details. As Berliner notes,

> Performers' attention to the artful regulation of their interaction expresses itself most formally in the creation of musical arrangements ... worked out for each piece in advance of music events. Arrangements represent varied degrees of planning and impose different compositional constraints upon improvisers.[47]

An improvising musician can neither do nothing or anything, but there is a large set of options as she is the bridge between the pre-composed and the not-yet played.

4. The Criticism That There Is Too Much Repetition

However, the last thought above should remind us of caveats that really do seem to qualify the freedom of the improviser, and they may seem to do so in ways that add fuel to the formalist fire. The formalist will insist that improvisational jazz practice is much more hidebound than indicated by the abstract schema presented earlier. The alternatives for improvisers are not wide open, but are circumscribed by the character of the music's materials. As we explained in greater detail in Chapter 7, improvisers do not create *ex nihilo*. Jazz improvisers must master a stock of musical figures and phrases out of which they gradually learn to construct solos of their own. They also internalize a cache of musical forms – e.g., meters and chord progressions – that function as frameworks for the direction improvised solos will take. Most obviously, in mainstream jazz, soloists are guided by the underlying harmonic motion exemplified by the song played at the head. A Sonny Stitt blues solo will be guided by a very different chord progression than that guiding a Chet Baker performance of "Body and Soul." Even Keith Jarrett's famously "free" piano improvisations were typically built upon a vamp of familiar chords.[48]

If we take a certain kind of case as a paradigm, the distinction between improvising music and performing an established musical work seems stark. Free improvisation, for instance, seems to inhabit a world of its own completely unrelated to playing tunes or compositions. Normally, however, while improvising a solo, a jazz improviser is either embellishing or drawing materials from a musical work – a Broadway show tune, for example, or an old standard. Such tunes must be included along with the elements of the framework within which improvisers improvise. In mainstream jazz, they supply the chord progressions that players track. A clarification is important here: in previous chapters we argued that many genuinely improvisational performances are not instances of any musical *work*, with everything that this concept implies. The music of these performances is not reidentifiable in multiple instances. On the other hand, when improvisers begin with a standard tune and then move on to "play the changes" without further direct reference to the established melody, the improvised portion is the element that is not reidentifiable.

At this point, the formalist launches the counterargument: consider how little complexity there is in the 32-bar AABA show tune, or in the 12-bar blues form. Surely, the simplicity of such forms cannot help but negatively affect the jazz that results from performing them. While it would be tempting to counter that jazz musicians often come up with ingenious variations on songs and song structures (e.g., Lennie Tristano's reworkings of standards like "Pennies from Heaven" or "I Can't Get Started"), it misses the point. We are not pursuing the issue of how jazz performers breathe new life into works in the course of their performances of them. If that were our goal, we would have no reason to turn to jazz: the argument could be made with respect to popular music more generally.[49]

Suppose we grant the relative simplicity of the pieces that are bases for much jazz improvisation. Despite this simplicity, there is no reason to grant that the improvised music that results from playing them will itself be routine in character. As Barry Kernfeld observes, basic jazz forms are simple because they are aesthetically *unimportant*: "Forms are the least significant building blocks of jazz ... What matters is how those molds are filled."[50]

A well-known distinction by Kendall Walton between a work's *standard* features and its *variable* ones helps here.[51] By some measure or other, instances of almost any kind of music could be deemed monotonous. A string quartet could be monotonous in its use of strings. Bach's music is monotonously duple or triple in meter.[52] But of course, such observations reflect inappropriate ways of measuring. A better way to do so is by reference to deployment of standard features as a framework for exploring variable features. Consider some cases.

Case 1. Reviewing Charlie Parker's Savoy studio recordings, the jazz writer Max Harrison came up with the following results: of some fifty recordings embracing some thirty titles, twenty-two rely on the phrases or chord progressions of familiar simple tunes, e.g., "Back Home in Indiana," "Honeysuckle Rose," and the blues. Nine of them use "I Got Rhythm" chords. Parker's range of favored keys was also quite limited. A broader survey of more than 250 items of his whole recorded output shows them all to be based on equally standard materials. However, the results of Parker's use of them is hardly routine. As Harrison explains, Parker's solos "develop their ideas – in terms of harmonic inflection and rhythmic variation as much as melody – with a precision quite foreign either to popular song writing or to ... [a] reshuffling of stock phrases."[53] Parker found ways to begin a basic linear shape on different beats of the bar, to play it upside down or backwards, and to leave incredible scope for rhythmic variation, particularly at slower tempi, where, departing from the quavers and semiquavers which dominate faster playing, he made figures "blossom" into demisemiquavers, grouped in quintuplets, sextolets, etc. Parker does not simply shuffle through his materials mechanically, but rather looks for ways to exploit them with constantly fresh effects. And it is easy to strengthen the evidence about the case. The alternate recording "takes" that the Savoy and Dial record companies made of Parker's performances often take very different courses from those on the original record releases. So a characterization of musical materials does not tell how a player will use them.

Case 2. To illustrate the same point, compare the approaches of two tenor saxophone players improvising on the same song. When Coleman Hawkins and Lester Young jammed together on the same material, their contributions were in stark contrast – their approach is so different "in almost every particular" that they inspired rival schools of playing.[54] Shared material: very different results. When improvisation goes beyond the basics of expressive ornamental embellishment, it is to be valued not because it provides access to the song – as an expressive instantiation of the work – but rather as a performance in relation to a musical schema extracted from that work. Most of the expressive and aesthetic impact of the performance derives from the choices of the performance – from how the players fill out the schema or pattern, as informed by their tone, melodic sensibility, rhythmic play, and a host of other variables that reflect their personal histories as players.

Case 3. The argument can be further illuminated by reflection upon the jazz avant-garde – initially dubbed "free jazz" – as first instanced in the late 1940s by Lennie Tristano and then in the 1960s by Ornette Coleman and Albert Ayler, and subsequently developed by such players as David Murray and Manfred Schoof.[55] As its fans understand, the label "free" doesn't really apply here without qualification. Setting up no expectations whatsoever, sheer free improvisation would bear no musical significance at all. True, free jazz operates on bases substantially different from those of mainstream jazz. However, like all jazz, it exploits a stock of materials. Where the latter is predicated on harmonic motion, swing, etc., free jazz places a greater emphasis on such qualities as texture and dynamic level. More significantly, Gary Giddins and Scott DeVeaux note that "critics routinely pilloried the avant-garde for rejecting jazz conventions, [but] it ultimately proved to be the most inclusive form of jazz in history."[56] Yet, again, a recitation of materials does not tell us what an improviser will do with them. To contrast two of the earliest free jazz players, Coleman emphasized emotionally expressive lines rooted in the blues tradition, whereas Cecil Taylor's percussive piano work "was virtuosic and intellectual," but with less overt relationship to African-American music.[57]

Every developed art form involves the interplay of standard, variable, and contra-standard features. Thus, evaluations of achievement in a stylistically rich art, such as jazz, are meaningless unless they can track the interplay of these categories of features. Assigning proper weight, in each performance, to what is standard – that it's a quintet performance of "My Funny Valentine," or that it uses a standard blues progression – is the precondition for attending to what is unique, perhaps even surprising, in a performance.

5. The Criticism That There Is a Lack of Form

Let's now turn from the formalist's charge that much of the music is monotonous to the complaint that it tends to be disorderly. This charge returns us directly to the Kantian analysis of perfection with which we started this chapter. Normally, an artifact is produced according to "the concept of what sort of thing it is supposed to be," and the resulting object can then be evaluated as more or less perfect by reference to the concept under which it was produced. Kant's point was developed by one of his first advocates in the English-speaking world, Samuel Taylor

Coleridge. Concerning poetry and, by implication, other art, Coleridge wrote, "[N]othing can permanently please, which does not contain in itself the reason why it is so and not otherwise."[58] To be "legitimate," all parts of an artwork "must mutually explain and support each other; all in their proportion harmonizing with, and supporting [their] purpose." Nothing can be superfluous; nothing can be a random choice. From this perspective, the forced choices and risk-taking of jazz improvisation generally result in a random and disappointing assemblage of inexplicable musical gestures.

The criticism is not without merit, as the description of the Miles Davis performance at the beginning of this chapter suggests. Against this charge, we begin with a point analogous to the one made at the end of the previous section: it is conceptually confused to single out the defects of specific performers or performances if the underlying claim is about the putative defectiveness of the music as a whole. For every example of a lacklustre or badly formed jazz solo, we can cite a beautifully crafted solo – Coleman Hawkins's "Body and Soul," Bix Beiderbecke's "Singin' the Blues," and Charlie Parker's version of "Embraceable You," to name some famous ones. However, it also has to be admitted that the special status of these splendid cases almost marks them as small miracles. Even Parker is not as reliable a producer of musical order as a formalist might wish. However, just as we had resources for mitigating the sins of the first type, we can bring arguments to bear on the present charge.

Jazz has characteristics that seem inherently "wrong" to the ears of a formalist, even by comparison with the modest but reasonably well-made show tunes that the music often uses. In jazz these materials are profoundly disturbed by agendas coming from different quarters. Let us consider two applications of this thought, both of which depend upon a recognition of the cultural matrices out of which the music arises and within which it flourishes.

5A. Non-Conformism

The first application is found in the approach adopted by one group of jazz scholars in the late twentieth century. They explain and justify the putative defectiveness of jazz by situating it within a specific social context. One might call the position *subaltern non-conformism*. In much jazz, we hear what Nathaniel Mackey terms a "fractured" subjectivity reflecting the special circumstances of African-Americans under the conditions of social repression.[59] For example, Mackey cites the anger in the "willfully harsh" tone of players like Albert Ayler. In the words of Jed Rasula, the "voices" in jazz can sound "*dis*unified, … strategically contrapuntal," because they are intended to "glance off and … evade the dominant code."[60] In hard bop, to mention one more example, the expression of African-American defiance and "bitter sarcasm" were advanced – in the view of the white critical establishment – by means of monotonous and "regressive" music.[61] So, we have to admit that many jazz players actively resist the primary formalist criteria of excellence. However, as we have been saying all along, formal criteria are not the only ones for aesthetic success. Where formalism emphasizes aesthetic values considered in isolation from other factors, there is an equally important school of philosophical aesthetics that emphasizes the interplay of aesthetic and expressive properties.[62] Subaltern non-conformism is a variant of this position, asking listeners to be sensitive to sources of musical significance in jazz that expresses African-American alienation.

There is much to be said for this approach. Of course, it faces the problem of providing criteria for deciding when a performance really does bear the kind of meaning that gives it non-formal value – rather than being, simply, disordered music with little or no significance. Does Don Cherry make a mistake when he "hits a clinker" at the four-minute mark of "Lonely Woman,"[63] or does he make a strategical intrusion to mark his independence from the group? More importantly, subaltern non-conformism surely has limited application: there is no reason to accept it as the explanation of everything that sounds like a "clam." Just as there are "slips of the tongue" and malapropisms in the act of speaking, there are errors in jazz improvisation.[64] The argument that we should be more appreciative of Albert Ayler's anger in his playing will hardly help us appreciate the apparent roughness of jazz performers to whom we have no reason to attribute social alienation at all – white jazz figures like clarinetist Pee Wee Russell, for instance, whose "daring and nakedness and intuition" often strayed far from the path of musical logic.[65] We might retreat to the position that Russell was a hipster who adopted the *persona* of the alienated subaltern, an act of racial cooptation that we have discussed in Chapter 5 as the minstrel hypothesis. But now the wedge that invited us to value some musical disruption as expressively valuable will hinge in the opposite direction, and will ask us to concede that a vast swathe of jazz innovation is improperly grounded in African-American experiences. What, then, are we to say of jazz performances that do not exhibit this kind of disorder at all?

As we argued in Chapter 5, we think that the minstrel hypothesis becomes vacuous when indiscriminately applied to popular music, whether to white jazz performers or to popular musicians in general. We grant that subaltern non-conformism is a prism through which to understand some jazz performances. However, we must be prepared to say that many other prisms are needed, as appropriate to different movements and performers. Erected into a principle, non-conformism would marginalize such cases only on penalty of espousing an objectionably narrow essentialism.[66] However, we did not retreat from an essentialist definition of jazz in Chapter 3 in order to embrace an essentialist interpretive framework at a later stage.

5B. Syncretism

Whatever be the virtues of non-conformism for our understanding of the features of *some* jazz performances, the problem we are addressing is a more general one.

This suggests that we need to broaden the position just described into a general framework that might be called *syncretism*.

This amended appeal to socio-historical context also maintains that the formalist's demand for more formal consistency in jazz presupposes European criteria that are too narrow. The syncretist argues that the distinctive features of jazz result from the interaction of culturally distinct practices — or families of practices — some European, some African. So, the claim against formalists is that they bring inappropriate criteria to bear on forms of music that result from this interaction. It is *not*, however, the view that familiar, European formal criteria play *no* role in the success or failure of a jazz performance. Nor is it the view that "European" formal values will be characteristics of performances by white players such as Dave Brubeck and Bill Evans. Charlie Parker's playing displays both an African-American approach to rhythmic propulsion and a concern, very much like J. S. Bach's music, for polyphonic voice-leading.[67]

From the perspective of syncretism, we can understand the presence of some apparent disorder in jazz as a byproduct of the way the European melody is deflected in it by African influences. Unlike European melodies, African ones are typically "end-repeating." When African melodies are varied, the part that changes is usually the beginning, while the endings remain comparatively similar to each other. This is particularly noticeable in vocal blues. To the Eurocentrist's ear, the music seems to be running out of ideas just when it is supposed to be most charged with them. A more charitable view — even on the formalist's own grounds — would be that the common endings bring unity to the previous variety. But this does not explain why the vast majority of jazz solos, within performances, end without any sense of arrival or purpose. William Day summarizes this tendency:

> "When you solo, tell a story," the old advice of the jazz musician goes. But stories have endings, familiar ways of tying things together; so it can surprise us to notice that the exemplary jazz soloist has not devised such ways, that he does not see the end as having special importance.[68]

Clearly, we cannot entirely rationalize jazz melody while remaining within the formalist perspective. For instance, melody in jazz is deflected by rhythmic agendas that have partly African roots. Consider the way Louis Armstrong would repeat a three-note figure many times — as in the wind-up solo of "West End Blues." If we regard the music from the point of view of the characteristic features of European melody, we will not get the point of the effort. If we hear it the right way, the music seems bursting at the seams with its powerful rhythmic inflection. For related reasons, the achievement of a collective groove often takes precedence over other modes of organization.[69]

The most difficult features of jazz melody for the Eurocentric ear to appreciate, however, are those that reflect the relationship between jazz melody and speech; a connection that clearly reflects African practice.[70] For instance, African music brings "call-and-response" effects to jazz, e.g., the echoing pairs of riffs one hears particularly in swing music. To the formalist, insensitive either to the ground of such practices in linguistic practice, or to their rhythmic function, such devices can seem pointlessly repetitive. In jazz, horns and voices have mirrored each other almost from the beginning. Instrumental lines will often be intentionally pushed off course to convey the effect of an expletive, a sob, or a laugh. Voices in jazz learned to sound like horns, as in scat, while horns learned to "speak." The strategy by which horn players sound conversational becomes particularly pointed when several of them dialogue with each other. In such cases, the formal musical values of abstract sound-structures give way to quasi-linguistic ones.

All this is not to say that repetition is foreign to the Eurocentric ear or that all Eurocentric music is formalist. But in jazz, especially with respect to the call-and-response use of horns, the difference is stark. So, what may be a matter of music gone wrong from one point of view is part of the expectations of a seasoned listener of jazz.

According to one view of this linguistic dimension of the music, jazz performers often engage in what Henry Louis Gates calls "signifyin'."[71] To signify in speech is to engage in a distinctively evasive kind of African-American repartee. The effect — which listeners on the other side of the social line are intended *not* to get — is typically satirical or mocking. In this vein, Robert Walser devotes an essay to recuperating the Miles Davis performance cited at the beginning of this chapter by arguing that the trumpet man was "playing off on" white pop singer Tony Bennett's approach to that famous jazz standard.[72] At this point, the syncretist's argument begins to subsume that of the non-conformist. The salient features of jazz are resultants of the intersection of distinct practices and intentions, which become transfigured in the music by their interaction. Contrary to the formalist, the peculiar harmonic, rhythmic, and melodic values that give jazz its special interest are emergent ones, not just more of the same values already well established in European music.

6. Risk

Even if we bracket much of the apparent disorder in improvised jazz by appeal to the strategies discussed so far, the formalist may still object that much of the music is fraught with a kind of disorder that cannot be placed in a better light by these means. As indicated at the beginning of this chapter, we need to frame this residual element in the right way in order to articulate what might be said in mitigation of it.

Improvisation involves risk. In a situation involving risk, something of value must be at stake — typically, the formal character of the musical product. However, the situation in jazz is distinctive. The risks one takes in building a bridge — to consider a case of a different kind — do not typically make themselves felt in the resulting bridge and the stakes here may be too high. In the case of jazz improvisation, however, this is exactly what does happen. The risk-taking process itself can become part of the target of our appreciative attention. But that is not all, as noted earlier. In the bridge-building case, plans can be revised in the middle of the project if trouble arises. With improvised music, as stressed earlier, all attempts at revision become part of the music played. To frame this delicate situation correctly, we need to augment the formal account of the parameters of improvisation in section 2 with the concept of a *regulative ideal* – or, more precisely, a small hierarchy of such ideals, because some take priority over others. However, as in the case of the bridge, we think of improvisation, not as composition, but rather as construction. Unlike the constructed bridge, in improvisation, there is no blueprint. With this contrast in mind, let us now consider three levels of regulative ideals in jazz improvisation.

6A. Primary Level

An improviser (a) presents music intended to be worth hearing, by (b) determining a significant number of its features *as* he or she plays. Players may not always satisfy (a) while satisfying (b). However, it is a regulative ideal that an authentic player will aim to do both. If so, then even at this basic level – the *primary level*, let's call it – even players like the putatively uninventive George Brunis and Kenny G take some risks.

6B. Secondary Level

In one of his essays, Hodeir concentrates on a particularly unexpected F# in a famous recorded performance of "Bags's Groove" by Thelonious Monk.[73] Such an example illustrates a *secondary* regulative ideal beyond the primary obligation. A distinctive feature of jazz is the way its players look for opportunities to make daring moves. In its reflection of this goal, the title of one of Whitney Balliett's collections of jazz criticism – *The Sound of Surprise* – is particularly apt.[74]

This second-level ideal appears to govern musical practice in much improvised music outside jazz as well as in. Incidentally, the unexpected in jazz improvisation is quite different from the unexpected in a composed work. As we discussed in Chapter 9, we can look forward to the same "surprise" in a musical work on subsequent hearings. However, this is not the case with genuinely improvised music. We anticipate that some readers will immediately disagree with this statement because they will be thinking of their favorite jazz recordings, where, of course, an astonishing passage can be heard again and again.

In connection with this secondary ideal, consider Sargeant's vivid description of collective improvisation:

> When ... players ... are not quite sure what is going to happen next the music takes on the aspect of a tussle in which individual players may actually try to unhorse each other, as well as the audience, by means of conflicting

rhythmic impacts. When players, dancers and audience alike are hanging desperately to their sense of rhythmic orientation on the one hand and are violently disturbing it (or listening to it being violently disturbed) on the other, the result is jazz in its purist form.[75]

When we say the players are really "cookin'" we are applauding the heat and the mixture of ingredients, but with a loose and flexible recipe.

Interestingly, in such a context, instrumentalists do not have to reach out very far musically in order to unbalance other players. A musician working by himself, however, has a private project, namely, to outdo himself.

A daring player may pick notes that carry him to the edge of or even beyond the bounds of what is acceptable in that style. Or he may go to or beyond the limit of what he is able to further develop. In other words, undertaking to put his musicianship to test, there will, obviously, be occasions of failure. Indeed, in taking radical chances, the more likely it is that pursuit of this regulative ideal will interfere with the realization of even modest first-level aims. On this score, singer Carol Sloane shares the story of how, night after night opening for Oscar Peterson at the Village Vanguard, she embarrassed herself by trying to impress Peterson in response to his nightly request for "My Ship." But Peterson withheld his approval until she "sang it straight as a dime." The problem, she realized, was that "I wasn't ready to do what I thought I should do." She was taking too many risks and realized it was better to "pull back" until she gained more experience.[76] Understandably, many jazz improvisers only rarely exhibit this kind of daring; and few are so adventurous all the time. It is no wonder that some performers will choose to play it safe, preferring to offer a safe and polished solo to the paying customers. In light of this, consider Whitney Balliett's description of the playing of trombonist George Brunis, that his solos on a certain July evening in 1972 were "still intact, note for note, thirty-five years after he invented them."[77]

6C. Tertiary Level

Finally, while we cannot safely generalize the point across the world's improvised music, every jazz improviser acknowledges a *tertiary* regulative ideal to break out of the hand-me-down repertoire he has internalized. All players have heard the kind of advice Charlie Mingus was always giving, namely to reach "beyond their formulas."[78] Miles Davis once went so far as to forbid Herbie Hancock from playing any "butter notes" (i.e., obvious choices, given the musical framework); Hancock found that his playing was revitalized by the limitation.[79] Under this tertiary ideal, players do not merely strive to surprise us while working within an inherited style, but look for ways to push beyond those boundaries and by doing so, surprise comes naturally. Such revisions typically meet with resistance. Bandleader Cab Calloway was not sympathetic to the young Dizzy Gillespie's attempt to break out beyond his formulas into the new harmonic territory of bebop. (Fellow jazz musician Jonah Jones says that Calloway complained that he wasn't going to have any of Dizzy's "Chinese music" in *his* band.[80])

Most improvisational efforts fall between the options sketched by the first two levels. But it is standard within the institution of jazz that players will look for opportunities to go beyond them. There is obviously no recipe for how to do this. Something like courage is required.[81] But even the most willing revolutionary may be able to accomplish nothing useful if the time isn't right for it. We can, of course, cite exemplary cases of such breakouts. Looming above all others – according to most accounts – was Louis Armstrong, whose approach to rhythm took the music away from the ragtime-era syncopation that had earlier defined it, and thereby liberated the soloist to become a freely swinging performer. Beyond Armstrong, the obvious short list of such cases includes Charlie Parker, Ornette Coleman, and John Coltrane. Coleman, for instance, broke with the steady "netted" rhythm of mainstream jazz in favor of a constantly varying tempo *rubato*.[82]

Now every jazz player knows that even the approximate realization of these regulative ideals is frustrated by practical considerations. Think of Benny Goodman's players during the band's sensational run at the Paramount Theater and the Pennsylvania Hotel in 1937, when they were obliged to play as many as ten shows a day. Under such pressure, they had little alternative but to work out basic solos on tunes like "Sing, Sing, Sing," and to play them repeatedly with only slight variations. (The problem was compounded whenever players were obliged to repeat solos note for note because they had become record hits.) However, jazz improvisers have always understood these demands for what they were – compromises of their real aims. Once a musician establishes a certain style, not to mention a well-known rendition of a popular jazz piece, it may be difficult to break the mold. To a certain extent, this is true in other forms of art and entertainment, even in painting. But, as so much of jazz is the environment for improvisation, the jazz improviser becomes a different kind of performer from the musicians, jazz or otherwise, who play it safe.

Moving beyond regulative ideals to the realm of pragmatic strategies of jazz musicians, there is an additional species of risk-taking that merits attention: dependence on alcohol and narcotics. The association of jazz and narcotics – and not just alcohol – dates from the start of the Jazz Age. As early as 1919, one song about jazz associates it with "dream pipe dope ... opium."[83] It is a sad legacy that not all jazz greats led lives that were healthy, wealthy, or wise. Many of the important figures in jazz, black and white, male and female, had fallen on hard times – heroin addiction being the hardest fall. Charlie Parker, Miles Davis, Billie Holiday, Chet Baker, Sonny Rollins, Anita O'Day, and Bill Evans, to name only a conspicuous few, found heroin and had to struggle in and out of its use.[84] It is impossible to say how much of this derives from the intense and itinerant lifestyles of musicians, and from other socio-economic pressures. But drug use is also encouraged by the belief that it stimulates musical creativity and stamina, and that it is especially conducive to improvising.

It is widely held that the relaxing effects of opiates are beneficial because they block out stage fright, personal issues, and "other distractions," thereby generating a state of mind fixed solely on the music.[85] Some musicians sought the way "it seemed to slow things down," and many subscribed to the view that it could "make you *hear* better."[86] On the other hand, Elvin Jones stresses that there is a wide gap between subjective self-evaluation and the objective effects on the music – between "what you think you are under drugs and what you really are."[87] Although it took him some time to realize it, he came to see that playing while high "destroyed" his time-keeping abilities. And while there are many anecdotes about how well Charlie Parker played after injecting heroin, we also have the recorded evidence of how drug addiction interfered with his timing and concentration, most notoriously his "disturbing" attempts to record "Lover Man" and "Gypsy" on July 29, 1946.[88] Without moralizing, we can say that the alleged benefits of drug use have all too frequently derailed musicians from their musical aims. In the words of the often-quoted summary of Red Rodney, "It ruined most of the people" who used.[89] Direct interference with performance skills was compounded by the non-musical distractions of deteriorating health, the struggles of drug rehabilitation, and legal troubles (including, in a number of high-profile cases, periods of incarceration). The general consensus is that Miles Davis and Sonny Rollins played better after they were free of drugs, and that Charlie Parker and Billie Holiday succeeded despite, not because of, their heroin addictions.

7. Compensations

Let us now bring the foregoing to bear on the unresolved dimension of the formalist's complaint. It isn't that the formalist is just wrong. Nor is it simply that what the formalist proposes is incomplete. The formalist's values are values we listeners prize, as do jazz musicians. However, those values are systematically qualified by other aspects of the music that are no less interesting. We can understand the problem better with the help of a particular kind of example.

In the long-playing record era, when jazz soloists could begin to stretch out in their recorded solos, some gained a reputation for unusually consistent playing. The critic Nat Hentoff once drew attention to the remarkable coherence of Paul Desmond's alto sax lines, for instance. In his playing, Hentoff said, we heard a mind moving with "eerie swiftness."[90] This sounds like a description of music to which no formalist could object. Hentoff's point is that Desmond seemed able at once to invent both a germinal musical idea and a set of well-realized implications of it. The whole gave the effect of having been composed at leisure. But the description is curiously problematic. Just because Desmond's mind moves with such eerie swiftness, we are not sure we hear it really moving at all. Perhaps Desmond has a phenomenal memory for solos that he worked out in advance, and they merely *feel* improvised.[91] If we knew that a genuine spirit of improvisation was absent, we would reclassify the kind of thing we were witnessing and would significantly downgrade our estimation of his performance. Philosophers, and philosophers of art in particular, are familiar with cases of perceptual indiscernibles, which belong to entirely different categories and require diverse responses and interpretive strategies. Only out of any context would they be mistaken for the same thing.

Now, Hentoff may be guilty of slight hyperbole in his description of Desmond's playing. However, for the sake of argument, assume he is correct. If so, then we may feel that this adds to Desmond's lustre: he is able to cover his tracks, so to say, by embedding his explorations seamlessly into the well-wrought music he plays. But if we never hear Desmond groping, or recovering his balance, then we may wonder just how daring he really is. The point is not to resolve the case definitively. It is an illustration of a general tension built into our reception of this kind of music. It reflects, in part, the importance we place on the *process* by which improvised jazz is made as well as on the sonic result.

We can be interested in how a bit of unfamiliar music of any sort will go. We can do this without having a sense of any actual activity transpiring before us at all. Indeed, there may be none – as with a piece of computer or tape-generated music. With improvised music, too, we obviously have an interest in how the musical line will proceed. However, we are also interested in the player's activity itself. We are interested in his on-the-spot gambits and responses. If things are going well, we wonder if he can sustain the level. If he takes risks that get him into trouble, we worry about how he will deal with it. If he "pulls the fat out of the fire," we applaud. Wynton Marsalis points to the beginning of Coltrane's "Resolution" (on *A Love Supreme*, 1965), where "the rhythm section stumbles and the band almost falls apart. Instead of stopping, they regroup and go on to record one of the most swinging tracks in jazz history."[92] Our overall interest in such music is predicated on both aspects of it – the quality of the result *and* the adventurous character of the actions that generate it.

The situation has a paradoxical quality. With many performances, the tidier a player's performance, the more routine it is liable to sound. The more ambitious the performance, the more likely it is to be messy. In the degree to which a player's performance takes on the smooth quality Desmond's playing exhibits, its searching character will correspondingly tend to slide from view. To the extent that this searching quality is evident, the more likely we are to register disorder in the music.

The problem we are addressing here, note, is distinct from a purely formal trade-off in jazz that is superficially similar to it. It has often been noted that group improvisation in early New Orleans music faced the difficulty that the players could only preserve some harmonic order because the musical parameters were restricted harmonically. A variant problem arose in the bop era, when the criterion for what notes were harmonically acceptable for soloists to play was greatly expanded. The trade-off was that accompaniments often had to be pared down in order to avoid unwanted clashes with the player out front. However, the double bind of which we are speaking here cannot be reduced to this formal problem. It is a problem that can be identified in solo performances, where no problem of coordination arises.

Clearly, the dimension of the music just reviewed is complicated by aspects of the music that syncretism and non-conformism profile. However, granting that those perspectives explain why certain features of jazz should be seen as immunized against standard formalist criteria, it remains the case that jazz improvisation is subject to contingencies that reflect its sheer improvisational character. This is one of the most fundamental reasons for calling the music "an imperfect art." But the constant risk of imperfection is a vital dimension of the music, for along with it come compensations for those listeners whose attention is not controlled by strictly formalist considerations. These compensations will be minimized if the risk of imperfection is also minimized. We call attention to three such compensations that improvisation brings to jazz. (We recognize that they are also present in jazz that is experimental in other ways.)

First, there is the general compensation that comes from expanding audience focus beyond the character of the musical product to include the *activity* of generating it. The listener who cannot do this can easily remain bewildered by the music's chaotic aspects. And he can miss the excitement of savoring that the music is being carved out as it is being played – which happens to be, after all, the improvised string's *raison d'être*. With deference to the other improvisational performing arts,[93] an aesthetician might say that a jazz improviser is the artist who comes closest to exemplifying art as *activity*, and not merely as disinherited *product*. The phenomenology of our appreciation of such music is striking: we find ourselves slipping back and forth between our hopes for the ultimate quality of the music and our fascination with the activity by which it is generated – even when those actions appear to threaten other qualities of the resulting music. The tension contributes to the music's fascination, rather than detracting from it.

Second, compensations also arise from our appreciation of the ways players convert their confrontation with the problem we have described into an individualized feature of style. Miles Davis's playing, for instance, typically consisted of short, meditative bursts of notes interspersed with pauses. The pauses are not merely the breathing spaces demanded by playing a wind instrument. They allowed Miles partly to transform hesitations about what to play into music already played.

Third and finally, there is the compensation that derives from the off-the-wall moves with which players try – and often manage – to redeem the missteps for which their daring is responsible. The capacity to repair a misstep is, Ingrid Monson observes, "one of the most highly prized skills of an improviser."[94] However, if it were a category mistake to identify these missteps as imperfections, so that they are not genuine imperfections, then it would also be a category mistake to prize this skill in jazz improvisers. It is not an extramural perspective that identifies imperfection followed by improvised correction: this is what jazz players experience, too.[95] We conclude by returning to a classic example that we have discussed before.

In the early notes of the famous *a cappella* introduction to his Okeh recording of "West End Blues," Louis Armstrong leads off with a thrillingly nervy trumpet flourish. But one can sense that right from the start he's going too quickly into those first notes. Armstrong's musically beautiful third-measure solution seems to be as spontaneous as the gesture that got him into trouble in the first place. He slows down the overall tempo just a little and, as Gunther Schuller notes, in such a way as to place the new notes in a definite rhythmic relationship to the previous tempo, so that he preserves an underlying pulse through the change.[96] Much of the beauty of the passage reflects, first, his spontaneous plunge into the unknown and, second, his equally spontaneous solution to his self-created problem. The moment is a brief one. It is a good example of the accidents that arise from taking risks, and then taking advantage of those accidents. But it is out of such stuff that the finest improvisational jazz is made.

Notes

1 René Descartes, *Meditations on First Philosophy: With Selections from the Objections and Replies*, ed. John Cottingham (Cambridge: Cambridge University Press, 1996), Third and Fourth Meditations.

2 Immanuel Kant, *Critique of the Power of Judgment*, ed. Paul Guyer, trans. Paul Guyer and Eric Matthews (Cambridge: Cambridge University Press, 2000), 112–113.

3 Kant, *Critique*, 112.

4 For examples concerning harmonic relationships, see Paul F. Berliner, *Thinking in Jazz: The Infinite Art of Improvisation* (Chicago: University of Chicago Press, 1994), 250–251.

5 Ted Gioia, *The Imperfect Art: Reflections on Jazz and Modern Culture* (Oxford: Oxford University Press, 1988).

6 Barry Kernfeld, *What to Listen for in Jazz* (New Haven: Yale University Press, 1995), 161.

7 The performance is on *My Funny Valentine: Miles Davis in Concert*, Columbia CS 9106.

8 John Mehegan, quoted in John Szwed, *So What: The Life of Miles Davis* (New York: Simon & Schuster, 2002), 50.

9 The full session of November 26, 1945, can be heard on Charlie Parker, *The Complete Savoy Studio Sessions* (Arista Records, 1978).

10 Theodor W. Adorno, "On Popular Music," *Studies in Philosophy and Social Science* 9 (1941): 17–48. On this and Adorno's views about popular music in general, see Lee B. Brown, "Adorno's Critique of Popular Culture: The Case of Jazz Music," *Journal of Aesthetic Education* 26:1 (1992): 17–31, and Theodore Gracyk, *Rhythm and Noise: An Aesthetics of Rock* (Durham: Duke University Press, 1996), chap. 6.

11 Winthrop Sargeant, *Jazz, Hot and Hybrid*, rev. ed. (New York: Da Capo, 1976), 247.

12 Berliner, *Thinking in Jazz*, chap. 9.

13 Henry Martin, *Charlie Parker and Thematic Improvisation* (Lanham, MD: Scarecrow Press, 2001), 116.

14 Martin, *Charlie Parker*, 99.

15 Gunther Schuller, "Sonny Rollins and the Challenge of Thematic Improvisation," in *Musings: The Musical Worlds of Gunther Schuller* (Oxford: Oxford University Press, 1986), 86–97, at 87.

16 Krin Gabbard, "Introduction: The Jazz Canon and its Consequences," in *Jazz Among the Discourses*, ed. Krin Gabbard (Durham: Duke University Press, 1995), 1–28, at 13.

17 R. A. Sharpe, *Philosophy of Music: An Introduction* (New York: Routledge, 2004), 57.

18 This line of argument is criticized in Daniel Martin Feige, *Philosophie des Jazz* (Berlin: Suhrkamp Verlag, 2014), 30–31. However, his criticism assumes that "imperfection" is inherently second-class. We, however, see it as a *pro tanto* negative value, one that would, by itself, be a defect but which might, given the right circumstances, contribute in some positive way to the overall achievement. In this respect, imperfect playing is like funky playing.

19 The classic essay on this problem is Laudan Nooshin, "Improvisation as 'Other': Creativity, Knowledge and Power – The Case of Iranian Classical Music," *Journal of the Royal Music Association* 128:2 (2003): 242–296.

20 Sargeant, *Jazz*, 253–278.

21 E.g., André Hodeir, *Toward Jazz*, trans. Noel Burch (New York: Grove Press, 1962), 163; Roger Scruton, "Why Read Adorno?" in *Understanding Music: Philosophy and Interpretation* (London: Continuum, 2009), 205–227, at 224.

22 Ingrid Monson, *Saying Something: Jazz Improvisation and Interaction* (Chicago: University of Chicago Press, 1996), 134.

23 Monson, *Saying Something*, 86–87, 103–104; see also Robert Walser, "Out of Notes: Signification, Interpretation, and the Problem of Miles Davis," in *Jazz Among the Discourses*, ed. Krin Gabbard (Durham: Duke University Press, 1995), 165–188.

24 Peter Kivy, *The Fine Art of Repetition* (Cambridge: Cambridge University Press, 1993), 329.

25 Kivy, *Fine Art of Repetition*, 341.

26 Miles Davis, *In Person Friday and Saturday Nights at the Blackhawk, Complete* (Sony Legacy 2003).

27 Julian Dodd is the most prominent contemporary proponent of this position; see his *Works of Music: An Essay in Ontology* (Oxford: Oxford University Press, 2007), 205, see also 6. Dodd's argument depends on the premise that musical works (including Coltrane's *A Love Supreme*) are uncreated, eternally existent types, and that this is a "default position" (3, 5) that has not been dethroned by counterarguments. Like its ancestor position, formalism, this strikes us as a thoroughly Eurocentric perspective. See also Ben Caplan, "Review of Julian Dodd, *Works of Music: An Essay in Ontology*," *British Journal of Aesthetics* 47:4 (2007): 445–446.

28 The best introduction to the general position is Stephen Davies, *Musical Works and Performances: A Philosophical Exploration* (Oxford: Clarendon Press, 2001), chap. 2.

29 Dodd, *Works of Music*, 174.

30 Construed as an uncreated, eternally existing type, the sound pattern "ə ləv səprim" has no semantic dimension: its meaning is only *contingently* related to American English.

31 Arthur C. Danto, *The Transfiguration of the Commonplace: A Philosophy of Art* (Cambridge, MA: Harvard University Press, 1981), 2–5.

32 The best example of such a theory is that of R. G. Collingwood, *The Principles of Art* (Oxford: Oxford University Press, 1958). The strict evaluative standards of expression theory are seen in Collingwood's extended analysis of T. S. Eliot's "Sweeney Among the Nightingales" (333–336); the poem's value depends on the degree to which each detail contributes to its expressive particularity.

33 Quoted in Monson, *Saying Something*, 67. Worried that undue emphasis on extemporaneous improviser interaction reduces improvisation to "a glorified love-in dressed up as art," Gary Peters recommends understanding improvisation as an engagement with the past (*The Philosophy of Improvisation* (Chicago: University of Chicago Press, 2009), 3).

34 Bruce Ellis Benson, *The Improvisation of Musical Dialogue: A Phenomenology of Music* (Cambridge: Cambridge University Press, 2003), 187–188.

35 Philip Alperson, "On Musical Improvisation," *Journal of Aesthetics and Art Criticism* 43:1 (1984): 17–29, at 23.

36 Stefan Caris Love, "The Jazz Solo as Virtuous Act," *Journal of Aesthetics and Art Criticism* 74:1 (2016): 61–74; Love cites Berliner, *Thinking in Jazz*, 192–220.
37 The remark – "It was when I found out I could make mistakes that I knew I was on to something" – is frequently quoted without citation, but it first appeared in Martin Williams, "Ornette Coleman – The Meaning of Innovation," *Evergreen Review* 4 (15) 1960: 123–134, at 126.
38 This is not only true of jazz. In Iranian instrumental music, the unpredicted phrases are most prized. See Bruno Nettl, *The Radif of Persian Music: Studies of Structure and Cultural Context*, rev. ed. (Champaign: University of Illinois Press, 1992), 191–192.
39 Walser, "Out of Notes," 344, 346. Despite Walser's emphasis on Davis's signifying with his playing, his extreme focus on Davis at the expense of the rest of the quintet is an ironic example of Monson's point about the intrusion of "standard" values.
40 Quoted in Keith Waters, *The Studio Recordings of the Miles Davis Quintet, 1965–68* (Oxford: Oxford University Press, 2011), 17; originally quoted in an article in *Down Beat* (1974). For a different interpretation of the significance of Hancock's anecdote, see Feige, *Philosophie des Jazz*, 80–81. For more on musical "saves" in jazz, see Berliner, *Thinking in Jazz*, 210–216.
41 Gioia, *Imperfect Art*, 60. The description is prompted by Bill Evans's liner notes to Miles Davis's famous recording, *Kind of Blue* (Columbia CS 8163). Evans borrows the idea from a description of a form of Asian visual art in which the artist is required to be spontaneous.
42 We are sensitive to the question of which pronoun to use here – "he," "she," or "s/he." The problem is exacerbated in this case by the fact that women are still, unfortunately, in the minority in the jazz business. To use "she" or even "s/he" gives the misleading impression that the facts are otherwise.
43 Quoted in Berliner, *Thinking in Jazz*, 192, emphasis added.
44 Lewis Lockwood and Alan Gosman, *Beethoven's "Eroica" Sketchbook: A Critical Edition* (Champaign: University of Illinois Press, 2013).
45 See Berliner, *Thinking in Jazz*, 376.
46 However, see Jean-Paul Sartre, "I Discovered Jazz in America," trans. Ralph de Toledano, *Saturday Review of Literature* (November 29, 1947): 48–49. Sartre saw jazz as a kind of metaphor for his existentialist vision of human life.
47 Berliner, *Thinking in Jazz*, 289.
48 See Peter Elsdon, *Keith Jarrett's* The Köln Concert (Oxford: Oxford University Press, 2013), 70–71.
49 Such an argument can be found in Alison Stone, *The Value of Popular Music: An Approach from Post-Kantian Aesthetics* (New York: Palgrave Macmillan, 2016).
50 Kernfeld, *What to Listen for*, 73.
51 See Kendall L. Walton, "Categories of Art," *Philosophical Review* 79:3 (1970): 334–367.
52 For this very reason, Indian composer Vishnudas Shirali dismissed a Mozart symphony as "baby music ... for little children." Anecdote related in Jonathan Cott, *Dinner with Lenny: The Last Long Interview with Leonard Bernstein* (Oxford: Oxford University Press, 2013), 137.
53 Max Harrison, *A Jazz Retrospect* (New York: Crescendo, 1976), 15–17. See also Martin, *Charlie Parker*, chaps. 3, 4, and 5.
54 Gary Giddins and Scott DeVeaux. *Jazz* (New York: W. W. Norton, 2009), 251–252.
55 A short overview is Alyn Shipton, *A New History of Jazz*, rev. and updated ed. (London: Bloomsbury, 2007), chap. 17.
56 Giddins and DeVeaux, *Jazz*, 472.
57 Giddins and DeVeaux, *Jazz*, 461; their comparison is expanded here.
58 Samuel Taylor Coleridge, *Biographia Literaria*, ed. G. Watson (London: Dent, 1965), 172.
59 See Nathaniel Mackey, "Other: From Noun to Verb," in *Jazz Among the Discourses*, ed. Krin Gabbard (Durham: Duke University Press, 1995), 76–99, at 87.

60 Jed Rasula, "The Media of Memory: The Seductive Menace of Records in Jazz History," in *Jazz Among the Discourses*, ed. Krin Gabbard (Durham: Duke University Press, 1995), 134–162, at 155.
61 David H. Rosenthal, *Hard Bop: Jazz and Black Music 1955–1965* (New York: Oxford University Press, 1992), 128–129.
62 E.g., Jenefer Robinson, *Deeper than Reason: Emotion and Its Role in Literature, Music, and Art* (Oxford: Clarendon Press, 2005).
63 Giddins and DeVeaux, *Jazz*, 453.
64 Love, "Jazz Solo," 64–65.
65 Whitney Balliett, *American Musicians II: Seventy-One Portraits in Jazz* (Jackson: University Press of Mississippi, 1986), 134.
66 Essentialisms are not all of the formalist kind, as explained in Lee B. Brown, "Afrocentrism Old and New: The Critical Theory of Jazz," *Journal of Aesthetics and Art Criticism* 57 (1999): 235–246.
67 Martin, *Charlie Parker*, 15–20.
68 William Day, "The Ends of Improvisation," *Journal of Aesthetics and Art Criticism* 68:3 (2010): 291–296, at 293. Day reads the tendency to avoid "endings" on solos as a way of signaling that mutual responsiveness is more important than closure (296).
69 See Monson, *Saying Something*, chap. 2, and Berliner, *Thinking in Jazz*, 349–352.
70 See the seminal essay on the matter by Jeannette Robinson Murphy, "The Survival of African Music in America," *Popular Science Monthly* (September 1899): 660–671.
71 Henry Louis Gates, *The Signifying Monkey: A Theory of African-American Literary Criticism* (New York and Oxford: Oxford University Press, 1988). Gates spells the colloquial "signifyin'" ("signifying") for purposes of his own that do not concern us here.
72 Walser, "Out of Notes."
73 Hodeir, *Toward Jazz*, 177. The performance is Monk's solo on Prestige 7109.
74 Whitney Balliett, *The Sound of Surprise: 46 Pieces on Jazz* (New York: Dutton, 1961).
75 Sargeant, *Jazz*, 241–242.
76 Wayne Enstice and Janis Stockhouse, *Jazzwomen: Conversations with Twenty-One Musicians* (Bloomington: Indiana University Press, 2004), 305–306.
77 Whitney Balliett, *New York Notes* (Boston: Houghton Mifflin, 1976), 31.
78 Rosenthal, *Hard Bop*, 137.
79 Berliner, *Thinking in Jazz*, 250.
80 In the documentary film *The Spitball Story*, 1997, directed by Jean Bach.
81 For development of this point, see Love, "Jazz Solo," 69–70.
82 See his own words in Michael J. Budds, *Jazz in the Sixties* (Iowa City: University of Iowa Press, 1978), 69.
83 Catherine Tackley, *The Evolution of Jazz in Britain, 1880–1935* (New York: Routledge, 2017), 24.
84 A list of other jazz musicians whose careers were complicated by drug issues includes Joe Pass, Fats Navarro, Jaco Pastorius, Red Rodney, Dexter Gordon, Gerry Mulligan, John Coltrane, Hank Mobley, Max Roach, and Jackie McLean.
85 Martin Torgoff, *Bop Apocalypse: Jazz, Race, the Beats, and Drugs* (New York: Da Capo, 2017), 174; a very similar view is articulated by Elina Hytönen-Ng, *Experiencing 'Flow' in Jazz Performance* (New York: Routledge, 2013), 142–143.
86 Geoffrey C. Ward and Ken Burns, *Jazz: A History of America's Music* (New York: Knopf, 2000), 358.
87 Quoted in Balliett, *American Musicians II*, 466; Larry Coryell makes a parallel point about the "fallacy" that drugs improve playing (*Improvising: My Life in Music* (New York: Backbeat Books, 2007), 21).
88 Carl Woideck, *Charlie Parker: His Music and Life* (Ann Arbor: University of Michigan Press, 1998), 129–130.

89 Ira Gitler, *Swing to Bop: An Oral History of the Transition in Jazz in the 1940s* (Oxford: Oxford University Press, 1985), 282.
90 Nat Hentoff, quoted by Gioia, *Imperfect Art*, 88–89.
91 See Andy Hamilton, *Aesthetics and Music* (London: Continuum, 2007), 202–203.
92 Wynton Marsalis with Geoffrey C. Ward, *Moving to Higher Ground: How Jazz Can Change Your Life* (New York: Random House, 2009), 72.
93 See Aili Bresnahan, "Improvisation in the Arts," *Philosophy Compass* 10:9 (2015): 573–582, at 576–577.
94 Monson, *Saying Something*, 176; see also 156–170.
95 Monson, *Saying Something*, 176; Berliner, *Thinking in Jazz*, 379–383, 395–409.
96 See Gunther Schuller, *Early Jazz: Its Roots and Musical Development* (Oxford: Oxford University Press, 1968), 116–118, for his acute and patient analysis of how Armstrong's restructuring stands in a deliciously "right" relationship with the original meter.

References

Adorno, Theodor W. "On Popular Music." *Studies in Philosophy and Social Science* 9 (1941): 17–48.
Alperson, Philip A. "On Musical Improvisation." *Journal of Aesthetics and Art Criticism* 43:1 (1984): 17–29.
Balliett, Whitney. *American Musicians II: Seventy-One Portraits in Jazz*. Jackson: University Press of Mississippi, 1986.
Balliett, Whitney. *New York Notes*. Boston: Houghton Mifflin, 1976.
Balliett, Whitney. *The Sound of Surprise: 46 Pieces on Jazz*. New York: Dutton, 1961.
Benson, Bruce Ellis. *The Improvisation of Musical Dialogue: A Phenomenology of Music*. Cambridge: Cambridge University Press, 2003.
Berliner, Paul F. *Thinking in Jazz: The Infinite Art of Improvisation*. Chicago: University of Chicago Press, 1994.
Bresnahan, Aili. "Improvisation in the Arts." *Philosophy Compass* 10:9 (2015): 573–582.
Brown, Lee B. "Adorno's Critique of Popular Culture: The Case of Jazz Music." *Journal of Aesthetic Education* 26:1 (1992): 17–31.
Brown, Lee B. "Afrocentrism Old and New: The Critical Theory of Jazz." *Journal of Aesthetics and Art Criticism* 57 (1999), 235–246.
Budds, Michael J. *Jazz in the Sixties*. Iowa City: University of Iowa Press, 1978.
Caplan, Ben. Review of Julian Dodd, *Works of Music: An Essay in Ontology*. *British Journal of Aesthetics* 47:4 (2007): 445–446.
Coleridge, Samuel Taylor. *Biographia Literaria*, ed. G. Watson. London: Dent, 1965.
Collingwood, R. G. *The Principles of Art*. Oxford: Oxford University Press, 1958.
Coryell, Larry. *Improvising: My Life in Music*. New York: Backbeat Books, 2007.
Cott, Jonathan. *Dinner with Lenny: The Last Long Interview with Leonard Bernstein*. Oxford: Oxford University Press, 2013.
Danto, Arthur C. *The Transfiguration of the Commonplace: A Philosophy of Art*. Cambridge, MA: Harvard University Press, 1981.
Davies, Stephen. *Musical Works and Performances: A Philosophical Exploration*. Oxford: Clarendon Press, 2001.
Day, William. "The Ends of Improvisation." *Journal of Aesthetics and Art Criticism* 68:3 (2010): 291–296.
Descartes, René. *Meditations on First Philosophy: With Selections from the Objections and Replies*, ed. John Cottingham. Cambridge: Cambridge University Press, 1996.

Dodd, Julian. *Works of Music: An Essay in Ontology*. Oxford: Oxford University Press, 2007.

Elsdon, Peter. *Keith Jarrett's* The Köln Concert. Oxford: Oxford University Press, 2013.

Enstice, Wayne, and Janis Stockhouse. *Jazzwomen: Conversations with Twenty-One Musicians*. Bloomington: Indiana University Press, 2004.

Feige, Daniel Martin. *Philosophie des Jazz*. Berlin: Suhrkamp Verlag, 2014.

Gabbard, Krin. "Introduction: The Jazz Canon and its Consequences." In *Jazz Among the Discourses*, ed. Krin Gabbard, 1–28. Durham: Duke University Press, 1995.

Gates, Henry Louis. *The Signifying Monkey: A Theory of African-American Literary Criticism*. New York and Oxford: Oxford University Press, 1988.

Giddins, Gary, and Scott DeVeaux. *Jazz*. New York: W. W. Norton, 2009.

Gioia, Ted. *The Imperfect Art: Reflections on Jazz and Modern Culture*. Oxford: Oxford University Press, 1988.

Gitler, Ira. *Swing to Bop: An Oral History of the Transition in Jazz in the 1940s*. Oxford: Oxford University Press, 1985.

Gracyk, Theodore. *Rhythm and Noise: An Aesthetics of Rock*. Durham: Duke University Press, 1996.

Hamilton, Andy. *Aesthetics and Music*. London: Continuum, 2007.

Harrison, Max. *A Jazz Retrospect*. New York: Crescendo, 1976.

Hodeir, André. *Toward Jazz*, trans. Noel Burch. New York: Grove Press, 1962.

Hytönen-Ng, Elina. *Experiencing 'Flow' in Jazz Performance*. New York: Routledge, 2013.

Kant, Immanuel. *Critique of the Power of Judgment*, ed. Paul Guyer, trans. Paul Guyer and Eric Matthews. Cambridge: Cambridge University Press, 2000.

Kernfeld, Barry. *What to Listen for in Jazz*. New Haven: Yale University Press, 1995.

Kivy, Peter. *The Fine Art of Repetition*. Cambridge: Cambridge University Press, 1993.

Lockwood, Lewis, and Alan Gosman. *Beethoven's "Eroica" Sketchbook: A Critical Edition*. Champaign: University of Illinois Press, 2013.

Love, Stefan Caris. "The Jazz Solo as Virtuous Act." *Journal of Aesthetics and Art Criticism* 74:1 (2016): 61–74.

Mackey, Nathaniel. "Other: From Noun to Verb." In *Jazz Among the Discourses*, ed. Krin Gabbard, 76–99. Durham: Duke University Press, 1995.

Marsalis, Wynton, with Geoffrey C. Ward. *Moving to Higher Ground: How Jazz Can Change Your Life*. New York: Random House, 2009.

Martin, Henry. *Charlie Parker and Thematic Improvisation*. Lanham, MD: Scarecrow Press, 2001.

Monson, Ingrid. *Saying Something: Jazz Improvisation and Interaction*. Chicago: University of Chicago Press, 1996.

Murphy, Jeannette Robinson. "The Survival of African Music in America." *Popular Science Monthly* (September 1899): 660–671.

Nettl, Bruno. *The Radif of Persian Music: Studies of Structure and Cultural Context*, rev. ed. Champaign: University of Illinois Press, 1992.

Nooshin, Laudan. "Improvisation as 'Other': Creativity, Knowledge and Power – The Case of Iranian Classical Music." *Journal of the Royal Music Association* 128:2 (2003): 242–296.

Peters, Gary. *The Philosophy of Improvisation*. Chicago: University of Chicago Press, 2009.

Rasula, Jed. "The Media of Memory: The Seductive Menace of Records in Jazz History." In *Jazz Among the Discourses*, ed. Krin Gabbard, 134–162. Durham: Duke University Press, 1995.

Robinson, Jenefer. *Deeper than Reason: Emotion and Its Role in Literature, Music, and Art.* Oxford: Clarendon Press, 2005.

Rosenthal, David H. *Hard Bop: Jazz and Black Music 1955–1965.* New York: Oxford University Press, 1992.

Rudrauf, Lucien. "Perfection." *Journal of Aesthetics and Art Criticism* 23:1 (1964): 123–130.

Sargeant, Winthrop. *Jazz, Hot and Hybrid*, rev. ed. New York: Da Capo, 1976.

Sartre, Jean-Paul. "I Discovered Jazz in America," trans. Ralph de Toledano. *Saturday Review of Literature* (November 29, 1947): 48–49.

Schuller, Gunther. *Early Jazz: Its Roots and Musical Development.* Oxford: Oxford University Press, 1968.

Schuller, Gunther. "Sonny Rollins and the Challenge of Thematic Improvisation." In *Musings: The Musical Worlds of Gunther Schuller*, 86–97. Oxford: Oxford University Press, 1986.

Scruton, Roger. "Why Read Adorno?" In *Understanding Music: Philosophy and Interpretation.* London: Continuum, 2009, 205–227.

Sharpe, R. A. *Philosophy of Music: An Introduction.* New York: Routledge, 2004.

Shipton, Alyn. *A New History of Jazz*, rev. and updated ed. London: Bloomsbury, 2007.

Stone, Alison. *The Value of Popular Music: An Approach from Post-Kantian Aesthetics.* New York: Palgrave Macmillan, 2016.

Szwed, John. *So What: The Life of Miles Davis.* New York: Simon & Schuster, 2002.

Tackley, Catherine. *The Evolution of Jazz in Britain, 1880–1935.* New York: Routledge, 2017.

Torgoff, Martin. *Bop Apocalypse: Jazz, Race, the Beats, and Drugs.* New York: Da Capo, 2017.

Walser, Robert. "Out of Notes: Signification, Interpretation, and the Problem of Miles Davis." In *Jazz Among the Discourses*, ed. Krin Gabbard, 165–188. Durham: Duke University Press, 1995.

Walton, Kendall L. "Categories of Art." *Philosophical Review* 79:3 (1970): 334–367.

Ward, Geoffrey C., and Ken Burns. *Jazz: A History of America's Music.* New York: Knopf, 2000.

Waters, Keith. *The Studio Recordings of the Miles Davis Quintet, 1965–68.* Oxford: Oxford University Press, 2011.

Williams, Martin. "Ornette Coleman – The Meaning of Innovation." *Evergreen Review* 4:15 (1960): 123–134.

Woideck, Carl. *Charlie Parker: His Music and Life.* Ann Arbor: University of Michigan Press, 1998.

INDEX